[signature] S. Hancock

Utah State U.

1972

THE NATIONAL PARKS

Freeman Tilden

The National Parks

A REVISED & ENLARGED EDITION
of the classic book on the national parks,
with new information & evaluation on all of the
NATIONAL PARKS, NATIONAL MONUMENTS,
& HISTORIC SITES

Foreword by George B. Hartzog, Jr.
Director of the National Park Service

New York / Alfred · A · Knopf

1 9 7 0

Frontispiece:
Sunset storm over Mount Moran. Grand Teton National Park. [Photo: B. D. Glaha]

To the Interpreters
of the National Park Service,
steadfast in their efforts
to reveal the truths
that lie behind the appearances.

FOREWORD

THE PUBLICATION, in 1951, of the first edition of *The National Parks: What They Mean to You and Me* heralded good things for the National Park Service and the public it serves. And it was superb evidence of what has been rightly termed Alfred Knopf's "love affair" with the national parks. From the House of Knopf have come a number of fine books on conservation; and from Mr. Knopf himself, distinguished service as chairman of the Secretary of the Interior's citizen Advisory Board on National Parks, Historic Sites, Buildings and Monuments.

But primarily the book brought to a new focus the talents of a sensitive and thoughtful observer, Freeman Tilden, who approached the subject of national parks with a rare understanding. In this book, and in his other writings, Mr. Tilden has enriched our literature, helping people appreciate the National Park System and the benefits the parks can bring to the people of America, and of the world.

The 1951 edition dealt only with the natural areas of the system. This new edition includes the entire spectrum of natural, historical, and recreational areas—more than tripling the coverage and making it the most comprehensive book of its kind.

This is a book, too, that conveys the "feel" of the parks to readers who may take pleasure from simply knowing they share in park ownership, as well as to the millions who enjoy them first-hand. This creative essence of the parks is especially well conveyed through a judicious selection of new illustrations.

Regarding these, Mr. Tilden has said: "This is the first book ever published on our parks for which the pictures have been chosen, invariably, on the judgment not of whether they were pretty pictures (though most of them are) or examples of the photographer's skill (though they are mostly highly professional), but of whether they INTERPRET. For every illustration in this book I have used the criterion: Does this picture somehow contrive to convey something of the spirit, the essence, of the area? I dare not say that the results are 100 per cent, but I do think they represent a very high degree of success."

They do, indeed.

I would like also to suggest something of the enormous expansion in responsibilities that has taken place in the years since 1951. A program to save the finest of the nation's shoreline areas, given vigorous impetus under President Kennedy and President Johnson and Secretary Udall, has resulted in a network of national seashores along the Atlantic, Gulf, and Pacific coasts and national lakeshores on the Great Lakes. The Land and Water Conservation Fund Act of 1964 has enabled us to acquire lands needed for the many new parks.

Major impoundments behind the giant dams have become full-fledged recreation members of the system; they answer a need recognized as long ago as 1925, when Director Stephen Mather's annual report foretold the demand for areas that would provide specifically for healthful outdoor recreation. His concern was only that such areas be clearly differentiated from the national parks and monuments, on which the fullest protection of natural features for human enjoyment and inspiration was paramount. That distinction has been faithfully observed.

There have been other significant changes affecting the system. Now in progress is the identification of potential units of the National Wilderness Preservation System within the National Park System. The establishment of Ozark National Scenic Riverways shows the way for what many hope will be a nationwide system of national rivers—free-flowing streams in unspoiled settings, providing for a unique kind of outdoor recreation. And the Bureau of Outdoor Recreation has been established in the Department of the Interior to correlate the activities of federal and state agencies in the park and recreation field.

And our management problems have become increasingly complex as we have watched visits to the national parklands increase from 37 million in 1951 to 139 million in 1967.

And yet, the policy that governs the preservation of park resources remains essentially unchanged. We still strive to attain for the parks the goal so eloquently expressed by Director Newton B. Drury in his 1951 Introduction: "to conserve them, not for commercial use of their resources but because of their value in ministering to the human mind and spirit."

This book, which interprets so well one of the priceless cultural resources of this nation, will do much to help us keep that goal steadfastly in mind.

GEORGE B. HARTZOG, JR.
Director, National Park Service

CONTENTS

Contents

Contents

Contents

THE NATIONAL PARKS

OLYMPIC

NORTH CASCADES
● NORTH UNIT— ROSS LAKE
SAN JUAN
ISLAND ★ LAKE CHELAN
SOUTH UNIT
COULEE DAM

WATERTON LAKES
NATIONAL PARK

WATERTON-GLACIER
INTERNATIONAL PEACE PARK

GLACIER

O C E A N

C A N

N

WASHINGTON
MOUNT RAINIER

FORT CLATSOP

● FORT VANCOUVER
WHITMAN
MISSION

◐ McLOUGHLIN HOUSE

● NEZ PERCE

MONTANA

FORT UNION TRADING POST

NORTH DAKOTA
■ THEODORE ROOSEVELT

OREGON

IDAHO

● BIG HOLE

CRATER LAKE

★ OREGON CAVES

WESTERN

CRATERS OF THE MOON ★

★ CUSTER BATTLEFIELD
BIG HORN CANYON

YELLOWSTONE

DEVILS TOWER ★

SOUTH DAKOTA

MOUNT RUSHMORE
JEWEL CAVE ★
★ BADLANGS

PIPESTONE

LAVA BEDS
REDWOOD ★
▨ WHISKEYTOWN—
SHASTA-TRINITY

LASSEN VOLCANIC

★ GRAND TETON

WYOMING

MIDWEST

WIND CAVE

GOLDEN SPIKE ●

FORT LARAMIE ●
SCOTTS BLUFF ●

★ AGATE FOSSIL BEDS
● CHIMNEY ROCK

NEBRASKA

OMAHA

NEVADA

★ TIMPANOGOS CAVE

FLAMING GORGE

● MUIR WOODS
★ JOHN MUIR
SAN YOSEMITE
FRANCISCO
★ DEVILS POSTPILE

INT ★
YES

LEHMAN CAVES ★

UTAH

★ DINOSAUR

ROCKY MOUNTAIN
SHADOW MOUNTAIN

HOMESTEAD ★

KINGS CANYON ★
PINNACLES ★
SEQUOIA

DEATH VALLEY ★

CEDAR
BREAKS ★
BRYCE
CANYON ★
ZION ★

CAPITOL
REEF ★
CANYON-
LANDS ★

ARCHES ★

★ COLORADO

COLORADO

★ BLACK CANYON OF THE GUNNISON
CURECANTI ●

BENTS OLD
FORT ●

KANSAS

FORT LARNED ●

NATURAL BRIDGES GREAT SAND
★ HOVENWEEP DUNES ★
RAINBOW ● YUCCA
BRIDGE HOUSE ● MESA VERDE
NAVAJO ★ AZTEC RUINS

CALIFORNIA

PIPE SPRING ●
GLEN
CANYON

LAKE GRAND
MEAD CANYON

★ WUPATKI

CANYON DE CHELLY ★

★ CAPULIN MOUNTAIN

CHANNEL ISLANDS ★

JOSHUA TREE ★

SUNSET CRATER ★
WALNUT CANYON ★
TUZIGOOT ★

● HUBBELL
TRADING POST

★ CHACO CANYON ● FORT UNION

BANDELIER ●

SANTA FE ★

SANFORD
★

OKLAHOMA

PLATT
ARBUCKLE ▨

★ CABRILLO

MONTEZUMA CASTLE ★
PETRIFIED
FOREST ★
EL MORRO ★
★ PECOS

ALIBATES FLINT
QUARRIES AND TEXAS
PANHANDLE PUEBLO
CULTURE

ARIZONA

TONTO ★

CASA GRANDE RUINS ★

ORGAN PIPE
★ CACTUS
SAGUARO
★
FORT BOWIE
★

NEW MEXICO

GRAN QUIVIRA ★

GILA CLIFF DWELLINGS ★

★ WHITE SANDS

SOUTHWEST

PACIFIC OCEAN

TUMACACORI ★ ▨ CORONADO

CHIRICAHUA ★

CARLSBAD CAVERNS ★

GUADALUPE MOUNTAINS ▬

CHAMIZAL ▨

TEXAS

● FORT DAVIS

BIG BEND

▨ AMISTAD

SAN JOSE
MISSION ◐

PADRE
ISLAND

ALASKA
WESTERN

M E X I C O

MOUNT McKINLEY

Nihau

Kauai

Oahu
Molokai
Lanai Maui
Kahoolawe ■ HALEAKALA

PACIFIC OCEAN

KATMAI ★

GLACIER BAY ★

SITKA ★

PACIFIC OCEAN

HAWAII
WESTERN

Hawaii

CITY OF REFUGE ◐

HAWAII
VOLCANOES

J. P. TREMBLAY

NATIONAL PARK SYSTEM
REGIONS, REGIONAL OFFICES, AND AREAS, 1970

D A

ROOSEVELT CAMPOBELLO

ST. CROIX ISLAND ★

MAINE

ACADIA

ISLE ROYALE

GRAND PORTAGE ★

LAKE SUPERIOR

PICTURED ROCKS

WISCONSIN

NESOTA

ICE AGE △

MICHIGAN

LAKE MICHIGAN

LAKE HURON

VT. N.H.

SAINT-GAUDENS

JOHN FITZGERALD KENNEDY
SALEM MARITIME
DORCHESTER HEIGHTS

MINUTE MAN

SARATOGA

LAKE ONTARIO

★ FORT STANWIX

MASS. ADAMS

CAPE COD

EFFIGY MOUNDS ★

OWA

HERBERT HOOVER

CHICAGO PORTAGE

INDIANA DUNES

ANSLEY WILCOX HOUSE

NEW YORK

ROGER WILLIAMS

TOURO SYNAGOGUE

CONN. R.I.

NEW YORK CITY AREA

VANDERBILT MANSION

CASTLE CLINTON NATIONAL MONUMENT
FEDERAL HALL NATIONAL MEMORIAL
FIRE ISLAND NATIONAL SEASHORE
GENERAL GRANT NATIONAL MEMORIAL
HAMILTON GRANGE NATIONAL MEMORIAL
ST. PAUL'S CHURCH NATIONAL HISTORIC SITE
SAGAMORE HILL NATIONAL HISTORIC SITE
STATUE OF LIBERTY NATIONAL MONUMENT

HOME OF FRANKLIN D. ROOSEVELT

DELAWARE WATER GAP

MORRISTOWN
EDISON

PERRY'S VICTORY AND INTERNATIONAL PEACE MEMORIAL

ILLINOIS

JOHNSTOWN FLOOD

HOPEWELL VILLAGE

PENNSYLVANIA

THEODORE ROOSEVELT BIRTHPLACE

N.J.

PHILADELPHIA

GLORIA DEI CHURCH NATIONAL HISTORIC SITE
INDEPENDENCE NATIONAL HISTORICAL PARK

ALLEGHENY PORTAGE RR
FORT NECESSITY

GETTYSBURG
EISENHOWER

MD.
DEL.

NORTHEAST OHIO

INDIANA

MOUND CITY GROUP ★

WASHINGTON

NATIONAL CAPITAL

AREAS ADMINISTERED BY NATIONAL CAPITAL REGION

JEFFERSON NATIONAL EXPANSION MEMORIAL

GEORGE ROGERS CLARK

LINCOLN BOYHOOD

KENTUCKY

SHENANDOAH

W. VA.

RICHMOND

RICHMOND

YORKTOWN
COLONIAL
JAMESTOWN

VA.

APPOMATTOX

BOOKER T. WASHINGTON

PETERSBURG

POPLAR GROVE

MISSOURI

FORT SCOTT

GEORGE WASHINGTON CARVER

OZARK ◇

★ WILSON'S CREEK

ABRAHAM LINCOLN BIRTHPLACE

MAMMOTH CAVE

CUMBERLAND GAP

BLUE RIDGE PARKWAY

ANTIETAM NATIONAL BATTLEFIELD SITE
ASSATEAGUE ISLAND NATIONAL SEASHORE
BALTIMORE WASHINGTON PARKWAY
BATTLEGROUND NATIONAL CEMETERY
CATOCTIN MOUNTAIN PARK
CHESAPEAKE & OHIO CANAL NATIONAL MONUMENT
CUSTIS-LEE MANSION NATIONAL MEMORIAL
FORD'S THEATER LINCOLN MUSEUM
FORT McHENRY NATIONAL MONUMENT
FREDERICKSBURG NATIONAL BATTLEFIELD SITE
FREDERICKSBURG & SPOTSYLVANIA NATIONAL MILITARY PARK & CEMETERY
FREDERICK DOUGLASS HOME NATIONAL MEMORIAL
GEORGE WASHINGTON BIRTHPLACE NATIONAL MONUMENT
GEORGE WASHINGTON MEMORIAL PARKWAY
HAMPTON NATIONAL HISTORIC SITE
HARPERS FERRY NATIONAL MONUMENT
HOUSE WHERE LINCOLN DIED NATIONAL MEMORIAL
LINCOLN MEMORIAL NATIONAL MEMORIAL
MANASSAS NATIONAL BATTLEFIELD PARK
PENNSYLVANIA AVENUE NATIONAL HISTORIC SITE
PISCATAWAY PARK
PRINCE WILLIAM FOREST PARK
SUITLAND PARKWAY
THOMAS JEFFERSON NATIONAL MEMORIAL
WASHINGTON MONUMENT NATIONAL MEMORIAL
WHITE HOUSE
WOLF TRAP FARM PARK

WRIGHT BROTHERS

FORT RALEIGH

CAPE HATTERAS

ANDREW JOHNSON

GUILFORD COURT HOUSE

FORT DONELSON

GREAT SMOKY MOUNTAINS

NORTH CAROLINA

CAPE LOOKOUT

TENN.

STONES RIVER

SHILOH

RUSSELL CAVE

COWPENS

KINGS MOUNTAIN

MOORES CREEK

ARKANSAS

BRICES CROSS ROADS

CHICKAMAUGA & CHATTANOOGA

SOUTH CAROLINA

HOT SPRINGS

TUPELO

KENNESAW MOUNTAIN

FORT SUMTER

ARKANSAS POST

NATCHEZ TRACE PARKWAY

HORSESHOE BEND

OCMULGEE

GEORGIA

VICKSBURG

MISS.

ALABAMA

SOUTHEAST

FORT PULASKI

FORT FREDERICA

LOUISIANA

FORT CAROLINE

CASTILLO DE SAN MARCOS
FORT MATANZAS

ATLANTIC OCEAN

CHALMETTE

FLORIDA

DE SOTO

GULF OF MEXICO

EVERGLADES

★ FORT JEFFERSON

PUERTO RICO AND THE VIRGIN ISLANDS
SOUTHEAST

SAN JUAN

ST. THOMAS

ATLANTIC OCEAN

VIRGIN ISLANDS

Puerto Rico

St. Croix

BUCK ISLAND REEF

CHRISTIANSTED

CARIBBEAN SEA

⊕ International Park
○ National Battlefield
◖ National Battlefield Park
◕ National Battlefield Site
† National Cemetery
◒ National Historical Park
◓ National Historic Site
▥ National Lakeshore
▨ National Memorial
◪ National Memorial Park

▲ National Military Park
★ National Monument
■ National Park
◇ National Scenic Riverways
▨ National Seashore
△ National Scientific Reserve
═ Parkway
▨ Recreation Area
◉ Regional Offices

PART

ONE

[I]

The Life Community

[1]

THE VALUE OF THE NATIONAL PARKS to the scientist, the student, and the researcher is with some, perhaps not with many, a touchy subject. I sometimes meet an enthusiast who delights in the parks as "pleasuring-grounds," who squints horribly when I happen to mention the scientific importance of the wilderness areas. "I see," he says. "You are one of those fellows who wants to keep everybody out of the parks so that the long-haired, nearsighted professors can prowl around in them, working up material for a master's degree."

Now, it happens that most of the men of science with whom I am acquainted are not long-haired. Some of them are as close-cropped as a freshly sheared Angora goat, while others have had most of their hair removed permanently by nature. As for their physical condition, I recommend that anyone who doubts their stamina follow a geologist up a canyon with pack and specimen bag, or travel with a wildlife expert on a snowshoe trip in the high mountain country, with the temperature something below zero and a gale blowing. But this is aside. If there were any plot afoot to deprive me of the pure fun of loafing and inviting my soul in these lovely preserves, I should be the first to raise a howl of protest.

It so happens that park management that provides the maximum of spontaneous, lazy enjoyment to visitors is also ideal for the natural scientist and the student. What the average person loves about the primeval parks is the feeling of elbowroom, bigness, far horizon, freedom. You can get these sensations in the highest degree only when the areas are large enough; and this condition is the very one that makes them of value from the scientific

The young moose is curious and unafraid. Isle Royale National Park. [Photo: William W. Dunmire]

point of view. For the historian of the future, they must not be flooded out by river dams and "improvements" or by other encroachments that seem of vital importance at the moment but later may be recognized as wasted effort and money, even commercially. For the student of plant and animal life, their value depends upon their being large enough to constitute a home. Half a home may still be a home for humans; in the economy of the wilderness it is just about no home at all. Humans are able to juggle with their environment or quit it at will for another. Only to the faintest degree is this true of the animals and plants that, with the spectacular features, constitute the attraction of the national parks.

At this point I want to introduce a word not yet in common usage. The word is *ecology*. It ought not be a hard word to take, since we are already accustomed to the word *economy*, which comes from the same root. Economy, in its original meaning, was just the art of running a *home*—household management—and perhaps the political economists would do well to remember this fact before they go on star-gazing expeditions. Ecology, in our present context, is the study of animal and plant life in their *home*—in their environment—over long periods; and therefore their relationships with other forms of life which share that home. These make up a community. We used to study natural history differently; each form of life was observed for itself, or its kind, without much reference to its intricately poised habitat.

Some biologists dislike the expression "the balance of nature" because it seems to imply the desire to attain a certain status of relationship between living creatures and then to freeze that condition. It could not be done even if anyone wanted to do it; and the Park Service, in its wilderness management, does not attempt it. What is desired is that the flowers and shrubs and trees, the hoofed animals and the rodents and the insects shall have the opportunity to adapt themselves to changing natural conditions as best they may. The fittest will survive; or rather, since nobody yet knows who the fittest are or in just what sense they are fittest, at least the survivors will survive, without man's interference. And it is the maintenance of this freedom that will always be the root of the greatest pleasure to those who go to the national parks merely to see and to admire.

Letting nature take its course is, and always will be, an ideal. Once man comes into the picture, an approximation to the ideal is as near as you can get. Even if the national parks were closed to the public, which is an absurdity since they were set aside for the public, you would still not have ideally natural conditions. The people and activities on the fringe of the areas would make a difference. And park management sometimes implies a direct interference with nature. Once, when I was in Yellowstone, lightning set six forest fires raging in the dry woodlands of the park, and half the ranger force and half the naturalists were out fighting. Since it is nature's way to touch off a blaze with her celestial torch, why not let the forests burn? The answer is so obvious that the question is not worth debating. In geologic time—a few hundred million years—it would not make any difference whether Yellowstone was a smoking waste. As mankind may not be here that long, it is common sense to keep the trees if we can.

There will be interference with wildlife for the same reason, but it will be resorted to only when it is imperative, after careful study, and when a little evil is sure to prevent a greater one.

[2]

MY MANY FRIENDS among the men of the natural sciences—the gentle sciences like zoology, botany, and geology—do not scold me when I commit an anthropomorphism. An anthropomorphism is the misdemeanor of ascribing to the lower forms of life feelings that only *Homo sapiens* is supposed to entertain. If you say that an Eastern white pine *prefers* a sandy soil, or that a yellow lady-slipper *likes* damp woods, that is anthropomorphism. Preferences and likes have nothing to do with the matter; they grow in those places because of their adaptation.

Sometimes, however, my specialist friends surprise me. Once, down in Big Bend National Park, I sat listening to a mockingbird for at least twenty minutes. Something about the bird's manner convinced me that he was deliberately trying to impress me with his virtuosity. He would stop, cock an eye at me, and then, as if to say: "Wait a minute, you haven't heard anything yet; listen to this one!" he would pour out his silver notes. Finally he jumped to another branch and said: "Don't go yet. This is the one I like best myself!" I never heard a tenor at the Metropolitan who more plainly seemed to be playing to the audience.

I told this to a park naturalist who happened to be down in the Bend. I wanted to hear that good old word *anthropomorphism*. Instead he smiled and said: "I don't know; you might be right. Anyway, I don't know *why* birds sing."

I'm not so sure I like the physicists, among the men of science. It took me thirty-five years to adjust my mind to the existence of a thing known as an atom. Just when I had it well in mind, these ferocious fellows took my atom apart, leaving me not only without my atom, but with an uncertainty about my mundane future. But among the men of unexplosive science I feel at ease. I respect their proficiency, and they envy me the ease of my amateur standing. I have an advantage: I can laugh when I make an erroneous conclusion. Nobody cares.

I will tell you a secret about the specialists. In their hearts they always carry the wistful memory of the rank amateur. They know too much. Of course, they get pleasure out of their work, just as anyone gets pleasure from work well done. But the anatomist often wishes he could look at an animal specimen without knowing where all its bones and muscles are; and I knew two accomplished biologists in Washington who regularly reverted to amateur type by going to a little island in the Potomac River, peeling off their clothes to their shorts, and becoming ignorant and happy aborigines. These fellows pay the price: the law of compensation is pitiless. They wish they could go into the national parks once in a while and say "Oh!" and "Ah!" and ask silly questions the way we visitors do.

There is a touching story about David Starr Jordan, the great ichthyologist and onetime chancellor of Stanford University. He had an astonishing memory for the names of the students and could greet them familiarly when he met them on the campus. One day, when walking with a faculty member, on meeting some undergraduates he failed to call them by name. His companion was surprised and asked Jordan if he had really forgotten. Dr. Jordan replied: "Yes, I have forgotten, deliberately. I mustn't let myself remember their names. I've found that every time I remember the names of two students, I forget the names of two fishes."

Poor man! As a specialist he was forced to choose between young men and fish, and professionally he had to choose the fish. It was the excise tax of specialism.

But the top men of the natural sciences have one great advantage over us amateurs: they have discovered humility. The smatterer prances around in his paddock of misguided opinion and hates to say "I don't know." The farther these specialists go in their knowledge, the more modest they are inclined to get. And what is more charming, as a bit of intellectual conduct, than the pronouncement made back in Darwin's time by his friend Thomas Huxley?

Men of science do not pledge themselves to creeds; they are bound by articles of no sort; there is not a single belief that it is not a bounden duty with them to hold with a light hand and to part with it, cheerfully, the moment it is

---

A blinding flash reveals the flower stalk of the agave. Big Bend National Park. [*Photo: M. Woodbridge Williams*]

really proved to be contrary to any fact, great or small. And if in course of time I see good reasons for such a proceeding, I shall have no hesitation in pointing out any change in my opinion, without the slightest blush for so doing.

Thus it is with the men who have in their care the management of the wildlife in the national parks. Ecological successions work themselves out over great periods when they are let alone. Park management implies arrangements for relatively short periods and depends upon conclusions that simply cannot be fully demonstrated. They may be verified someday. Meantime, though the principles are sound, the practice will be a common-sense best possible.

[3]

THE COMMUNITY OF LIFE in any given locality is governed by a number of factors, but chiefly by the climatic zone in which the living organisms are struggling to adapt themselves. This is the "struggle for existence" noted by Charles Darwin. But it is wrong to think of it in the sense of a fight among animals. As conditions change, those forms which cannot adjust themselves must migrate if they can; otherwise they go under. Thus there is a biological succession which ends in a balance that will be maintained, with minor fluctuations, over a long period.

If you live near a pond or lake, you have the whole picture under easy observation. Perhaps the pond was gouged out by glacial action; it may have been dammed behind a moraine; it may be the cut-off section of a meandering river which once made almost a circular detour at that point. In any event, the tendency of the pond will be to fill up and disappear. Soil will be washed in along the edges, dust will be blown in, and plants will press toward the water.

When the water in the pond was deep enough, fish could thrive in it. Along the edges frogs and salamanders lived. In the shallower water, pond lilies grew. When the soil conditions were right, cattails and rushes began to appear. Behind them in this march toward the center would come marsh grasses; and in time these would give way to meadow grass, and finally shrubs and trees might begin to take the place of the grasses. With no interference by man, in time not only will the pond disappear, but where the pond was there will be vegetation exactly like that of the surrounding country. If the pond was in a forest, trees will grow there; if in a prairie, it will become prairie. All the animal life that wholly depended upon the pond's remaining a pond will have gone, and other animals will have moved in from the surrounding country.

This illustration does not pretend to cover the whole ground, but it will suffice to suggest what is continually happening. It is a "balance of nature" in which the scales are constantly moving up and down but are heavily weighted on one side or the other only when humans introduce artificial conditions.

Does this seem remote from human affairs? On the contrary, it touches our lives at every point. In the first place, the history of mankind shows that we have been, in some respects, helpless pawns in this game. It was no accident that the first savages began to tame wild animals. They tended to exhaust their supplies of wild game and fish, and dependence on hunting and fishing became too precarious. But with the growing population even the pastured animals were not enough, and the more resourceful people supplemented them with agriculture; and these men in turn were bound to be succeeded by those who could create devices for better living, with a greater range of communication in which to think of even better tools and methods.

The farmer uses "ecological" principles all the time. If he is a graduate of an agricultural college, he uses them knowingly. But even if he has never been to college, his cut-and-try experience, in addition to what he learned from his forebears, leads him to manage his affairs in consonance with them. And he has observed one thing in particular: when you interfere with the delicate balance of nature, the result may not be exactly what was expected. Or, at least, there is a price tag attached to it, and the cost of interference may be too high.

For example, ranchmen do not like the badger because it makes big burrows on the prairie land that are a menace to horses and their riders. But if the superior rights of man are vindicated by a wholesale slaughter of the badger, it is then observed that the number of ground squirrels has greatly increased, and these animals destroy crops and compete for forage with the livestock. The badger had been keeping the number of squirrels in check.

It is not necessary to detail other similar instances. Every rural dweller can cite dozens of them that closely affect his daily life; and even the city dweller who is at all observant can add some from his own experience.

[4]

NOT SO LONG AGO predatory animals—the wolf, the cougar, the bobcat, the coyote, and such—were considered an unmitigated nuisance even in the national parks, to be either extirpated or held to a bare representation. It is easy enough to see why. A predator may be loosely described as any animal that kills game that man himself wishes to kill. The emphasis was on maintaining a good crop of game animals, and even if hunting was not permitted within the parks, the game could migrate outside. The psychology was against the cougar who pulled down a fawn, even though that was his natural right.

As late as 1918 a distinguished naturalist writing of the wild animals of Glacier National Park said in the caption on a photograph of two dead cougars: "Picture of two cougars that will kill no more game. The only good mountain lions are those gathered in by hunters and trappers. Some effective means should be taken for their destruction." Yet within ten years deer and elk were starving in great numbers, because for lack of predators they had become too numerous for their food supply.

Of the Canada lynx the naturalist wrote: "Their presence adds little of interest to the Park. They could certainly be well spared in the interest of game protection." Of bobcats: "It is fortunate that they do not reside in the Park in great numbers. They are not safe animals to have in a region where the increase of large game is to be encouraged." Of other animals he wrote: "It is to be hoped that the presence of the gray wolf may be eliminated before many years." "It would not be difficult for one or two reliable and skilful trappers to keep the number of coyotes in the Park to a practically harmless minimum." What a "practically harmless minimum" might be, the naturalist did not say. Possibly it could be represented as one castrated male specimen.

"A few martens would do no harm, but *the delicate balance of species is not easily maintained by hard and fast laws of man.*" The italics are mine, because I do not know what can be made of this statement. Here we are confronted with the concept of a "balance of nature" with a deliberate plan to upset any such natural adaptation as much as possible. Apparently in 1918 it was held possible by good thinkers to maintain the "balance of nature" by putting the thumb on the scales.

One thing is certain: in the national parks there must be a striving, even if it falls below the ideal, to maintain a complete haven for all the kinds of life known to belong there and to exclude those which do not belong there, or else we should forget the whole thing and put the animals people like best on display at convenient hours, patching up the ecological holes as they occur, as the improvident farmer mends his roof. But in that case they are not wilderness parks—and Americans do seem to enjoy wilderness parks.

[5]

MUCH OF OUR EARLIER HISTORY lives today within the boundaries of the national parks. Some of our best literature has its roots there; and it is not too much to hope that some of the best to come may spring from these scenes.

But there may be a far greater consideration. Man is a trustee of animal life. "Some animals are antiques," as J. Arthur Thomson, an eminent biologist, Regius Professor of Natural History at Aberdeen, reminded us, "like the giant tortoises of the Galápagos islands," and there is an *impiety* in obliterating ancient milestones.

> Some animals reveal secrets, as the New Zealand lizard disclosed the story of the pineal eye, and as the spectral tarsier the trend of brain evolution toward man, and there is an impiety in defacing our own history. Others, again, like the osprey, are simply masterpieces, and there is impiety in destroying the great works of art.
>
> Many creatures, often humble ones, are wrapped up in the bundle of life with ourselves. Their threads enter our web, often in very subtle ways. And careless introduction may be as disastrous as ruthless elimination.

Professor Thomson would hardly be suspected of peddling treacle. So, for the final words on this subject, I am glad to lean heavily upon him. If I said the same thing, I might be charged with an amateur sentimentality.

> . . . But there is an attitude even more humane than that of scientific conservation. It is the evolutionist attitude. These creatures are our kin. With Emerson, we may see the worm "mount through all the spires of form, striving to be man." We are solidary with the rest of creation, which once included our ancestors. These animals are distant collaterals of the human stock, our remote relatives.

This might explain why so many people feel a sense of ease and relief, and a contentment they cannot impart, when they are in the wilderness parks. They could be strayed members of the wild community who left home years ago and made good in the big city, now coming back to see what the old place is like.

It would be fine to have as little change as possible!

[II]

The Meaning of the National Parks

[1]

IF A GREAT WATERFALL, in a setting of natural beauty, is in question, it is much easier to explain that you are going to harness it for waterpower than to explain why you are forgoing that industrial use in favor of preserving it as a thing of beauty and inspiration. If it is a mountain meadow, capable of fattening sheep, that is under discussion, the commercial use of it is obvious. Not so obvious is a proposal to let wild animals have that forage. You are inviting someone to listen to what sounds like a distant drum; and the first human impulse is always to "take the cash and let the credit go."

To understand the full scope of the purposes and activities of the National Park Service requires considerable thought. The good reasons that lie behind some of the park policies are not always instantly apparent. They need interpretation; then they become clear enough.

The word *conservation* may itself be misleading. The Park Service and the Forest Service are both dedicated to conservation, in the general sense of the term. Forest conservation was a direct answer to the atrocious greed and waste that had once characterized private exploitation of timberlands in the United States. The national forests, except for the reservation of primitive areas, are set aside for wise current use, which includes selective cutting, study of growth and plant disease, regulated grazing by domestic animals, recreational pleasures, and hunting of certain game. These multiple uses are admirable, and they have the advantage of being easily understood; everyone has some firsthand knowledge of conservation of this sort. It is primarily, though not wholly, economic. The language is that of dollars and cents.

Where the sun filters through, the young redwoods get a chance. Muir Woods National Monument. [Photo: George Grant]

Now, you need only set foot in a forest area in a park to come abruptly against a clear-cut concept of conservation. Suppose you are driving through Yellowstone. There are places along the road where you see a wild disorder of fallen trees—lodgepole pines, perhaps—so thickly intertwined that it would be hard to make your way through them. Your first thought might be, and perhaps has been: "This debris should be cleaned up. This is an awful mess." But you would be wrong. It is *not* a mess. It should *not* be cleaned up. Any such suggestion means that you have not grasped the meaning of the national parks.

When a tree falls in a national park, it will lie where it fell. Of course, if it falls across a road in such a way as to spell trouble or becomes a menace to visitors, it is removed. It is not necessary to indulge in absurdities in order to fulfill the general plan. The tree undisturbed will decay and become forest mold and supply the nourishment for future growths. It harbors sustenance for animal life. It is nature's way. Whether those trees in Yellowstone are an eyesore or something agreeable to look at depends on what you are looking for. If you like to be in a wilderness, the sprawled trees are in harmony with all else, and beautiful. If you prefer a botanical garden or a manicured private estate—both of them good as such—then there is no quarrel. But each concept must be itself.

In the national parks there is no harvesting of timber. There is at present no hunting of wild animals. There is no mining of minerals. There is, or should be, no grazing of domestic animals. There are no shows, or what are commonly known as "amusements." There is no attempt to make profits. The parks are operated on funds appropriated by Congress, and the receipts from visitors go into the miscellaneous receipts of the Federal Treasury, so that the balancing of income and outgo, common to business enterprises, does not exist.

This scheme of land use, so far removed from the average person's economic experience, may glancingly seem strange and remote. And so it is. It is a new theory in the world, of management of the public land for a superior kind of pleasure and profit; for the perpetuation of the country's natural and historic heritage, untarnished by invasion and depletion other than that of invincible time. No wonder, then, that it is a difficult story to tell. Worse, it is one of those efforts at public relations and interpretation where, by telling only a part, a false impression is almost surely created.

The meaning of the parks is known and reverenced by. hundreds of thousands of those thoughtful Americans who spur to the defense of the integrity of the system whenever it is threatened by selfish and unimaginative private designs. The number grows every year. But so splendid is the master plan, so wide its implications, so novel in the history of civilized man, so successfully impractical—like one of the things that cannot happen, but do —that a half century is really a short time for full realization to be widespread. This book aims to be of help.

[2]

IN TRYING to convey the ultimate meaning of the national parks, perhaps I should first explain what they are not.

The national parks are *not* merely places of spectacular scenic features and curiosities. This seems a strange statement in the face of the advertised lure of wonders like the geysers of Yellowstone, the incredible blue of Crater Lake, the unrivaled erosion picture of the Grand Canyon of the Colorado, and the falls of the Yosemite. But nearly all the national parks, and many of the wilderness monuments, would justify their existence even if they did not possess so great a scenic merit. The scenery is inspiring, unforgettable; but the meaning goes deeper.

The national parks are not merely places of physical recreation. If finer and more re-creative recreation can be found anywhere in the world, the spots have not yet been revealed. But the word *recreation* covers a host of activities, and many of them can be had in municipal, state, or other areas, in the national forests, and in similar locations. I cannot understand why anyone should travel long distances to the national parks for physical recreation as such, but if they represent a special dividend, deriving from a larger appreciation and a higher use, then visiting them becomes a most desirable thing.

The national parks are not merely attractions whereby travel facilities are stimulated; railroads, buslines, and garages made busy; hotel and other accommodations and eating places made profitable; and the hearts of local chambers of commerce made glad. I say this with no intent to reflect on any of these incidental corollaries of the system of national parks. To see and enjoy the parks, one must first get to them. There must be housing and food, or at least campgrounds and a commissary to provide for them. Inside the parks there must be concessions of many kinds; outside the gates there will be a growth of businesses that cater to visitors. Any concessioner and any owner of facilities at the gates and on the highway, who supplies the public with good wares and services at a reasonable price is doing his part toward the enjoyment of the parks. Such businesses are not only legitimate, they are absolutely necessary. But private enterprise being as eager as it is, it is sometimes necessary to issue a reminder that the national parks were not established to afford profit to anyone. That there are profits to be made is wholly adventitious.

Finally, the national parks are not in the least degree the special property of those who happen to live near them. They are national domain. Yellowstone and Yosemite belong as much to the citizens of Maine as to those of Wyoming and California; Isle Royale to the New Mexican as much as to the people of Michigan. The people of the states in which national parks happen to exist are rightly proud of them, and should normally be the first to rise against any spoliation of them; but pre-emption and settlement of land that happens to border on the present parks, or any that may be created later, imply no title to any rights in the preserved area beyond what belong to any American.

Now that I have mentioned a few things the national parks are not, it is cheerful to turn to what they are.

[3]

WHEN YELLOWSTONE NATIONAL PARK WAS ESTABLISHED in 1872, it was as "a public park or pleasuring-ground for the benefit and enjoyment of the people." Whatever Congress meant by those words, it is fairly easy to surmise what was in the minds of men like Langford, Hedges, Hayden, and Folsom—pioneer preservationists. It occurred naturally to the exploration party that the wonders of the region were no ordinary creations of nature—that the volcanic phenomena especially were of world significance, and that consequently any private interests that could gain ownership would reap large profits. It is not likely that these men had in mind a "recreational area." The whole reach of the Rocky Mountains was a place where you could have even more physical exercise than you wanted, including running. The idea of a complete game sanctuary would not have occurred to them. They were not interested in the harboring of grizzlies, wolves, and other "varmints."

It seems clear to me that "public park or pleasuring-ground for the benefit and enjoyment of the people" meant simply the opposite of what these early conservationists feared might happen: "private park or pleasuring-ground for the financial benefit of a few." It is true that the discussions of the bill in Congress brought forth many various points of view. It was even said

Martin Volcano. Katmai National Monument. [*Photo: Lowell Sumner*]

that the forests of the region were what was most worth preserving. But I see no point in reading into the words meanings not necessarily there. The reason given was ample enough at the time.

In the the act of Congress that set up the National Park Service, some forty-five years afterward, the field of purpose was much widened. The words of the act should be well remembered, for the National Park System operates today under that organic law, which orders the conservation of "the scenery and the natural and historic objects and the wild life" in the national parks, and the provision "for the enjoyment of the same in such manner and by such means as will leave them unimpaired for the enjoyment of future generations."

This is what the national parks are for—not a part, but the whole of the stated purpose. This, with the implication of policies and methods to achieve the stated ends, is the full meaning of the national parks. It is no longer "conservation." It is *preservation.* Or it may be called conservation in another and newer sense: the conserving of resources that are not to be expressed in terms of money, but embrace the moral, spiritual, and educational welfare of the people and add to the joy of our living.

The Romans had their lares and penates—their protective and benevolent household and neighborhood gods. At the risk of being too precious about it, I should say that perhaps our American lares and penates can best be discovered in the national parks.

So we see that the national parks are really national museums. Their purpose is to *preserve,* in a condition as unaltered as is humanly possible, the wilderness that greeted the eyes of the first white men who challenged and conquered it. It is to ensure that the processes of nature can work, without artifice, upon all the living things, as well as the earth forms, within their boundaries. It is to keep intact in the wilderness areas all the historic and prehistoric evidences of occupation by our predecessors. And in doing these things, the extra reward of recreational value emerges as a matter of course.

John Muir wrote, in 1898: "Thousands of nerve-shaken, overcivilized people are beginning to find out that going to the mountains is going home; that wildness is a necessity; and that mountain parks and reservations are useful not only as fountains of timber and irrigating rivers, but as fountains of life." With every passing year, the truth of the statement is emphasized.

During one of the debates in the Senate, at a time when the fortunes of Yellowstone Park were balancing dangerously, George Vest of Missouri told his hearers that "there should be to a nation that will have a hundred millions or 150 millions of people, a park like this as a great breathing place for the national lungs." Vest, no doubt, was recalling what Lord Chatham once noted—that "the parks are the lungs of London." The Senators must have smiled sardonically when a future population of 150 million was predicted. California did not then number 600,000. Yet see where we are already!

The physical size of the preserved area in the National Park System has nothing to do with the designation. Acadia National Park, in Maine, contains only 28,000 acres. Katmai National Monument in Alaska contains more than 2,697,000 acres. Why is part of the Grand Canyon area known as a national park, while a contiguous area, dedicated to the same purposes and managed with the same ideals, is called Grand Canyon National Monument? The answer to this question is simple. A national park can be established only by act of Congress. A national monument can be set aside by Presidential proclamation. Since the lands so set aside must be already federally owned, it really means that the change is only one of new purpose and management: commercial use has been supplanted by cultural uses.

The total area of all the lands administered by the National Park Service has grown to more than 27 million acres. It sounds like a great deal, and as the Hollander or Belgian would see it, it is. But it is actually less than one per cent of the total land area of the country. By far the greater part of the territory preserved, invaluable as it is for the spiritual enjoyment of our future generations, contains little that could be used for commercial purposes, so far as anyone now knows. The great virgin forests, where they exist, are of course sources of lumber and pulp, and somebody is always eying them avidly across the fence; but the lands are not rich in minerals and are not generally suitable for agricultural production.

Sometimes, but not as often as formerly, you may hear the comment that in the management of the wilderness parks the Service has become overscrupulous, overscientific, in its zeal for preservation of all the natural features; that too much stress is placed on the good of future generations and too little on current fun and use. There is even a suggestion that the professors want to embalm the parks or preserve them in alcohol for laboratory analyses. Considering the fact that the number of visitors tends to outrun all the facilities for sheltering and feeding them, and that it is always increasing, this is amusing. But the idea of emphasizing constantly the highest uses of these places and stressing their cultural value is not new at all. It was

---

Overleaf: Paradise Valley campground. Mount Rainier National Park. [Photo: Bob and Ira Spring]

a long, long time ago that Senator Wilkinson Call of Florida, speaking of Yellowstone, said: "The Park and the natural curiosities there, and the game, were set aside to be preserved for future generations, for the *naturalist* and the *philosopher*. We cannot estimate the value of the preservation of the almost extinct animals of the western continent, to *science*."

An Indiana Congressman named Cobb, speaking also of Yellowstone, was even against having any large hotels in the park. "People can go there and camp out," he said. "They would delight in doing so; it is the very thing visitors would enjoy." He thought it unwise to improve the park in any way, lest its "natural charm should be destroyed."

Perhaps Cobb was a campfire man. At any rate, his comment was particularly interesting to me. I have personally tried every kind of accommodation afforded in the parks—the great hotels, cabins, and tents—and observing other visitors as well as consulting my own feelings and those of my children, I am inclined to think that the campers and hikers manage to get the most out of the experience. But there is something for every taste.

In 1885 a party of Congressmen made a junket to Yellowstone. They reported: "The Park should so far as possible be spared the vandalism of improvement. Its great and only charms are in the display of wonderful forces of nature, the ever-varying beauty of the rugged landscape and the sublimity of the scenery. *Art cannot embellish them.*"

The Park Service would hesitate to use such dogmatic declarations today, for fear of being charged with too austere an attitude in its management; yet the *Congressional Records* of a long-gone period are replete with similar statements. To be sure, it must be admitted that there were plenty of legislators who, far from having such tender feelings, were for exploiting whatever natural resources there were, and having no parks at all.

World War II in particular put the parks to a great test. In a great conflict, where the very existence of a nation may be the stake, it is inevitable that the way of life and all natural resources will be subordinated to one end: the successful prosecution of the war. That the parks came through practically intact in their basic integrity, however much they may have deteriorated for lack of money and manpower, is really a heartening testimony that their meaning is understood and cherished. War is a time when the heads of the armed forces keep cool heads and the civilians run high temperatures. It is also a time when, under the color of necessity, profitable invasions into public lands may be made, which establish footholds for continued private profit.

Olympic National Park contains some magnificent virgin stands of Sitka spruce. There was a need for this kind of wood for the manufacture of certain types of aircraft, mostly in Britain. What a pleasant coincidence! How convenient! The Park Service admitted that if the sacrifice of the wonderful trees was necessary to win the war, of course they must be logged. But it asked: Is it necessary? Have all the facts been obtained? Have all the avenues been explored? It was not found necessary to destroy the trees. Other sources of the spruce were found. The Olympic trees still stand, to be seen and admired by generations to come.

A deposit of the vital mineral tungsten was known to exist in Yosemite National Park. Doubtfully, the guardians of the park gave way to the demands for a mining operation there. Was it necessary? The net result was that just fifty-five tons of ore were taken out, and the work ceased.

A demand was made that grazing of cattle should be permitted upon park lands in California as a wartime measure. Indeed, a bill was introduced in Congress that would have permitted grazing of livestock upon all national parks and monuments during the war and for "six months thereafter." It might have been a long six months. The Park Service again asked: Is it necessary? Would the amount of food produced justify the damage to the features of the parks? A similar demand had been made during World War I. It had then been found that if all the demands of California cattlemen had been met, the maximum amount of beef produced would have added less than one half of one per cent to that state's supply. So when the same challenge appeared in World War II, it was agreed that "each case would be considered on its merits." The merits were not found to be transcendent, nor the motives wholly guileless.

Throughout such dangerous periods the Park Service was sustained and fortified by public sentiment, expressed partly through the many conservation societies that are alert to the needs of the national parks and to the potential dangers. But behind those organizations perhaps there was further force. Today there is a more general understanding of the meaning of the parks by the whole people. It may be that the "public relations" of the Park Service have been, over the years, far better than it realizes.

[III]

That Elderly Schoolma'am:
Nature

[1]

IT HAPPENED at Crater Lake National Park, in Oregon.
Just inside the rim of the crater stands the Sinnott Memorial Observation Station, cunningly ensconced so as to give visitors the best possible view of the lake and its surroundings, which suggests the origin and subsequent geologic story of the region. And to make understanding as easy as possible, the memorial is equipped with exhibits, field glasses fixed upon key points, and a large relief map.

On this relief model, with a scale of one foot to six miles, are depicted the prominent features of the landscape—Wizard Island, the Phantom Ship, the deep glacial valleys, and other important landforms that are part of one of the finest of our preserved natural wonders.

One day in summer the park naturalist, just then inside the memorial, was introduced to a man of middle age whose appearance at once whispered: "Here is a man who is different." It was not his clothes, though he was fastidiously dressed. It was not his face, though the face lighted up with fine intelligence at the introduction. But there was something about the gloved hands, the walking stick hung by a curved handle on his arm, something about the erectness of his posture, the grip of his hand, that set the naturalist wondering. A pair of very dark glasses that the man wore forced the conclusion that the man was totally blind.

Blindness was not mentioned; it did not need to be. But when the visitor asked gently: "Will you describe Crater Lake for me?" the naturalist knew that he had a task before him. This man had come to *see* Crater Lake. Perhaps

The "phantom ship," sailing in the bluest water. Crater Lake National Park. [Photo: Joseph Dixon]

his friends back home had vainly tried to describe it to him; now he was here to see it for himself.

The poignancy of the situation gave a tug at the heart of the naturalist. How convey to a blind man the distances, the heights, the highlights and reflections, and the forests on the crater walls—to say nothing of that blue of the water which has no counterpart? For even we who have our normal sight fall far short of full appreciation of this picture—we see only in part and understand only in part.

The naturalist had an inspiration. Perhaps, after all, he could make his visitor see what he wished. He knew that with the blind the other senses usually become compensatingly acute. He knew, too, that the Danish poet Henrik Hertz was voicing no sentimental illusion when he wrote, in his *King René's Daughter*:

> In the material eye, you think, sight lodges!
> The eye is but an organ. Seeing streams
> From the soul's inmost depths. The fine, perceptive nerve
> Springs from the brain's mysterious workshop.

He knew that this is just a simple truth, demonstrated every day in his experience: for every park naturalist observes that of the millions of visitors with reasonably normal eyes, there are all grades of sight, from seeing astonishingly much to seeing not much at all.

"I think I can show you Crater Lake, sir," said the naturalist, "if you will take off your gloves and put your hands in mine."

The gloves came off.

As the naturalist told me: "I took his hands and moved them around the crater model in relief, trying to convey through his sensitive fingertips and through his quick, eager mental perception the general shape of the crater and the variations of its rim skyline. By putting his thumb tips together, with hands extended, the little fingers accomplished the scaled diameter of the lake.

"I asked him if he had an idea of distances. He said that he could relate distances to those he experienced in walking. It was obvious that when he knew the scale spanned by his hands, he could sense the great expanse covered by the crater and its water.

"Then we moved the fingertips up the modeled face of Llao Rock, the two inches on the model representing the sheer face of almost twenty-two hundred feet of drop. He understood that there were two thousand more feet of the crater below the surface of the water. His fingers told him the conical shape of Wizard Island. The tiny depression at the summit of the cone gave him not only that special feature, but the type of many other craters too. He could *see*, through his fingers, the lava flows that extend from the base of the island cone. And then we traced out the U-shaped glacial valleys and compared them with the V-shaped stream-cut valleys in other parts of the park. Then, with a model block, I could explain to him that perhaps—we do not certainly know—this whole mountain peak, where now the crater and lake exist, was another of the great volcanic cones that rise along this long mountain uplift—not unlike Mount Hood, Mount Rainier, and others—but that this one suffered a strange collapse. It was so evident that he saw it all.

"But then, as we finally must, we came to the great outstanding quality of Crater Lake—its color. How encompass that? How convey the importance of the reflection of the sky, the action of the wind, the refracted sunlight, and all those known and unknown factors which result in this blue to end all blues? And how suggest its crystal clearness?"

Suddenly the man said, with a little catch in his voice: "I do remember —I think—yes, I know I do remember something of the blue of the sky— when I was a little boy—it comes back to me now."

Well, the blue of Crater Lake is not that of the sky, of course. It is not the blue of anything—except Crater Lake. But *blue* he could recollect, and perhaps in that "mysterious workshop of the brain" he charted the color better than the naturalist could possibly know.

"He thanked me and was led away," said the naturalist. "He went away with a smile on his face. And I shall not forget that smile. He had not only seen Crater Lake. He had extended his power of seeing—which was an achievement beyond price."

[2]

WELL, we are all of us somewhat blind, even those who believe their eyesight is faultless. In viewing natural objects and scenes, the total amount we discern is nearly nothing compared with what there is to see. Even the trained naturalist, whose business it is to make the fullest use of his senses, will readily admit that he is living a life of constant discovery. And when it comes to understanding the why and the how of what we do manage to see, which is vital to a feeling of its reality, we all need what help we can get.

The National Park Service had scarcely come into existence before the need was felt for a program of interpretation. It can be called, and correctly enough, an educational program, but to call it so is to invite a misunderstanding of its true purposes. Very few persons visit the national parks to study. They do not want to take a course in botany or geology. They want to look at the spectacular displays, the flowers, the birds, the wild creatures; they want to idle, browse, inhale deeply, hike, go horseback riding, take pictures, mingle with folks doing all these things, and forget their jobs or their routine existence.

That is all they want. Rather, that is all they think, at first, they want. But almost all of them find that it is not enough. They see the eruption of the Old Faithful geyser at Yellowstone; or in early summer they watch the tremendous gush of water of Yosemite Falls; or at Mount Rainier they see the avalanche fawn lilies pursuing the retreating snowbanks. These things are no longer something just to look at; they are something to wonder about. The birds and the flowers ask for a little intimacy. Nature holds out a hand. There are few who do not grasp it. There are secrets. There are few who do not want to penetrate some of them.

Good books about nature, and descriptive of places and things few of us can hope to visit, are precious, and we should feel poor without them. But at best, if it remains a matter of reading or of pictures, the acquaintance is secondhand. In the national parks, whoever wishes it can greet these things in their homes; it is firsthand. Nature is the teacher; the classroom is outdoors; the textbooks are the very things you see. And what the interpreters of the National Park Service really do is to arrange an introduction to the schoolma'am and lead visitors to the place where class is in session.

The great fun is in seeing everything "in place." Mr. Squeers, master of Dotheboys Hall, in Dickens's *Nicholas Nickleby*, was a cruel, bullying, cowardly rascal; but I have always thought that his explanation of his teaching method, while selfish, had great merit. He said that he taught the boys to spell *winder* w-i-n-d-e-r, and then go and wash it! To see a natural wonder "in place," in its surroundings, with the bright sky overhead and the mountains over yonder and the good earth underfoot—that is something that cannot be had from books.

All over the Western country you are likely to come upon bits of petrified wood—not of the gorgeous hues of the logs in Petrified Forest National Park, but easily identifiable as fragments of trees that once grew in places perhaps now desert, but formerly inundated by some invading sea. One day I toiled several miles up a sweltering dry creekbed just to have a look at the stump of a petrified tree of which I had been told. It was not much to look at. What had been the trunk was hardly more than a foot above the ground, and even that part was badly broken. But the roots of the tree were there. It was *in place*. That was the very spot where it had actually sprouted, grown, and later been overwhelmed. I felt rewarded. It was a thrill. No vagrant chips could satisfy like that.

In some such way the interpretative work in the parks carries on its policy of introducing visitors to the schoolma'am, the original teacher. By means of guided trips, in the company of a naturalist ranger; by the creation of nature trails, so selected and labeled that visitors may go exploring by themselves; by campfire talks, observation stations, museums, and other devices, visitors to the parks may take as much as they please of the opportunities to observe and learn. In this school there are no marks, no examination papers.

To go on a walking trip with a naturalist guide, or better still to make a three-day trip on horses into the backcountry not accessible except in this manner, is to have an enthusiast for a companion. These naturalist rangers are all-around fellows. They must be resourceful, tactful, patient, and understanding. If the blind man who was shown the crater of ancient Mount Mazama had happened to be on the trail with a naturalist, he would have found that sight, however precious, is not the only desirable sense, for the guide would have made plants come to keen perception by their odors and tastes; trees by the feeling of their bark; birds by their call notes and songs. Even many rocks can be recognized, or guessed, by touch, especially when one knows the kind of rocks that might be expected to occur in a locality.

Many visitors to the parks prefer to wander and inspect alone or with a companion or two. For these the "self-guiding nature trails" have been created. These paths find their way along objects or to places that the average visitor is most likely to wish to see, and the labeled rocks or plants or trees answer the questions the stroller would ask a guide if one were present. They indicate, too, such features as the superb polish and striations made by the glaciers of Yosemite, or the former locations of the retreating Nisqually Glacier at Mount Rainier National Park. All the major parks have these self-guiding trails. They will never quite take the place of a guide. Animals and birds, for instance, cannot be labeled, and naturally it is impossible to identify any but salient features. But for those who dislike to join larger parties, the self-guiding nature trails are admirable.

Who can forget the campfire talks in the high country, when the blaze from burning logs sends flittering gleams and stalking shadows into the branches of the surrounding trees, and the night air has just the amount of invigorating nip to put edge on the appetite for this wilderness experience? The setting is perfect; and here is a ranger who talks from no schoolbook study, but from a rich experience with the forests, the birds and other animals, the upland streams and fish, and the threading canyons. They are informal, these naturalist talks, but they have meat in them. They are chat, but never chatter. They call for questions from the audience, and the questions seldom fail to come. Visitors who gather round some of these campfires in the larger places are not numbered in the hundreds, but in the thousands. The talks are given not only in the campgrounds, but in the hotels, lodges, and museums.

[3]

FINALLY, TO SUPPLY THE INFORMATION that will make a visit to the parks and monuments the fullest possible experience, there are museums and observation stations.

The observation stations are just what the name implies, but they may also have something of the quality of museums. The station at Yavapai Point, on the South Rim of Grand Canyon, one of the first to be erected, was the result of the most careful study. In a very real sense the whole of Grand Canyon is a museum, and so is every other park and monument. Likewise any point where you happen to be is an observation point. But for those who believe they have neither the time nor the inclination to explore the details of the canyon, the observation station at Yavapai seems to be almost ideal.

First you have a glimpse of the wide range of the great chasm and that first shock of its vastness. Then you may go out upon the parapet at Yavapai and look through the telescopes for closer views of points of special interest. Through one telescope the rushing, muddy Colorado can be seen; through another the top of Cedar Mountain; and still others show the differences in the rock structure of the walls. At hand are references to these very details. Here is a sample of the silty river water—you may see how enormous is the quantity of land material being poured toward the Gulf of California. Here is a "formation column." You have seen these formations through the glass; now they are at your fingertip, in the shape of actual slabs of rock from the canyon walls. Here is a "fossil column," which reveals the evidences of life still remaining in those stratified cliffs. And here are several large sandstone slabs showing the footprints of animals, reptiles, and land-water forms that ages ago crept along on the plastic surface which at that time—but only at that time—was the level of the land hereabouts. It will be more of an adventure, certainly, if visitors go down into the canyon and see similar footprints where these animals crawled along, on the very spot—the thing *in place*—but if not, then these sandstone fragments are the next best things.

Museums anywhere, everywhere, are a problem. The museums of the National Park Service, those of the wilderness areas and those of the historical classifications, are without doubt the finest of their kind in the world. Into them has gone superior intelligence, taste, painstaking accuracy, superb craftsmanship, and, indeed, art.

Much as they are used, and really popular as they are, the museums of Yellowstone, Yosemite, Rocky Mountain, Lassen, and the other wilderness parks and monuments should have even more visitors than they do. It is not expected that everyone who visits the parks will go to the museums. Not all who visit the parks even see the major features. I know of one man who went in by the Cody Gate of Yellowstone, spent two weeks in camp at Fishing Bridge, and saw nothing but that locality. He was well and happy all the time and said he had had a great vacation.

There is, however, such a thing as "public resistance" to museums of any kind, and it has been a source of discussion not only in this country, but in Europe as well. It has even been suggested that the name *museum* be changed to something else; and although this may sound absurd, you have to consider that the naturalists are aiming at telling the story of the parks to the greatest possible number, and the end to be achieved is the finest pleasure of the public and the noblest uses of the parks. The name is unimportant.

I understand well why some people dodge museums, especially if they have visited unfortunate samples. I have been through historical-society museums that left me dazed and dizzy. Each article displayed was valuable in its way, and possibly a treasure, but the whole setup was inchoate. It is really bewildering to find a letter from Napoleon to Josephine reposing beside a stuffed albino squirrel. If you add to those a fireman's hat just above a first edition of Fenimore Cooper, and both of these in front of a Revolutionary musket, the display becomes almost crushing.

You will not find museums of the National Park Service of that kind. They limit themselves to what is local, coherent, important, authentic. They tell a story, and having told *that* story, they stop. They tell the story in a way which requires no special knowledge to understand. Because they are the work of enthusiastic experts and artists, they stimulate the imagination without diffusion. They amplify many confidences that nature makes in low whispers.

[IV]

Audit of the Treasure

I HAVE OFTEN BEEN ASKED which are the best national parks. The answer is easy. There are no "best" parks. There are your favorite parks and mine and those of somebody else. These wilderness areas are highly individualized, and the choice is a matter of taste. If you were fortunate enough to be able to visit all of them, you would find yourself most in sympathy with one, or two, or three, perhaps without knowing exactly why.

It is true that some of the parks are more spectacular in their showing of natural elements than others. But each park is an expression in its own manner —a de luxe edition, so to speak—of some manifestation of natural forces. I believe that as visits to the areas increase, the proportion of hobbyists grows in relation to the number who come for the merely spectacular. Thousands return again and again to Mesa Verde, in Colorado, because they have developed an interest in the story of the prehistoric peoples; and for the same reason they visit as many as they can of the Southwestern monuments because they want to read other chapters of the same book.

For those who love to explore the roadless regions on horseback, there are parks that are pre-eminently trail parks. Wild-flower lovers find in the more northerly high mountain country a season-long profusion of bloom so impatient that the plants can scarcely wait until the snow recedes, but actually thrust up through the white cover. Bird lovers know which parks present the best opportunities for their favorite sport; and the hardy hikers and mountain climbers have a wide range of choice. The desert has its own following. So has the dense forest wilderness. Fishermen willing to forgo the easy armchair approach and pack back to the less-visited streams and lakes

---

Rising from a carpet of goldenweed bloom. Joshua Tree National Monument. [Photo: Josef Muench]

will have their just reward. In a word, there is adventure for everybody. The person who wants to "see something different for a change" can draw upon an inexhaustible fund.

Our wars revealed in a touching way the love of the American people for their national parks and, in particular, the place that certain aspects of wilderness have in the hearts of those who know them. In the files of the Park Service are letters from young men and women of the armed forces, indicating the dreams they had during their exile on land and sea or at the scenes of the bloody conflict: "When I get my furlough, I want to come back and rest in Yosemite." "I'm counting the days, if I can have a little luck, before I get back to Mount Rainier. . . . I never realized before . . ."

Looking back at that period, with ordinary means of travel impeded or stopped altogether, it was a trying time in the parks—undermanned, short of funds, and faced with the threat of permanent invasion for destructive purposes—yet altogether perhaps it was a good thing. Perhaps short of such a crisis the basic mission and meaning of the national parks would not have been revealed so quickly. In that time of stress, the healing qualities and the power of mental and physical restoration inherent in the wilderness places were suddenly and sharply defined. Early in the spring of 1941 the Army recognized the tonic possibilities of wild areas for soldiers on leave; and as the war went on, the parks were used more and more for convalescence and for the recuperation of jaded, shocked, and frustrated young souls, as well as for maneuvers, tests of equipment, and training for Arctic and other climatic conditions. And the armed services authorities were, on the whole, most understanding in their attitude toward the use of the parks. Deterioration under war conditions was inevitable, but a minimum of irreparable damage was done.

Yes, there is something for every taste in the great cluster of park jewels. What will you have?

In dealing with the wilderness parks and monuments, I have decided, and not without a good deal of doubt and reflection, to group them according to what has seemed to me best presents the essential character of each one. The grouping is arbitrary, and is obviously open to some objections. But I feel that the advantages of treating the parks in this manner will outweigh any disadvantages. The categories are:

1. Primeval forests.
2. Volcanic scenes.
3. Earth-building and erosion.
4. Caves.

5. Desert and desert-mountain areas.
6. Work of the glaciers.
7. Tropics.

The defect of this grouping will appear at once. There are scarcely any areas that do not show a variety of the earth forces that have been at work over the ages. Earth-building and erosion are common to all. There is not one square foot of surface in our country where, unless hidden by human constructions, the evidences are not clear. The identical wasting powers that created the Grand Canyon are to be observed in your own back yard, if you have one. But some parks and monuments present the results of these forces on such a magnificent scale, with such overpowering color and stunning scenic drama, that it seems to me fair to exclaim: "Here is erosion!"

Mount Rainier is an extinct volcano; yet its twenty-six active glaciers form the largest single-peak glacier system in the United States, if we except Alaska. The Tetons of Wyoming owe their alpine form to the chiseling of mighty glaciers; yet they are the most dramatic, if not the greatest, example of uplift and block-faulting to be seen in the country. And though Big Bend National Park is primarily a desert picture, the Chisos Mountains, which are part of its lure, are volcanic in origin. So we could go on taking exceptions to an impertinent grouping like this.

But it seemed to me that any method was better than the usual hodge-podge of describing one park after another, leaving each to stand apart from all the rest, with no emphasis on the most arresting and stimulating fact of all: that they are all parts of the same drama; that each is a scene within the whole, and vital to appreciation and enjoyment of the whole.

So, to begin the most fascinating quest that I can imagine for any human —a journey into unity as shown in the national parks—let us go first into the primeval forests.

PART

TWO

[I]

Green Sanctuaries

IN THE WOODS, TOO, *a man casts off his years, as the snake his slough,*
and at what period soever of life, is always a child. In the woods is
perpetual youth. Within these plantations of God, a decorum and
sanctity reign, a perennial festival is dressed, and the guest sees
not how he should tire of them in a thousand years. In the woods we
return to reason and faith.

—RALPH WALDO EMERSON

1. APPALACHIAN ADVENTURE

IN WRITING OF THE NATIONAL PARKS and monuments, especially of those where the wilderness aspect is most pronounced, it is easy to glide over the human impress that gives them a part of their significance as pages in the Book of America. It is true that man has had nothing to do with the creation of the scenic beauty and the natural marvels we see within these areas. Indeed it is sadly true that man has done much in the past, before they became wards of the government, to deface and alter the primitive scene. But when all is said, our people have moved restlessly through and within and around these places; they have fought and bled, pioneered and hungered, created homes, raised children, laughed and wept, and lived and died—and all this cannot well be forgotten.

We are now approaching two of the Eastern national parks where the human story is the very woof of the fabric that delights both the eye and the imagination. In both the Great Smokies and Shenandoah, though visitors

The forested mountains seem to go on and on into infinity. Great Smoky Mountains
National Park. [Photo: Great Smoky Mountains Natural History Association]

may easily wander into forested recesses that seem to have been untrodden, there is always the feeling that these ancient hills are still peopled with sinewy backwoodsmen, roving with squirrel guns, cultivating a tiny patch in the wilderness, and living off the land like an army on conquered ground. It is a feeling justified by the facts, for here we have the Park Service dedicated to a dual purpose of preservation: to keep the natural scene unimpaired and to keep the human story accessible and vivid.

First as to the Appalachians themselves. If there were ever historic mountains, considered either as a range or as a system, they are these. Here are some of the oldest uplands on earth. The crushed and folded formations of their oldest rocks are part of a mountain chain that once extended from Nova Scotia down into Alabama and possibly swung far southwestward of that apparent terminus. The intensity of the forces which thrust out of the Southeast and carried older rocks over younger rocks, a phenomenon similar to that which the tourist sees in Glacier National Park, is beyond human understanding. How high were the peaks of those earlier Appalachians? Impossible to know; but there is evidence that they were like the modern Alps or—not to go so far away—the Tetons of Wyoming. They could have been much higher than that, even; we do not know how rapidly they were torn down while they were still rising.

But those Appalachians passed away millions and millions of years ago; they were planed down almost to sea level; and the mountains that we now so much admire were warped up gently, with long periods of quietude, at a much more recent period. They are the highest elevations of the eastern part of the continent. From the northern end of the Appalachian Trail to the southern end, the foot traveler will find plenty of ruggedness in these deep-cut flanks, where thousands of mountain torrents pour sparkling water toward the rivers and the sea. But seen from the air, or from any distant vantage point, the Appalachians are innocently sleek, almost velvety. In the Southern mountains particularly, the climate is so bland and the rainfall so ample that even when the ancient ledges come to the surface, or where the bold face of a precipice occurs, the vegetation so clothes the whole scene that the eye sees only forests after forests, billowing away and away to the horizon.

2. GREAT SMOKY MOUNTAINS NATIONAL PARK
[North Carolina–Tennessee]

IT IS REALLY AMAZING that when the twentieth century opened, part of the southern Appalachians where the mountains form a high divide between

North Carolina and Tennessee was almost an unknown land. It just does not seem possible, but so it was. Populous cities had come into being not far away. The streams that flowed through the foothills were already furnishing power for busy factories. Speaking impulsively, most people along the eastern seaboard would have told inquiring strangers that everything on their side of the Mississippi was mapped and known. But the Great Smokies were still sleeping peacefully and sending up from the lush vegetation a bluish perpetual haze, a filmy veil as mysterious as the mountains themselves. Their name was old and inevitable. The first men who ever saw them could not fail to use those words—Great Smokies.

A small group of geologists and botanists had packed their way into the dense forests. It was known that few spots in the world had a richer variety of plantlife than this. The highest peaks (sixteen within the park rise more than six thousand feet) were covered with a magnificent primeval cloak of spruce and fir. On the mountainsides was an unbroken cover of deciduous trees, permitted by a genial climate and ample moisture to attain unusual size. Growths that farther north in the Appalachians are only shrubs here become trees. The serviceberry or shadberry of my own home in the northern Appalachians is never more than a big shrub or a small tree, a thrice-welcome harbinger of spring with its lacy white early bloom. Here it reaches a massive size that makes it almost unrecognizable.

In all Europe there are not as many species of native trees as are to be seen in the Great Smokies—130 native tree species and more than 1,300 varieties. And what great flowering plants some of them are! First in the spring, the dogwood; then in May, the mountain laurel; in mid-June, the flame azalea and the rose-purple rhododendron, with the magnificent blooms of the white rhododendron to come a few weeks later. Most of the gorgeous blooming is in the forest, of course, for the forest is nearly everywhere. It is said that at least 40 per cent of the one-half million acres within the park are in the original forested condition. And this, mind you, in the "settled" East. No wonder there was a movement to preserve this wild beauty so that it could be enjoyed by all future generations!

The establishment of the park was authorized by Congress in 1926, and North Carolina and Tennessee began to acquire lands with state funds and with donations, to be matched dollar for dollar by John D. Rockefeller, Jr., through the Laura Spelman Rockefeller Memorial, in honor of his mother. There were no federally owned lands to form a nucleus in the undertaking. All was privately owned and had to be acquired the slow and hard way. But finally 461,000 acres were amassed, and the park was formally dedicated in 1940.

There are larger parks. For those who love the forest land there is none so gifted with feminine softness of outline. You feel like stroking those velvet vistas shown in a photograph taken from one of the mountain crests. And when autumn comes and the broad-leaved trees assume their brighter finery, then is the time that millions of pilgrims come to see the painting of the foliage, as millions have done before.

One of the strangest natural features in the Smokies is the presence of the unexplained "balds," mountaintops that are not forested but have a grassy and heath growth. Naturally, the views to be obtained from these spots are unobstructed and panoramic. Elevation seems to have nothing to do with the presence of the balds, for those called Andrews, Silers, and Parsons are not much higher than many of the wooded peaks.

A hike along the seventy-one-mile stretch of the Appalachian Trail, with eight trailside shelters spaced for easy one-day walks, is the high point of Appalachian adventure, but for less active visitors there are plenty of short trips leading to ingratiating corners of peacefulness and charm.

To visit this lovely national park without learning and observing something of the people who have lived in these mountains since the earliest days of America would be to lose much of the flavor of the holiday. Aside from the Cherokees, who camped and trailed in this forest fastness long before the white man came, the people of the mountains constitute a part of the oldest white immigrant stock that settled the English-speaking New World. That the Indians are still here—several thousand of them on the Qualla Reservation, adjoining the park—is an accident. They have survived from the refugees who took sanctuary in the deep woods when in 1838 their fellows were herded by the soldiers to be driven westward from their ancestral home.

The chief interest, however, is in the pioneer white stock that went into the mountains in colonial days and remained there, in remote freedom, while the rest of the eastern seaboard was achieving what is called progress. English, Scotch-Irish, and Irish most of them were, and their dialect has been sometimes described as "Elizabethan English." Probably that is too fancy a claim; but certainly the mountain folk use many words and phrases of the time of Elizabeth the Virgin that have elsewhere ceased to be current. More important, they retain the love of the spoken word, not more for bare utility than for the satisfying expression of their simple and strong emotions. They are natural singers and balladists, and I would almost say a bardic people.

Always clouds, always that dim mystical look. Great Smoky Mountains National Park. [Photo: Josef Muench]

When the tension in Cade's Cove becomes too great, Uncle Dave Meyer whittles. Great Smoky Mountains National Park. [Photo: Allan Rinehart]

Love and death, the fine-pretty world around them, the seasons, the birds and beasts, their sorrows and joys are expressed with a clarity like that of an etching. I give you a sample recorded by Percy MacKaye, the distinguished poet, who has known these people well:

"Yea, Sir, hit war the first cold spell that come, right when the grapes is about all gone and the rest of the berry tribe, between the turnin' of the weeds under and the dyin' of food; and thar comes in a gang of jay-birds, and they fills the mind of the bird poetry."

Could there be a more adequate or poetic thumbnail picture than that, of the end of summer and the coming of the frost?

Now, for comparison, listen to Mistress Quickly, the hostess of Eastcheap, describing the death of Sir John Falstaff in Shakespeare's *Henry V*:

"... A' made a finer end and went away an it had been any christom child; a' parted even just between twelve and one, even at the turning o' the tide: for after I saw him fumble with the sheets and play with flowers and smile upon his fingers' ends, I knew there was but one way; for his nose was as sharp as a pen, and a' babbled of green fields."

The dialect is not quite the same, truly; but in respect of the neat turn of phrase and the singing quality, Mistress Quickly, as I feel it, is still living in the Appalachians. I say still living, but her time will be short now. The mountaineers of today are being planed down like their mountain peaks; the impact of education, refinement, and gadgets is the eroding force. In a few years they will be ashamed to speak poetry and sing homespun songs. Better see something of them now, when it is not wholly too late! They are as hospitable and kindly to strangers as the Bedouin Arabs are alleged to be. There is no people, and there is no place, in the midst of which the life of a well-disposed person is safer.

When these people came from their cramped life in Europe and tasted the liberty of the hills, where there was no exciseman to tax their windows and no recruiting sergeant to press the King's shilling into their helpless palms, they must have thought themselves transported to the very Eden of their deeply religious imagination. Perhaps that is why they were content to remain isolated, to live a hard existence scratching a patch of hillside, to weave, to forge, to swing an adz—to do everything for themselves the laborious way —but in freedom. True, they were free to starve; but they were also free to sing, to dance, to pray, to hunt, to fish, to drowse and dream on the sunny side of the cabin—to let the world go hang.

Now, it happens, too, that they brought from the cold north of Europe a taste for certain liquids that may be distilled from grain. In the New World they discovered that the Indian corn, or maize, a plant easily raised on these hillsides, would produce a mash, and afterward a distillation, which gives a divine jolt when it passes the esophagus, going in either direction. Thus "co'n whiskey" became one of the notable products of the region. I am informed that it still is. The government thinks that such industries should be supervised and pay a tax. The mountain people do not agree. There has long been friction on this point, which after all concerns not personal but political morals, if you are so adept as to separate these. You will not be taken for a "revenooer," a revenue officer, if you keep away from any little column of smoke you should see rising from a neck of woods outside the park.

These Southern mountaineers were responsible for the defeat of the British forces under Colonel Ferguson at Kings Mountain in 1780. Equipping themselves, at their own expense, and wonderfully handy with a musket, they wasp-swarmed down from their corn patches and helped make possible the final humiliation of Cornwallis at Yorktown. They could shoot. Indeed they could. In the course of years they developed such skill that when Great Smoky Mountains National Park was established, the animals native to the region were pretty well gone. Since then, under protection, the bears and deer and smaller game-creatures have come back in good numbers. Poaching by these rugged individualists is a problem. The hill folk are not fundamentally lawless, but use and wont over the centuries are hard things to hurdle in a few years. Tact and firmness are called for on the part of the Park Service personnel, and that they show both is evidenced by the slow, sure progress in carrying the gospel of preservation to the park's border dwellers.

No, the mountain folk are not really lawless. On the contrary, when their sentiments are touched and their confidence is gained, there are no gentler people. I recall, one day at the park headquarters, pointing to a certain shrub that grew at the base of the main building, and asking the naturalist for the name of it. He gave me first its botanical name. Then he smiled and added: "But the natives call it 'hearts-a-bustin'.' That is short for 'hearts-a-bustin'-with-love.'"

Hearts-a-bustin'! Hearts-a-bustin'-with-love! In that name you see the sentimental side of the mountaineer. More than that, it seems to carry the fragrant essence of the wild, flowered park itself.

3. SHENANDOAH NATIONAL PARK
[*Virginia*]

LIKE ITS SISTER APPALACHIAN PARK farther to the south, Shenandoah National Park was created from privately owned lands. These were bought by the state of Virginia, and contributions were received from public-spirited people everywhere in the nation. The pennies, nickels, and dimes of the schoolchildren of the Old Dominion were the mites that went to swell the funds for acquisition.

Nor were these conservation-minded donors the only ones who gave. To rid the proposed park of private owners, so that it could be properly administered according to the policies of the National Park Service, it was necessary to buy the quitclaims of six or seven hundred mountain families and relocate these people outside the boundaries. Many did not want to leave. After all, one's home is a home though it may be made of chinked logs and have pullets and pigs coursing at will through the kitchen. They came to old Hezekiah

Lam, aged eighty-three, and told him that the government wanted his land. Man and boy, Hezekiah had been in these mountains so long that he could tell you from just smelling a tumbler of new-made corn likker just what "holler" it was made in, the name of the man who made it, and the approximate date when it ran through the still.

"I ain't so crazy about leavin' these hills," said Hezekiah, rubbing his rheumatic leg, "but I never believed in bein' agin' the government. I signed the papers they asked me. No; I didn't read 'em. I reckon I could've if I hadn't lost my specs. I allus said these hills would be the heart of the world."

Bless your old heart, Hezekiah; you have gone from us, maybe to a place where a man can use Indian corn for what you thought its noblest purpose, without putting an excise stamp on it. Where Hezekiah farmed his little hillside patch, the trees are coming in now. You can still discern, from one of the outlooks on the Skyline Drive, the furrows, grassed over, where the corn was hoed. In these hills the forest moves in quickly when it has a chance. Except, of course, on those queer "balds." Big Meadows is one of them.

The farmer shocks his corn at the forest edge. Shenandoah National Park. [Photo: M. Woodbridge Williams]

I was wandering over Big Meadows not long ago, meditating on why trees never come up on such places. I soon gave up this mad pursuit of knowledge and went into the excellent hotel, and out on the stone rampart just in time to see a young bald eagle—an infrequent visitor—hovering overhead. It was coming autumn. The proprietor told me that the telephone was ringing frequently, people asking whether the leaves had begun to turn. He said he was booked solidly through October by people who wanted to come and see that miracle of coloring which comes to the trees of Shenandoah.

The three hundred square miles of mountain and ridge that Shenandoah National Park comprises extend from Front Royal at the north to near the entrance to the Blue Ridge Parkway on the south, at Rockfish Gap, about seventy-five miles. At no point is the park very wide, and since the idea was to include not only the spine of the range but also the infinite number of ridges that shoot out from it easterly and westerly, the surveying of the boundary must have made the engineers mildly insane. The general effect is that of tracing the skeleton of a fish—preferably a shad, that osseous labyrinth which has mortified many a diner who wished to exhibit a delicate performance at table.

Shenandoah is notably different in aspect from the Great Smokies, but the adjacent mountain people are essentially the same. Here are no great expanses of virgin forests. There are a few pockets of primeval hemlock and some very ancient oaks that have escaped the ax, but mainly it is modern growth. Oak, especially the fine chestnut oak, predominates, but there are gums and locusts, hickories and walnuts, maples and—I was going to say chestnuts. Alas, the wonderful American chestnut, once one of the most valuable and cheerful Appalachian trees, has never recovered from that fatal blight which came upon it. Not only children and squirrels in our Eastern states but especially the mountaineers who lived in the Blue Ridge country looked forward to the nutting as they longed for Christmas. All that remain of the chestnuts in Shenandoah are the ghostly trunks that rear themselves among the oaks, resisting the weathering of time, and a few hopeful sprouts that still come from the old roots, but do not long survive.

For the motorist, there is a constant succession of well-placed overlooks, now to the west, down to the foot of the ridges, into and across the Shenandoah Valley to the dimmer heights of the Alleghenies; then to the eastward, down into other hollows and ridge ends, with cultivated fields beyond. At times the road travels along on a spine so narrow that you can look off to both east and west. It is one of the most restful scenes in our country.

I know a man who tells me he greatly prefers Shenandoah to the Smokies.

"Down there," he said, "I feel shut in; I can't see anything but woods. I was born in the dense woods, up in New Brunswick, where the primeval trees were always knocking at your front door, and, for me, give me a place like that Skyline Drive where I can look off and see human habitations and feel the nearness of humankind."

Well, that is a point of view. Other folks feel that Shenandoah entirely lacks the wilderness quality they seek. It goes to prove one thing, at least: that there is something for everyone in our national parks. And not only is there something for everyone: there is even something for everyone's changing mood. The variety is unbounded.

One evening I sat in a club in Washington, talking with a group of men about Shenandoah National Park. I had just returned from a trip down there, and I was full of what I had seen. Some of the group knew the park well; some had never been there. One man sat a little aloof, with a quizzical smile, and I began to suspect he knew much more about Shenandoah National Park than any of the rest of us. I was right; he did. I think he would prefer to remain anonymous, so I will call him Smith. No; come to think of it, I can't call him Smith, because his name *is* Smith. I shall call him Jones.

Finally, when it came his turn, Jones said: "Well, I have some pleasant recollections of Shenandoah. I put in one of the best holidays of my life down there. You see, I had done the Skyline Drive many times, but I was still curious about the two hundred miles of trail that the government folders talked about. And I thought I'd better learn something about the folks that lived around there.

"I went down to a little place called Arcadia and got myself a horse. A good little Virginia mare she proved to be, with plenty of spirit and well gaited. She shied at everything from leaves and bits of paper to the mention of General Sherman, but we got along very well. Her name was Tuckie.

"My saddlebags carried what I needed for overnight stops, but I figured on eating where I could find meals. I crossed the Lee Highway one fine October afternoon and got into the park by going southward around the foot of Pine Mountain on a dirt road at the mouth of Kettle Canyon. This is the place persons going to the Skyland resort before the days of the drive used to start for the four-mile climb up the steep mountain on horseback or in carriages to an elevation of thirty-six hundred feet. George Freeman Pollock, the genial story-telling showman and host, founded Skyland, and his years of efforts to save the park from spoliation by fire and lumbering interests made the park possible. He was one of the ardent pioneers in the movement to make a national park. On horseback he used to rout out his guests with a bugle in the morning, and in the evening he would more than likely put on a rattlesnake show. I stopped off at Skyland the first night.

"Next day I crossed the Skyline Drive and the top of the Blue Ridge and went down the White Oak Canyon Trail. The canyon got its name from the magnificent stand of large white oak and the six falls, each more than fifty feet in height. The stream drops about fifteen hundred feet in falls. I also took the Limberlost Trail, which led me to the Limberlost Swamp area, in which are growing grand red spruce, Canada yew, and enormous hemlocks. Descending on down the mountain trail, you come into a vast meadow, and Old Rag Mountain comes towering into view.

"Down the Robertson River there were a lot of mountain cabins. I rode into one yard where they were having an old-fashioned apple-butter bilin'. A young couple were stirring the slow-boiling, chopped apples in a forty-gallon kettle. By an old tradition, this is a duty performed only by young courting boys and girls. A day's bilin' produces about thirty or thirty-five gallons of apple butter.

"When I got as far as Syria, it had become misty and cold, so I turned in for the night. They were picking apples in the orchards thereabouts, on hillsides so steep that you needed a ladder on one side and you had to reach down to pick them on the other. Next morning I crossed the Robertson River and came to the Rapidan road at about the place, I think, where Stonewall Jackson camped on his way to Fredericksburg. All this region is historic ground. The Confederate troops made valuable use of their familiarity with these mountain trails and passes.

"It began to get steep as I climbed up a mountain. I've forgotten the mountain's name, but I remember there was one spot where I could almost look down the stone chimney of a cabin. An old wagon trail followed the Rapidan, through a forest of mostly hemlock, and then I got directions at Graves' Mill for a section called Fletcher's Store, by way of a pass between Buzzard's Rock and Kirtley Mountain. I was up at least two thousand feet there. Coming down a steep road on this jaunt, I stopped at a house and asked a woman who was on the porch if I was on the right road. She told me I was. I hadn't gone far before I heard a horn—an automobile horn—blowing. It kept on blowing long after I was out of sight. I'm sure now, looking back on it, that the horn was to warn somebody down in the woods tending a co'n-likker still that there was a stranger in the vicinity.

"Well, that gives you a sketchy idea of the mountain country I traveled for seventy-five miles before I got back to Arcadia. I could have spent weeks on the trip if I had accepted the invitations of these hospitable mountain

From Skyline Drive the visitor looks down. From the Great Valley the mountains loom above him. Shenandoah National Park. [Photo: M. Woodbridge Williams]

people, wherever I stopped to ask the way, to spend the night with them and share their food, whatever it happened to be. Oftentimes when I was coming down a mountain trail, I would be seen by folks in the hollow below, and they would relay my approach, from one cabin to another, by a sort of yodeling call. One of the great views I had was from a place called Devil's Tanyard. From there I could look down into three or four 'hollers' where ridges branched off the mountain like wagon spokes."

Mr. Smith—I mean Jones—hoisted himself out of his chair and concluded: "Well, I have to go now. Hope I haven't bored you. Really, nothing exciting happened. It was just the mildest kind of adventure, in a beautiful and interesting wild country, different from anything we commonly see. But try it sometime. I think you'll like it even better than driving along on the top and looking down."

Mr. Jones went out. There was a silence. Then somebody said:

"He really knows something about those mountains. He *saw* them. We just *looked* at them."

4. ISLE ROYALE NATIONAL PARK
[*Michigan*]

THE TERM WILDERNESS PARK is perforce an elastic one. Almost all the national parks are essentially primitive areas, where nature is left to go its own way; and it is true that even in places of heavy visitation like Yosemite and Yellowstone you have only to step a little aside from the spots where people congregate and the paved access roads to find yourself in a wilderness where you may cruise and meditate in a peace unbroken save for the company of the lowly creatures who enjoy it all tax-free. Still, with the necessary developments which make possible a public enjoyment, every park must be something short of a wilderness. It is obvious: it is unavoidable.

Isle Royale National Park, a rock fortress in Lake Superior, clothed with dense woods and dotted with many lakes, is perhaps the nearest thing, except for the Alaskan areas, to a true wilderness. You can reach Isle Royale only by boat, or by chartering a seaplane. When you get there, you find no roads, no wheeled vehicles, and only limited lodge facilities, concerning which it is well to inquire and make reservations in advance. There is nothing to prevent your taking your dinner jacket with you, but it will suffer the indignity of appearing alongside red sweaters and mackinaws, worn, you may find, by bank presidents, university dons, and others who know that even in summer the nights in the park get cool and the waters of Superior breathe frostily. Hiking clothes and boots are *de rigueur*.

Even the trails of Isle Royale lack the sophisticated touch. They are entirely practicable for good hikers—they are marked with metal tags, except where they cross open spaces, when stones or posts show the way. Explicit directions should be obtained from park headquarters before starting on a hiking trip. Several memorable excursions can be made by going by boat one way and returning afoot, and this is probably the ideal way to see the main island, which combines a land-and-water adventure.

The main island, for which the park is named, is about forty-five miles long and nine miles across at its widest point. The park really comprises an archipelago, for there are two hundred small islands in the group, not count-

---

Quiet haven at the edge of wilderness. Isle Royale National Park. [Photo: Abbie Rowe]

ing a multitude of mere rock projections from the lake. The northeastern end of Isle Royale consists of five chains of islands and peninsulas, which together form four long harbors of such deep water that they resemble fiords. On Mott Island, facing the longest of these fiords, Rock Harbor, the park headquarters, is located. The park is closer to Canada than to the nearest point in Upper Michigan, and is only one or two miles from the international boundary.

From the earliest pioneering time to the day in 1940 when the Secretary of the Interior accepted from Michigan the deed to all the hitherto privately owned land and thus created Isle Royale National Park with the addition of public domain that had been set aside in 1923, this ancient stronghold, flanked by its rock bastions and deep moat, has had a highly varied career. Long before summer cottages ever dreamed of going there, the exploiters had swarmed over it, testing its resources—first the fur traders, then the miners, lumbermen, and fishermen. At one time there were six fur-trading posts—at least one belonging to the Hudson's Bay Company, others of the American Fur Company. Intensive trapping practically exterminated the beaver and other fur-bearing animals, but under protection, now that it is a national park, they are restored to their enjoyment of the Animal Bill of Rights.

For a number of years Isle Royale has been the perfect laboratory for the study of the predator-prey relationship—in this case the moose and the wolf. Early in the twentieth century, it is known, the moose came over from the mainland before there were any timber wolves there. They found ample browse and flourished. By the mid-thirties there were as many as three thousand of the great animals. But, with no predator to keep down the exploding population the inevitable happened. They ate themselves out of house and home. A report of the Michigan Biological Survey of 1905, giving a "complete list" of mammals on the island, did not mention the moose, although it included the woodland caribou, now no longer seen.

About the time of a second starvation cycle, timber wolves crossed the fifteen-mile stretch of ice from Canada, and a new and brighter period began for the *prey*. It sounds odd to the nonscientist, but it is simply the fact. The predator, under natural conditions, corrects imbalance. Conditions such as exist in Isle Royale are, it has proved, nearly perfect, not only for the correction, but for the study of it by the biologist. L. David Mech, who was Dr. Durward L. Allen's first student when the Purdue University studies began, reports that "at this time the condition of the moose herd is health. A good measure of its health is its productivity. Aerial and ground surveys have shown that the Isle Royale moose are among the most productive in the country. No other herd bears such a high proportion of twin calves." And of course with the volunteer effort of the wolf, the browse supply is likewise in good shape. Their favorite haunts are Washington Creek, McCargo Cove, and Lake Eva. The sight of a moose on the edge of a pond at twilight, his awkward shape looming out of the still water, and his head completely hidden as he browses on succulent underwater plants, is a thrilling one. A nearer acquaintance is not suggested.

All over the main island are vestiges of the copper mining that began with aborigines who hollowed out the first open pits where they observed the metal outcropping from the rock. With only crude stone instruments, which they had brought from the mainland, they had enough rude inventiveness to break up the tough country rock with fire and water, after which they could batter out the big masses of almost pure copper for use in creating utensils. Isle Royale inherited a share of native copper, which is not common, along with the Keweenaw Peninsula of Michigan, where it was mined until the supply diminished below the profit point.

Mama Moose and children navigating Rock Harbor. Isle Royale National Park.
[Photo: William W. Dunmire]

The white man later took out enormous chunks of the metal from Isle Royale's ancient rocks. One of these masses was exhibited at the Centennial Exposition in Philadelphia in 1876. It weighed 5,720 pounds. There were periods when mining was active, but it was mainly a story of blasted hopes and hardship, like most of the mining ventures in our southwestern desert. Neither did it have any beneficent effect upon the landscape of the island, for much of the primeval forest was burned deliberately in order to expose the hoped-for metal, which might lie beneath the forest duff.

Isle Royale is one of those areas where every inch of soil is precious. The predominant rocks are extremely ancient lava flows, which may be as much as a billion years old. Whatever accumulation of soil there may have been in the hundreds of millions of years that passed before the great ice sheet moved down and overrode the island, the final retreat of the great glacier must have left it bare. And thereupon began a long series of changes in the water level of what is now Lake Superior. These changes are recorded in benches cut out by waves, and by beach lines, which show that the island was at times submerged completely, merely a reef of greenstone rock in the great body of water. As the "modern" Lake Superior found new outlets for its water, Isle Royale gradually rose higher and higher from the lake level, until it achieved its present condition. But it was all the work of lazy Time, and the years between each stage of emergence and the next, indicated by those beach lines, is difficult to grasp.

Because of that broom wielded by the ice sheet, because of the low mean annual temperature of Isle Royale and the added fact that the rainfall and snowfall are very moderate, the growth of plants on the island is not rapid, and recovery from fires is slow. Yet for the scientist, and especially the ecologist, it is one of the most interesting of all the national parks. So many questions can be raised concerning the occurrence of the plant and animal forms that now exist! How did certain mammals get there after the glacial ice had finally gone? The swamps and bogs of the earth are perhaps the most revealing testimonial areas of life-economy, and Isle Royale has its full share of them.

There were certainly caribou on the island once. A small group was seen by trappers, years ago, five miles out from the Canadian shore, headed for the island, and other men saw caribou on the ice at Rock Harbor after the ice had broken up. But how did the mice, the squirrels, and the weasels get there? Possibly by driftwood rafts? The conjectures are fascinating.

Then, too, in the dense cedar-tamarack swamps, with their low temperature at all seasons, it was once reported that "perennial ice" had been found

Seventeen wolves on the ice—nearly the whole wolf population of the island. Isle Royale National Park. [Photo: William W. Dunmire]

beneath a layer of turf, not in one spot, but in several. It could hardly fail to suggest the possibility of what would be called a "relict" of glacial ice, though the masses would have to be rather large, I suppose, to maintain the supposition. No doubt the existence of a glacial remnant is improbable; but the mere fact that the year-round ice was there is highly suggestive. It emphasizes the far-north aspect of the park. With an annual snowfall a quarter of that which visits Mount Olympus, in Olympic National Park, what would Isle Royale be like? Or, not to indulge in anything so fanciful, suppose the mean temperature were just a few degrees lower than it is? What new cycle of life-adaptation would ensue? A small rare fish taken from the stomachs of trout caught off Isle Royale has been described as "doubtless a relic of a former arctic marine species." There is no lack of engaging speculations in this extraordinary environment.

But the fishermen will be more interested in fishing. I have not fished in Lake Superior, nor in the lakes of Isle Royale, but from what I have heard I should imagine that this place does not prove disappointing. There are trout on the offshore reefs, and fishing boats may be rented at the developed centers. On guided trips fishing tackle is supplied. I have even seen a report somewhere that in some of the smaller inland lakes there are more fish than should be there. I suppose that means they outrun their food supply. It sounds like the dream of a devotee, but there may be a hidden drawback somewhere. Possibly these places are hard to reach. Incidentally, the ranger force at Isle Royale, engaged in protection work, is not numerous enough to undertake the interpretative services offered in many parks, but to the extent that the men have time, they will be glad to inform and to help all visitors.

Scenically, if you like the northern forest scene—that in which the immaculate canoe birch mingles with the balsam and the other evergreens; where the sugar, red, and mountain maples splash the landscape with their paintpots in autumn; where, in tramping, there is not a single three-mile path of monotony, because the forest changes are rung by stands of maples, stands of birch and poplar, cedar, and tamarack, then jack pine, then alders and willows, and back to evergreens again—if you like this scene, and love to hike in it and search for the surprises it holds, then you will find in this remote wilderness of Isle Royale exactly what you seek. You will not have to rough it much—not more, I assume, than you will prefer to.

5. SEQUOIA AND KINGS CANYON NATIONAL PARKS
[California]

AS A NARRATOR, LEMUEL GULLIVER, a seafaring man, had the fault of letting his timidity lead him into understatement. He tempered the accounts of his adventures in strange places for fear that he might be disbelieved. This was especially true of his sojourn on the island of Brobdingnag. I have this lesson before me as I begin to write of Sequoia and Kings Canyon National Parks, which, administered as one park, present a Sierra scene that complements and emphasizes the beauties and wonders seen by so many millions in Yosemite.

Gulliver, left behind by his fleeing shipmates, found himself in a land where the wheat fields were composed of stalks forty feet high; where "the trees were so lofty that I could make no computation of their altitude." The house cats were larger than oxen; the King's kitchen was six hundred feet high; the King's horses were sixty feet tall. The human inhabitants of Brobdingnag were proportionately large. Gulliver was at first taken by them to be an insect.

We who have been in Sequoia and Kings Canyon, as well as in the backcountry of Yosemite, know well how Lemuel Gulliver felt. To enjoy it is the easiest thing in the world. To comprehend the magnitude of it all is quite another matter. The first feeling of a new visitor to this Brobdingnagian scene may well be one of puzzlement. He has heard of trees so huge that the lumber in a single one of them would be sufficient to build 100 five-room houses. He has been told of looking down from a certain rocky eminence almost a sheer mile, and of canyons whose granite walls rise abruptly 5,000 feet from a plunging river at the bottom. He has seen on a map, perhaps, that seventy-five of the mountain peaks exceed 11,000 feet in height, twenty are more than 12,000, and seven, including the master of them all, Mount Whitney, are more than 14,000 feet above sea level. He gazes about him. What about it? Is this all true? It doesn't seem so colossal as he expected.

The reason is clear. There is no effective scale. Everything is gigantic except the visitor himself and his companions; and because the human life against this background is as a mustard seed lost in a square mile, it is no scale at all. Comparisons must be made from like to like or they fail to register. This is notably true of the giant sequoias. Standing at the base of one of these trees, the newly arrived visitor has no perspective. The statistics—height, diameter, circumference—mean almost nothing at all. It is only when you have lived with these trees for a while and have seen them in their relation to the community of which they are the biggest living things but where there are other giants too—sugar and ponderosa pines, cedars and firs—it is only then that you will appreciate the grandeur and significance of the sequoia patriarchs. It is a revelation never to be forgotten.

Since these two national parks cannot adequately be pictured for those who have never visited them, we must fall back on statistics that will intimate what may be expected there. It is customary to begin with the Big Trees, and I suppose it is really necessary. Yet it would be almost tragic to leave anyone with the impression that, having seen some of the sequoia groves, he has seen all that Sequoia and Kings Canyon have to offer. On the contrary, this region, the mightiest section of the Sierra Nevada, offers trail experiences, some easy, some difficult, which go far beyond anything that can be had elsewhere if you are looking for titanic proportions. The trail enthusiast can here ride over the top of the mightiest mountain peak in the United States proper, or if he is a practiced hiker, he may cross it afoot. It is not easy, but it is done. This is really extraordinary. Here is a peak that towers 14,495 feet. Many mountaintops not nearly so high are closed to any but the most skillful alpinists.

We shall come back, a little farther on, to those 400,000 acres of unbroken wilderness which lie between the southern tip of Sequoia National Park and the northernmost limit of Kings Canyon National Park, a territory with the wildest grandeur the eye can look upon. But for the moment the Big Trees must have their say.

When John Dryden wrote that ringing line "The monarch oak, the patriarch of trees . . . ," he knew nothing of the existence, in a faraway land called California by the Spaniards, of a kind of tree that could dethrone his monarch without half trying. Dryden had in mind some English trees that were truly venerable, such as the Damorey Oak in Dorsetshire, blown down in 1703 and found to be more than 2,000 years old. But it was a comparatively young monarch. We do not know how ancient some of the greatest of the standing sequoias may be, but the rings of trees that have been cut frequently exceed 3,000, and some of the larger trees may be between 3,500 and 4,000 years old. Thus they were aged trees when Dryden's oak was an acorn. They had gone into their patriarchal period when Rome, the Eternal City, was a settlement of shepherds from the Alban Hills. They are older than any human historical reference to which we can turn with a feeling of true kinship with the men who left the record.

This *Sequoia gigantea*, growing only on the western slopes of the Sierra in central California, is one of three survivors of a genus that once flourished throughout the world. Its near relative, the coast redwood—a fine grove of which may be seen in Muir Woods National Monument—makes luxurious stands from Monterey County to Oregon. The only other species now alive, the metasequoia, or "dawn redwood," located and examined in China a few years ago by Dr. Ralph Chaney of the University of California, may possibly be the tree of which so many and such widespread fossil forms have been found. As a genus, the sequoia was certainly as abundant once as the pine is today. The roster noted above embraces all that are known to exist as living trees. What happened to them? Who knows? Probably a number of factors were involved—changes of climate and creation of desert areas, volcanic lava flows, the movement southward of polar or mountain ice sheets. For the most part they disappeared with the passing of the mighty reptiles of a moist, warm geologic period.

If the Ice Age finally put an end to most of the Big Trees, that would explain why the remnant in the Sierra escaped. It would not explain why they have never been found there as a continuous forest cover, but always in groves, living in association with other trees, and numbering in each group

Snow comes to the giant forest. Sequoia National Park. [Photo: R. Badarocco]

from as few as six to as many as several thousand. There are approximately sixty-three of these groves.

Looking back to our earliest knowledge of the presence in our country of such magnificent trees, it is rather amusing to note the almost complete ignorance of them as late as 1853 by a botanist as famous as was Dr. Jacob M. Bigelow, who was attached to the Pacific Survey party led by Lieutenant Amiel Whipple. The sequoias were known to exist, to be sure. Probably Captain Joseph Reddeford Walker saw them as early as 1833. But when Dr. Bigelow arrived in California, he found that a local amateur had taken the trouble to send specimens of bark, wood, leaves, and cone, with a full description, back to Washington by way of the Isthmus of Panama. The specimens never arrived.

Meanwhile a certain Mr. Lobb, collecting for some botanical society in Scotland, sent specimens to Dr. John Lindley in London. Lindley pronounced the tree a new genus and called it *Wellingtonia gigantea,* in honor of the Duke of Wellington. Dr. Bigelow was greatly annoyed. He had already made up his mind that it was a new genus, and proposed to call it *Washingtonia.* Bigelow had nothing against the Duke, but he wanted no foreign interloper claiming the tree of trees. He reported sourly: "Well, let England have the empty name. *We* have the tree!"

But there was no international incident. The Hungarian botanist Stephan Endlicher had studied the coast redwood and declared it to be an entirely new genus, which he called *Sequoia sempervirens;* and now a Frenchman came along and recognized the Big Tree as another species of sequoia, calling it *gigantea.* Endlicher had named the tree in honor of the Cherokee chief who created for his people a syllabary of eighty-six symbols representing each sound in the language spoken by them. There is a statue of this extraordinary Indian in the national Capitol. Well is it deserved. Uneducated, and speaking no English, Chief Sequoyah was no less touched with genius than any of his forerunners who made writing and printing possible.

But how little Bigelow knew of this tree, which he declared one of the wonders of the world! He relied upon hearsay, probably never seeing more than a small grove near the headwaters of the Calaveras. "The whole number of these trees in existence, young and old," he wrote, "does not exceed 500, and all are comprised in an area of 50 acres. I am impressed with the belief that the species will soon be extinct." (He was providentially wrong about

Looking down into Paradise Valley. Kings Canyon National Park. [Photo: Weldon F. Heald]

this; the ax and saw of the lumberman were stayed in time.) There are probably not less than twenty thousand Big Trees with a diameter of more than ten feet, and it is heartening to note that 92 per cent of these are either in national parks and national forests or in the custody of California. It would be well if the other 8 per cent should somehow come into preserves. Not a single *Sequoia gigantea* should be cut. They represent a unique survival; the patriarchs are probably the oldest living things; they belong to our remote and future histories. In a wider sense they should even be regarded as wards of the world.

Although it is unique in other respects, what makes the giant sequoia the true monarch of the plant world is its massiveness. The vast volume of wood in these trunks is caused by the fact that they rise from the ground without the taper that characterizes most trees. They are prodigious clubs rather than Brobdingnagian walking sticks; you might almost call them cylinders. Hence, though no Big Trees approach anywhere near the record of the tallest coast redwood, or even the tallest Douglas firs, in total volume they stand supreme. The General Sherman tree, in Sequoia, reaches a height of 272 feet, with a diameter at the base of 30 feet and 7 inches. But consider! At the height of 120 feet the trunk has still a diameter of 17 feet, and the first large limb, nearly 130 feet from the ground, is close to 7 feet in diameter. Even as I write these words, which are the statistics of qualified engineers, I keep asking myself if it can be really so. A tree with a limb far bigger than the trunk of any tree that grows in my own well-forested countryside?

The General Grant, in the Grant Grove section of Kings Canyon National Park, is even thicker at the base than the General Sherman, but not quite so tall. This Grant Grove section, by the way, was the first stand of sequoias to be given national-park protection, and the reason may be seen in the cut-over areas nearby. Magnificent sequoia groves, more extensive than anything now preserved, were ruthlessly destroyed before the butchery ended. Vandalism is a harsh word, and I should certainly not apply it to any ordinary deforestation, even when it has been proved to be inept and unwise; but here among the sequoias it is doubtful if the destruction even resulted in any monetary profit commensurate with the effort involved. And near Big Stump Basin you may see a tree that was nearly cut through and then abandoned, as though the children tired of their play. Strange to say, this tree refused to fall, and the cut is steadily healing. The powers of recuperation of a maimed Big Tree are a phenomenon in the plant world.

You may also see the Centennial Stump, all that remains of a huge tree that was cut up in sections and shipped to the Centennial Exposition in

Philadelphia in 1876. It was a bright idea, undoubtedly; but the promoters were rewarded by having most of those who saw it pronounce it an absurd fake. No tree like that ever existed!

At Sequoia National Park the center of activities is at Giant Forest. This was the favorite of John Muir, and a discovery of Hale Tharp, who found a huge hollow log there and fashioned himself a comfortable cabin from it. Not far away is the Crescent Meadow, likewise beloved by Muir, who esteemed it the loveliest spot in all the Sierra. Giant Forest Village has a strategic location, with easy foot trails or short drives to many things of admiration—recalling that the original meaning of the word *admiration* was "wonder." Moro Rock, Beetle Rock, Sunset Rock, the Tokopah Valley, Crystal Cave, the Muir Grove, Admiration Point—all are readily accessible.

Nine miles along the Colony Hill road from Giant Forest is the site of the lumber mill of the Kaweah Cooperative Commonwealth Colony, whose lumbering activities, oddly enough, had much to do with the establishment of Sequoia National Park. Even the site is worth visiting, and not alone for its location in the midst of grand prospects of canyon and mountain. Kaweah Colony was a belated example of an outburst of experiments in communal living which began in the early part of the last century and flourished in numbers, if not in durability, like dandelions in the commuter's lawn. Of such gestures toward the equitable life, the famous Brook Farm was a blue-stocking example—Ralph Waldo Emerson, declining an invitation to join Brook Farm, said dryly that he preferred to own his real estate in Concord.

Noble as were the motives of the leaders in these communal enterprises, and undeniable as it is that the theory is sound and only lacks the existence of people who can live according to a sound theory, nearly all the communities started with clay feet. Some of the colonies were planted upon soil that was hostile even to beans; others, believing that they held the master key that would unlock all economic closets, gravely repeated all the practical errors that had preceded them, and added some of their own.

Kaweah, instituted with such high hopes in the glorious Sierra forest country, was no exception. It should have occurred to the founders, who were going to attain the upright social existence by cutting down trees—trees, by the way, that they later found they did not own—that people who depend for their thrift upon eating up a forest will have no resource when the forest is gone except to eat up each other. The colony, however, did not last long enough to experience cannibalism, for the day soon came when a detachment of U.S. cavalry came in and ordered an end to the timber operation.

[69]

That was the finish of Kaweah Commonwealth, but you may be sure that the devotees dispersed with the conviction that only bad luck prevented the consummation of a success that would have astounded and allured the world; and that many of them hastened to form or join other experiments of the kind. I once met, in the single-tax colony at Fairhope, Alabama, a number of enthusiasts who had lived successively in half a dozen such communities, dutifully remaining with each one long enough to give it a decent interment. The concept dies hard, especially among folks who are naturally good and humane; and doubtless the world stands always in need of a little Arcadian madness.

Of these two great parks, Sequoia and Kings Canyon, only a small part— but that sufficiently revealing for those who have only a few days to spend —can be reached by automobile. Beyond is the wilderness of mountain, lake, stream, flowered meadow, imposing canyon. The way to see what this fastness holds is the way pioneers saw it, and such a holiday is for those who have the time and the willingness to plod, browse, and associate with the things of the wild. To cover the longest trail trips afoot is, of course, for the most vigorous. Slightly less arduous would be to let a donkey carry the grub and the pans and bedding, as did the old-time prospectors. When you get well acquainted with a sad-faced burro and learn to speak his language, he can be an excellent companion. Behind his mournful face he conceals a fine, albeit occasionally annoying, sense of humor.

Those who want to rough it deluxe—camping out under the easiest conditions—may procure the services of seasoned guides, packers, and camp cooks. In these circumstances it will still be a retreat into the primitive.

In Sequoia the rock-carved passages of the Kaweah and the Kern, and in the neighboring park the stupendous canyons of the forks of the Kings, reach upward toward the hundreds of lakes of the Sierra and tumbling tributary streams that have wild fish in them—wild fish eager to fight when they feel the barb. Even the novice can get his fish here, but he has honestly earned them by going back where no serried ranks of highway fishermen are crowding the landscape. This statement is prompted by the fact that I have just been looking at a photograph, reproduced in a sportsmen's magazine, showing "opening day" on one of Pennsylvania's streams. The sportsmen, poor wretches, are lined up shoulder to jowl as far as the camera lens can reach. What that sort of thing would do to the "natural economy" that exists along

---

Big Trees along the Generals Highway. Sequoia National Park. [*Photo: Howard R. Stagner*]

a riverbank in a wilderness area requires no special scientific knowledge to understand. For real sport, with a tingle in it, the streams and lakes of the high Sierra are an Izaak Walton domain.

Then, in these backcountry places, the glimpses of the native animals come naturally and almost surely into every tramping experience. The black bear, harmless when you leave him alone, is common at about the elevation of Giant Forest. Mule deer are plentiful and, if anything, too tame. They tend to move down into places where they can be fed tidbits by sentimental people. The sentiment is a natural one; the limpid eyes of the deer are almost irresistible when he approaches for a handout; but let us resist the impulse. A toffee-fed deer is going to be a sick deer later, an easy victim for the predator. The hiker will not see bighorn and cougar, probably, but they are there. And almost surely the golden eagle will be found soaring over the craggy peaks.

The John Muir Trail, all the way from Sequoia up to Yosemite, finds its way along the ridgepole of this Sierra stronghold, seldom dropping below the 8,500-foot elevation. Lucky are those who have the time and the passion for a trail adventure like this one.

Yes, in these two magnificent parks we are all, without exception, Gullivers arrived in Brobdingnag. Yet, really, I do not wish to overemphasize the smallness of man in relation to the immensity of the natural scene in which he finds himself. The skill and daring that through his will and hand have transmuted the stubborn raw materials of earth into comfort and dominance form no less a marvel, perhaps, than any of the elements he has wrought upon. Man is able. I congratulate him, and he will think my congratulations no more than his desert.

Still, when he stands at the foot of the Grizzly and the General Sherman sequoias and considers not so much their bulk as their meaning and history, or when he gazes from the pinnacle of Moro Rock at the flowing harmony of the crests of the Kaweahs and the mountains of the Divide, or when he is engulfed in the magnificence of the canyons of the Kings, it would be no confession of weakness, but rather an affirmation of true strength, to consider a certain brief utterance set down many centuries ago. These occur in the third verse of Psalm CXLIV, in a book that may be consulted, I think, at any good public library; and before delivering it, the attendant will considerately dust it off.

6. OLYMPIC NATIONAL PARK
[*Washington*]

THERE IS A LEGEND TO THE EFFECT that Jupiter, aghast at the growing skepticism of his people and angered at the gibes of scurrilous writers like Lucian, pulled up stakes from his mountain in Greece, emigrated to the New World, and took up residence in the western part of Washington State, on a peninsula fronting upon the Pacific Ocean and the Juan de Fuca Strait.

I do not vouch for this tale. But it must be said that there is some evidence to substantiate it. There certainly *is* a mountain in the peninsula—where Olympic National Park is situated—called Mount Olympus, and nothing is more natural than that Jupiter should have kept up the ancestral name and style. There is on this Mount Olympus a blue glacier of transcendent beauty, and, as every schoolgirl knows, blue was Juno's favorite color. Everything about the area suggests that it is a place a god like Jupiter would choose.

This is not all. You remember—do you not?—that the Romans paid respects to Jupiter under many titles, corresponding with his various supernatural powers. He was, among other things, Jupiter Pluvius (Rain-Bringer). If you needed rain, you resorted to the appropriate temple and asked for a shower. There was a small charge for the service. But if you wanted the weather to clear, you went to the temple of Jupiter Serenator (Fair-Weather-Bringer). If all went well (there was trifling fee), the sun began to shine. What happened when the farmers wanted rain and the rest of the people planned a pantheistic picnic, I do not know. My informant is silent.

Now, it *may* be a coincidence that the weather conditions on the Olympic Peninsula suggest that Jupiter is locally sometimes Pluvius and sometimes Serenator. On the western side of Olympic National Park the yearly precipitation may exceed 140 inches. It is the wettest winter climate in the United States. As for Mount Olympus itself, it has been estimated, from the runoff, that the total snowfall might be at least 250 feet in a season. Yet the easterly slope of the park is the driest place on the west coast outside of southern California, and even drier than some parts of that irrigated land.

The meteorologists explain this phenomenon glibly. They say that the Olympic Mountains reach up and squeeze dry the moisture-laden clouds that come in from the Pacific before they can get over to the eastern side. This

---

Overleaf: Here and there the sun finds an opening in the rain forest. Olympic National Park. [Photo: George Grant]

explanation would eliminate the need for Jupiter altogether and is therefore destructive modernism. I am tolerant, however. If my neighbor prefers to worship a barometer, I am content. Let us look to the results.

Olympic National Park, which has been set aside as part of the cultural wealth of the United States, for the admiration and enjoyment and education of generations to come, is indeed a wilderness. It contains a temperate-zone rain forest that is unique. There are other rain forests in the world. Darwin described the jungle of beech giants in Tierra del Fuego. There is a temperate rain forest, predominantly of a kind of yew, in New Zealand. But this forest of evergreen cone-bearing trees of the Olympic Peninsula is one of the world's wonders.

There are no words competent to picture such a forest. Photographs give merely a feeble suggestion of such plant fecundity, the result of a happy combination of climatic conditions and soil. Even actually seeing it, walking in it, observing the community life that goes on within it, leave one with a sense of unreality and incredulity. There diffuses through the forest in its heaviest portions a greenish-white light that becomes in other spots a glow of misty warm ivory when the sun strikes in upon some broad leaves like those of the maple, which have a transparent quality in comparison with the light-devouring conifers.

Pile carpets of moss cover the ground; moss dangles from the branches; ferns climb from the bases of the trees to join the mosses above; at first venture the silence is frightening. It is not only the luxuriance of the vegetation that is bewildering. There are pygmies in this forest that would be giants in many places; and the giants here are in troops, in regiments, in armies. The largest known Douglas fir, found on the Queets River, is seventeen feet eight inches in diameter four feet above the base. Here are considered to be the largest red cedar, twenty feet in diameter; the largest Western hemlock; and the largest Alaska cedar. There is a Sitka spruce that as yet has no discovered rivals for size. That any soil in any climate could support such a total of growth in the space provided for it is a challenge to belief.

It is called a rain forest, and that is just what it is. But the name suggests to the imagination a perpetual drip and driving rain, like a Gustave Doré picture, or like the weather that made the army swear so terribly in Flanders. Do not be alarmed. To be sure, there is copious rainfall, annually. How could there be a rain forest otherwise? In winter the word *copious* may be an understatement. At Quinault Lake in one twenty-four-hour period, twelve inches of rain bucketed earthward. The rivers that course to the ocean are subject

Ruby Beach, on the log-strewn ocean strip. Olympic National Park. [Photo: George Grant]

to great fluctuations, and are awe-inspiring when in flood. Even in summer the Pacific may send spongy clouds in upon the peninsula without much warning.

But in summer and early autumn there may come days upon days that smile invitingly upon those willing to take the potluck of the wilderness and follow on foot or horseback some of the five hundred miles of trail that find their scenic way through the forest and into the mountains to the choice meadows, blooming from June through October.

The hiker who wants to pack a few necessaries and a bedroll and really test his kinship with the wild can find trailside shelters at convenient points. The Oregon jay will be watching you from point to point as you plod along the trail. He will not abuse you in seven avian languages, like Steller's jay, but as soon as you strike one of these rustic shelters, a half-dozen of him will drop in on you before you have unpacked. He will propose a partnership. Beware of partnerships. If you have any success, your partner's infinite sagacity was responsible. If you do not, it was due to *your* stupidity. You will enjoy the company of this alert bird, but you must maintain your sturdy independence.

A jay's nest found in these woods contained the portion of a Seattle newspaper that carries the dateline—April 4. Any bird that lays a cornerstone and deposits evidences of current history therein is worthy of respect and—suspicion.

There is no lack of wild animals to be seen from the roads and trails. Outstanding, of course, is the fine Roosevelt elk. In summer, these animals are in the higher country, but when snows come, they move down into the valleys to browse on the vine maple, which forms such an important undergrowth in the dense forest. The elk bulls are sturdy fellows, weighing from seven hundred to a thousand pounds. They seldom go down to tidewater and have an odd way of concentrating in some of the valleys and rarely visiting others. The Columbian black-tailed deer and the mule deer are also abundant, though the latter was introduced from the pine country of eastern Washington.

While in the rain forest, visitors should note the extraordinary features of tree growth. First of all will be observed the way in which so many of the living trees have taken root on fallen logs and old stumps. Though this habit is also characteristic of the coast redwood of California and seems to be connected with the difficulty the seeds may have in sprouting in the thick mat of moss that carpets the forest, here the adaptation may be seen in most dramatic form. For example, a Sitka spruce, three feet in diameter, and a Western hemlock may be seen making a twin growth out of the stump of a Sitka spruce that went down more than a century ago. Another instance is twenty-three trees, twenty-one of them hemlocks, one a spruce, and the other a maple, which have taken root on one giant fallen log. They line up like a platoon of soldiers.

But it is high time to leave this temperate-zone jungle and take the trail up one of the river valleys toward the cluster of mountains that rise in a scattered way—there is no definite range—in the center of the park. These rivers, most of them crystal-clear, which come plunging down from the mountains to flow into the Pacific, do not travel long distances to their goal, but they carry a surprising amount of water from the melting snow and ice of the peaks. It is not far to timberline in these mountains, generally not more than five thousand feet, which is a low timberline compared with that

Cove of quietude. Olympic National Park. [*Photo: Joseph Dixon*]

of most of the Western parks. At timberline are the alpine meadows, with their profusion of flowers, and from these bright spots it is no great distance to the perpetual snow. There are probably a hundred glaciers in these peaks, though many of them are small. Mount Olympus has seven major glaciers on its upper flanks.

Though one of the great charms of Olympic National Park lies precisely in its lack of "developments," and though the best things are reserved for those willing to take at least short and easy jaunts on foot, there is still much beauty and strangeness to be observed from the approach and mountain roads. Deer Park, in the northeastern section, can be reached by a road that climbs to six thousand feet and affords splendid views of the mountain cluster of the Juan de Fuca Strait and of Vancouver Island. Some of the finest of the rain forest, along the Hoh River, may be seen without leaving your car, but it would be better to put on your galoshes and get a more intimate sense of this marvel of tree growth by following some trail a short distance into the wilderness.

It is the same here in Olympic as anywhere else; good fishermen get fish, and the others say there are no fish left in this wicked world—at least, none in places where a fellow can go and get them without any inconvenience to himself. Hence has arisen the great clamor for the planting of legal-sized fish that, reared in the cloistered luxury of a hatchery, will have, when transplanted to the streams, all the desperate fighting quality of aquatic rabbits, and the high flavor of wet newspaper. These educated trout, dumped into a river to take their chances with rough-mannered wild fish, have been known to jump into a fisherman's basket and beg to be taken back to boarding school, where they were so happy with the rest of the girls, with chopped-liver hors d'oeuvres three times a day and nobody ever speaking a rude word. Sport fishermen will understand what I mean by this; others should order their fish by mail.

7. MUIR WOODS NATIONAL MONUMENT
[California]

MOUNT TAMALPAIS, IN MARIN COUNTY across the Golden Gate, is the holy mountain of the native San Franciscan. Hence it is that sometimes Fujiyama is spoken of (though not by Japanese) as the Mount Tamalpais of Japan. There is no likeness in appearance. It is a matter of reverence: the famous Bohemian Club performs its devotional exercises in its tutelary grove on the Russian River.

Muir Woods National Monument

In the days before the Bay and Golden Gate bridges were built, the dwellers in Marin County who got up early to catch the Sausalito boat were regarded with some respect even by those San Franciscans who spoke sneeringly of the commuters from Oakland and Berkeley. The voyagers who came in on the Sausalito ferry had a spicy aroma, of cinnamon and cloves, like the old-time salts from the South Seas. They were all able-bodied seamen —survivors of many a dense fog. There were giant commuters in those days. Transportation is now rapid and—colorless. ¡Ay de mi!

At the foot of Mount Tamalpais, the aforesaid holy mountain, is Muir Woods National Monument, donated to the people of the United States by Congressman William Kent and his wife, Elizabeth Thacher Kent. They tied only one string to their noble gift: that the beautiful valley of redwoods, when proclaimed as a national monument, should bear the name of John Muir, who loved these trees with all the ardor of his great Caledonian heart. A request granted before it was asked! No name could have been more fitting. Nimble John, clambering everywhere in California and seeing everything, had made the sequoias almost as much his own as Chief Sequoyah's.

These coast redwoods, which launch their great spires skyward all the way from Monterey County to just across the California-Oregon line, are cousins of the mighty giant sequoias of the High Sierra. They are called *sempervirens*—evergreen—and aside from the great difference in the manner of growth, particularly in the shape of the trunk, there are a number of other distinguishing characteristics when the two trees are more closely examined. The foliage of the *gigantea* of the Sierra somewhat resembles that of the juniper; the other is nearer to the hemlock. The bark of the giant is a bright reddish brown, while that of the coast redwood is a dull chocolate. Finally, the cones of the *sempervirens* are very small, only one third as large as those of its relative.

Which is the nobler sequoia—*sempervirens* or *gigantea?* Not Solomon himself could judge. For if the *gigantea* is one of the oldest living things on earth, and if its girth is far greater than that of the coast redwood, the latter breaks all forest records too. The *tallest* living thing known to exist is a specimen of the coast redwood.

This tallest tree is not in Muir Woods, but the trees there are quite tall enough and varied enough in their habits to afford a perfect demonstration. Here in Muir Woods, for example, you may see dramatic instances of how the coast redwood propagates itself. It does not need to spring from seed, coming up very readily from stumps, from the roots of veterans, or even obligingly from burls, as many people know who have put these lifeless-looking tree warts in a bowl of water and seen the green shoots emerge from them. You may see an albino redwood of great size, and instances of albino shoots; and circles of large trees, with a patriarch in the middle of each ring, where fire ran through these woods two centuries ago and the wounded tree made haste to send up a liberal progeny from its roots, in case the worst should arrive.

In northern California, where the redwood growth is most intense, there are great stands of these trees, almost exclusively. The giants grow so close together as seemingly to leave no room for anything else and to allow no sunlight to come through the canopy of their tops. Yet enough sun does filter through to allow a rich ground cover of ferns and flowering plants, especially the oxalis; and where the redwoods are not quite so dominating, the Douglas fir, tan oak, and madroña may add a modest companionship to the scene, as they do at Muir Woods.

To visit Muir Woods National Monument is to have an adequate sample of the typical redwood forest. If the tallest redwood there is only 246 feet, with a diameter of 17 feet, the Statue of Liberty is not much taller, and Niagara Falls nowhere near so high. It must be owned, too, that the greater forests to the north do not have quite such an intimate touch as the moderate acreage of Muir Woods. Wandering along the trail among the Muir trees, most visitors have a sense, even among these giants, of kinship and friendliness. They have this feeling, too, in driving over the Redwood Highway, which winds for many miles among the towering trees.

But in those dense uncut forests which reach from Dyerville to the Smith River, where California and the Save-the-Redwoods League have created precious reserves that will never feel the saw and ax, the wilderness is uncompromising. To go into that overpowering, silent cathedral of the Smith River redwoods—into, let us say, the National Tribute Grove, which has been set aside to honor the men and women of the armed services of World War II—is to leave human vanity in the sunlight just outside. The beauty and majesty of it is inspiring, and also a little crushing.

The wilderness, as an old friend of mine says, is "strong medicine." He knows. He has lived with it more than most men. Going into the *true* wilderness for a long sojourn alone, you had better pack in your saddlebags, besides chocolate bars and changes of socks, a maximum of character and integrity, and a willingness to go to a school of stern discipline. The wilderness can

Sometimes the seedling redwood is an albino. Muir Woods National Monument.
[Photo: George Grant]

ennoble the Jedediah Smiths and John Muirs; it can also disconcert and dilute.

Of course, for a holiday land cruise, the wilderness, especially in the company of a guide who has both skill and imagination, is pure tonic. At all events, singing the praises of the wilderness *merely as such* is much like congratulating the Cosmos. The Cosmos will not feel obligated. Even so good a physicist as Sir James Jeans, who patiently explained the Universe to itself, never received any acknowledgment from it while he lived. Since then his relations may have become more chummy.

So do not demand any immediate mental or spiritual profit from a visit to the wilderness. All in good time. The wilderness simply *is*. That is the best reason for preserving our finest examples of it.

Muir Woods is the best kind of introduction, I think, to the larger California State wilderness redwood preserves. It is redwoods-in-cameo.

Deer are quite common in the monument, but except in early morning and late evening you are not likely to see them till autumn, when they come down from the surrounding hills. When the winter rains have set Redwood Creek to flowing briskly, you may see mature salmon and steelheads fighting their way up the rapids to the spawning beds within the monument. Naturally, you are forbidden to catch them. It is a great sight; after a first greedy impulse, you will not want to catch them.

8. PETRIFIED FOREST NATIONAL PARK
[*Arizona*]

THE FOREST THAT WAS, 135 million years ago, stood on the banks of an ancient stream in northern Arizona when the face of that now mountainous country looked very different from what it does today. In the days of the Forest That Was, it expanded as a flattish lowland, not much above sea level. On the flood plains grew ferns and rushes, and cycads that looked somewhat like modern palms; and among these floundered giant saurians and salamanders. Somewhere upstream, on slightly higher ground, grew pines. They were not wholly different from our modern pines, but were rather more like certain pines now living in South America and Australia.

The Forest That Was is now again the Forest That Is. But how changed! No longer standing upright with anchors of root and with branches and leaves. Those Triassic pines are now scattered helter-skelter—some in whole logs, some in broken sections—over an area perhaps a hundred miles from where they grew. They are now stone trees—stone of such hardness that it will scratch all but the hardest alloy steels.

Petrified Forest National Park

Petrified trees, they are called; and this is Petrified Forest National Park, preserved first as a monument under the Antiquities Act so that Americans of the future may see and study the greatest natural phenomenon of its kind. For these are not merely fragments of petrified trees, such fragments as can be seen in many places, particularly in the Southwest, where every heavy summer rain washes them from the soil. This is the greatest and most colorful concentration of petrified wood ever yet revealed on the earth's surface. Most petrified wood is brownish or slaty in color, if not black. These stone trees are of nearly the hues of the rainbow; indeed, one of the six "forests" within the area is called the Rainbow Forest. Their colors are practically the colors of the Painted Desert, part of which is in the northern part of the park. The reason for this similarity is evident when the story of the trees is unfolded.

Are everyday folks interested in geology? They certainly are interested in the phase of geology expressed in Petrified Forest. The yearly visitation here greatly exceeds that of many other national parks, and few of the monuments

Hansel and Gretel at doorway of the witch. Muir Woods National Monument.
[Photo: Donald Reeser]

anywhere nearly approach it. It is true that the trees are near one of the most heavily traveled cross-country highways; but it is also true that the area is not near any populous cities, where people might run out merely to spend a Sunday afternoon. Visitors to Petrified Forest definitely come to see the trees; and having seen them, they wish to know more about them. In the Rainbow Forest Museum there is a fine exhibit of polished wood, revealing the coloring in all its brilliance, as well as local fossils and a diorama that graphically shows the way it all happened. In summer, a short talk is given at regular periods in this museum, and there are naturalist guided tours through the nearby forest.

There must be something especially mysterious and romantic about the petrifaction of a tree, especially when it also becomes a mineral rainbow. There seems to be no other reason why such great numbers of people are lured here. Yet, dramatic as was the occurrence that created this wonder, it was one of those natural sequences which can be traced without difficulty. These trees, when they were living things, were swept into the rivers and carried downstream, finally to be buried in the sand and mud in the spot where they are now, and will be for many thousands of years, because they will continue to be constantly exposed by erosion. Their progress downstream was probably a slow one. In that journey the pines lost their bark, their branches, and most of their roots.

If nothing further had happened, the forest giants would have decayed, or at most would have become some sort of coal, under pressure. But the something else happened. Distant volcanoes threw up vast clouds of fine cinders, which were carried by the wind and deposited upon the muds and sands in which the trees were buried. For ages this story was repeated—more trees, more burials, more volcanic ash. Indeed, hundreds of feet below where the petrified trees are seen today, there are probably hosts of others that will someday come to view.

To turn these trees to stone it was required that the ground where they lay should be flooded with waters containing silica in solution. The volcanic ash supplied this silica as it was leached. It also supplied the minerals from which the paint was mixed. Iron and manganese were in that amorphous dust which finally settled to earth to become later a kind of claylike rock called bentonite—a rock that takes up water like a sponge and becomes a fine mud that easily creates "badlands."

135,000,000 years ago these stone logs were part of a great forest. Petrified Forest National Park. [Photo: George Grant]

Out of these badlands the stone trees were washed; to the north, the wild coloring of the Painted Desert was produced. The tourist who, leaving the main highway and running up to Desert Inn, looks out for the first time upon this kaleidoscope of reds and orange, of purple, blue, and yellow, stretching away into the distance, can only gaze in silent wonder. There are rare times, in the early morning, when the rosy fingers of the dawn dabble with just such colors along the horizon; and many a cross-country motorist, getting an early start for a long day's pull, has hauled over to the side of the road and watched the shifting miracle awhile. It is something like that.

Another thing that makes this silicified wood so prized is the presence of lovely quartz crystals, which, as fluid silica, sought out the crevices in the petrifying wood and solidified as gemstones of water—clear amethyst, amber, green, black, red. The logs literally became warehouses of jewels. But the lapidary must get his gems from other sources than this park. Naturally, it is forbidden to remove any of this precious petrified wood, no matter what the size of the fragment. Does this seem stingy? Simply consider what would happen if each visitor took away a few pounds. These forests are not growing. This particular alchemy of nature has been completed. The supply is exhaustible. That is why it comes as a shock to learn that the incident which hastened the creation of the earlier monument was the erection of a mill to crush these petrified trees into abrasive material. Imagine that!

Besides the petrified trees and the Painted Desert, visitors to this park will not fail to see the evidences of an occupation, many centuries ago, of a prehistoric people. The story of these early settlers follows generally that of northern Arizona as a whole: first the rude pithouses and excavations, then the later developments of stone houses and pueblos. But these people have left behind something else—some curious picture-writing on the sandstone rocks.

In 1200 or thereabouts, there was no particular hurry in northern Arizona. A pleasant way to spend a month was to chisel geometric designs or pictures of frogs, birds, antelope, snakes, footprints on a cliff or boulder. Some of these petroglyphs seem to convey a message, and some seem quite aimless. Nobody has yet found a clear interpretation of them. One of the best examples of the picture-writing is called Newspaper Rock, found near Rainbow Forest. Do not miss it. As to what this chiseled "newspaper" means, your guess will be about as good as anyone's.

Another feature of interest is the evidence of the use of the petrified wood for tools and weapons of these aborigines. Many objects fashioned from the agatized trees have been found, and near Rainbow Forest and Third Forest are several ruins of houses that were built of blocks of petrified wood. One of these, Agate House, has been partly restored and can be reached by the Third Forest Trail.

In the First Forest is Agate Bridge. Where a great stone tree trunk lay, a gully was created by erosion, so that finally the log became what might be called, if one labored, a natural bridge. In time, if nature had her way— which, so far as is practicable, she is intended to do in the wilderness parks and monuments—this unsupported log would break under its own weight. It would therefore no longer be a bridge. By building a support under the log, it could be made to persist for many years. Eventually, however, all this scenery of northern Arizona will undergo a change. So far as the park is concerned, other logs will appear, and gullies will be created under them. The last time I was at Petrified Forest, I thought I saw something artificial supporting Agate Bridge. In such cases, however, my admiration of the National Park Service being what it is, I always conclude that my eyesight is faulty.

In easily eroded soil the buried trees come to view over the years. Petrified Forest National Park. [Photo: George Grant]

[II]

Forge of Vulcan

AMONG THE WONDERS *of mountains there is Etna, which always burns in
the night, and for so long a period has always had materials for
combustion, being in the winter buried in snow, and having the ashes
it has ejected covered with frost. Nor is it in this mountain alone that
Nature rages, threatening to consume the earth. . . . In so many
places, and with so many fires, does Nature burn the earth.*

—PLINY THE ELDER (A.D. 77), *Natural History*

1. YELLOWSTONE NATIONAL PARK
[*Wyoming–Montana–Idaho*]

[1]

IN 1870 CHARLES SCRIBNER, a book publisher, began the issue of a monthly
magazine, with Dr. J. G. Holland as editor. Illustrated throughout by
wood engravings, the initial number, containing a poem eighteen pages long
and a provocative article about the ocean, indicated a stern purpose to lift
the morals of the reading public or, where those were too heavy to lift, at least
to agitate. This worthy publication, *Scribner's Monthly*, had hardly been
born when Dr. Holland began hearing tales of extraordinary discoveries in
the Western states. It was related to him that a certain General Washburn,
with a gentleman named Langford and others of a party escorted by soldiers,
had spent more than a month in the little-known mountain wilderness that
lay south of Montana Territory and had seen strange things.

Old Faithful seen against its forested background. Yellowstone National Park.
[Photo: M. Woodbridge Williams]

Dr. Holland was no amateur editor and he had heard about strange things from the West before—things that were more strange than true. The sturdy trappers and frontiersmen who for years had been risking their scalps in the remotest spots of the Rockies, the Patties and Sublettes and Colters and Jedediah Smiths, were probably taciturn and uncommunicative men as a class; but Jim Bridger and the later comers loved to astound the tenderfoot. There was a feeling east of the Mississippi that the Ananias family had emigrated to the wide-open spaces and multiplied exceedingly. The fact, however, that this expedition of Montanans had been given a sort of official color by the presence of a cavalry lieutenant encouraged the editor to invite a contribution from Nathaniel Pitt Langford, who later was to be the first superintendent of a newly created Yellowstone National Park.

Langford, who had kept a diary of the expedition, obliged with two articles, which were published in 1871. There is evidence that the editor, mindful of his responsibility to pure and impressionable young minds, toned down the descriptions considerably. The existence of Yellowstone Lake was already known; Langford's report of its extent could be set down to bad eyesight. Such matters as a mountain of volcanic glass and a stupendous canyon with a waterfall higher than Niagara might pass muster as innocent illusions, and hot springs of a sort were entirely credible. But when the writer passed into the field of vents in the surface of the earth which suddenly shot tons of water two hundred feet into the air; one such monster that obligingly erupted every hour on the hour; fountains of boiling water that played continuously; explosions of multicolored muds that plastered the landscape; hills made of solid brimstone; ice-cold streams with hot stones on the bottom; a valley of smokes, or a hillside that looked like a New England factory town with its belching chimneys—well, it was what Artemus Ward would have called "2 mutch." A blunt reviewer said that "this Langford must be the champion liar of the Northwest," and many readers of the monthly gently reminded Dr. Holland that his prospectus had guaranteed a moral tone.

Langford was made to feel a kinship with David Folsom, who, with two companions, had seen some of the geysers in 1869 and on his return to Helena was invited to relate publicly what he had experienced. Folsom replied that up to the moment his local reputation for veracity was good; he thought it would be well not to trifle with it. He did prepare an article about his trip for the *Western Monthly* of Chicago. By some who knew its content, it was considered an act of Providence that before the magazine could mail out the issue containing the story, the building burned down. C. W. Cook, one of Folsom's companions, sent an article to *Lippincott's Magazine*, timidly report-

In 1916 "we had our pictures taken at Jupiter Terrace." Yellowstone National Park.
[Photo: courtesy Marietta Sumner]

ing what they had seen. He received a polite rejection slip: "Thank you but we do not print fiction."

Looking back upon it, it seems strange that the marvels of the Yellowstone should have aroused such incredulity. This was no unknown land, like the canyon of the Colorado before Powell revealed its majesty. John Colter, the soldier of the Lewis and Clark Expedition, and afterward famous as a trapper, had visited part of the region in the early days of the century. Other traders and trappers knew Yellowstone Lake and had seen geysers, boiling springs, and mudpots. Jim Bridger, with a bit of charcoal on a buffalo hide, mapped out the general lay of the land with fair accuracy for Lieutenant J. W. Gunnison about 1850. Father de Smet, Captain Charles Reynolds, and Walter De Lacy either had seen some of the spectacles or knew of them from guides. But until the definite sanction of an official report had been seen and digested, the skeptics were unrelenting.

This official report was the work of a shavetail in the Second Cavalry, stationed at Fort Ellis. His name was Gustavus C. Doane. He was the one detailed, "with one sergeant and four privates," to escort the surveyor general of Montana and his party to "the falls and lakes of Yellowstone and return." The commanding officer at Ellis had not been happy about furnishing an escort for a group of wonder-seekers. The Indians were giving trouble; the Crows especially were thumping the drum. The garrison was already weakened with so many soldiers in the field. If the civilians from Helena had not been territorial bigwigs with some influence, they would have been invited to go sightseeing at their own risk and expense. It was fortunate that they had an order from General Winfield S. Hancock, describing the trip as "an important military necessity"—which it was not.

Fortunate indeed, because it resulted in the classic report of Second Lieutenant Doane, describing, day by day, what the party saw in Yellowstone. Volumes have been written since on the wonderland that became a national park, more accurate in detail, more specific in scientific observation; but there will never be anything finer, fresher, or more responsive than the military document of this young soldier. He tried to remember that, after all, he was just on a tour of duty, and that the cavalry was no place for hearts and flowers. When somebody "reckoned" that a geyser eruption, such as that of the one they called the Giantess, had reached a height of three hundred feet, he straightway triangulated, and declared it to be not more than two hundred and fifty. "Our whole party was wild with enthusiasm"—but Doane had to measure. But little by little the professional detachment began to be swept away and the lieutenant opened the floodgates of his admiration. Yet he did not strive for words and he did not reel with superlatives. It was as though nature, in some of her strangest moods and forms, was speaking to him and he was translating as best he could.

There were several men in that Washburn party who could write very acceptably. Washburn, Langford, Hedges, and Everts all published journalistic material, and no newspaper ever carried better special correspondence than the Helena *Daily Herald* during the period when that frontier newspaper was publishing their accounts. But Doane had an eye and a gift. He climbed the peak now known as Mount Washburn on a day when the pure air of the high country revealed everything with crystal clarity. He saw the snowy summits above the Gallatin Valley, and from them traced almost an unbroken circle of mountains, of which he thought the Tetons were a part. He noted that this circle was broken through in places for the passage of rivers; but he felt that he knew, at this first view, what that circle, with the great basin below him as he faced southward, meant.

"A single glance" he said in his report, "at the interior slopes of the ranges, shows that a former complete connection existed, and that the great basin has been formerly one vast crater of a now extinct volcano. The nature of the rocks, the steepness and outline of the interior walls, together with other peculiarities, render this conclusion a certainty." Well, with whatever amendments the geologists might later make, Doane had gone straight to the heart of Yellowstone. There may have been thirty or forty volcanoes. There are sixteen vents known in the Absaroka Range alone. Wherever Doane went in the next three weeks—to the hot springs, to the geysers, to the mudpots, and even to the great canyon that had eroded through volcanic material of many kinds—it all made sense. It fitted the picture he had seen from Washburn peak. The wonder of it lay behind the individual spectacles, the outbreaks of fiery force from the earth's entrails. He thought there must be "springs of all kinds in the valley to the number of at least 1500," and he was certain they had seen far less than remained to be seen.

Doane stood on the brink of the great canyon of the Yellowstone, first at a point where the upper fall could be viewed, then the lower. The wild beauty and power of the cataracts stunned him. As the dazzle of it receded, he began to think of comparisons, as we all naturally do. But Doane showed the taste that makes for the perfect enjoyment of national parks. "There can be no standard of comparison between such objects, either in beauty or grandeur," he said. His memory, however, naturally summoned up pictures of Niagara and Yosemite and the Shoshone Fall, and each one conveyed to his imagination a special quality. Niagara was "overwhelming power"; Yosemite was "altitude"; Shoshone, in the desert, was "going to waste." So he bathed his eyes with the beauty of the upper fall of the Yellowstone and decided that it embodied the conception of Momentum; and the lower fall—that was Gravitation. As a visitor to Yellowstone National Park you will rightly pay no attention to Doane at this point. Still, you see that this was a strange young second lieutenant, out West fighting Indians. If you had called him a poet, he would have been surprised and might have been annoyed, but of course that was what he was, at the moment. The Yellowstone had drawn it out of him.

For the record, it appears that the Washburn party was never in much danger from the Indians, Crows or other. One gets the impression that Indian scares were already being used to dispossess the red man from land he regarded as his own. Indeed, a multiplying gang of white desperadoes was operating in the Montana Territory who were more to be feared than the aborigines. It is also evident that there were plenty of white men who knew the Yellowstone region like survey men. These men were simply not inter-

Sheep on Mount Washburn. Yellowstone National Park. [Photo: Bob and Ira Spring]

ested in geysers, waterfalls, or gorgeous rock and hot-spring colorations. They had gold and the fur market in mind.

An incident that occurred during the Washburn exploration points up these facts. One of the party, Truman C. Everts, had very unfortunately established himself as a pathfinder by taking a short cut back to camp and reaching there before his companion arrived by the blazed trail. This convinced him, it would appear, that he was a Jedediah Smith or Kit Carson. The next thing that happened to him was that he was lost, and he remained lost in the wilderness for thirty-seven days. The Washburn party had to return to Helena without much cheer for his family and friends. Everts, by his own account—which he miraculously lived to write for a magazine— besides being handicapped by poor eyesight, was a man who could have strayed on an atoll. He entrusted all his effects, including his matches, to a

horse, and the animal departed. Had he remained where he was, he would have been quickly found; but he started a pilgrimage on foot, which always took him a little farther from his pursuers. They caught up with his trail, only to find that he had gone in a new direction. He had a field glass in his pocket, the only thing he had not confided to the horse, but it was nearly two weeks before he remembered that you can make a fire with a lens if the sun is shining. He slept once in a bear's den, and only the fact that the bear was visiting and did not get home that night prevented a brutal eviction proceeding. All this is not to belittle Everts's intelligence. It simply means that certain men are naturally forest-wise, but most others had better stay with the guide; and this is something all visitors to the great primeval national parks might profitably bear in mind.

The point is this. When a reward of six hundred dollars was offered for the recovery of Everts, two experienced frontiersmen started on a search and found him, in the last stages of physical exhaustion, within a few days. No, this was no trackless wilderness, nor was it so dangerous as was commonly believed; it was simply that until Folsom, Cook, and Washburn, Hedges, Langford, and Doane went into the region with eyes for the grand qualities of it, and the ability to publish their discoveries to the world, the Yellowstone was merely a place where animals wore valuable skins, and a pushful prospector might strike it rich if he could survive the wear and tear.

[2]

THE MARVELS OF YELLOWSTONE having been revealed to the country, there was the rush that might be expected, on the part of ambitious individuals, to capitalize and sell admission tickets. It was government domain and presumably could be filed on. It looked like good tourist country, and there was gold in those hills, or was thought to be. A railroad into the region of the spectacles was soon projected.

A little group of idealists, however, who knew the real present values and sensed greater ones not so apparent, were sure that with ruthless private exploitation these values would be degraded. There were not many of them, but what they lacked in numbers they made up for with the reiteration of whippoorwills. Led by members of the 1870 party, who themselves gave up lands and potential wealth they might well have claimed, these idealists stormed Congress, gained disciples in the House and Senate, and demanded that this region should become a national park, to be preserved forever for all the people.

The demand could hardly have been made, from the viewpoint of federal finance, at a worse time. The backwash of the Civil War was making itself felt in our economy. The public lands were regarded by otherwise respectable people as a legitimate grab bag. It was still a pioneer country, except for the selvage along the Eastern seaboard, and words like *aesthetics, natural beauty*, and *spiritual values* were received with a squint. Man must eat; man must thrive; spiritual values should be left for posterity. It was all quite natural. The unnatural thing was that such idealism prevailed.

At any rate, for once the insistent angels had their day, and on March 1, 1872, Yellowstone National Park was established by act of Congress. The area was set apart as a "pleasuring-ground for the benefit and enjoyment of the people," and the act provided for "the preservation, from injury or spoliation, of all timber, mineral deposits, natural curiosities or wonders . . . and their retention in their natural condition." True, it was many years before the legislation and the money necessary to carry out properly the noble design were forthcoming, but the course was set.

It may be said that the proponents of Yellowstone had, as leverage, the precedent of Yosemite, which was set aside by Congress in 1864 as an area to be preserved under the protection of California. There has been much heartburning over whether this was, in effect, the establishment of a national park, and therefore whether Yosemite was not the first. We may leave the matter with the historian, who will cheerfully dot all the i's and cross the t's for us. Such matters obscure the real phenomenon, which is that the concept of setting aside such places of natural beauty and geological significance had never before been carried out in any young country in recorded history. It was the Magna Charta of national cultural behavior. The few instances of zealous preservation in ancient times had only a religious background.

That was a wonderful thing: that a hustling, restless, dollar-chasing young nation, with much of its population swarming like locusts over rich virgin land, should have been able to pause long enough to look into the future with such spiritual prudence; it had not happened before.

For this forethought and insight we can thank those who made the preservation of these treasures possible. For the scenic loveliness, for the solace and healing quality of the wilderness places, and for their prodigies of form, color, and animal life—nature at her grandest and simplest, with all that belongs in the picture and as little as possible that does not—we can take no credit. We happen to be the fortunates who live in a spot on the earth's surface where nature has been notably lavish and experimental, if sometimes boisterous and explosive. So we have, taken as a whole, perhaps the best that all the world affords. But if we cannot claim authorship, at least we are trying to safeguard the rare volume—not against the ravages of time, for that would be a foolish hope; not against change, for change in nature is order, and life is adaptation; but against all but the wholly unavoidable intrusions into the book's integrity.

[3]

If YELLOWSTONE NATIONAL PARK had no geysers and hot springs of such variety, color, and power, the great canyon and falls of the Yellowstone would still make it one of the world's most inviting attractions for tourists and for students of nature's manifestations in the grand manner. If it lacked the canyon and the plunging water, it would still be the largest of all parks for the refuge of every kind of wildlife that belongs to its type of geographical and climatic condition. But as it has all these, in addition to other allurements, the whole being maintained in as natural circumstances as the presence of humans will permit, there is no wonder that it attracts each year nearly a million people.

"In as natural circumstances as the presence of humans will permit." There, of course, is the constant challenge to the preservation of the primitive. There is the constant headache of administration. The act of Congress that established Yellowstone National Park and led to a great system of national parks and monuments was really a wonderful document, but the twin purposes it embodied are essentially in contradiction. Enjoyment and use in the present, with preservation in their natural condition for all time—how do you contrive that?

The contradiction shows its problems in all the primeval areas, in greater or less degree. But in Yellowstone nobody is to be satisfied with a telescopic view of the geysers and boiling springs. The great thrill is to stand close by them, watch for eruptions or changes, revel in the color of their craters and in the forms of their terraces, and above all to have the shocking but joyous adventure of putting your boot soles closer to the interior fires of the earth than you can do at any other spots on the globe save two. And these other places, Iceland and New Zealand, while wonderful enough, make a poor display compared with the vulcanism of Yellowstone.

But because myriads come year after year, to see and experience, what happens to the natural conditions? The sinter, or mineral deposit of the springs, is softer than that of the geysers, which is tough silica; but even the siliceous material stands no chance against the millions of feet that tread it. If you resort to wooden catwalks to keep the boots from the lovely mineral, where is your "state of nature"? The Washburn party did not record any catwalks when they saw the geysers in their time. This is but one example of a disconcerting problem of managing the national parks for the welfare of the whole people and for posterity. Again and again in visiting the other parks we come upon it; the National Park Service can only strive to approximate the ideal.

[4]

EVERYTHING THAT MEETS the eye in Yellowstone, unless you chance to be in a wooded spot away from steam vents or the sight of the rim of mountains, expresses the volcanic tumult that was here. You look upon the cliffs of black obsidian, a lava rock that either cooled so quickly as it flowed that it had no time to form crystals or was perhaps too viscous to do so. This was the favorite material of the Indians for arrowheads. You see the great depths of rhyolite, through which the canyon is partly cut, and, not being held to strict scientific account, you can fancy it as being once a granite, like that of the New England hills, being melted and poured out in a new rock-form, not pepper-and-salt, but so close-knit that only the microscope reveals the crystals.

Then you gaze up at the columns of basalt, jointed so neatly as to look like man-made architecture; and beneath and above these columns are other kinds of eruptive or flow material. Off in the distance you see the marching crests of the Absarokas—more volcanic rock, a sort of basalt. There are evidences of the belching of ash from craters—not really ash, of course, like coal or wood ashes, but finely pulverized material, which must have covered a vast terrain with dust when it was blown into the upper air. There are breccias that were hurled out of the craters when the eruptions were most explosive and were consolidated by ash showers that followed, or by later seeping waters. All are volcanic—all are the product of ferocious violence, originating in the terrific heat beneath the earth crust.

Compared with that former violence, the present activity in the form of steam, boiling pools, and geysers is vulcanism at senility, speaking in a weak voice and approaching extinction. Or is it? The geologist may know it; you may know it; does the earth know it?

Something else claims your attention as you look incredulously into the hot springs of so many shapes and temperatures. The mineral deposits have built charming encrusted basins, over the edges of which the water flows or trickles. But on the sides and along the edges of these basins something has painted colors—reds, bluish grays, browns, pinks. You surmise that they may be mineral pigments from the water; but it is not so. Living organisms have made the decorations. It seems impossible that life, as we know life, could exist at such temperatures. But microscopic forms of plant, of bacterial life, and the tiniest of one-celled creatures, diatoms, flourish in this environment. You begin to sense the community scheme of existence—algae clinging to the rock habitation, diatoms clinging to the algae. It is what impressed the young Charles Darwin when he was examining a salt lake in Patagonia. "How surprising," he said, "that any creatures should be able to exist in brine!" They were worms, crawling among crystals of sulfate of soda and lime. "And what becomes of these worms when the surface is hardened to a solid layer of salt, in summer? I saw flamingoes wading about in search of these worms, and the worms feed on infusoria or confervae. Thus we have a little living world within itself, adapted to these lakes of brine." So, here in Yellowstone, are these little worlds.

What you see in the hot pool is a miniature. The larger tapestry is hung all around you. The magnificent herd of bison in the Lamar Valley, the thousands of elk and deer, bands of mountain sheep, antelope, grizzly bears, black bears, and from these larger mammals down to the very smallest, including the animals that prey on other animals, all are included in the picture. Those that are there belong there; none are there that do not naturally inhabit that kind of country. No domestic creatures, except necessary work animals, compete with the wild for the grazing and browsing. They are living their spans, long or short, according to their ability to survive, not according to favoritism. The cougar belongs to the community as much as the deer, and so does the coyote.

There are flaws in the carrying out of this plan, no matter how good the design. Wherever the wild animals receive protection against humans, no matter how huge the domain set aside for them, some of them multiply beyond their food supply. A minimum of artifice must be resorted to, but the approximation to normal life conditions in this vast wildlife refuge is so nearly perfect that it can be said that visitors to Yellowstone see what the first pioneering intruders into the wilderness saw.

The great moment for most of us is when we come upon these animals unexpectedly. You may travel a long distance without seeing any except the ubiquitous black bear. The beasts are going about their affairs, and it gives them no thrill to have their pictures in the newspapers; so there is no guarantee, particularly if you stick to the tourist track, that you will see much of the great wild population. But you may be lucky enough to stumble suddenly into the fellowship of the primeval. That will be something to remember.

Thomas Moran painted the canyon of the Yellowstone. No artist was ever more at ease with Western scenery than Moran. But he was not satisfied with his work; he felt that he had not caught it. Its delicacy, which tends to make the observer forget its size, derives from the happy proportions of rock, tree, and water, with their color and intimacy, especially at the two favorite spots for viewing it: Artist's Point and Inspiration Point. Under a noonday sun the walls of the canyon glare in yellow and white; but actually, as is

As the great pioneer photographer saw the Falls in 1871. Yellowstone National Park.
[Photo: William Henry Jackson]

revealed by coming closer, the volcanic gases and waters have blocked and streaked the rock with everything from the yellow of grapefruit to the mellowed brick of an ancient manse, and from pearly gray to jet black. Where the river has found tougher rock, it leaps for something easier to grind: and so, seeming to come from nowhere, with a sudden spring, the water drops more than a hundred feet at the upper falls and nearly three times that height at the lower. The falls at Tower Creek, some twenty miles to the north, would themselves be regarded as notable, anywhere. Here the drop is 132 feet, over great boulders.

While the forest growth in Yellowstone is not extraordinary, as Olympic and Sequoia and Muir Woods trees are, the park has a fine unspoiled cover, mostly of evergreens, which is permitted to go through its cycle of birth, decline, and fall without benefit of tree surgery. There are several pines, alpine and Douglas fir, Engelmann spruce, and the juniper of the Rockies. Perhaps the typical tree is the lodgepole pine, which is not a showy tree, but has one great merit: a lumber-mill operator can stand beside it without feeling obliged to estimate how many board feet of lumber it would make.

But there were once forests in Yellowstone—forests after forests, and forests after more forests—and some of them were very different from those seen now. There were pines, to be sure, but not these present pines; there were sequoias, but none exist here now; there were broad-leaved trees that must have enjoyed a much warmer climate than that of the present. These forests are gone, but they are still here: a riddle until you recollect that they are petrified trees. The original wood has disappeared, but mineral matter replaced the organic material of the tree form, ring for ring, cell for cell. There is a place in the park where a succession of twelve forests, each buried in volcanic dust, each rising on the ruins of the next older, can be studied in a vertical section of two thousand feet of rock. A fine standing specimen, readily accessible, can be seen just off the main road between Tower Junction and Mammoth. It remains just as it was overtaken by the storm of ash.

Many visitors to Yellowstone find the profusion of wild flowers one of the chief attractions of the park. The varieties, seasonally decorating the open spaces with splashes of color, are generally characteristic of the high Rocky Mountain country, but especially noteworthy is the fringed gentian. This delicately beautiful plant, whose bloom emulates the sky, has been chosen as the "park flower," not only for its appeal to the eye, but because it is to be seen throughout the entire visitor season. Beginning in June on the warm earth of the geyser basins, it is still to be enjoyed when the last visitors are leaving in late September.

2. HAWAII VOLCANOES NATIONAL PARK

[*Hawaii*]

"THE PRESENT PREDICTION for Kilauea is that it is on its way to a new period of activity, which may bring back the full firelake of the great pit and pour out new flows on the mountain flanks."

So I wrote in 1950 when I was preparing the manuscript for the first edition of *The National Parks*. It was not my personal opinion, of course; I was dependent upon the prognosis of the experts in volcanology. Well, Kilauea obliged within a few years. On November 14, 1959, fire fountains began to play from a rift on Kilauea's Iki Crater. It was the most spectacular eruption ever witnessed in Hawaii—possibly in the entire world. One of these flaming fountains reached a height of 1,900 feet. Lava poured into Kilauea Iki to a depth of 414 feet. Today that lava is cool enough to walk on, but below the crust will be at high temperatures for years.

Less than a month after Kilauea Iki's fountains subsided, a new vent opened near the village of Kapoho in the Puna district, twenty-eight miles away. This flow buried most of the village, entered the ocean, and added some acreage to the island. Since 1961, eight eruptions have occurred—three in Halemaumau and five along the east rift zone.

One of the greatest flows from Mauna Loa began on the first night of June 1950. Emitted from a fissure thirteen miles long, this highly fluid lava raced to the sea at a speed of nearly six miles an hour. This outbreak lasted for twenty-three days, producing enough cubic yards of lava (quoting one of our statistically minded friends) to pave a four-lane highway four and a half times around the earth. It is consoling to feel sure that this is only a hypothetical highway. At best, highways have a way of obliterating fine landscape features.

Twelve years after Captain Cook discovered the Hawaiian Islands, a native chief of considerable ability was trying to bring the largest of the volcanic group under his sway. He had ideas about making himself king of the whole cluster of islands, and in 1791 he succeeded, becoming King Kamehameha I. But in 1790, when this story opens, the fighting was brisk on the island of Hawaii.

Whether the troops were those of Kamehameha or of the opposition, it is sure that on a certain day part of an army was on the march past Kilauea volcano. The soldiers tramped in their bare feet. It may have been a ragamuffin army, but to be in bare feet would not prove it, nor would the weapons they carried be any indication of their combat quality.

In the desert six miles southwest of Kilauea's crater you may still see the prints of those bare feet as they were imprinted in a layer of volcanic ash on that day in 1790. Most of the soldiers were killed; perhaps even those whose footprints can now be seen failed to escape. They were the victims of a surprise attack. As they were passing the home of the fire-goddess Pele —she whose delicate strands of pumice-hair are swirled up from the boiling lava lake of Kilauea—the crater let go with one of its violent steam explosions. The assault must have come without the slightest warning, for the islanders were familiar with the vagaries of their fire mountains. The blast of rock and of rock dust was lethal. Whoever the soldiers were, they had a right to expect something better from Pele. Every army, Hawaiian or other, being so undoubtedly in the right, deserves the assistance of fire-goddesses. This was treachery and ingratitude.

Hawaii National Park, which originally included both those now known as Hawaii Volcanoes and Haleakala, was voted by Congress in 1916 to preserve, free from exploitation or other abuse, the most accessible and best-studied of the areas in the world where volcanic activity is great. The craters here, both the active and the dormant, may be approached with what may be called reasonable safety. That means that there cannot be any guarantee about volcanoes; but I should think the danger about the same as that of being struck by lightning while riding in your automobile, which, as you know, is much less than that of being killed by slipping in the bathtub.

Kilauea is a low dome built up by many layers of lava erupted from the central crater, as well as from lines of craters east and southwest of the summit. Because the neighboring Mauna Loa towers so much above it, Kilauea might seem to be a crater in the side of the greater mountain. It is in fact probably older than its colossal companion. Within the broad depression at its top is the vast pit, Halemaumau. For most of the years during which this pit has been observed, the "House of Everlasting Fire" has contained a lake of active lava, sometimes rising and overflowing, sometimes sinking from sight. Always the sinking has meant the collapse of the pit walls in great avalanches. When the sinking has been so violent that water has rushed through the cracked walls, then have come tremendous explosions of steam. It was one of these that caught the native soldiers.

Eruption fountain bursts from Kilauea Iki. Hawaii Volcanoes National Park. [Photo: National Park Service]

The Kilauea Ridge, though not high, effects a marked difference in the scenery on the windward and leeward sides. Along and below the northeast rim and the Chain of Craters Road is a tropical rain forest watered by the copious rainfall of the trade winds. Here visitors pass through a jungle of tree ferns and ohia trees, the latter rich with scarlet pompon bloom. In the area of Twin Craters and the Thurston Lava Tube, where for many years there has been no new covering of lava, the ohias become a forest of giants. The way in which vegetation moves in, where there is plenty of moisture, may be seen along the Chain of Craters, where a young rain forest is recapturing the fields.

South and west of Kilauea is a different scene. This slope of the ridge is cut off from the trade-wind rains, though it gets a heavy general storm on occasions. The rim road enters the upper edge of the Kau desert, and except for scrubby ohia plants and the bushes of the ohelo berry, which was held by the Hawaiians to be sacred to Pele, the strange lava formations are seen in all their nakedness. From here to the seacoast is a wild expanse of the successive products of Ilauea—crusted volcanic ash, barren lava, and dunes of drifting ash and pumice. There is a road through the desert, and several long foot trails traverse it, but hikers should not set out into this waste without getting detailed information from park headquarters.

From the 4,000-odd feet of Kilauea to the 13,680 feet of Mauna Loa is a rise from tropical forest to a volcanic crater where ice remains the year round in places protected from the sun.

Mauna Loa actually rises from the Pacific Ocean floor to a height of little less than 32,000 feet—18,000 feet of its bulk is beneath sea level. So it is in truth a "mountain mass" with its lava-covered flanks extending over more than 2,000 square miles of the island surface.

Obviously it makes no difference to the furious caldron of molten rock below the earth crust—fingering here and there for a weak spot, a fissure, a new or old vent—whether that vulnerable place happens to be in an ocean deep or in an Indian's cornfield in Mexico. One can only wonder what the ocean must be like, locally, in times of great cone-building activity in its depths. A suggestion of it is seen when the lava from Mauna Loa rolls down into the sea, and the ocean becomes deep green and appears to be steaming in ever-widening areas.

The Hawaiian lava flows have given several terms to the science of vol-canology. When the lava flows slowly, like cool molasses, the upper portions harden while the interior continues to move forward. This results in a field of sharp, irregular blocks that were tumbled over one another as they were carried along. The thin, fast-moving lava, which spreads out in twisted and ropy forms, with glistening surfaces, sometimes in glowing tones of blue, purple, and bronze, is called *pahoehoe* (pah-hoay-hoay), and fine examples of this are seen also at Craters of the Moon National Monument in Idaho.

Traveling clockwise from the park headquarters, visitors pass lush jungle, raw craters, and great areas of devastation; you will see pumice piled high from recent eruptions, and lava flows only a few years old. Along the road you will come to trails and overlooks—Byron Ledge Overlook and its exhibits, Thurston Lava Tube with a trail through jungle and part of a tunnel through which once rushed glowing lava, the overlook at Kilauea Iki, the boardwalk Devastation Trail, Kilauea Overlook north of the Hawaiian Volcano Observatory, and Sulfur Bank.

The Thomas A. Jaggar Memorial Museum at park headquarters has exhibits, relief models, and paintings on the story of the park. Daily programs

The fiery breath meets cool air and vaporizes. Hawaii Volcanoes National Park.
[Photo: Robert T. Haugen]

include a talk by a park naturalist and a color film of recent eruptions. The Wahaula Heiau Visitor Center contains another museum.

Hawaii Volcanoes National Park now has an entrance from the sea—a magnificent new road that rises from the Kalapana Black Sand Beach and rugged seacoast of Puna, up over the cliffs to Kilauea Crater some twenty miles distant. The National Park Service has proposed an extension of the boundaries of Hawaii Volcanoes National Park to include the summit region of Hualalai and to connect these areas with each other and with City of Refuge National Historical Park at Honaunau by a scenic parkway.

3. HALEAKALA NATIONAL PARK
[Hawaii]

ON THE ISLAND OF MAUI, in the Hawaiian group, is the 10,000-foot Haleakala, an old volcano considered to be in its last stage of activity. Is it? Or is it just taking one of those long naps? The occurrence of earthquakes on the island suggests that someday it could renew the business under new management.

The Hawaiian natives called this mountain House of the Sun, from a legend about the demi-god Maui, who climbed to the summit of Haleakala, snared the rays of the sun, and forced it to travel more slowly in its course so that his mother, Hina, might have more sunlight each day in which to do her work. When we talk of mythology we are usually thinking of the Greeks and Romans, but the truth is that primitive people everywhere made their first timorous attempts to explain natural wonders by inventing myths.

The great depression in the summit of Haleakala is attributed partly to erosion and partly to glacial work during the Ice Age—even though Maui is but little more than twenty degrees from the equator. Subsequent eruptions have dotted the crater floor with great cinder cones and flooded the area with laval flows, some of which poured down the valleys to the sea. The tallest gaily colored cone, Puu O Maui, rises a thousand feet from the floor.

Sometimes visitors, arriving at the airport, find that thick clouds are obscuring the mountain. These trade-wind clouds drift in through the great Koolau Gap and override the high western rim. Meeting in the center of the crater, they leave the high north rim, Hanakauhi, an island in a sea of vapor. Patience. The clouds will probably blow away. Sometimes in late afternoon an observer standing on the western rim will see his shadow cast against a crater cloud and surrounded by a circular rainbow—an effect similar to the famous "specter of the Brocken" long famous in the Alps of Germany.

No roads lead into the crater, but there are well-marked trails. However,

Lava pours into the sea. The islands were built just so. Hawaii Volcanoes National Park. [*Photo: Robert T. Haugen*]

at this elevation, one must be in the pink of condition to make a one-day trip of it, even on horseback. A wiser plan is to get a permit from a park ranger and stay overnight in one of the crater cabins, each of which has twelve bunks, potable water, a woodburning cookstove with fuel, and kerosene lamps. Reservations are required, naturally.

In the northeast part of the crater, which gets as much as 150 inches of rain in a year and where soil conditions are favorable, there are luxuriant grasses, trees, and ferns, in startling contrast to the lean and hungry appearance of the rest. On the walls and within the crater the rare silversword grows. Its long, narrow leaves gleam like frosted silver, and each plant produces one flower stalk, sometimes six feet high, bearing hundreds of small purple flowers. When the seeds have matured, the plant dies, just as does the agave of the Southwest desert of our mainland. They say that fifty years ago, the silversword covered many acres of the crater floor with transcendent beauty. It was almost exterminated by visitors who thought it would look better growing somewhere else than on the islands of Maui and Hawaii, where, in all the world, it was found native. But under the protection of the National Park Service, this botanical rarity is recovering.

Near Paliku Cabin, the Hawaiian goose, the nene, which had nearly become extinct, has been reintroduced. Among the native birds are the apapane, iiwi, amakihi, pueo (Hawaiian short-eared owl), koae (white-tailed tropic bird), and kolea (American golden plover). The many other birds are species that have been introduced to the island. The only mammals are a native bat and exotic nuisances like wild pigs and goats, mongooses and rats. To migrate naturally from any mainland point to these volcanic isles of the Pacific, mammal forms would have to be hardy sailors indeed.

4. CITY OF REFUGE NATIONAL HISTORICAL PARK
[Hawaii]

THE IDEA OF FLEEING to sanctuary, and thus taking advantage of the fact that a sacred shrine must not be blemished by violence, is almost as ancient as religion itself. Immediately one thinks of Orestes taking refuge from the Furies in the temple of Apollo at Delphi after he had killed his mother to avenge the murder of his father. Or, nearer to us in time, we recall that as late as the reign of James I in England, a person accused of any crime except treason could go to the nearest church or churchyard, be free from arrest there, and upon promising to quit the country from the nearest seaport, receive safe-conduct to the seaport.

The concept of such haven has been universal, but in this City of Refuge at Honaunau, on the largest of the Hawaiian islands, we see today the remains of a sanctuary that was clearly far different from anything else of its kind. Here, on a twenty-acre shelf of lava rock with the ocean front on two sides and a great wall of dry-laid stone on the other two, was an asylum which could accommodate great numbers of men, women, and children, even defeated warriors escaping the hard fate of the loser in ancient island days— extermination, root and branch.

All such sanctuaries have been violated, and no doubt the City of Refuge was no exception, since that would account for the great wall, ten feet high and seventeen feet wide. The city sometimes needed, no doubt, more than the aura of holiness to prevent invasion and vengeance. The thousand-foot-

Giant ferns. Hawaii Volcanoes National Park. [Photo: W. W. Dunmire]

Growing only here, the silversword is the grand monarch of the sunflower family. Haleakala National Park. [Photo: National Park Service]

long wall dates from the time of Chief Keawe-ku-i-ke-ka'ai, who ruled Kona about A.D. 1550, but such refuges are common to the islands and date from a much earlier period of native existence.

5. CRATER LAKE NATIONAL PARK
[*Oregon*]

FIRST THE LAKE WAS CALLED Deep Blue Lake. Later it was rediscovered and named Blue Lake. Two soldiers from Fort Klamath stumbled upon it, never having heard of it, and christened it Lake Majesty. Finally it became Crater Lake. To me, this final name is the best one. "Deep Blue" does not describe its color. "Blue" does not describe its color. "Majesty" was a reverent attempt to capture the flying perfect with a word. But where the attempt so obviously can never have fulfillment, it is better to accept defeat and resort to the accurate commonplace. It is, certainly, a lake in a crater.

Crater Lake is a thing of the spirit. It must be so, for I have never met anyone who did not express it in one way or another. Long before I ever saw it myself, I heard about it as I sat talking one day in a London club, from an Englishman who had just returned from a round-the-world trip. He was a rich sportsman, especially a dry-fly fisherman. He had been jogging in the Orient, had come over to Puget Sound and fished, and then, before returning to England, had visited Crater Lake. I recall a foolish tinge of jealousy that I, an American, should be learning of this place of beauty from a European. This man said to me: "I have seen beautiful things all over the world. I have never seen anything that touched me so strangely and deeply as Crater Lake. As I sit here, I can still see *that blue*."

The cause of the color of Crater Lake has long been a subject of speculation and inquiry. Some have thought it was due to the reflection of the sky, but it is the same whether the sky is clear or clouded. Then it was suggested that there was something peculiar about the mineral content of the water. Chemical analysis indicated no such thing. A small quantity of the water does not exhibit the color characteristic. The generally accepted theory is that a scattering of light, in this water of such clearness and depth, separates and reflects the blue rays and absorbs those of other colors. I suppose the men of science know. I suppose they have wrested the secret of the purple from the murex. But I recall a saying attributed to a wise man of the sixteenth century: "Blue is not merely a color; it is a mystery."

If the blue of Crater Lake is mysterious, not much less so is the volcanic bowl in which the water rests. There is no peculiarity about the existence of the volcano itself. It is one of many that at a fairly recent period burst into activity in the uplift known as the Cascade Range. There is a line of them stretching from northern California to Canada. Seeing them even from a distance, you have no doubt that Lassen, Shasta, Rainier, St. Helens, Baker, and Adams are the results of repeated outpouring of lava, rocks, and ashes. But something strange happened to Mount Mazama, where Crater Lake nestles, and the best geologists are puzzled.

Mount Mazama is what may be called a "theoretical" mountain. Many cubic miles of what once constituted the conical peak are not there. There is every evidence that they were once there. How high the mountain was is not certain, but it may have been twelve thousand feet above sea level at its highest. If so, it was about the same height as Mount Adams.

Did Mazama suddenly blow its head off? Volcanic peaks have done that very thing. Katmai in Alaska did, and so did Krakatao. But if Mazama did, where is the evidence? There ought to be fragments around the rim of the present crater, and the surrounding country should be well covered with the materials hurled out. They are not found.

The only conceivable explanation is that the top of the mountain collapsed, falling inward and disappearing into the pit, which is now in places almost four thousand feet deep, half of which depth is the lake itself. Vast quantities of pumice lava extend more than eight miles northeast of Mazama. This came from the heart of the volcano, and it is believed that after this eruption the crater poured out rock broth that raced down the sides of the mountain at great speed and traveled thirty-five miles to the south and southwest. If, then, during these violences cracks had appeared in the flanks and base, it is possible that the leakage of incandescent lava into these fractures drew enough material away so that there was no support for the upper part of the cone. This is the best of the theories advanced up to now, and there is much evidence to support it.

The volcano did not die at once. There must have been sufficient activity left to produce the cone called Wizard Island, which rises above the surface of the lake, and there may be other cones that do not come to the surface.

Then comes the question of the existence of the lake within this great pit. Lakes in volcanic craters are known in other places in the world, but they have nothing of the magnitude of this one, nor have any of them appeared under such conditions. It seems to have required a set of factors of exactly the right kind to create and maintain a lake of such dimension which, without inlet or outlet of stream water, would maintain its total volume with only a slight variation throughout the year and across the years. The gain from snow and rainfall and the loss by evaporation and seepage are almost perfectly balanced.

Less than fifty years ago Crater Lake was almost, if not quite, devoid of the aquatic life one expects to exist in a great body of water. It was not until Judge William Gladstone Steel, whose efforts later succeeded in having the park established, had hiked and toted minnows nearly fifty miles from the Rogue River and put them into the lake that fish of any kind have been there. Even then there was no food for them in the mysterious blue water, which lacked even vegetation. The problem was solved by planting freshwater shrimp, and when it was found that these little creatures throve, trout could be introduced. The fishing now is considered by many anglers to be the finest in all the parks.

From the air we see the whole caldera—the collapsed volcano called Mazama.
Crater Lake National Park. [Photo: Delano Photographics]

There is much else in this lovely place to lure visitors. Of the larger animals there are black bear and Columbian black-tailed deer, as well as mule deer and elk. The smaller animals are abundant, but there are few reptiles because of the high elevation. The golden eagle and the Southern bald eagle have nesting places here, and Llao Rock is the home of falcons. California gulls and Farallon cormorants come over from the ocean.

Virgin forest, mostly of cone-bearing trees, and meadows of wild flowers are on the slopes that ascend to the rim of Crater Lake. During July and August visitors will find beautiful displays of alpine blooms on the road between park headquarters and Rim Village and along the trails on the crater rim. The flowering season is short, so there is a rapid succession of blooms during July and August. Winter sets in early and lingers; in the winter of 1932–3 there were seventy-three feet of snow—feet, not inches. Fifty feet is about average. The suburbanite whose back creaks when he shovels a path from the front door to the street after a snowfall of some eight inches should stop his unreasonable plaints. He is enjoying an open winter.

Despite the snow upon snow, and the snow upon that, Crater Lake National Park is accessible all year, and the slopes are ideal for skiing. It is only necessary for winter visitors to take the usual precautions in motoring in the high Cascade Mountain country.

6. LASSEN VOLCANIC NATIONAL PARK
[California]

THE ARRANGEMENTS FOR INTERNMENT of Lassen Peak as a deceased volcano were made back in the time of President Taft, when that chief executive proclaimed two national monuments in the little-known wilderness at the southern end of the Cascade Range in California. One monument was intended to preserve the peak itself, the other to preserve a perfectly formed cinder cone, colorful and symmetrical; and both were in the heart of a country clad with beautiful evergreen forests. The idea was a good one, though at that time only a little group of people had the slightest interest in it, and those were mostly Californians motivated by local interest and pride. In the rest of the country you would have found few with more than a vague notion of the location of the new monuments.

Some people knew that since the white man moved westward to the Pacific there had been volcanic activity in the chain of peaks stretching from Shasta into the state of Washington. In 1843, when Frémont pushed his way across the continent, Mount Baker and Mount St. Helens were both in mild eruption, casting a spray of volcanic dust over the surrounding country. In 1858 the clouds over Baker were seen reddened by activity from the crater. Rainier and Shasta were both known to emit hot vapors from fumaroles on their summits. But the mountain named for Peter Lassen, the Danish emigrant pioneer of Alta California, had, so far as anyone knew, slumbered peacefully so long that it was fit and proper to put up a marker: "Here sleeps . . . once a volcano . . . exact age unknown. Requiescat in pace."

One feature of the landscape might have given the mourners pause. Directly south of Lassen Peak was a basin that hot sulfuric acids had eaten out of solid lava rock. Here were steam vents, hot springs, and mudpots. Visitors to Lassen Volcanic National Park today know the place as Bumpass Hell. It somewhat resembles the thermal areas of Yellowstone National Park. Bumpass, an oldtimer of the region, discovered the basin during a hunting trip. In 1865 he took a Red Bluff editor to see it and cautioned him to step carefully, as the ground was treacherous. So saying, Bumpass broke through the thin crust and plunged his leg into the boiling mud beneath. He was so annoyed, as well as burned, that he forgot to swear. This was remarked as a pioneer phenomenon almost equal to the brilliant coloring of the basin itself. But for years few except the most adventurous climbers or the straggling homesteaders at the base of Lassen ever saw this thermal exhibit, and the mountain slept on.

At five o'clock in the morning on May 30, 1914, Mount Lassen, without the slightest warning in the way of mutterings or twitchings, woke up. The next day the forest supervisor of the area reported to a newspaper at Redding, fifty miles distant: "Mount Lassen is in eruption from a new crater on the north slope close to the summit. The new crater is 25 feet wide, 44 feet long, with deep fissures radiating in all directions. Lava and ashes have been shot up to a depth of a foot to two feet. The new volcano is in eruption today."

For several days the eruptions were heavy, though of short duration. By June 11 the crater had enlarged from about 600 to 1,500 feet, and in the ensuing months ashes and steam rose as high as 20,000 feet above the mountaintop, so that they could be seen all up and down the Sacramento Valley. For nearly a year the new Lassen crater puffed and fretted away, at no time as violent as the eruptions of the Hawaiian and Alaskan volcanoes, but doing very well for an embalmed curiosity. It still had some surprises in store for its first birthday observance.

On the night of May 19, 1915, a party was watching the volcano from the west side of the mountain when they saw a red line appear at the notch in the crater rim. With tremendous explosions, lava spilled through the notch and down the slope for a thousand feet. During that night the snow, which was still deep on the northeast side, was melted and sent a mud torrent rushing down Lost Creek and over the divide into Hat Creek, sweeping everything before it. There was no loss of life because the very few persons who lived in the valleys were warned, but in a few hours the meadowlands on both creeks were an indescribable mass of rocks, logs, uprooted trees, and other debris. In places the river of mud was at least twelve feet deep. Boulders weighing twenty tons were swept for several miles by the slippery torrent, and one of these, ever afterward called the Hot Rock, was said to have sizzled in the surrounding water for a whole day. And still old Lassen had something left to say.

In Lost Creek Valley before the 1915 eruption, there had been an estimated five million feet of primeval forest timber. Three days after the mud tore down into the creek valleys, some minor mudflows took place on the north and west flanks of the mountain. But these were not important. What was important was a sudden terrific blast that came from the crater at a low angle and swept down the northeast flank. The nature of such a blast, which in this case was perhaps like a quick puff from crusted-over soft coal when the stove lid is lifted, can hardly be realized when it comes on such a ferocious and sweeping scale. It was perhaps a little like that which overwhelmed St. Pierre, in Martinique.

The trees on the slopes of Raker Peak went down like rows of corn. They lay uniformly with their tops pointing straight away from the crater and up the hillside. Every tree had its bark on the crater side sand-blasted; trees that were broken off left stumps smoothly rounded and polished, and grains of volcanic sand were driven into the trunks a full inch. The curious thing about this prodigious blast was that no fires were kindled—or at most only one or two were reported—so that the temperature of the crater's breath must have been low. This Devastated Area is now one of the things visitors to Lassen Volcanic come to see. To view anything similar of such recent occurrence is nowhere else possible within the United States proper.

One of the great experiences in Lassen Volcanic is the climb of Cinder Cone, the velvety sides of which make the going slow, but not really difficult. Once at the edge of the crater, you look down upon a painted river of volcanic sand, which stops abruptly against a sheet of helter-skelter lava. To the southwest looms Lassen itself, serene and ermine-cloaked, posing as an innocent mountain again, but possibly harboring thoughts of further mischief later on.

Behind it all is the story of a very ancient volcano from which the Lassen scenery has stemmed. Three miles southwest of Lassen Peak once stood a mighty mountain known as Tehama, whose top towered more than four thousand feet over the present Sulphur Works, in the southwestern corner of the park. A succession of quiet lava flows had built this Tehama mountain. Later it collapsed inward, perhaps as Mazama did to form Crater Lake. Brokeoff Mountain, with its precipitous sheared side, is the largest remnant of this old crater rim.

Lassen Volcanic National Park is pre-eminently the place for people who are in no hurry. It is, truly, a relatively small area, as wilderness parks go.

About 1980 the volcano may take up unfinished business. Lassen Volcanic National Park. [Photo: William L. Perry]

But hikers and horseback riders will have the best of it here, and without exertion that would tax the strength of anyone in fairly good physical condition. Lassen Peak itself is not a difficult climb, and, except as a challenge to youth, there is no particular reason for climbing the craggy sections of the western side of the park. The eastern half is the reposeful place for ambling, meditating, and filling the eye with the soft beauty of little gemmy lakes in a setting of evergreen forests. Those who set up camp in one of the fine areas set aside for the purpose and who give themselves plenty of leisure to follow the trails will be as richly rewarded in Lassen as in any of our primeval parks.

We were taught in school to say that nature "abhors a vacuum." She also seems to dread nakedness, though wherever lava has issued forth or sand has blown into great dunes, the process of covering bare spots will be hard and long. Here in Lassen you can see the great clothing arrangements at work. You walk through a forest of luxuriant pines, to come abruptly against a wall of lava rock. From the bare flanks of Cinder Cone you have to go only a short distance to find parklike stands of mature pines growing up through the ash that showered from the crater fifty years ago. The charming little lakes are after all but intruding jewels set in bars of slag that came hurtling out of Vulcan's forge. The evidence of violence is at hand everywhere in Lassen, but you step aside no great distance into soothing softness.

Fishing is excellent in Lassen. The rainbow trout is the most abundant, but there are also Loch Leven and Eastern brook trout. Down at the hot pools of Devil's Kitchen it is said that you can catch a trout from the nearby mountain stream and, without removing it from the hook or moving far, toss it into the natural pot and cook it. You *can* do so, but I do not advise such blasphemy. *Boiled* brook trout! Oh, no!

As the snow melts in spring and early summer, Lassen Peak Road is cleared and skiers are able to follow the snowline to the road summit. At this time, cross-country skiing is most popular. The timber-free slopes of the high country are ideal for the sport.

7. HOT SPRINGS NATIONAL PARK
[*Arkansas*]

A BELIEF IN THE THERAPEUTIC VALUE of hot springs is very ancient. It will never be known, I suppose, just where lies the borderline between the curative powers of the waters and the delightful social experience of exchanging symptoms and other personal history with a similarly minded group.

Eruption of Lassen Peak, 1915. Lassen Volcanic National Park. [Photo: R. I. Meyers, copyright by B. F. Loomis]

In England for more than a century a large segment of "society" was built up around the famous town of Bath and its thermal springs. Many a sober merchant overworked diligently to the end that he might give his wife and family the distinction of being seen for two weeks among the aggregation that "took the waters."

But our American Indians believed in the magic of hot springs, too, and there are plenty of legends to the effect that various tribes battled over the undisputed use of certain thermal localities. Among these places was undoubtedly the present Hot Springs of Arkansas, the oldest reservation set aside by act of Congress for the perpetual use and enjoyment of the people, with freedom from exploitation. So, in a sense, it may be called truly the first national park. The Indian legend continues to the effect that after warring for some years over the possession of the forty-seven springs grouped at the base of Hot Springs Mountain the tribes took a large view of the question and decided that the Great Spirit had meant the benefits for all the sick. I see no advantage in being skeptical about this, unless one is a specialist in Indian manners and customs.

Hot Springs National Park contains about a thousand acres in the region of the Ouachita Mountains of Arkansas. The climate is unusually equable, with mild winters and summers that are very tolerable owing to the low humidity. The slopes and crests of the park are traversed by excellent roadways, and there are miles of forest trails, bridlepaths, and footpaths.

One does not need to be ill to enjoy Hot Springs. It is a restful place, and if one is merely in a run-down condition, where nature needs only a bit of the feeling of partnership, one can sit on the hotel porch and consider the words of Lucretius, a poet who was very far from being cynical:

> Tis sweet when tempests roar upon the sea
> To watch from land another's deep distress
> Amongst the waves—his toil and misery:
> Not that his sorrow makes our happiness,
> But that some sweetness there must ever be
> Watching what sorrows we do not possess.

This graceful translation is W. H. Mallock's.

The government wishes it to be generally understood that while baths can be taken, on permit, at any of the bathhouses receiving water from the hot springs of the park, it is recommended that the advice of a physician be procured. The waters are not beneficial in all diseases, and the ailing are urged not to diagnose their own cases and prescribe for themselves, the principle being the same as that one often mentioned in legal cases: that he who acts as his own lawyer has a fool for a client.

8. PLATT NATIONAL PARK
[Oklahoma]

NEAR THE CITY of Sulphur in southern Oklahoma is a pleasant little national park among gently rolling hills, well wooded, with a number of streams, springs, waterfalls, and cascades. This is Platt, named for a Senator Orvill H. Platt of Connecticut, who was distinguished for his interest in the Indians. Platt National Park is within the holdings of the Chickasaw Nation of the old Indian Territory.

I am in some doubt about the category in which Platt should be placed. In a way, this is a penalty I have to pay for dividing my book into arbitrary groups dealing with certain major characteristics. This area has many springs, some of sulphur and some of bromide; but they are cold springs. A hot spring falls naturally into the field of volcanism. Seemingly a cold spring does not. After some mental anguish over this point, I have evolved the pleasant theory that perhaps these springs were once hot, but the underlying fires have gone out. I do not invite any correspondence on this, especially from geologists. Can we not rely, once in a while, on pure intuition?

While the waters of the springs are for the use of all visitors, they should be taken extensively only on the advice of a competent physician. The National Park Service maintains and protects the waters according to the best possible standards, but there are no provisions in the park or in the city of Sulphur for free consultation on treatment of diseases.

Pavilion Spring, Bromide Spring, and Medicine Spring are among the best-known of the mineral waters. These springs are in the valleys along Travertine and Rock Creeks. In the eastern end of the park, along Travertine Creek, are two natural springs that together flow more than five million gallons of pure water a day. It is said that these springs, named Buffalo and Antelope, were so called because of the animal herds that formerly came there to drink.

Campgrounds, with water, lights, and other facilities, are maintained at three places in the park. There are also several attractive picnic sites, two of them capable of accommodating large parties. Within the park is a complete circuit drive of eight miles, and there are horseback trails. Saddle horses are readily available nearby.

9. Lava Beds National Monument
[*California*]

A RAGGED BAND of Modoc Indians, never more than seventy-one in fighting strength, and without benefit of warpaint and feathers, managed to maintain a campaign against the U.S. Army for six months, during which the white men suffered two costly defeats. This was in 1872–3, in the northeastern corner of California, near the Oregon border. It was the same old story: the Indians did not want to be relegated to a reservation—and the Modocs were particularly unwilling because they were to share it with their hereditary foes, the Klamaths. So Lava Beds is historic grounds in the development of the West.

But that was not the basic purpose for the proclamation setting aside the bewildering area for preservation. This national monument presents another exhibit of the strange ways of volcanoes. And the reason why a small force of Indians was able to cope with large numbers of their enemy is the same reason why the region so well deserved to come into the National Park System. Those natural rock trenches and caves from which bullets could come so unexpectedly, those forts which did not have to be built, that wild, broken terrain where one armed man could hold off a dozen—all these had gushed and belched from flaming volcanoes centuries before. For the Indians this was a ready-made Maginot Line.

From a distance Lava Beds looks like fairly level country. The whole region is high. Symmetrical cinder cones dot the landscape, and if you come from the southwest you look toward the towering precipices that mark the front of the great Columbia River lava flow. Once you are in the monument, the scene is entirely changed. Most of the fantastic devices of flowing molten rock are to be seen here. Chasms a hundred feet deep are walled by contorted masses of lava, which as it cooled or was thrust forward by an incandescent stream pouring from behind twisted itself into every conceivable shape. Where fountains of gas-inflated lava once played like those of Kilauea in Hawaii, there are now deep "chimneys." One of these, on the main road northwest of Indian Well, is three feet in diameter and more than a hundred feet deep.

Some of the lava flowed like thick, frothy molasses from deep cracks in the earth crust. The surface hardened, but the interior continued to flow, so that when the drainage was complete, horizontal tubes were formed. Sometimes the surface of these tubes fell in and they became serpentine trenches, with bridges marking places wherever the roof remained.

After the lava tubes drained, the space between the fiery floor and the roof filled with hot gases, which remelted and glazed the ceilings and side walls with drip-pendants of many colors. Along the main road, which traverses the monument, are many large caves. At Captain Jack's Cave, named for the Modoc Indian leader, the road crosses a natural bridge of such height that from a distance an automobile on the bridge seems to be suspended in air.

Skull Cave has three levels. The roof, rising seventy-five feet above the floor, is beautifully domed. The lower story is a river of solid ice. Many skulls of bighorn and pronghorn were found here, indicating occupancy by Indians of long ago. They killed their game on the surface and took it downstairs to the freezer.

But there are no bighorn in Lava Beds now. Their trails are still visible, but before the monument was established, domestic sheep and cattle claimed the little forage that existed. During a snowy winter, however, many Rocky Mountain mule deer come to Lava Beds from the neighboring high country.

10. CRATERS OF THE MOON NATIONAL MONUMENT
[Idaho]

IF THERE WERE rocket excursions to the moon (and who says there may not be?) I would not buy a ticket, even if the return trip were guaranteed. Admittedly, it would be exciting, but it would be too depressing. At less expense, and with much more pleasure, I can visit Craters of the Moon National Monument in Idaho, not far from the town of Arco, and see much of what the moon has to offer; and that same night I can get back among sweet forests and verdure such as the moon never had. The moon has an excessive supply of volcanic wreckage. The choice specimens of such hot riot included in the Park System are just about enough: a leaven sufficient to give us an understanding of those prodigious earth forces.

Some national park volcanic areas show certain features of the vagaries of eruptive work, some show other effects; Craters of the Moon has nearly everything. It is all dead now, this field of tumult which came blasting out of the Great Rift—that series of fissures in the earth crust which constituted a zone of weakness allowing the incandescent dough to well up from the depths. But what a scene of activity it must have been a thousand years ago, or even five hundred years ago, when it was sputtering out! Lava cones, cinder cones, spatter cones, and bombs! Not all volcanoes manufacture bombs. These did. Exploding lavas sent big and little blobs of magma high into the air—high enough so that some of the bombs took a streamline teardrop shape on the way down and hardened with slender tails. It rained stone pollywogs at intervals. Other bombs curiously resemble bread crusts, still others are ribbonlike.

Overleaf: Where lava swirled over the landscape and created grotesque forms. Geologically speaking, these lava flows are recent. Craters of the Moon National Monument. [Photos: Franz Lipp]

The lava sheets flowed down upon forests, felled the trees, and encased them. The heat consumed the wood, but the moisture of the trees had coolness enough so that the lava hardened quickly. Here are the molds that resulted. They are perfect casts of the trunks and even the roots of the overthrown trees.

It is a scene of desolation, if you like; but it is beautiful in its terrible way. If you look closely at the pahoehoe lava—the kind that has a ropy, billowy quality—you will see that some of it, notably the Blue Dragon, shows an iridescent glow in the sunlight. The curves of the billows are graceful. It flowed like a river, this lava, and in places it shows low falls such as you see in a sluggish, wide river where the water has met a tough rock dike across its path.

Then, too, vegetation has come in, even in the relatively short period since the ground was smoking. Already the limber pines and aspens and chokecherries arc of fair size, and shrubs spring from the cracks where soil has accumulated.

A loop road southward along a portion of the Great Rift provides access to many points of interest. There is adequate camping space in the monument, and a limited number of tourist cabins, with provision for meal service, during the season.

11. SUNSET CRATER AND WUPATKI NATIONAL MONUMENTS
[Arizona]

IT MAY HAVE BEEN just about the time that the Normans, under William, invaded England and conquered it that Sunset Crater began pouring out lava and cinders upon the country around. As you stand at the foot of this thousand-foot cinder cone, its summit tinted with red and orange, you can imagine the terror of the Indians who lived in the vicinity. You can see the little groups of farmers and their wives and children hastily grasping whatever of their possessions came to hand and leaving their pit houses to be buried under the ashes that rained upon their heads as they fled. The imagination does not have to be stretched in creating this picture, for Sunset happens to be one volcano, of the many in the Southwest, where eruption has been very accurately dated, by a combination of tree-ring comparisons using the beams from the buried houses and archaeological evidences. It is in north-central Arizona, and is part of the great San Francisco Mountain volcano field, the highest peak of which, Humphreys Peak, rises 12,600 feet.

The prehistoric people were driven away by the firemountain, but they must have remained somewhere in the general vicinity, for it is certain that they came back. What was more natural? It had been home. They had been happy there; they had raised their families there. They felt no differently from modern Italians when Vesuvius and Etna have calmed down after a terrible outburst destroying houses, vineyards, and orchards; soon they are back again with renewed confidence. And so these prehistoric people came timidly back after the volcano seemed tired and the lava had cooled. They discovered that all was not on the debit side; the very ashes and cinders that had buried their homes had actually improved the lands they had farmed. Once they could raise crops only in favored little pockets that held moisture. Now the layer of ashes permitted rain and snow to soak into the soil and be held there. Now they could produce good crops of corn and beans almost anywhere.

Somebody has said very aptly that this started a prehistoric land rush.

Scene of a prehistoric "land rush." Capulin Mountain National Monument. [Photo: Edgar P. Bailey]

The ancient grapevine telegraph spread the news that volcanoes were not such bad demons after all. Within a few years after the eruption as many as four thousand Indians were occupying the fields covered by ash. New customs and new arts were introduced as strangers came from long distances to settle.

But again Fortune turned her head. The same winds that had whipped the ashes from the crater of Sunset and spread it around as a mulch now began to blow it away. First from the higher places, then from the level lands, the light cover began to disappear. The farmers were back where they had started; and there were many more of them now, dependent on the crops. In the end, the coyote howled mournfully at night on the mountainside, and there was nobody to hear him.

For years after Sunset became harmless, there were still hot springs and vapors rising from the crater vents. It was these that, by the deposit of minerals, painted the crater rim with the glowing colors that suggested the mountain's name.

At the height of their most flourishing period, the villages that clustered in the cinder-blanketed area of eight hundred square miles developed a culture which is called Wupatki, the Hopi word for "tall house." From an original small pueblo this one grew to a habitation of more than a hundred rooms, capable of housing as many as three hundred persons.

In the valley below the Wupatki village was a "ball court" of stone masonry. What kind of a game was it? We can only conjecture. Was it purely a physical recreation, the pleasant use of leisure, or was there a religious element, as there was in the Olympic games of the early Greeks? Within the monument are about eight hundred ruins; notably, besides Wupatki, those of the Citadel, Lomaki, and Wukoki and the less accessible ruin of Crack-in-the-Rock near the Little Colorado River.

12. Devils Tower National Monument
[Wyoming]

THOSE WHO HAVE DRIVEN through the Black Hills to Yellowstone National Park by way of Spearfish and Sundance must have caught glimpses from the highway of a strange-looking peak rising in lonely majesty from the rolling ground along the Belle Fourche River. If they were in too much of a hurry to ask about this mountain and to discover that its significance in the American scene is so great that it was the first national monument to be established, their haste cost them a fine experience. For this fluted stone

The Sioux called it "Grizzly Bear's Lodge." Devils Tower National Monument.
[Photo: Franz Lipp]

column, rising 1,280 feet above the bed of the Belle Fourche and 865 feet above its apparent base on the hilltop, is a piece of modernistic volcanic sculpture. And it is a geological mystery.

The Sioux Indians called the tower Mateo Tepee ("Grizzly Bear's Lodge") and had a legend that the columns of the rock were the result of clawmarks of a grizzly bear that tried to climb the sheer wall to get at some Indians on the top. He was a larger bear than ordinary. The Sioux explanation does not satisfy the geologist. But neither does his own. For the tower could have been the lava neck of an old volcano, the walls of which have been weathered away; or it could have been part of a great sheet of molten rock that found its way between layers of other rock—what is called a "sill." But either way, it has to be explained how the surrounding material was disposed of so easily.

The diameter of the tower at its base, where it is surrounded by rock fragments—fallen bits of the fluting—is about a thousand feet. The flat top of the tower is about an acre and a half, on which there are not only grasses and shrubs but also mice, pack rats, and chipmunks, who must have climbed up in past days and found the place agreeable enough so that they never came down.

In the mythology of the ancient Greeks, there were two brothers, Prometheus and Epimetheus. Prometheus, as his name implies, did his thinking first, and then acted. His quarrel with Jupiter was disastrous for him, but at least he went into the venture with his eyes open. It was a calculated risk. Epimetheus was the other sort: he acted first and did his thinking afterward. He was the counterpart of the modern snagwit who sits out on a limb and saws it off between himself and the tree trunk. On his way down, it occurs to him that he should have had a plan. In practical affairs epimetheans are more deadly, to themselves and others, than smallpox.

A young parachutist, some years ago, decided to make a landing on top of Devils Tower. He made a very good landing. He then began to think of going down. He was surprised when he walked around the edge of that acre and a half and found no flight of stairs. It went straight down, like the side of the Washington Monument, so far as he could see. Actually, the tower had once been conquered by an expert who took advantage of breaks in the flutings for footholds. It had been climbed by a promethean—the kind of alpinist who takes calculated risks. Such a man may have an accident, but he tries to provide against all the contingencies.

The parachutist spent six days and five nights—thinking—on top of the tower, and was then rescued by a party that included National Park Service men and was led by the very man who had climbed the mountain before.

For most of us, Devils Tower will be much more interesting viewed from the base. There is a fine trail all around it, and a little museum at headquarters, where the volcanic mystery is framed clearly and the natural and the human history of the region are happily pictured.

13. CAPULIN MOUNTAIN NATIONAL MONUMENT
[New Mexico]

FROM the top of Capulin Mountain, in the northeastern corner of New Mexico, visitors may look into four other states: Colorado, Kansas, Texas, and Oklahoma. Unusual as this experience is, it is only an incident of political geography. The real attraction is the picturesque mountain itself, an imposing example of an extinct volcano with a crater whose symmetry is almost perfectly preserved. The latter fact indicates that, as geologic time goes, the volcano was active at no very distant date. The high angles of the slopes of the mountain also attest this conclusion.

Possibly Capulin came into action during the last period of wild volcanic outbursts in western North and South America. All around it can be seen other fire-mountain peaks. Northwest of it are mesas topped with black lava. Perhaps a series of lava flows at long intervals overspread much of this country, followed by a final effort in which Capulin, among other volcanoes, began to hurl cinders and rocks. Rising from a base of already high land, the peak is about eight hundred feet high; but it was its regular form that made it a landmark, like the volcanic Spanish Peaks back of Trinidad, Colorado, eagerly sought by the eyes of the immigrant trains following both branches of the old Santa Fe Trail.

Capulin not only is beautiful in its form, but, owing to its general elevation above sea level, is clothed with lush grassland and with a forest of pine and juniper. Sometimes one may see the golden eagle hovering over the peak.

Nearby is the famous Folsom site—the spot where in 1926 a discovery was made that revolutionized the notions of the length of time humans have been on our land. Rather, it might be said that it was an additional discovery, but it was so well authenticated that it assumed major importance.

A field party from the Colorado Museum of Natural History, while excavating the fossil bones of bison, found a finely chipped stone lancepoint. This aroused the greatest interest; but on the strength of one such find, conclusions were naturally reserved. Then four more similar points were found, always, as it looked, associated closely with the bison bones. In all, nineteen of these well-formed lance-points have been discovered, and it is now reasonably supposed that the owners of the weapons killed some of the extinct bison, particularly since every one of the animal skeletons lacks the tailbone. It would seem that the ancient hunters skinned their prey and "took the tail with the hide," literally.

Capulin is accessible all through the year except when, rarely, the road to the summit may be blocked by a heavy snow. The road spirals around the cinder cone, and ends at a parking area on the western side of the crater. Near the western base there is a picnic ground, but water and supplies are not available in the monument. The towns of Capulin and Folsom, however, are nearby.

[III]

Discipline of the Desert

I HAVE CROSSED *wide tracts of desert, and I count the hours of undisturbed
musing, of still possession of Nature unbroken by sound, and of
beneficent repose that I have enjoyed there as among the happiest of my life.*

—GEORG EBERS

1. BIG BEND NATIONAL PARK

[*Texas*]

MEMORIES OF OUR LAST FRONTIER, where the Rio Grande makes its big
vagrant swing, dallying with the compass, wondering which way to go.

I remember the sweet, clear days in the basin of the Chisos Mountains in
the latter part of May, when the agaves—or century plants, if you must call
them so—came into their prodigious bloom. Outside the mountain circle the
desert was already growing hot, but here, at the foot of Casa Grande, in the
shade of a weeping juniper, no human lot could have been more fortunate
than mine.

A miracle was taking place—a miracle worth coming thousands of miles
to see. For those agaves, which had lived their term of eighteen or twenty
or twenty-five years on these slopes of crumbled igneous rock, were now
ready to flower, to seed, and to depart. Without warning, except perhaps
to skilled botanists, a great stalk overnight begins to thrust up from the
tightly clasped heart of the fleshy leaves. From that moment until the last
petals have fallen, the agave is a marvel of purposeful intensity. The rate
of growth of that stalk, which may measure half a foot in diameter at the
base, is almost unbelievable, in a climate where the rainfall is so niggardly.

But the agave is reckless of consequences. Like a miser who has hoarded,

---

*The yucca struggles for survival against the shifting sands. White Sands National
Monument. [Photo: Fritz Henle]*

skimped, haggled, and starved and then in a burst of profligacy enjoys one great moment of life, the agave goes to its end proudly and grandly. For this is the bloom of death. Almost before the seeds have rattled down, to be snatched by furry animals and birds before they have time to sprout, the leaves that were so plump and fresh in their smooth green with just a touch of blue sky in the color have turned ashen and then yellow and then sere. *Morituri salutamus!* And what an unforgettable salute when the sides of the Chisos, all the way up from Green Gulch to the foot of the bare rock faces of Casa Grande, Ward, Pulliam, and Emory, are flying the standards of the amaryllis family! Look at them from the basin and you seem to see a host of deployed giants seeking to take the heights by storm.

I would not suggest that these Big Bend agaves are finer than those of Mexico or some other place, but if you go down into that wild frontier in the loop of the Rio Grande—into this national park which was given by the people of Texas to the nation—you will find *Agave scabra* something to feast the eyes upon. Perhaps it will not be the season of bloom when you are there. No matter; the plant at any time is a triumph of symmetry. Even the stiletto that is carried on the end of each leaf, if you will examine it, is as lovely a piece of burnished carbon as ever was turned on nature's lathe. On many of the younger leaves there is a decorative motif, like tiny finger-prints, along the margin.

There is a little sister of the century plant, called the lechuguilla, which all across this rocky soil contends with the other desert plants. It is from the fibers of this plant that the native Mexicans weave ropes and harness and halters, saddlebags, and a hundred other useful things. These and the sotol and the wild pineapple and the creosote bush; the ocotillo and the allthorn; tarweed and cactuses and Mormon tea—these give the answer to the imper-tinence of those who ask: "What can possibly live in such a desert?" They say: "*We* do. And if you keep your domestic animals off our necks, we will settle, one day, amongst ourselves, we and the wild animals, where each of us shall live." These brave, self-reliant green things I remember.

I remember the full moon rising over Casa Grande, and the sun setting in a blaze at the Window. For there is one break in this mass of dissected lava, forming a great bowl, the very bottom of which is the basin. Looking toward the west, out across Burro Mesa and into Old Mexico, there is a V-shaped opening, with a vedette on the left, guarding the entrance. This is the Win-

Across the desert expanse the Chisos Mountains rise, ghostlike. Big Bend National Park. [Photo: M. Woodbridge Williams]

dow. The whole mountain mass rises abruptly from a peneplain, and when you are in the basin you are at an elevation of five thousand feet. The highest peak on the rim of the bowl, Mount Emory, is nearly eight thousand. Emory was the peak that the members of the boundary-survey party in 1852 "long and anxiously watched." It was their beacon—this and the Boquillas Finger, which sticks up above the long regular line of the Sierra del Carmen, on the east side of the park.

One winter morning I looked up at Casa Grande and Toll Mountain. From where I stood there is an apparent cleft between them, and I saw a huge waterfall—a thousand Yosemites—pouring down from that cleft. It was fog. A great bank of it had crept up the eastern side of the Chisos, found a path, and was pouring down in a cascading stream into the bowl. I remember this; and I remember coming down one afternoon through Persimmon Gap and reaching that point on the road from Marathon where the Chisos suddenly comes into view. And I saw then the Chisos rising out of a mist like a medieval walled city. You would have said it was the Cité of Carcassonne in Provence.

What simple incidents thrill us in the desert! A few weeks before, I had been standing at the corner of Broadway and 42nd Street, in Manhattan, with a mind thoroughly confused at what was going on in the world. I could make nothing of it. Whatever the mad scramble meant, I, at least, was being jostled out of the orbit. Now, in the desert, in the lovely basin of the Chisos, things began to make sense again. I remember that. And I remember what complete sense the herd of flagtail deer made. When I drove back to the cabin, I frequently met them—fifty or more—browsing quietly not far from the road. One of them had only three legs. They gazed at me with that quizzical expression from behind their black burglar masks, and then, not seeming frightened, but just for the lark of it, scampered up the mountainside, with three-legs always well to the fore. They stopped for a while, looked at me again, and then scampered a little farther up.

I remember those merry flagtails, and I remember harvesting some of the curious seeds of the mountain mahogany, which have a spiral feathery tail. The barbed seed vessels, when ripe, are blown along the ground and finally gyrate into the earth at some favorable spot. I planted some of them, to save them the trouble of so much gyrating. I wonder if any of them came up. If you go down there—or *when* you go down—please look for them, will you? I can give you the exact location. Anyway, it is pleasant to remember something of so little utility and so much good will.

Dog Canyon, too; and a little canyon that I called Puppy Canyon, be-

*The Rio Grande finds its way through these narrow slits. Big Bend National Park.
[Photo: M. Woodbridge Williams]*

cause it presents a geological picture you do not often see—a canyon that
is just in the formative stage. Dagger Flat, where the yuccas have found a
condition absolutely to their taste; and here the Giant Dagger, which will
be the object of a favorite pilgrimage for visitors to the park, outdoes in
size and magnificence all the other yuccas of the region. There are at least
five species in all to be found there.

I remember—and who could forget?—the mouth of Santa Elena Canyon,
that dark, winding slit in the Mesa de Anguila, a tilted fault-block of hard
limestone through which the Rio Grande has cut a narrow channel with
precipitous walls. The sheerness of the drop of Santa Elena Canyon from rim

to river has scarcely any equal in the topography of the West. For nearly ten miles the river has been flowing through this great chasm. Suddenly, near where Terlingua Creek flows in, it emerges into full daylight, making a charming picnic spot, and an easily accessible one for fishermen. For there are big fish here in the Rio Grande.

Santa Elena is one of the three great canyons through which the Rio Grande has carved its way. The others are Mariscal and Boquillas. I learned from the notes of Dr. Parry, botanist with the boundary survey, that they ran the Mariscal in India-rubber boats, "one of which was capsized in shooting a sharp rapid." Santa Elena and Boquillas canyons they left alone, wisely enough, for they were on important business, not men out for adventure. All the canyons have been successfully navigated, but it is not a feat recommended for the average person.

We linger awhile at the mouth of beautiful Santa Elena, to loll under an alamo and hark back to the day in late July 1860 when a body of tired, ragged, discouraged soldiers, led by a shavetail named Echols, came down the creek now called Terlingua and gazed in wonder at the mouth of the canyon. It was a strange sight. Thirty men, some jaded packmules, and twenty camels! The native wildlife of the district must have goggled at the sight of camels in Big Bend. The camels, said Echols, had done nobly. They had stood the journey from Camp Hudson better than the mules; better even than the men. On July 3 the whole command had been in imminent danger of death from thirst; water was found on July 4, and that was a day of celebration. But all the hardships were forgotten when at last the soldiers came out upon the river and saw its rush-covered bottom lands and the trees along its banks.

It was Jefferson Davis's idea, when he was Secretary of War, to use camels for army transport across the deserts of the West. They never had a real chance to prove themselves. First the Civil War intervened. Then the transcontinental railroads pushed across the country. The last of the camels were turned loose upon the desert and finally disappeared.

The picturesque little quicksilver-mining town of Terlingua lies just outside the boundaries of Big Bend National Park. Terlingua—what does the name mean? We used to wonder about it, among the things we talked over, around a fire on a winter's night in the Bend. Some thought it meant "three languages." But what three languages could they have been? The name is not Spanish, as presently spelled. Lieutenant Echols called the creek

Santa Elena Canyon releases its hold on the Rio Grande. Big Bend National Park. [Photo: M. Woodbridge Williams]

Lates Lengua, which was the way he caught it from his guide. Was it really Las Tres Lenguas, which might mean three strips of land, as, for instance, the sand-bar tongues in a creek delta? Who cares? But it is so pleasant to speculate about unimportant matters! It is one of the enjoyments of the desert.

We must be moving down the river.

I remember Mondays at the little post office and store at Hot Springs. Monday was mail day. The nearest railroad station is at Marathon, and the postman drove the hundred miles down once a week, stopped over in Hot Springs, and went back on Tuesday. Mrs. Margaret Smith, a frontier woman who could face a cougar with equanimity, kept the store and with her son and daughter maintained a rendezvous for the scanty population in the south end of the area, as well as for the straggling denizens on the other side of the river. Monday was a great day for these latter folk. The rules were relaxed and they could come across if they had legitimate trading affairs or were expecting letters—or for no particular reason, probably, if they were known to the border men as trustworthy. For you must know that between the Rio Grande at this point and any town or city of Old Mexico is a vast expanse of land about which the average Mexican knows as little as we know of Tierra del Fuego. The Mexican border patrolmen used to come across on a Monday to get their paychecks from the U. S. Treasury, and perhaps they still do. The mail from Mexico City came round by way of Laredo or some other border station, then over to Marathon, and so down into the Bend. *That* is frontier!

For years hopeful invalids had come from other places in Texas to soak in the hot springs along the riverside. I once found a man immersed in one of these tubs. I asked him if he thought the waters did him any good. He replied that he didn't think so, but they *might*, and it gave him a chance to get away from home for a few days.

I remember footing it along an exposure of gray-white limestone where the living-rock grows. The living-rock is a cactus, and one of the queerest of the whole great family. In the crevices of this limestone it takes root. The limestone is full of fissures. So the cactus decides that it, too, will be full of fissures. The cactus resembles the rock, and the rock resembles the cactus, and I assure you you can be looking directly at one of these plants and never see it at all, so perfect is this imitation.

Sometimes, over Casa Grande, the clouds pour like a waterfall. Big Bend National Park. [Photo: M. Woodbridge Williams]

I remember the lime-rock hillside, not far from Hot Springs, where the resurrection plant grows. Here is a strange little fernlike growth that has learned to tailor its suit according to the amount of material on hand. One day you pass by and there is nothing on the hillside but what appears to be dried-up herbage; then comes one of the grudging rains of the desert. Two days later you pass the spot again, and the hillside is green and flourishing. A week later all may be sere once more. But the little plant can sit out the longest drought.

A few years ago we used to wonder if the pronghorn could ever return to its old home in Big Bend. Great numbers of pronghorn formerly lived in this region, feeding on the good herbs, especially the tobosa grass of Tobosa Flat and along the Tornillo creekbed. But the hunters shot them out, and a few that escaped the gun were no match for the sheep and goats and for the sheet erosion, which was partly natural and partly due to the trampling of the "hoofed locusts," as John Muir called sheep. If sheep deserve this harsh epithet, what shall we say of goats? Goats are long-haired Japanese beetles, at the very least. Anyone who has wandered around the Basin of the Chisos and seen the mountain-mahogany and the Apache plume literally torn to pieces by these terrific foragers can well believe that a few goats on the island of St. Helena, in a few years, converted a forest to a tangle of inedible sedge grass.

And, finally, I remember the way night comes to the Big Bend desert. You arrive somewhere along the Tornillo Wash late in the afternoon and busy yourself with the thousand things to do and see. You are about south of massy Chisos, and to the eastward you look, on your far left, at the Dead Horse Range, and in front of you at the regular line and banded cliffs of the Sierra del Carmen. Seemingly a part of the Carmen range, but really having nothing in common with it, is the towering Fronteriza—in Old Mexico. And what appears to be a volcanic peak—Picotena, I think it is called —is also on the alien side of the Rio Grande.

Your own shadow begins to lengthen. The dark line slowly crosses the wash, deepens the color of the vanadium yellow on the low cliffs on the eastern side, and begins to approach the foot of the Carmens. Those bands of gray and reddish yellows and brown, as seen in the full sunlight, now begin to change. First a pink flush suffuses the whole escarpment; the grays take on the tone of magenta, the reds deepen, and there seems to be a violet haze coming over all. It deepens to a purple as you watch. The lower part of the Carmen is turning a velvety black, but on top the last rays of the sun set up a riot of colors for just the flicker of a minute—and night settles down.

Creosote bushes and candelillas, etched so sharply against the yellow sands a few minutes ago, now soften into vague blurs and withdraw. It is time to be going. But you go with a rested mind and a sort of renewal of faith.

Thus I remember a few things about Big Bend, and if I have here indulged myself with a little excess of the personal pronoun, it has not been to celebrate myself, believe me. I wanted to convey the general notion that in these national parks there are so many gentle, refreshing, unspectacular experiences of eye and soul, which, taken home, are a treasury from which memories can be withdrawn, long afterward, with delight. For these recollections, though dimmed, can always be rekindled, just as I am doing now— I, who am writing these words thousands of miles from the desert and looking out a window upon a landscape so different: pines, oaks, sugar maples, and beeches and the lush tall grasses of an Eastern spring.

The national parks are operated for profit—this kind of profit.

2. Death Valley National Monument
[*California–Nevada*]

When death valley, with its surrounding mountains, was proclaimed a national monument in 1933, there must have been great wonderment on the part of those who knew the region only by hearsay. Why set aside a strip of wilderness notorious for undrinkable water, uncrossable bog, billows of drifting sand, and the bleached bones of blasted hopes? If the idea was to preserve the memories of the ill-advised emigrants who suffered and died there in the great trek of '49, why not just fence off a piece and call it a national cemetery?

Fortunately, those who knew the real value of this strange page of American geography were able to have it set aside and to save it from any further commercial exploitation. For if you consider its winter climate alone, the future of Death Valley was assured. From October until May the weather conditions are as nearly ideal as nature is willing to provide. Imagine a year with 351 clear days! This, to be sure, was an exceptional year, but the average annual rainfall is slightly less than one and a half inches. *That* is true desert.

This rugged area of nearly two million acres, which lies east of the Sierra in California along the southwestern Nevada boundary, is a bundle of contradictions. Almost anything you would guess about it is either not true or only partially true. It is one of the driest spots in the United States, yet it is rather well supplied with water—though you may not like the taste of all the water. More than five hundred square miles of the valley are below the level of the Pacific Ocean, and the lowest spot, at Badwater, is 280 feet below sea level; yet not far from that very depression towers Telescope Peak, 11,325 feet above the valley floor. Telescope is therefore higher above its immediate surroundings than any other mountain in the conterminous United States— higher in this relation than Mount Whitney. The aridity would seem to forbid the existence of any considerable life of any sort; yet the fact is that not only is animal life abundant, but there is plenty of plantlife too; and under exactly the right conditions, which occur at irregular intervals, the parched soil comes to life and mantles itself with such beauty that the mass blooming will one day be an event to be teletyped over the country by the press associations.

This desert bloom occurs on the alluvial fans, in the dry washes, and in the canyons. No one can predict the flowering with certainty. The intervals recorded are somewhere between five and ten years—there was a mass bloom- ing in 1935, again in 1940, and in 1947. In a brief period the annual plants must produce their seeds and cast them where they will lie dormant till some favorable time of moisture. The seeds not only retain their vitality, but even tend to produce too many plants in some years. A botanist, observing the crowding plants near Daylight Pass, noted that every plant developed at least one flower spike, even if it was reduced to only a single flower, and even if there were only two resulting seeds—a beautiful example in the desert of the provision for the survival of the species!

Nearly three hundred feet below the surface of the ocean you would expect there should be fish. Very well; there are. And they are salt-water fish, too; at least, they belong to an order that lives in both fresh and salt water. Desert sardines, they are called, and they are found in Salt Creek and Saratoga Springs. Are these minnows survivors fom a period, perhaps of glacial time, when the drainage of the region was altogether different and a fish could be cool and composed on a summer day? There are those who think so; and anyway, their presence here is something that needs explaining.

Let us get the overall picture of this extraordinary sink and its forbidding mountain barriers. The valley is boxed, east and west, by precipitous slopes —the Amargosa Range on the Nevada side, and the Panamints on the other. From Dante's View or Zabriskie Point, on a day when the haze permits, the High Sierra can be seen. Some optimists have believed they could make out Mount Whitney, but there is a frailty that leads folks to see what they wish to see. Certainly, so far as low humidity may help, this is the ideal place to look long distances. From a perch on the Panamints it seems impossible that the valley floor is seven thousand feet or more below the viewer. It is almost touchable with the finger.

The geologists are chary about coming to conclusions about the creation of the deep sump. One thing is certain: it was not eroded like the Grand Canyon. There is no sign of the work of glaciers. To some degree the most ancient history of the region follows the general sequence of changes that took place in the Southwest—the thrusting up and planing down, the advent of oceans, with marine life, the raging of volcanic action, and the creation of limestones and sandstones from sediments of torn-down mountains. But at some point in the dim past—yet a past nearer to our own little wafer of time—the forces that created Death Valley worked the effect we see today. Was it a stupendous folding of the earth crust that left the valley at this sunken point? Or was there a vast block that dropped down between two great fractures of the earth crust? Now that this desertland is becoming more accessible to study, the correct scientific picture will some day be drawn.

Meanwhile visitors will be more interested in the coloring. Not even in the Grand Canyon is there quite such a dazzling variety of tints and shades—the dark and jet-black volcanic masses, the red and gray granites, and sandstones that mineral pigments have painted green, red, pink, and blue. And in this almost rainless land there is one mocking relic of a time when water must have been plentiful. Not far up the canyon from Natural Bridge is an extinct waterfall. The rock is grooved to a depth of ten feet, and the fall was as much as twenty feet wide. Not a trickle ever goes down that chute now. It must have been a very different climate when cascading water wore away the stone.

Until the Bennett-Arcane party crossed the salt flats and camped for three ghastly weeks (December 22, 1849, to January 16, 1850) in the vicinity of Bennetts Well, Death Valley was a land unknown to the white people of the United States. A small tribe of the Shoshone Indian nation had lived for some centuries in the Panamints, trading a pretty meager existence for security, and migrating back and forth from the high land to the low. It is possible, too, that the Spanish freebooters from Mexico knew the locality, for they went into the byways in their search for loot; but they left no record of such knowledge. It was not until some of the forty-niners came back to look for gold and silver in the barrier mountains that any whites deliberately braved the hardships of life in the valley.

Stout-hearted, determined, and utterly self-reliant were these prospectors who crossed and recrossed the salt floor of the valley and climbed the mountainsides, with burro for companion, and hope springing eternal, looking for the rich finds alleged by gossip and campfire yarn to be awaiting them. Some of them, indeed, found pockets of gold; many of them found only happiness and death—happiness because they learned to love the absolute freedom of the nomad life, with a beckoning fortune awaiting them in the very next "porphyry"; death because they wagered too heavily upon their iron nerve, missed the waterholes, let their burros stray, or stayed too long into the hot season and were driven mad by a furnace blast that has been known to touch 134 degrees in a modern thermometer shelter.

Now this is changed. No, not all; but the valley is readily accessible to visitors, and there are enough good roads so they can see the salient features. Where the prospector prodded his burro along, and a few years ago a few adventurous souls with motorcars blew their tires and cursed their day on villainous cart tracks, now sightseers roll comfortably in buses because they are there in the proper season.

For five or six months, Death Valley is a joy and a delight. There are signs for the prudent motorist, such as: WARNING: DO NOT ATTEMPT THIS ROUTE WITHOUT AMPLE SUPPLIES OF WATER, GAS, AND OIL. There is a camp-ground, maintained by the National Park Service near the mouth of Furnace Creek, in a side canyon surrounded by hills of high color. Restrooms, water, tables, and parking spaces are provided for tenters and trailer folk. There is no firewood, so visitors should bring an adequate supply or an oil stove for cooking.

Just inside the monument, on the new highway between Trona and Wildrose Canyon, there is a service station, with cabins, where supplies may be had. This is controlled, under franchise, by the government. All the other accommodations—the luxurious hotel and ranch at Furnace Creek, Stove-pipe Wells Hotel, near the Sand Dunes, and limited accommodations at Scotty's Castle—are on private land and are not Park Service concessions.

Scotty's Castle is almost as great a paradox in this setting as the "sardines" in Salt Creek. A two-million-dollar edifice, placed in a singularly unpromising location—except for the water supply—it reflects, perhaps, the strange build-ing whims that take possession of humans. Years ago I used to observe in Los Angeles a man who had constructed a small hut in the top of a tree; he pulled up his rope ladder at night against inconvenient visits. And once in the south of France, near the Spanish border, I saw an unfinished house in which the floors had been purposely constructed to make an angle of, say, thirty de-grees. The owner was called away for examination before the place was finished, and did not return. The lady across the street told me that he was an "original."

But Scotty's Castle is certainly worth seeing. Perhaps it constitutes a study in diffidence—the desire to live in such a way as not to attract attention. If so, it is as unobtrusive as a symphony conductor's bandaged thumb.

Because you may never see them, you must not conclude, after a visit to Death Valley, that animals in this real desert are scarce. They are really abundant, but most of them get about only at night, and all of them are wary. A notable wildlife feature of the monument is the several hundred head of desert bighorn that live in the high country. In some parts of their range these wild sheep have become extinct, but under protection here they are holding their own in numbers. The wild burros you may see are of course the progeny of those brought in by prospectors, who were turned loose or escaped. They fend for themselves as burros can.

There are a dozen or more species of lizards, from the big chuckwalla to the anemic-looking gecko; and besides the rodents like the antelope ground squirrel, kangaroo rats, and pack rats, the kit fox and the coyote are sometimes seen. Then, of course, there are snakes. Somehow most of the people I know associate snakes with the desert. They are there, but personally I have seen

A great boulder is being pushed across the slick playa by the wind. Death Valley National Monument. [Photo: Josef Muench]

ten snakes in the East and the humid South to every one I ever saw in the Southwest. This may be merely a singular personal experience.

There are two kinds of rattlesnakes in the area, neither of which you are likely ever to see; but campers should of course take reasonable precautions against the vicious little sidewinder, which goes abroad at night. No, the dangers from venomous creatures are negligible in this desert. The great danger is to rash adventurers who might disregard sage advice and go off the trail on excursions for which they are neither practically nor mentally equipped. For, to be safe as an explorer of far corners in the desert, one must be in perfect attunement with the terrain, like the Bedouin and our own desert rats. And even then there are accidents. So be wise: learn the desert little by little, and you may come to love it so well that you will want to live nowhere else.

I have heard people, crossing the Mojave on the Santa Fe and looking from the train window, say with a shudder: "How can people live in such a place as this?" The desert dweller has an answer to that, a retort not at all impolite. He merely shrugs and says: "How can people bear to live anywhere else?"

Jim Dayton was for some years caretaker of the Furnace Creek Ranch. One August day he started, alone, on one of his periodic trips to Daggett, 160 miles away. Later he was found lying under a mesquite, his four horses dead, and his dog still alive on guard. Jim was buried where they found him.

Some years later Shorty Harris died. By his own request he lies beside Jim Dayton. There is a marker on the spot, which is worded as Shorty wanted it:

> *Here lies Shorty Harris*
> *A Single-Blanket Jackass Prospector*
> *Bury me beside Jim Dayton*
> *In the Valley*
> *We both loved*

No elegant elegy could tell better than this rude epitaph, touched with frontier humor, the affection of men for the desert.

3. ORGAN PIPE CACTUS NATIONAL MONUMENT
[*Arizona*]

SOMEBODY HAS REMARKED that a "whim of Nature" placed a section of the Mexican desert on the north side of the international boundary. I doubt it. I don't think Nature cares who says he owns the land, so long as the taxes are paid. The law of compensation sees that the taxes are collected. And claims for abatement are ignored at the bureau.

I didn't mean to quarrel with the phrase, though. It does well enough. It emphasizes the odd fact that when the boundary between the United States and Mexico was finally adjusted, the northern end of the Sonoyta Valley, which belongs climatically to the Sonoran desert, was clipped off, to give us a strip of desert unlike any other we have. Here, if you are an enthusiast for desert plants, is the spot for your venture into the exotic. Here you will see that wonderful cactus, springing up with unbranched arms to a height of nearly twenty feet, in great clumps of thirty or more stalks, which has been called the organ-pipe cactus. There is, indeed, some resemblance to the pipes of a church organ.

Here, in this desert garden, and just barely over the line in our country, you will see the equally bizarre sinita cactus—the cactus with whiskers. Near the tips of the older arms long, gray, hairlike spines appear, and continue to the ends, with occasionally a bare spot that looks as though the barber had started his work and been called away. Here along moist drainage chan-

Wearing a medieval jouster's coat of mail: the collared lizard. Organ Pipe Cactus National Monument. [*Photo: M. Woodbridge Williams*]

nels you will see plants you have not seen before, flowers like the ajo, or desert lily, which in blossoming time fills the air around it with a perfume much like that of the orange tree. All this queer assemblage of subtropical life in the country of little rain has been set aside for preservation for the Americans of years to come, under the designation of Organ Pipe Cactus National Monument.

Arizona, at the southwest end of which this monument is situated, is the richest state, I think, in the variety of its cactuses. Certainly it has many that can be found nowhere else. In recent years the interest in these brave, spiny marvels of adaptation has greatly increased, so that a huge mail-order business has grown up, and even a steady demand by the five-and-ten-cent stores. They look better, like all other wild plants, where they grow naturally; yet I think it rather a delightful little hobby. One of my neighbors is an elderly lady whose windowbox of assorted cactus plants is the joy of her life. She cannot travel, and she tells me that the plants take her to the desert on a magic carpet.

Of course you will never dig up a cactus or any other plant in Organ Pipe Cactus National Monument, or in any other national monument or national park. You will be tempted to; it is very human; but then you will remember that it is an unsocial act. You are a joint owner of these preserved places. You are a partner with about 190 million others. Partners of character do not raid a jointly owned property. They are anxious to protect, not to despoil. I hate lecturing, and I hate being lectured, on the subject of duty. Just consider that I am reminding the reader of a thing that I know from my own experience is easy, in the zest of meeting new and interesting plant-life, to forget. A mere jog of the elbow, may I say?

While Organ Pipe Cactus National Monument may perhaps interest you most because it is a wild desert garden, you may see plenty of wildlife, too, if you are fortunate. The desert wild hog, sometimes called the peccary, and by the Mexicans called the javalina, lives in the brush-covered plains. There are antelope, four kinds of them; and some of the wild sheep that were nearly wiped out by hunting in the thoughtless pioneering period are still living in the higher elevations of the monument.

It is historic ground, too. The early explorer Díaz went through here on his march toward the Colorado River in the conquistador days, and many years later Father Kino set up the San Marcel Mission at what is now the

_____

Nature's own cactus arboretum: Santa Rosa peak in background. Organ Pipe Cactus National Monument. [Photo: Natt N. Dodge]

town of Sonoyta, just over the border. The padre developed a route across the southwestern corner of the area, traces of which may still be seen.

Caravans of gold-seekers squeaked through these sands when the emigrants from eastern Texas and other Southern states joined in the rush toward the California diggings just about a century ago. Many forged through, after terrible hardships, and many paid the toll of Midas. The U. S. Treasury price of gold at this time is thirty-five dollars an ounce. The world's hoard of gold has cost far more than that. Far more.

When the desert poppies are in flower in Organ Pipe Cactus National Monument, they are of gold, too. And unstained.

4. SAGUARO NATIONAL MONUMENT
[*Arizona*]

LONG BEFORE I ever saw the superlative stand of giant cactus near Tucson, I had formed a passing acquaintanceship with the saguaro. Of course,

This cactus is happily named. Organ Pipe Cactus National Monument. [Photo: M. Woodbridge Williams]

I did not then know how impressive a saguaro forest could be, for the specimens I saw were at the northern edge of the range of this species, and could not compare either in number or size with those farther south. But I mention that first sight of the plant because something I observed on a rocky hillside not far from Apache Junction puzzled me no end, and later I was to find the answer in Saguaro National Monument.

I was spending a gloriously idle day, in the bright sunshine, browsing over what appeared to be bleak and barren ground, but was on closer examination rich in plant and animal life, like all the desert country. I was seeing the saguaros for the first time, with their leafless, fluted trunks, strange semaphore arms, sometimes contorted into imitative forms, some healthy, some dead. The dead saguaros reminded me of skeleton steel towers, into which the vegetable concrete might be poured.

Then it occurred to me that I should like to find a small saguaro, to take home to the East and rear to such size as it might attain in alien custody. I found none. It seemed strange. Big saguaros, middle-sized saguaros, but no little ones! Plenty of other tiny cactuses, but not the ones I sought. I remember that rodents were plentiful on that Arizona hillside. I had neither the wit nor the knowledge to put the facts together, and perhaps at that time there were not many biologists who could.

I know now. The great saguaro forest near Tucson is possibly a doomed forest. It is not renewing. True, it will be there for many years. But civilized human life moved in upon it. The life story of the strange plant reveals what has happened.

During the lifetime of the saguaro it scattered vast numbers of seeds over the ground, but few escaped the bright eyes of mice and other relishers or fell on a favorable spot for germination. The seedlings needed the shelter of a shrub, and even then the rodent life was thirsty and hungry for the tiny plants. Cattle had browsed off the shrubs; woodchoppers had cut down the trees for fenceposts and fuel; the stockmen had killed off the coyotes that had balanced out the rodents; and, the vegetative cover being gone, the humus and duff had been washed away.

And the saguaro has such a precarious infancy, too! About fifteen years may pass before the seedling is large enough to be noticed, and another fifteen years, maybe, before it is big enough to loom above its protective cover. Only at thirty years is it in a way to protect itself fully, with root system and spines. But in survival this object of such tender incubation becomes the greatest of all cactuses reaching a possible height of fifty feet and a weight of twelve tons. How long it can live is not accurately known. Perhaps two hundred years is its limit. It does not develop its flinging, admonitory, or knot-tying arms till it reaches a ripe age.

When the saguaro is in its prime, it is a tremendous natural storage tank for the meager rainfall of the desert where it thrives. No leaves for the saguaro! Leaves would mean a loss of precious fluid. Instead, the tough green skin of the fluted columns does the breathing, and the moisture gathered by the widespread root system is stored in the pulpy tissue between the vertical ribs. During one storm a ton of water may thus be put away by a single plant for a rainless day. As the tissue stores the water, it expands, so that when the tank is full, the huge stem puffs and rounds. Then, as the water is used, the deep-set wrinkles begin to appear.

Major William H. Emory, who ran the Mexican boundary, was astonished when he came into the neighborhood of the saguaro forests. "We encamped," he wrote, "in a grove of cacti of all kinds; amongst them the huge *pitahaya*, which was fifty feet high." To George Engelmann, the botanist of that time, Emory sent either specimens or descriptions of the various cactuses he found growing in southern Arizona. One of them was the bisnaga, or barrel cactus—the one that stores water in such a way as to furnish drink for men thirsting in the desert. This cactus, too, Engelmann told Emory, is called Pitahaya by the Californians, "but this appears to be a general name applied in Mexico and South America to all the large columnar cacti which have edible fruits."

The fruits of the saguaro are certainly tasty to birds, chipmunks, and ground squirrels, and in the early days the Pima and Papago Indians ate them fresh, dried them, and made syrup from them. The blossom, which has become the state flower of Arizona, is creamy white, appearing in clusters at the ends of the branching arms in May and early June.

In age, the giant cactus falls prey, it seems, to a strange disease, a bacterial enemy carried within the intestine of a tiny moth that flies at night. The larva of this moth lives only in the juicy pulp of the saguaro, and gnaws a tunnel that becomes the focus of the incurable rot that finally may slay the giant. Incurable? Well, not quite; for another of the natural balances here shows itself. The drone fly breeds in decaying saguaro pulp, and the bird called the gilded flicker, probing for the flies, opens the pockets of rot and clears out the lesion, thus performing what amounts to a surgical operation, enabling callusing and healing in many cases.

Defiant of drought, the giant cactus draws on its water storage. Saguaro National Monument. [Photo: Roger Toll]

The wonder of it! Bacterium to moth to larva to plant cell—spelling disease. Gilded flicker to lesion to drone fly—spelling surgery and cure. Could there be a more dramatic example of the community existence, over whose plodding, adapting course man seems to have no power except to thwart!

"It appears, however," says a well-known naturalist, "that it is only a matter of time until the famous Cactus Forest of Saguaro National Monument will gradually go down under the persistent efforts of the bacterium and the moth-carrier." If this should be so, then the preservation of the integrity of Organ Pipe Cactus National Monument becomes doubly important, for in that place there is a younger and healthy stand, not so showy as that at Saguaro, but promising well for the future.

5. JOSHUA TREE NATIONAL MONUMENT
[California]

FOR THOSE who are not skilled in botany, it is hard to believe that the Joshua tree belongs to the same family as the onion. They are both lilies. And the lily is the Smith family of the plant world. The rose family represents the Joneses.

In this great lily family there is a genus known as the yucca, and the yucca also takes a variety of forms, including the dagger and the Spanish bayonet. But one of these yuccas found the conditions of a part of the Southwest desert greatly to its liking and became a sizable tree: a queer sort of plant with burly arms crooked at the elbow, and so unsymmetrical that it looks as though it were constantly asking itself the question: "What shall I do next?" Some of these Joshuas are nearly forty feet high.

It has been said that the name was given to this giant yucca by the Mormons, who saw in its extended arms a symbol pointing to the promised land they were seeking. It may be so, but the promised land must have been in all points of the compass, for the Joshua tree points everywhere, including up and down. Though the tree itself may be no thing of beauty, when blooming time comes it sends forth a cluster of creamy-white blossoms a foot long at the very ends of its branches. Visitors look up at them with the feeling that nature's ends always justify the means.

Joshua trees are well scattered throughout the Mojave, but the finest stand, a real Joshua forest, is found east of Riverside, California—or south of

And the rocks are as bizarre as the trees. Joshua Tree National Monument. [*Photo: O. F. Oldendorph*]

Amboy, or north of Indio, according to the direction of approach. Here is Joshua Tree National Monument, a fine bit of desert with a fine climate almost any time of year. It was set aside by Presidential proclamation in 1936, to preserve not only the rare Joshua trees, but other rare plants and a remarkable assortment of wild animal life. Besides a limited number of mountain sheep, which will increase under protection, the coyote, the desert fox, and the bobcat, shy creatures, but sometimes to be glimpsed, live within the monument.

Here, in Joshua Tree National Monument, the landscape is entirely different from that of Death Valley and its mountain fringes. This segment of desert receives a minimum annual rainfall of perhaps five inches—not very much, surely. But in the desert Southwest a few inches more or less of moisture may mean a very different distribution of plant and animal life. The cactus family is better represented here, for example, than in Death Valley; indeed, there is an amazing stand of a kind of cholla vulgarly known as the Teddy bear. Next to the "jumping cholla," which has a reputation of throwing its missiles similar to that of the porcupine, the Teddy bear is perhaps the most formidable member of the tribe. There is much talk of snakes and Gila monsters and scorpions and tarantulas of the desert country. For my part, I would fear accidentally walking into the embrace of one of these barbed cactus monsters more. So when you see the army of them in Pinto Basin, be respectful. After you have concluded that you are not too close to one, stand away a little farther.

From a point on the ridge of the Little San Bernardinos, known as Salton View, you may have one of the greatest desert views of the country. You are at little more than five thousand feet above sea level, but the nature of the surrounding land is such that there is a panorama of mountain, valley, and desert. You see the Salton Sea of the Imperial Valley, the date gardens of the Coachella Valley, the great escarpment of Mount San Jacinto, and on some clear days you may even look into Old Mexico.

Gold mining and cattle grazing have left their scars on this bit of desert. The jackass prospector has gophered everywhere among the hills. Some rich finds were made, but in most cases the ores were not rich enough to pay for hauling them to faraway mills for reduction. As a Colombian mine owner said to me once, "Ah, *señor*, it takes much gold to run a gold mine." After a pause he added, clinchingly: "*Sí, mucho!*"

Like other desert areas, this Joshua country once had a much wetter climate. In Pinto Basin, in the eastern end of the monument, an ancient people must have lived along the shoreline of a stream that afforded the means of subsistence for many. It may have been twenty thousand years ago that a great dryness came and drove the primitive people out. The "pinto points"—flints used on an ancient throwing stick, which probably was used long before the arrow—found at the basin take us back into a past that makes our own national history seem like a single page torn from Time's diary.

6. White Sands National Monument
[*New Mexico*]

ONCE WHEN I WAS VISITING this unrivaled gypsum desert, not far from Alamogordo, and staring with renewed wonder upon the great dunes, which are not really of sand but of snow-white powdered alabaster, the superintendent led me aside and asked: "How can I tell the story of this White Sands National Monument?"

Truly, it is a nice problem in interpretation. I am glad to say that I was not flattered into trying to pull a quick rabbit out of my hat. The trick looks well, but on closer examination the rabbit is too often mangy. It was clear enough to me what the superintendent had in mind. There had been so many visitors, unprepared with a background of information, who had driven, looked around a few minutes, and then asked what the distance was to El Paso. And I thought what a pity this was. Because here is one of the choicest of the areas that have been set aside because of their notable scientific values. Relatively, too, it requires so little explanation to make it a great adventure in the mind, as well as an unforgettable picture to the eye.

Yet the question is how to condition the casual visitor so that he may look a little beyond the lovely dunes—fascinating in themselves—and give himself a full day's pleasure in contemplating this graphic example of the ebb and flow of surface which affects every living thing within its grasp. It is not easy to do. I have a few comments, which I do not value highly, but which might stimulate curiosity. Certainly I think visitors should go first to the fine museum, housed in the headquarters building. In many areas I would recommend that you first fill the eye with the scenic offering and later go to the museum. I believe White Sands is a place where the order should be reversed.

This is a great basin, stretching north and south between two ranges of mountains. There are thick beds of gypsum beneath the floor, and similar beds show themselves high up on the sides of the mountains, indicating that probably this whole section of country was once a plateau, of which the middle part sank. For a long, long time the rains and snows have carried the gypsum in solution from mountains to basin, while more gypsum "sand" is brought to the surface from the underground supply. The result is a vast alkali flat. But that is only the first result; for then the never quiet southwest winds pick up the particles and begin to whirl them into dunes—dunes that are ever on the move, assuming shapes that are never duplicated. A giant snow-white billow is here today—tomorrow it is moving on.

Whenever the drifting material encounters shrubs, like the yucca, it becomes a matter of life and death for the plants. As the sand moves in, the yucca exerts itself to keep its head above water, so to say. With each increase of an inch of sand around the stem, the plant adds another inch to the stem. Where dunes have receded from a spot, plants have been found with stems more than forty feet long. But the plants have their days of triumph, too. Sometimes when a dune has rested in one place long enough, the plantlife binds it down, as the Lilliputians tied up big Gulliver with ropes.

Observe how the animals have adapted themselves to life on this expanse of white. Obviously a dark-colored mouse or lizard would be an easy mark for an enemy against this snowy background. So in the life story of the species the survivors have been the white or pale-colored individuals. The proof of this is found in the surrounding hills. Whereas the pocket mouse of the basin floor is white, his cousin in the red strata has a reddish fur, and his relative on the beds of black lava a few miles north is nearly the color of that rock.

Incidentally, those who would like to prolong the skiing season can bring their boards to White Sands. On the steep sides of the dunes the finely pulverized gypsum offers a surface almost like that of a snow-covered slope in the northern regions.

Whenever I see the White Sands drifting, creeping, obliterating, irresistibly marching, I somehow think back to the great legendary character Kilroy, whose inscription was found in the later days of World War II in so many unexpected places in western Europe. On barns, on the sides of houses in French villages, on chunks of bomb-torn rubble in West Germany, later arrivals of the American armed forces found that classic announcement: "Kilroy was here."

Now, this has given me what I hope is a useful thought. The desire of humans to leave a record of their presence in any place of historic significance is ages old. I have no doubt that the Babylonians, visiting some site of previous human occupation, carved their names or initials on the plaster.

Creek bed of the Medano. Great Sand Dunes National Monument. [Photo: Robert T. Haugen]

But this *cacoëthes inscribendi*—this hankering for wall writing—is a sore trial to the National Park Service in its attempt to preserve the areas under its protection from impairment. The walls of the prehistoric Indian edifice at Casa Grande, in Arizona; the staircases of the Statue of Liberty; the stones on which the Indians, or some ancient dwellers, made their puzzling pictographs, are defaced by thoughtless people who wish to leave for posterity their names, addresses, and telephone numbers.

Here, upon the gypsum sands of this monument, is an opportunity for the satisfaction of this urge for personal inscription. With a stick or any pointed instrument, names, places, dates, and even poetic thoughts may be engraved upon the sides of the dunes. No harm will be done. No rules will be transgressed. The personnel of the Park Service will even be willing to offer suggestions for decorative motifs, including hearts impaled by arrows.

As for the permanence of these inscriptions, there is no guarantee, express or implied. But they will afford a relief not only to the desires of the inscribers, but to national parks where wall writing is sharply prohibited.

There is no proof that Kilroy was ever at White Sands, but I like to believe that Kilroy was here.

7. GREAT SAND DUNES NATIONAL MONUMENT
[Colorado]

IF I WERE AN AMATEUR PHOTOGRAPHER aiming to get an arresting shot that might find a wall place at the next salon in my neighborhood, I would lose no time in getting to the sand dunes. "Next to nudes, sand dunes are probably the greatest delight of camera-men who like to take the arty type of pictures called salon photographs," says *Life*, the pictorial magazine. *Life* should know. "Texture, pattern, tones and mood are the ingredients readily to be found in sand dunes."

To be sure. But I cannot imagine why the qualification "next to nudes" was used. Sand dunes *are* nudes. They are nature's presentation of that very texture and tone which even the loveliest human form does not quite equal. For excellent reason you seldom see a well-composed dune photograph that does not satisfy; and you seldom see even the most brilliant picture of a forest which leaves the observer quite convinced. The dune, though really never at rest, conveys the feeling of finality. The woods are busy and diffuse, advertising growth.

Great Sand Dunes, at the eastern edge of the San Luis Valley of south-central Colorado, should be the photographer's Mecca. They are not only the highest-piled dunes in the country, but they parallel for ten miles the base of the heavily forested, snow-capped mountain range called Sangre de Cristo, whose tallest peaks attain an altitude of fourteen thousand feet above sea level. Foreground and background are ready-made. Here, for instance, is a forest of dead ponderosa pines, standing stark against the sandline and skyline, victims of the irresistible tidal wave of dune that swept into them, smothered them, and covered them to the very tops. Then, later, the dune moved on, uncovered the victims of its blanketing power: went in quest of new victory. But the dunes themselves will be stopped dead at last, for when they reach the foot of the Sangre de Cristos, the winds drop them there, to assume bizarre forms of shadow and light. The burden is too great; the wind can transport them no farther.

The soil of the San Luis Valley, material that was deposited as silt in the bed of an ancient lake, is easily picked up by the southwest winds that blow almost continually and finally funnel out through gaps in the range. For centuries the dunes have been piled, shifted, sorted, and repiled, and the crests of some of them are now eight hundred feet above the valley floor.

Dunes are strange vagabonds on the earth's surface. They give the impression of willful, powerful giants, doing as they please. Actually they do nothing as they please. Their *padrone* is the wind, and they obey the boss without question, slavishly. In the formation of a single dune you will note the typical shape: gradual slope on the windward side, and a steep declivity on the protected side. If the dune is isolated, the wind sweeps past on both flanks and builds two long, pointed arms, resulting in that beautiful crescent which, with the front in a shadow, makes the heart of the photographer glad. Such crescents are called barchans, from a Turkish word.

The beginning of the dune is easy to explain. The blown sand accumulates around some object—grasses or bushes, perhaps—which starts the formation of a pile. But many have asked themselves why, when once the dune is created at a certain spot, the whole mass goes forward on the march, moving year after year till it comes to a place, like the foot of the Sangre de Cristos, where it can move no more. The answer is that the material of the gentle slope on the windward side is never at rest. Up that slope, unceasingly, sand is being carried and dumped over the crest. Soldiers, having thrown up a breastwork along their trench lines, could similarly move their breastwork forward, by shoveling the material at the base and throwing it just over the top. That is, in theory they could; in practice the enemy would resent the operation and take strong counter measures. But the process is the same.

[IV]

Change, the Unchanging

Now we have canyon gorges and deeply eroded valleys, and still the hills
are disappearing, the mountains themselves are wasting away, the
plateaus are dissolving, and the geologist, in the light of the past history
of the earth, makes prophecy of a time when this desolate land of Titanic
rocks shall become a valley of many valleys, and yet again the sea
will invade the land, and the coral animals build their reefs. . . . Thus ever
the land and sea are changing; old lands are buried, and new lands are born.

—JOHN WESLEY POWELL, *Explorations of the Canyons of the Colorado*

1. GRAND CANYON NATIONAL PARK
[*Arizona*]

THE GRAND CANYON OF THE COLORADO is probably the greatest visual
shock ever experienced by man. Only when the human observer is
wholly intimidated and his ego completely wrecked can the beauty and the
serenity of the canyon begin to work upon him. The camera, having neither
pride nor humility, and not feeling called upon to express infinitude in finite
terms, does very well. The camera says, simply: "This is what I see, of form,
color, and dimension." What it sees is, of course, very little, compared with
what is there; but at least it is not duped by the dictionary.

The best story of the impact of the canyon is that of the Texas cowboy
who had taken a job with an Arizona outfit that ran its stock on the plateau
not far from the South Rim. Nobody told him about the canyon; they
thought he knew. One day, rounding up strays, he came abruptly to the
edge and found himself staring into the abyss. He looked down, across, into.

Angel Arch. Canyonlands National Park. [Photo: M. Woodbridge Williams]

Then he took off his hat, wiped the sweat from his forehead, and exclaimed: "My God! Something has happened here!"

Very likely López de Cárdenas, who saw the Grand Canyon in 1540, made a similar remark. He also rode up to it in ignorance. But his thoughts were upon the loot of the Cíbola, those fabulous Indian cities so rich in gold and silver that the streets were paved with them, and Cárdenas cursed the obstruction to his march and moved on. Cárdenas had actually looked upon something far richer than the things he sought—a vein of beauty and wonder that never pinches out. But in those days the wilderness was only something to be exploited and plundered. For Coronado and his freebooters the greatest abyss in all the world was only a scenic nuisance. It is only fair to the conquistadors to say that this practical view survived them by many centuries. But the more than a million annual visitors to Grand Canyon, and the 145 million who delight in the other national parks, will witness that while the things of the flesh are necessary, the things of the spirit are important too.

When you come upon the Grand Canyon suddenly—and from the nature of the chasm you cannot otherwise come upon it—your feelings must be somewhat those of the Texas cowboy. Something has happened here! You may have seen rifts in the earth surface, from gullies to gorges of large proportion; they have prepared you for nothing like this. The normal world, the substantial footing you have felt entitled to, disappears before your stunned eyes, to pick itself up miles away. You look downward, and if you are where you can observe it, there is a straw-colored thread a mile below you, and that is a river. But unless you have been informed, you are not sure it is a river. It might be an optical illusion. Maybe the whole thing is an illusion. No matter what you have been told about it, and no matter how many pictures you have seen, you wince and instinctively look behind you to see if the earth you have had such confidence in is still there. There are mountains down there. They are in the wrong place. You should be looking up at mountains. You are looking down on their tops. It is disconcerting, when you have spent part of a lifetime establishing a metrical relationship between yourself and nature, to have the scale switched and the rules changed.

This is no doubt why your first thought when you resume thinking and ask yourself "What happened here?" is naturally in terms of a catastrophe. There was a weak spot in the earth crust, and a collapse. Maybe it was an earthquake. Of course, a geologist wouldn't think so, but you are not a geologist; you are just a puzzled observer. And you can take comfort, if you wish, in the fact that the geologists did not always know as much as they do now. There was a time when they laid great store by cataclysms—violent upheavals and submergences. Plodding study of natural phenomena has revealed the truth that the earth form is due in very minor degree to turbulence and shock. The Grand Canyon is the result of what David Starr Jordan, with a roguishness permitted to proficient men and women of science, called "the infinite laziness of nature." It has all been done without rest, but without haste.

As the feeling of sheer rebuff at the canyon fades, you begin to realize the color. Thomas Moran, whose painting of the canyon hangs in the nation's capital, was sure that no palette could approximate the endless tints and shades. He was not deterred from putting on canvas what he saw and felt, and because he was such a humble intimate of our Western scenery, many will find Moran's early pictures still the most satisfying of all interpretative attempts.

The Southwestern part of the United States is, as a whole, a region of brightness. The nature of the rocks, whether diffused as sand or in eroded sculptures, the scanty rainfall, and other natural agencies have combined to produce a color gaiety that dazzles, even at first annoys, the eye that has come from places of greens and somber browns. You do not have to go to national parks to see examples. They are nearly everywhere. There is a place on the highway west of Gallup, at about the boundary between New Mexico and Arizona, where, at a swoop, within what seems a few car lengths, the stage hands seem to have shifted the scenery. The rock forms have not greatly changed—the color has become entirely different.

But the Grand Canyon, with Bryce and Zion, goes far beyond anything else of the Southwest in this respect. Partly because you are here seeing colored forms almost in three dimensions; partly because so many differing rock formations are piled atop one another and all draped before your eyes; and perhaps mostly because of the number of ways the light from above can surround the objects in the abyss. whatever the reasons, the adventure in color here can never be forgotten. And this is so in spite of the fact that you will never have an isolated moment of coloring in memory. You could not, because though you were to remain for years at the North or the South Rim of the canyon, you would never see again what you saw a minute before. The scheme constantly changes. From the first shimmer of light that follows the darkest night, from actual sunrise in any of the infinite parts, through forenoon to noon to sunset—an infinity of sunsets, of course, all combining into the one that is sunset for the spot you stand on—never will there be a time when you can say: "There! That is it." It *was* it.

The time of day will make a difference. The time of year will make a difference. It will be different whether you are at Yavapai or Yaki or Bright Angel Point. It will certainly be something else to those who leave the rim and make the trip down into the gorge where the Colorado is now biting its way through a rock that seems to be the very root of ancient uplift. Not to make this thrilling voyage in time, space, and climate is to leave the Grand Canyon rather less than half seen. The vague novel of mountain, platform, butte, cliff, and box canyon—a mere hint so far as the poor eye can discern from the plateau above—is now to be read chapter by chapter, and the story becomes clearer. It is not an arduous trip; anyone in reasonably sound condition can make it in a guided mounted party. You had better be in prime physical form to attempt to do it afoot. Many a pedestrian sturdy in purpose but lacking in wind and muscle has gone gaily down the trail, to be humiliated on the return. It is undignified for *Homo sapiens* to have to be retrieved by a mournful-looking mule.

If you happen to go to the bottom of the canyon from the North Rim, you have dropped just about a mile in elevation above sea level, though the Colorado has still another half mile to fall before it reaches its mouth. But in this drop you have had an amazing experience in traversing the zones of organic life. Vertically you have made the equivalent of a horizontal trip from northern Mexico to the Canadian border, or nearly so.

So far as there is any accuracy or fairness in putting humans in categories, you may say that there are three classes of people who visit Grand Canyon, Yellowstone, Yosemite, or any other national park. Aside from specialists in the natural sciences, who will always resort to these places for study, these three classes are:

First, those whose interest is satisfied with visiting the famous areas, "seeing" them in the sense of looking at their outstanding natural features, seeing them in company with a lot of other people, and being able thereafter to say that they have been there, fishing or indulging in other sports where those are possible, getting out of hot lowlands in summer into cooler altitudes, getting away from a humdrum town life into something that at least stands for primitive experience—and for other similar reasons. The "seeing" is almost purely visual, and very incomplete. You could spend your whole life at Grand Canyon and not see it, even visually. Yellowstone is so vast an area that there are corners that nobody has ever looked at. But, not to chew words, the meaning is clear enough. The meaning in the instance of Grand Canyon is that you *have been there*.

Those in the second category remain unsatisfied with this kind of seeing. They ask themselves questions. How did it happen? What is the meaning of

Looking down into the geologic past. Grand Canyon National Park. [Photo: Wayne Bryant]

it? In what way does it touch their own existence? How does it relate to the places they come from? For such inquirers there are at every national park facilities for knowing, so far as knowing is possible. There are naturalist guides, brief lectures, museum exhibits, specimens of rocks, minerals, or organic life, explanatory maps, planned to put visitors in possession of the rudiments of the tale. The object is not so much directly to educate as to create a background that will add to the visual pleasure. Visitors can have as much or as little of it as they please. For most people, probably, a little suffices; yet a common expression heard from those who have just returned from one or more of the parks is: "I wish we had stayed longer and learned more about it."

There remains another group, who visit the national parks and make the most important discovery: they discover themselves. When they exclaim, "I didn't know there were such beautiful and interesting places!" what they are really saying is that they did not know they had within them such capacity for the realization of beauty and significance. They fall in love with the national parks, not for the spectacular features within them, but for the essence of them. They do not state this in self-conscious words, but they feel it. They cultivate the pleasurable hobby of dabbling, secondhand, in the greatest of all mysteries, partly revealed, but only partly, in the study of the natural sciences: our place in nature. Whatever can be learned of this mystery can be learned only where areas of size sufficient to preserve natural conditions in integrity are insulated from the march of utility.

These people are not geologists, or botanists, or zoologists. Whether the rock they are looking at belongs to the Ordovician or the Silurian period, or whether it was igneous or sedimentary before pressure and heat altered it, is not important to them. They will not grieve if they stumble in taxonomy. But they do want to know enough of the detailed story of the earth forces and organic life to be able to put them against the background of what they see and create a pattern. So far as they do go, it is fun, it is adventure, and it may be a passion.

To such folks the chief expression of Grand Canyon, beyond the beauty and the impact of its incredible vastness, is the geological story of how it came to be.

When you go up to the South Rim of the Grand Canyon from the town of Williams, you are making a gentle ascent up the slope of a tilted plateau. Across on the north side of the great chasm the land continues to rise, though more sharply. With the elevations at these three points in mind, you do not have to be a geologist to realize that something is wrong in the picture. The Colorado is taking its course *across* a slope instead of *down* one.

The upper reaches of the Colorado, and many of the tributaries, show the same perversity. They share this peculiarity with all the major streams in the central and southern Rockies, which seem to ignore the easy way in favor of the hard. The Arkansas, for instance, cuts profoundly through the Front Range in the Royal Gorge. The South Platte cuts through at another place. The Laramie, instead of following the lowlands north to the Platte, turns east and chisels through the mountains. And though seemingly the Green River could have passed around the Uintas, following valleys on the north side, it chose to carve a passage through them.

The answer is that the observer is now looking at a geographical picture bearing no resemblance to the one that formerly existed when the rivers began to flow. It is as though you arrived late at the theater, near the end of the play. The tag end of the action, if you lack a knowledge of what led up to it, is either misleading, or pretentious heroics with no good reason. But if you can figure in your imagination that when the Colorado, as well as these other Rocky Mountain streams, was in its infancy, the tough rocks of the deep canyons through which they now pass were buried thousands of feet below sedimentary material, you can see what has happened. The river made its bed when the bed was soft, and continues to lie in it.

As the river began to cut down, the land began to rise, responding to strange building and thrusting forces that originate far below the earth crust. And as the uplifting is never uniform, the result will be to accelerate the currents of the streams. Even as the land rises, erosion is taking place simultaneously: the washing of sand, gravel, and boulders into the river furnishes just what the water needs for cutting power. Thus it follows the course it originally found easiest, regardless of the nature of the rock that must be sawed through.

All the canyons, from Flaming Gorge on the Green down almost to the Gila River, where the Colorado is getting near to sea level, are thus explained. But impressive and colorful as these other canyons are, it is when the river enters that area which is now included in the national park that the marvels rapidly multiply. Here you come into a place that, aside from its majestic proportions, its beauty, and its almost frightening silence, is the prize geological sourcebook of the world.

To descend from the rims to the river, whose shouting increases with the snow melt in the mountains, is to go down the ladder of time, rung by rung, with each rung representing centuries, not years. And your excursion into time, tremendous as it is, is not even a true interpretation; for there must have once been a rim as much higher than the one on which you now stand as this one is now above the bottom of the canyon. If you go from the Grand Canyon to Bryce Canyon and Zion and rejoice in the flaming color of their rocks, you will see what was once superimposed upon the Grand Canyon rims, which time and the rain clouds have swept away.

But this is enough. It will be all you can safely view, and far more than anyone can comprehend. Will you descend, and thus go backward in time? Or do you prefer to climb the ladder and thus come forward toward the present year, which will have the relative importance, expressed in thickness, of a sheet of paper alongside the Empire State Building? Perhaps not that much; but let us not sink to the humility of nothingness.

We may as well begin at the river bottom and climb toward ourselves. Down there in the granite gorges the Colorado is now grinding its course

Overleaf: Kaibab Trail, below Yaki Point. Grand Canyon National Park. [Photo: George Grant]

through one of the oldest rocks known on this continent. It is not a granite, and perhaps was not unlike the other limestones and sandstones before the enormous pressure of an overburden, and heat from below, recrystallized and contorted it. Sedimentary rocks, miles high, once covered this schist, but they were not the rocks that lie above it today. These are recent: only a few hundred million years old. For between that dark, crumpled schist and the next layer above it occurs what the geologist calls an "unconformity." It means that this oldest visible rock had been uplifted and planed down flat by the elements before it sank beneath a sea. As it contains no fossil life, all you can say of its age is that it is even less comprehensible than what appears above it. It is possible that this rungless space in the time ladder represents a greater period than all the rocks from the Tonto platform to the rim.

But above this lowest rock appears, in wedge-shaped masses, seen near the mouth of Bright Angel Creek and elsewhere, another rock younger than the first, if the word *younger* does not become, in this relation, somewhat humorous. This tilted rock represents a deposit of something like twelve thousand feet of stratified sediments, which rested on the planed surface of the schists and gneisses. It, too, was elevated and planed down, so that between it and the next overlying rock is another unconformity—another signature torn from the record book and lost.

As from these most ancient rocks you climb the ladder to what is now the rim, you come to other missing pages, for the same reason always—that what was below the surface of a sea had been lifted up and eroded down. And about the only possible appreciation of the time involved is to keep referring it back to something now going on. If you live at the mouth of a river or at the edge of the ocean, how long, at the present rate, would it take to pile up twelve thousand feet of sand or mud? Or a thousand feet, or two hundred feet, or even ten feet? The foundation of the colossal statue of Rameses II was discovered in Memphis, Egypt, in 1854, beneath nine feet of silt deposits of the Nile. The statue being not more than three thousand years old, the rate of deposition had averaged not more than three and a half inches per hundred years. Although this is not a perfect yardstick, because the rate of erosion would not always be the same for every situation, it gives at least a feeble notion of the time element.

When you finally reach the South Rim, having come up through the layers of shales, limestones, and sandstones, some green, some gray, some red, buff, or tints that incline toward any of these colors, you reach what seems to be the end of the ladder. It is nothing of the sort. It is merely the place where the ladder has been sawed through and the upper part lost. For as you

Without that flowing river there is no true Grand Canyon. Grand Canyon National Park. [Photo: Philip Hyde]

look south from El Tovar to Red Butte, or east of Desert View to Cedar Mountain, you are looking at what remains, on this side of the canyon, of later rocks, which once had a total thickness of twice the distance from the present rim to the river.

The story, then, told by the ladder rungs on which you can put your feet is that of a succession of submergences beneath the sea and emergences from the sea; of mountain building and the tearing down of mountains; of rocks that have been ground to sand and mud and poured into oceans, to become rocks again, of a different kind, of a different color, and to take different forms in the erosion that never halts.

Years ago, when visitors to the Grand Canyon were not so numerous nor so well informed, a noted lecturer indulged his audience with this bit of feverish rhetoric: "The Grand Canyon of Arizona is Nature wounded unto death and lying stiff and ghastly, with a gash of 200 miles in length and a mile in depth in her bared breast, from which is flowing fast a stream of life-blood called the Colorado."

In a day when Barnum's press agent was describing an elephant as "the blood-sweating Behemoth of Holy Writ" this was probably not a bad funeral oration over Nature, as Nature appears at the Grand Canyon. The only trouble with it was that Nature was not even slightly wounded, her bared breast was not where the lecturer thought it was, and the funeral had to be postponed. Far from being sick, and lying stiff and ghastly, the Grand Canyon is all-beautiful, in perfect health, and possibly self-renewing. For all we know, the mountain-building forces may be still in progress here. Our time clock is built to tell hours, days, and even centuries, but it is no match for this dilatory progression. The canyon is not a passive thing: every inch of this area is pulsating with life. Gravitation is working on the walls incessantly; every rainstorm sweeps tons of material down toward the river; the weather bites into the softer rock, and the tougher rock above now overhangs; one night a great block drops and goes crashing down, but the noise is swallowed up in the vast web of silence. The Colorado moves to the Pacific.

Though it means nothing tangible to write down the symbols for a billion years, yet your excursion into time in the Grand Canyon has given you at least a sense of continuity: you have seen enough of the record to guess that it goes on and on in an orderly fashion, any appearances of disorder and catastrophic accident to the contrary. The rocks are not called organic, though something remains to be found out about that. But they are a part of the stream of life, of which you are an incident that need not be ashamed, though infinitely small.

When we remember that the national parks preserve not only the finest scenic and significant natural treasures of our country, but also the human record of discovery, occupation, and migration that has finally peopled the United States, we realize that the fullest enjoyment of visits to these areas calls for some knowledge of their first and continuing effect upon man. For this is the American story; this constitutes the richest American heritage; and valuable as are books, the actual presence in such places goes beyond reading. Here the American sees, feels, touches, and understands.

In Grand Canyon your joy and adventure are not complete unless, when you descend to the river and watch it galloping past, you can look back through the years to an August day in 1869 when a little party of battered men, under the leadership of a soldier who had lost his right arm at the Battle of Shiloh, were fighting for their lives near the end of a challenge that rates high in the drama of exploration.

These men, who had begun their river journey at Green River Station in Wyoming, were doing what could not be done. Pioneers had opened gaps in the wilderness, through which eager Americans were pouring to the Pacific—to the north, to the south, along well-set survey routes—and the railroad was fast displacing the pony express and the ox-team caravan. But the Colorado River, for many hundreds of miles, was an unknown world.

Its general course was observed well enough; trappers had been taking beaver in the lower reaches since the early years of the century, and they had trapped at accessible places in the upper tributaries. A steamboat coming from the Gulf of California had safely ascended above Callville, a Mormon outpost just below where the Virgin joins. Many a man had stood at the rims of the successive canyons, all along the line, and turned away convinced that the great stream would never be run. Lieutenant J. C. Ives, no milksop, after ascending the Colorado in 1858 to the mouth of Vegas Wash and then overland to the mouth of Diamond Creek, wrote, after a vain attempt to reach the rim: "It seems intended by nature that the Colorado River, along the greater part of its lonely and majestic way, shall be forever unvisited and undisturbed."

Captain Sitgreaves, of the Topographical Engineer Corps, some years before Ives, had been given airy instructions from Washington to "pursue the Little Colorado to its junction with the Colorado . . . and pursue the Colorado to its junction with the Gulf of California." He set out from Zuñi Pueblo, reached the Little Colorado and followed it down for some distance, and then washed his hands of the whole business as being "too hazardous." The fact was that the War Department had not the faintest idea of the country contiguous to the Colorado, or of much of the river itself.

Major John Wesley Powell started with nine men and four boats from Green River City, Wyoming, on May 24, 1869. That the venture was one of the greatest hazards, they knew. Powell did not credit the reports of trappers that there were high waterfalls and underground passages in the Colorado and its tributaries, nor was he deterred by the exhortations of friendly Indians that the Great Spirit would be affronted by this foray into his private domain; but hardships and danger were expected. One thing was certain: there would be places on the journey where, walled by precipitous canyon cliffs, there would be no turning back. Every twist of the madly plunging river would be a plunge into the unknown.

In the Canyon of Lodore one of the boats was smashed beyond repair, and a considerable part of their food supply and scientific instruments was lost. The upsetting of the boats and the hurling of the occupants into the cataracts became an incident of the day's course; for weeks their clothing was never dry. Sometimes at night they perched, or crouched, with scanty covering, on a narrow shelf of rock where sleep was impossible. There were rapids of foaming, jumping waves where the walls were vertical from the water's edge, with huge rocks in the channel. Then, by a most laborious process, the boats had to be let down, one past another, finally leaving one last man on a rock, from which he plunged into the water and was hauled out into a boat as he was being swept past farther downstream.

Whenever he could, Major Powell climbed the steep canyon walls to take observations. It seemed incredible that a man with one arm could have gone where he did. Only once, it appears, did he find himself clinging to a wall of rock and able neither to advance nor to retreat. With great difficulty he was rescued.

The party's flour was wet and dried so many times that it was in hopeless lumps, and musty. When their bacon spoiled, they boiled it and made it do; their sugar had melted away in every upset; but they always had coffee. Toward the end they were down to the thinnest rations, but they cheered themselves with each loss of food and stores by saying: "Well, the boats will be lighter, anyway, as we go on."

The final challenge came when they reached the granite canyons of the Colorado. Here they entered the positively unknown—not even a trapper professed knowledge of the next stage. The walls at their sides were more than 1 mile high. As Powell said later, "Here even the great river was insignificant in the vastness of the chasm, its angry waves were but ripples, and we were but pigmies." They had but a few days' rations left. But this last effort, which taxed their remaining strength and will, saw them through. At noon on August 29 they emerged into the Grand Wash.

"The river rolls by us in silent majesty; the quiet of the camp is sweet; our joy is almost ecstasy."

Major Powell and his party had the highest kind of courage when they set themselves adrift in the uncharted river: the kind of valor that is not to be confused with mere recklessness. For the adventure was long studied and the preparations as perfect as they could be, and though the drop of the Colorado from Flaming Gorge to the Virgin was known to be nearly a mile in altitude, which made it possible that there would be some place from which they could neither retreat nor go on without certain death to all, yet from what he knew of the nature of the rocks the geologist concluded that the chances were favorable.

A flicker of sun lights the North Rim. Grand Canyon National Park. [*Photo: Philip Hyde*]

Three men of the party died. Ironically, it was not the Colorado that caused their death. They had passed through the first granite gorge, frightfully buffeted and with provisions nearly gone. They did not know it, but they were nearly at the end of their labors. But when, after surviving the first black barrier, a second one just like it was seen, three of the men would go no farther. They were not cowards. They had not flinched from danger. But they had had enough. Their nerves were lacerated. They left the party to climb out of the canyon and make their way overland to the Mormon settlements, and were murdered by Indians on the Shivwits Plateau.

If the willful Colorado had had its choice, probably it would have preferred not to be at last humbled by a man who had only one arm. But, in return, when the game was up, the river and the canyons turned loose upon their master all their seductive loveliness and lure, forcing from him emotional outbursts that mocked at his scientific poise. In 1901, thirty-two years after his triumph, the major was writing: "The glories and the beauties of form, of color and sound unite in the Grand Canyon—forms unrivaled even by the mountains, colors that vie with the sunsets, and sounds that span the diapason from tempest to tinkling raindrop, from cataract to bubbling fountain."

2. CANYONLANDS NATIONAL PARK
[Utah]

I WOULD DESCRIBE CANYONLANDS as the place where the adjective died from exhaustion. Our language, as any language, has its limitations, especially when we attempt to ascribe a quality to natural objects, according as to how we *feel* about them. In contact with the examples of scenery created by the forces of nature, we may begin confidently with such modest adjectives as *large* or *pretty*, and proceed to *vast* and *beautiful*, but the end of that word game is always in sight. Sooner or later we have to admit our incapacity. We do it with the final adjective: *indescribable*.

After that, we stick to nouns. Note how the early venturers into the Canyonlands came to the rescue of their pride. Realizing that they could not describe, they named. The erosional marvels became Doll House, Elephant Canyon, Ernie's Country, Bagpipe Butte, Devil's Lane, Bobby's Hole, and The Sewing Machine. The pygmy in the presence of a giant loses nothing by assuming the jocular, and it may give him courage.

Canyonlands National Park, though it may seem limitless in extent to urban dwellers who find themselves within its maze of strange erosional

The Doll House. Canyonlands National Park. [*Photo: M. Woodbridge Williams*]

forms, is really only a small segment of a Greater Canyonlands that may be called the Colorado River Country. The region taken as a whole, far from being "unknown" to visitors of the National Park System, has in fact been visited by many millions of them. The Colorado Plateau includes three national parks—Grand Canyon, Zion, and Bryce—and many national monuments, with a total area of more than 800,000 acres, and as a geographical unit it even embraces Mesa Verde National Park in southwestern Colorado. These individual preserves are mostly not difficult to reach. They present, each in its manner, choice examples of the mighty dissecting forces—rushing streams, wind, frost, and rain—that together slowly abrade rock of varying resistance. But now, here in the heartlands, we are invited to see the rest of the exhibition, some of it even yet unexplored: needles and arches, mesas and buttes, quiet parklike bottoms, tumultuous river rapids, breakneck scarps, standing rocks sliced thick or finny. Above all, *standing* rocks. "Standing-up country" it has been called, since some baffled venturer threw up his hands and declared, "There is more of this place standing up than there is laying

down." He may, of course, have said *lying* down, but I have the feeling that he would have been inattentive to grammar.

Stark and rigorous as this land is, it could not keep acquisitive man from making traverse of it. The prehistoric "ancient ones" lived here. The prospector for gold and silver bet his stake and his life against its hazards; and in later days, after the magic element uranium became something quite other than the source of paint color, the feverish fellow with the Geiger counter rutted the delicate landscape with lines that will be seen for half a century, unless they are painstakingly erased—and even then, we shall continue to note the erasures. It is curious that land surfaces that seem at a glance so tough and repellent should scar as easily as a baby's skin.

The problem of providing access roads, trails, and visitor centers while preserving wilderness in this new national park should not be difficult, in the opinion of Secretary of the Interior Stewart Udall. He has viewed the domain from no ivory tower in the District of Columbia. He writes with intimate knowledge of its nature:

Here, careful development can allow visitors into the heart of the park in relative comfort without disturbing natural values, and still keep the wilderness areas accessible only by foot, boat or horseback.

Dry camps (to which visitors must carry their own drinking water) are available throughout the park. Salt Creek, in the Needles Country, provides water for travelers on horseback. For the present, overnight accommodations are expected to be provided by motels and lodges outside the park. Tourists need four-wheel-drive vehicles to negotiate much of Canyonlands. Unpaved but passable roads allow ordinary passenger cars to go as far as Grand River Point in the Island in the Sky, or to Squaw Spring in the Needles area. In the land between the rivers, the Island in the Sky will be the primary visitor-use area. Roads, overlooks and various interpretive devices, including a visitor center, self-guiding trails and a campground are planned. The White Rim road skirting the lofty Island in the Sky will remain a trail for four-wheel-drive vehicles.

Ultimately there will be hard-surfaced roads, but it will be a number of years before Canyonlands will be as accessible as other parks nearby. Even when the roads are built, they will not be allowed to dominate the landscape through which they pass. Where rivers and canyons divide major segments, access to the separate areas will be from outside roads, not by way of connect-

This was a rugged roadway for pre-Columbian folk. Canyonlands National Park. [*Photo: M. Woodbridge Williams*]

ing bridges and roads which would scar the landscape. Canyonlands will always remain a wilderness park. . . .

Visitors will have a wide range of recreational opportunities. Both the Green and the Colorado Rivers are navigable and this impressive country should be seen from the bottom up. A few river runners will challenge the rapids of Cataract Canyon down to the impounded waters of Lake Powell. Most visitors will be content with floating down the Colorado from Moab to Spanish Bottom, then up the Green River via Anderson Bottom to the town of Green River.

Even those visitors who have no special interest in geology will make their way to Upheaval Dome, at the northerly end of the new park. This is a natural feature that puzzled the professionals over a long period. Was it the huge crater of a volcano—about 4,500 feet from rim to rim and 1,600 feet deep? It looked like it, certainly. But there was no sign of igneous rock, or rock of any kind that would indicate alteration by volcanic steam and gas. Was it a so-called "crypto-volcano," then—resulting from a volcano that lay beneath the center of the crater, but never giving surface indications other than the depression? Finally it has been rather generally accepted by geologists that Upheaval Dome was created by the slow action of salt-doming. Such features do occur, but not commonly, throughout the world. There is still room for speculation on the part of the experts. The lay visitor will be content to look at the phenomenon. If he has any hypothesis he can confide it to a specialist, who will receive it, I hope, with a grave politeness.

Some time ago I fell to pondering: What will be the immediate physical and psychic responses of those who for the first time find themselves in this classical erosional miniature world of rim, bench, and stream bottom? In a sense, of course, this is unfruitful speculation: all the great scenic and scientific parks are many things to many persons. But Canyonlands is, it must be admitted, rather special.

As to form, texture, and color, these rocks of the canyon heartland are wilder, less believable, and more whimsically painted than one expects even in a region of "red rock." At times they flame. The gaunt, self-sufficing loneliness is disconcerting. Practically all people will call it beautiful, but they will not all be at home with this kind of beauty. I have a friend who says that the canyonlands have for him a lure like that of the siren, and yet when he found himself within this area he had the feeling of nightmare— as though he had eaten hot mince pie and cheese for dessert and dreamed the kind of dream where one is being pursued by an ogre, fleeing into one cul-de-sac after another, always finding a dead end. Which is only another way, I suppose, of expressing what the old-timers meant when they spoke of being "rim-rocked."

There will be those who will be less delighted visually than curious about how it all came to be. Though in the minority, they will be in the best of company, for Charles Darwin said bluntly, after his voyage around the world in the *Beagle*, that "group masses of naked rock, even in the wildest forms, may for a time afford a sublime spectacle, but they will soon grow monotonous. Paint them with bright and varied colours . . . they will become fantastic; clothe them with vegetation, they must form a decent, if not a beautiful picture." Darwin would have liked the Great Smoky Mountains better, but even there his word "decent" implies that he would have found the scenery merely "pretty good." But how he would have reveled in the marvels of the canyon-cutting and in such a puzzling occurrence as Upheaval Dome! Incidentally, Darwin detested travel as such. "No doubt," he said, "it is a high satisfaction to behold various countries . . . but the pleasures gained at the time do not counterbalance the evils. It is

Chesler Park. Canyonlands National Park. [*Photo: M. Woodbridge Williams*]

necessary to look forward to a harvest, when some fruit will be reaped." Well, it must be admitted that this man, wedded to laboratory exercises, reaped a great harvest. Besides, on the *Beagle* he was seasick for a good part of five years. That could color one's opinion about travel!

Some of the early pioneers, trying to wrest a living or strike a bonanza among these stark cliffs, not only didn't think the region beautiful; they cussed it out as willful and stingy. Captain John N. Macomb, who took a party into the country in 1859, reported: "I cannot conceive of a more worthless and impracticable region than the one we now find ourselves in." Yet the geologist with that same expedition, a man named Newberry, said that the view from one rim point called out "exclamations of delight from all our party." Macomb included? Possibly, because when he spoke of the worthlessness of the region he may have had commercial exploitation in mind. The military parties were not only seeking travel routes; they were to keep an eye out for material riches.

I was amused to read, in a "proposal" for a Canyonlands National Park, printed several years before the park was actually voted by Congress, a little paragraph that now sounds excessively timid. It was feared that "some people may be repelled, and call the scenery ugly; not because it is drab or dull, but because it is so different as to be incomprehensible to them and therefore hostile." Now that we have the fine park, we find it unnecessary to be so defensive!

Yet, though all conservationists and lovers of wilderness were heartened when Canyonlands National Park came into being, there was, and still is, disappointment that the area could not have been much greater than the present 257,000 acres. The 330,000 acres first requested was extremely modest. There were 800,000 acres of mostly federally owned land that could have been set aside. But even the 330,000 shrank to 300,000, then to the present acreage. "The Governor of Utah made it clear from the start," according to the Interior Secretary, "that he was opposed to park status that would . . . 'lock up' the resources and 'damage' his state's future economy." I think America will have come to maturity when it will be possible to erect somewhere—probably it will be west of the Mississippi—a great bronze marker which will read:

Beneath these lands which surround you there lies enormous mineral wealth. However, it is the judgment of the American people, who locked up

---

Fish-Eye Arch. Canyonlands National Park. [Photo: M. Woodbridge Williams]

this area, that these lands shall not be disturbed, because we wish posterity to know that somewhere in our country, in gratitude to nature, there was at least one material resource that we could let alone.

3. MESA VERDE NATIONAL PARK
[*Colorado*]

IT DID NOT RAIN.

Day after day the sun beat down upon the Green Mesa. The filmy white clouds drifted lazily around the circuit of the horizon line. At times, but rarely, the sky darkened over the higher lands to the northeast, and clouds crawled without conviction in the direction of the villages of the farm people. But instead of the forked fire that should have spoken with the voice of the Great Spirit, it came to nothing but flashes across the sky. It did not rain. It seemed to have forgotten how.

Yes, surely, occasionally a few drops fell. Once there was a sharp shower, which brought back life to the firing corn, and perked up the beans and squashes, and the villagers cried with joy and ran around repeating the refrain: "The rain has come. Now, after this, we shall have rain enough!" The priests wagged their heads triumphantly and said: "See, you of little faith! We have placated the Great Spirit. Get you about your business, and leave such matters to us."

But it amounted to little. Again the sun blazed down. Again the corn fired and the squash vines drooped, and the few showers that came were only enough to leave spots like tiny anthills on the dust of the gardens.

It did not rain; and the village people of the Green Mesa despaired and trembled for the future. And in winter it was the same. There was snow, but it merely put a thin cover on the ground, to evaporate speedily.

It was 1280—the year of the death of Kublai Khan, the great founder of the Mongol Empire, on the other side of the earth from the Green Mesa. The people of the mesa knew nothing of Kublai Khan nor of the Mongols, though they could possibly have originated over there—sometime in the dim past perhaps having crossed the Aleutian bridge and found their way down to the tableland and canyon country where they now lived. They had no record of their past, not even a bardic one—simply a vague notion that they had come from the direction of certain bright stars that move together, like a band of goats, around the sky.

Four years now, there had been a shortage of rain. Rain, but not enough rain. Some of the smaller trees were dying. The Spring of the Lame Deer,

Upheaval Dome, long a mystery to the geologist. Canyonlands National Park.
[Photo: M. Woodbridge Williams]

which had run so copiously, was noticeably depleted. Several lesser springs were down to a trickle.

There were those who were cheerful and hopeful. There had always been lean years. The weather would turn, and there would be good crops again. There were those who spoke darkly of some offense to the Great Spirit. There was an old woman who, when the Big House was receiving another addition (she was a girl then), had imprinted her hand in the ceiling plaster; and now she wagged her head and said that ruin was coming to the people of the Green Mesa. The village people had become proud—too proud. Pride—human pride—the Great Spirit would not too long tolerate. These jewels of turquoise and other colored stones; this delicately woven raiment; these pots fancifully decorated with black figures on a light-gray background: it was pride, pride. Their ancestors were content with little houses, with rougher garments, with pottery more for use than for show.

In the kivas—the ceremonial rooms—the elders and the men of magic consulted, divined, chanted incantations, made offerings, pitted their prayers against the elements. There was a raid by some nomadic ruffians who came out of the east to plunder and to kill. The Green Mesa people stood them off, as they had before; but there was less and less of value to defend. At the end of another five years the springs were really drying up. Large trees were dying. For lack of feed, the deer, rabbits, squirrels, and prairie dogs were getting scarce; even the mice were departing.

The old Cassandra shook her head and muttered: "Pride. Pride. Punishment. And I heard my grandfather say that it does not do to cut down all the trees. The Great Spirit does not like it. He refuses to let it rain when you have cut down too many trees. He said that. It is true."

The end came. Twenty-four years the drought lasted. There was no food. The last of the water supply was going. By 1299 it was certain that only death awaited the villagers of this no longer green mesa if they remained. Where to go? Nobody knew. There were messengers from the southeast now and then who brought news that though conditions were also bad in that direction—toward a great river that came out of the mountains and flowed to the end of the earth—yet things were not as bad as here.

So the people of the Green Mesa—not all at once, but village by village—left their houses and their garden plots, left all but the necessary things for travel, and went off to the southeast. What became of them? It was no small migration. Many, no doubt, perished, either from hardship or from attacks by brigand people. Along the Rio Grande in New Mexico today live many tribes of Pueblo Indians. Also, to the west, are the Hopis and other Pueblos.

Every nook and cranny among the rocks was turned to some use by these ancient dwellers. Mesa Verde National Park. [Photo: Fred Mang, Jr.]

Perhaps the people of the Green Mesa found a haven among the ancestors of these agricultural folk. There may be Green Mesa blood among the Jamez and the Isletas and the Zias and all the rest. But there remain only the ruins of a happy life once lived on the tableland and canyons of the Mancos country.

They are fascinating ruins, for they tell the story of the development of a people who began living in this region in the first century of our era, a peaceable, agricultural people who started with rude devices, though with certain skills, and rose from culture to culture till they attained an intricate social scheme, an elaborate religious organization, and some superb craftsmanship.

Mesa Verde National Park is the only area with *park* status that was set aside for preservation primarily because of its historical importance. But more people every year are becoming interested in the story of the prehistoric inhabitants of the Southwest, and Mesa Verde is the key to the fascinating puzzle of the vanished cultures whose ruins are preserved in the Southwestern monuments.

There are hundreds of ruins in Mesa Verde, although only a few have been excavated. The passage of centuries since they were built has weakened the structures, and before they finally came under the protection of the National Park Service some were badly damaged by thoughtless people who were unaware of their value. Visitors at Mesa Verde are not permitted to enter any cliff dwelling unless accompanied by a ranger. Violation of this regulation will not be tolerated. It is always with the utmost reluctance that the Park Service makes a rule of this kind. But the reason is obvious: preservation is authorized imperatively by acts of Congress, and preserving some of the structures would be impossible without this rule. But the rule does *not* apply to the ruins on the mesa top, which visitors may inspect at any time during the daylight hours if they have registered at the park entrance station or at the museum.

Visitors to Mesa Verde should see at least one ruin of each type: pit house, pueblo, and cliff dwelling. These, in order, represent the progress of the prehistoric people during the 1,200 years of their residence. They began as farming Indians, skilled in weaving baskets, but ignorant of pottery, houses, and any weapons except the throwing stick, or *atlatl*. The baskets served all purposes for which containers were needed. The people lived in shallow caves, in which there were places for the prudent storage of the things they raised on their mesa-top fields.

About A.D. 400, the archaeologists have found, there were important developments among the Green Mesa people. They had learned to make pottery and they had acquired the bow and arrow. They still made baskets; their pottery was plain; but they had taken to houses, even though these houses were shallow pits with head-high roofs of poles and adobe. Each pit house served as the home for a single family. The population must have been on the increase, for there are hundreds of villages on the top of the mesa and in the caves of the Four Corners region.

By 700, evidences show clearly, the people showed an increased tendency to group and form compact villages. The "pueblo" period had come. Their religious observances probably became more ceremonious, for each cluster of houses around an open court had its kiva. A strange development in this period was the adoption of a baby cradle, and as a result the heads of most of the people were flattened at the back, as the exhumed skulls show.

The final period was one of prosperity, of highly skilled construction, of artistic development—and of the penalties for all these things. They now had something worth stealing, and less peaceful Indians on their flanks probably made incursions upon them. They had to fortify against these enemies. It is also possible that the population increased to the point where crowding caused disease to spread. But there is no question about the superior culture the people had attained. It was in this final period that Cliff Palace, Square Tower House, Spruce Tree House, Long House, and other great buildings were erected.

Spruce Tree House, besides being wonderfully well preserved, serves as an example of the skill of the builders and the stage of social organization they had attained. A great many of the high walls still touch the top of the cave, and many of the original roofs are still intact. There were 114 living rooms in this apartment house and eight ceremonial rooms.

The reader may say, with a skeptical rise of the eyebrow: "No doubt your archaeologists are clever. Their studies and diggings have certainly been revealing. But—these Green Mesa people left no written records. There is no evidence that they had a calendar. And yet experts talk about the year

It was not really a square tower, standing alone, but a part of a ruined whole. Mesa Verde National Park. [Photo: Fred Mang, Jr.]

400, or the year 1200, as though they were speaking of the Battle of Gettysburg. How do they know?"

The answer is that the story of Mesa Verde, and of the other ruins left by prehistoric Indians in the Southwest, is partly written in trees. The great work of Professor A. E. Douglass, an astronomer who worked out a "calendar" through tree rings—using freshly cut trees for comparison with the wood found in ruins—has left little doubt of the dates.

The tree-ring technique is too involved to describe here. Briefly, it is based upon the cross-identification of annual growth rings of different trees from the same forest, extended to the different timbers of a prehistoric ruin, and then to fragments of charred ceiling beams in various other ruins. The work of Douglass and his associates lengthened our American calendar by so many centuries that it made the voyage of Columbus seem like a comparatively recent event.

4. PAGEANT OF THE SPECTRUM

A. ZION NATIONAL PARK
[*Utah*]

CAN THERE BE any better example of the way in which the demolition squads of nature produce stunning forms and revelations of color than this which greets visitors to Zion Canyon? Here is the Virgin River, the historic stream of the Southwest, which was named by the fur trader Jedediah Smith for one of his wounded comrades, and near the mouth of which the Mormon settlers planted an outpost in the days when their rugged followers were threading their way through the semidesert wilderness to the Zion of their dreams.

This Virgin, which with its numerous forks and tributaries can be a relatively innocent stream, can also be a very devil in its raging moments. At the present, the Virgin is removing three million tons per year of ground-up rock from within the boundaries of Zion National Park and pouring it into the Colorado River. It has been doing this for thousands of years. Presumably it will continue for more thousands. The river will cut its channel deeper, the precipitous walls will be wider, the colorings will be more profuse, because there will be more facets to show.

Even with such a stiff gradient—the Virgin system falls from fifty to seventy feet per mile, nine times as much as the Colorado in Grand Canyon—

you wonder, when you see the tiny creeks that act as feeders, how all this gorgeous destruction has been done. But there is a good key to the puzzle, a partial explanation. The river has able assistants in the nature of the rock and the cloudbursts of summer, but there is something else to be observed.

Suppose you have passed through the little Mormon village of Springdale and come to the south entrance of the park. For sheer surprise and the unfolding of wonders of form, this is the better way to come, though there will be no disappointment by any route. You see on either side of the Temples, the two great domes with crimson crests, and streaks of the same red down their sides. The Watchman, the Red Watchman, stands vigil over the valley. Somebody has called this other white summit, with its ruddy stains, the Altar of Sacrifice. We shall not quarrel with names, but its beauty required no gory reference. The strange white cones on the left are the broken top of the Streaked Wall.

Now, then, on your right is Bridge Mountain, called so because high up on its face there is a great flying buttress or natural bridge. In the face of that mountain, on the Pine Creek side, we are going to find the key to much of the demolition that produces gladdening sights. The famous Zion–Mount Carmel Road, after climbing almost eight hundred feet in three miles, by

Along the Narrows Trail—a high-walled garden spot. Zion National Park. [Photo: *Wayne Bryant*]

means of cleverly engineered switchbacks, plunges straight into the face of that canyon wall. The tunnel, much more than a mile long, has six openings, where visitors should pause and look. As the tunnel rises on a mild grade, each one of these openings forms a step in the ascent or descent.

When this spectacular tunnel was being built, the windows were cut first, and the debris from the borings was thrown into little Pine Creek below. Perhaps when you see Pine Creek almost dry and wholly innocuous, you will expect to see that rock rubbish which came out of the mountain wall. It is not there. In only a few months the floods that came down the creek as a result of rainbursts, pouring upon rock with no vegetation to hold back the water, had chewed up that rubble and whirled it on its way to Hoover Dam.

The north fork of the Virgin works upon soft material, for the most part. The amazing "architectural" shapes that everywhere greet the eye are due primarily to the attack upon the porous Navajo sandstone. A short, heavy rain on the rims above sends torrents of water pouring from the cliffs in large and small waterfalls. Frost and tree roots are forever sapping and mining. The weak sandstone itself disintegrates by chemical agencies. Over all, the Navajo formation is jointed both horizontally and vertically. So the destruction, beginning at the bottom and causing great slabs and blocks to fall, results in those sheer walls, which remain precipitous even when the canyon is widening. In these circumstances it was natural that startling massive figures should result.

Somebody has called Zion Canyon a Yosemite done in oils. In the mere matter of dimension of the valley floors, there is indeed a similarity, as there is in the bare fact of overtowering walls; but to me Zion Canyon resembles only Zion Canyon. A stream-cut chasm through granite, later grooved and polished by glaciers, such as is Yosemite, does not appear like a Southwest canyon cut angularly through sandstone, whether or not it is painted in oils. This gorgeous pageant of the Utah-Arizona country, it seems to me, cannot be compared with anything else we have.

To travel up the eight miles of road from the south entrance of Zion to the oasis called the Temple of Sinawava is to follow the Virgin between high walls, widening and narrowing by turns, till the Narrows are reached. Then for a mile there is a walk into the soft twilight, cool and green, where the canyon walls become a mere slit in the rocks, but with festoons of greenery and blooming flowers high up on their moist sides. What a stroll is this! And it should be a stroll, with ample time to feel it all. This, remember—this Southwest—is a country of much time. Depend upon it, the Great White Throne will be looking down at Sinawava when you get back to that lovely spot.

There are trails to East and West Rims, and from the top, looking down, a very different Zion is revealed. The relative proportions of the great mountain masses appear. From the valley floor, naturally, one cannot gauge the variation in heights. The coloring becomes something different.

You become aware that there is a constant deception in the color scheme. Some of the rocks are fooling you. They are getting their tints and shades from reflections, from subtle changes in the atmosphere. Angel's Landing, on the West Rim, is gleaming vermilion at the moment. Over to the left the Great White Throne is *not* white. What is it, then? Heaven knows. It is every color you ever saw, all in subdued, faintest tones—because it is getting the effect of every tint and shade from its surroundings.

Everyone says that the time to see Zion Canyon is when there is a full moon. For once everyone is right. It is not only the moon; it is the night, silent, windless, full of fragrances that have gone unnoticed in the lusty sunshine. It is a great moment in anyone's life when out of the darkness a filmy cloudlike apparition touches the peak of one of the cliffs above, and then, from this first torch, the lamplighters go speedily to work. The reds, pinks, creams, and yellows make themselves felt in the moonlight like ghosts of colors—but they are there.

A sweet retreat Zion Canyon must have been for the prehistoric cliff-dwelling people who once lived there, cultivating their crops of corn and beans and vines by the river and taking refuge in the face of the cliffs when need arose. Then, so far as humans were concerned, there seems to have been a long interlude, perhaps broken by the restless journeyings of the Spaniards, certainly by the indefatigable fur trappers and traders who sought out beaver streams. Then the Mormons.

Whatever former opinion may have been concerning the earlier domestic arrangements of these indomitable people who trudged into the desert and made it fertile and rich, nobody has ever had any doubt that they were pioneers of courage, intelligence, and utter self-reliance. They nosed everywhere; when roads were lacking, they built them, even down the wall of a canyon; impediments merely whetted their insistence.

They found Zion. Or, if you wish, they refound it. The early Mormon history, like all other, has become a medley of fact and legend. It is sure that among the first Mormons in this canyon was Joseph Black. Homesteading precariously there, Black was so thrilled by the beauties and colossal

Overleaf: A crossbedded sedimentary rock has its own austere beauty. Zion National Park. [Photo: M. Woodbridge Williams]

forms, the colors and the delicious carpet greenery of the valley, that he tried to do it justice in messages to his friends back in Salt Lake. Now, Salt Lake has fine mountains, fine streams, and canyons at its threshold, too; but they are not like what Black saw, and the friends thought Joseph a trifle mad. With gentle sarcasm, they called it "Joseph's Glory." But when they, too, had seen it, the place became known as Zion or Little Zion.

Zion was not a term, with these stern religious folk, to be used in a offhand way. Zion was an aspiration, a promise, a prayer to be fulfilled. So Brigham Young, though he acknowledged all the beauty of the canyon, shook his head. "It is *not* Zion," he said.

There was discipline, as well as giants, in those days. For many years the canyon was dutifully called Not Zion—presumably with accent on the *not*.

B. BRYCE CANYON NATIONAL PARK
[*Utah*]

EBENEZER BRYCE, A MORMON CATTLEMAN, was forewarned by the example of Joseph Black. When he suddenly rode up to the brink of the "canyon" now named for him, and the dazzling color of it, and its bizarre spires and pinnacles, burst upon him like a fairy tale—and that is probably the way he stumbled to the verge of it—he kept the damper on his enthusiasm. He wanted nobody to joke about "Ebenezer's Glory" or to ask whether the hot sun had affected his head. He shifted his quid, stared at the miles of marching pink and white castellations, and murmured: "A tough place to find a stray cow." At least, that is the tale, and it sounds entirely reasonable.

The Paiutes were familiar with this great horseshoe-shaped bowl cut into the pink cliffs of the Paunsaugunt plateau. They marveled at it, possibly regarded it with a sort of religious awe. The Indian was closer to nature than we are and felt himself more a part of it than we do. I once heard a simple but affecting account from a highly educated Sioux of the way he had been accustomed as a youth to go up to the top of a neighboring hill and greet the rising sun, merely standing silently, self-effacingly, letting nature flow through him. No words, no posturing, but a perfect intimacy. I can believe that the Paiutes looked down into Bryce Bowl with that same simplicity and reverence. It is said that they called the painted amphitheater "unka-timpe-

Naturally, somebody would waggishly call this "Wall Street." Bryce Canyon National Park. [Photo: M. Woodbridge Williams]

wa-wince-pock-ich." Not knowing the Paiute tongue very well, I assume that this is succinct. It is translated as "red rocks standing like men in a bowl-shaped canyon." *Red* is correct: it is the master pigment. But it is pink, red, less red, more red, and white, creamy white, ivory—oh, it is of no possible use to try to tell it in words. You have to see it. The delicacy of it is melting. The domes and spires and temples carved in the rocks of Bryce are rugged, even colossal, yet I feel that there is a tenderness and gentleness about them that is not common in rocks. You may feel differently after you have gone down by one of the many trails to the floor and find yourself hemmed in by an army of gaudy jinn.

Bryce is not really a canyon, but it came into the National Park System by that name, and it really makes little difference. In an area three miles long and about two miles wide the falling rains and snows, the wind, and the changes in temperature have cut down a thousand feet into the pink and white limy sandstone. The streams of the present plateau have done little, for those watercourses fall away from the rim. But the Paria and its rapid tributaries have cut deep into the face of the Paunsaugunt. The erosion is constant. The rim of the "canyon" is receding constantly, and the forms are constantly changing—new ones appearing, old ones softening down and altering shapes —though in any brief period the difference might not be apparent. New natural bridges are destined to appear; present arches will crumble and fall; but the colors—the corals, the oranges, the roses, all those pastels which now delight the eye by changing with every hour—will, I should suppose, be even more emphasized as the gnawing at the rocks goes on.

A series of fine horseback and foot trails has been built by the Park Service in the area under the rim. Inquiry should always be made before attempting a trip, as storms sometimes make the trails unsafe. Trails lead into Queen's Garden, the Silent City, Fairyland, Wall Street, Peekaboo Canyon, and other points. Horses and guides are always available. For those who do not wish to go below the rim—and this is almost unthinkable for people who are physically able—there is a delightful walk along the rim, with benches where one can sit. By all means follow some of the trails—but also, by all means sit. Meditate awhile about the Palette on which these colors were mixed.

C. Guadalupe Mountains National Park
[*Texas*]

In the days when the Butterfield stages bumped and rattled through this West Texas country, and changed horses at the Pinery station in the shadow of Guadalupe Peak, there were elk and turkeys and Texas bighorn in the mountain wilderness. The cougar and the bobcat saw to it that there was no population explosion on the part of the smaller animals. The Mescalero Apaches were fighting a bitter but hopeless battle against submersion in the westward flood of the whiteman's progress.

Prehistoric Americans had occupied these canyons perhaps as long ago as ten thousand years, and had hunted animals now long extinct. The Spanish conquerors noted the existence of the Guadalupes as they passed northwest of them along the Rio Grande, or up the Pecos. In the mid-nineteenth century military expeditions were surveying possible routes to the Pacific. Captain John Pope attempted to establish a post in the lower Pecos Valley in 1855, but gave up for lack of potable water. The Butterfield Trail was used for less than a year and was located far southward. The deeply cut mountains seemed to offer slight invitation for exploitation, so they slumbered through the years while traffic moved around them. Only in recent years have the geologists and other men of science revealed the significance of this region, in some respects unique. The world's best known fossil organic reefs are found here, and the greatest of them, the Capitan, has been described as the most extensive known to exist in our world.

A marine barrier reef here? Here, in Texas and the adjoining part of New Mexico? Well, of course this phenomenon has no element of surprise for the geologist; but most of us, who are not specialists, have to peer pretty dimly back through the passages of earth's long history to imagine the invasion by the ocean, in the period called the Permian, of this part of the continent. But so it was: a vast salt-water basin in a large part of what are now Texas and New Mexico. In the shallower water tiny, lime-secreting organisms created a barrier not essentially different from that which shelters the coastline of Queensland, Australia, today. When Guadalupe Mountains National Park is ready for visitors, there will be a museum in which the geological story will be graphically interpreted.

What we shall visit is a highland area that rises from about 3,000 feet in the Pecos Valley near Carlsbad, New Mexico, to the 8,751 feet of Guadalupe Peak. This is the highest point in Texas, though Mount Emory in the Chisos Mountains of Big Bend National Park is a worthy second. This highland is the northeast arm of the Guadalupe Mountain range, which resembles a great V, with two arms extending into New Mexico. One of the arms contains Carlsbad Caverns National Park, which will be a neighbor of only a few cross-country miles.

Though the geological features of the area come first in importance, the life communities are extraordinary in their zonal range. Here, within the space of a few miles, even a nonscientific observer will clearly note that four climatic zones are represented, from the character of northern Mexico to that of southern Canada. Here are agaves and cactuses at the foot of the mountains, but as elevation is gained, and with an increase in vegetation, we reach highlands with a cover of pines, alligator juniper, even a sampling of Douglas fir and groves of quaking aspen. There are spots on the highest peaks that show decidedly Canadian attributes. Roasting pits found at all elevations indicate that the early inhabitants followed the ripening of native plants from the valley floor in spring to the highest ridges in autumn. Many pictographs are found in the caves and rock shelters.

In 1961 the federal government received from Wallace Pratt a donation of 5,632 acres of land in the fine North McKittrick Canyon area of these mountains. It was thought at that time that the gift might someday be joined with Carlsbad Caverns National Park, but something even better than that awaited the preservation. It so happened that more than 70,000 acres of ranch land adjoining the Pratt holding were owned by J. C. Hunter, Jr., of Abiline, Texas, who ran a great herd of angora goats for the production of mohair wool. When one remembers John Muir's classic definition of sheep as "hoofed locusts," and that the goat is just as remorseless a feeder, that does not sound promising. But the Hunters, father and son, had shown an unusual affection for the land and an interest in preserving the more fragile features, as well as in restoring wildlife.

Since the early 1920's, an elk herd has been established—if not the identical species that were wiped out, at least a related species. The wild turkey has been restored. The little hunting that has been done has been strictly controlled. The section of the ranch used for goal raising was not the part of the area containing the best ecological values. Particularly, J. C. Hunter has employed strict conservation practices to protect the more sensitive terrain and its vegetation. Also it was his desire that when the ranch was sold, it should be preserved and protected for cultural and recreative public use. In 1965 Congress authorized the purchase of the land and the creation of one more national park.

Not least interesting to the conservation world is the fact that this is the first national park which has been acquired by purchase of private lands. Hitherto, either the land involved was already in federal domain, or was

Bristlecone pine may be the world's oldest living thing. Cedar Breaks National Monument. [Photo: Weldon F. Heald]

donated. True, in the case of this park there is a donated part, but the major part was bought—and at a bargain price.

D. CEDAR BREAKS NATIONAL MONUMENT
[*Utah*]

TWO MILES ABOVE SEA LEVEL, and still in the pink-cliffs formation, Cedar Breaks National Monument is, you might say, an appendix to the Red Book of the Utah-Arizona colorland. It is not a repetition of Bryce. There is naturally a similarity, but in this area which has been marked for preservation out of Dixie National Forest, we come upon something even more brilliantly colored, and on a greater scale, than the bowl of Ebenezer Bryce.

The climate here is superb. In summer, when the desert is seething with heat, there is perfect comfort at Cedar Breaks. The gathering clouds, though they do not gather to remain for any length of time, may bring flurries of snow in July. In July, too, there is enough moisture in the ground to provide rich displays of wild flowers. There are fine forests of fir and spruce, and meadows with carpets of blossoms that vie with the rocks of the amphitheaters—a competition for the admiration of visitors which, in July, is not common in the desert country.

Here the pink cliffs are nearly two thousand feet thick, and the rock shapes are bolder. The road skirts the rim in places, revealing from a number of outlooks the furrowed and corroded side walls, broken into massive ridges that radiate from the center like the spokes of a wheel. White or orange at the top, the cliffs, as they go down, are in rose and coral tints. There are chocolates, yellows, lavenders, and even purples. This is not one bowl, but really a series of them, or broken circles with the ends joined.

Someone has said: "If Cedar Breaks were anywhere but in this region, it would be picked as one of the world's greatest scenic wonders." It is true. It seems like the final lavish disbursement of a spendthrift of beauty.

E. DINOSAUR NATIONAL MONUMENT
[*Utah–Colorado*]

NOBODY KNOWS who may first have seen those monstrous petrified bones which protruded from the coarse-grained rock lying upturned along the north side of the Green River where it makes its swing from Colorado over into Utah. Possibly the aboriginal Indians saw and marveled at them, for there is ample and valuable evidence that prehistoric man lived in what is now

Dinosaur National Monument. Indeed, it was about the farthest north of the early "southwestern culture," and tree-ring studies have established habitation there at about A.D. 500.

The first man to report the quarry of bones of the fossil reptiles was O. A. Peterson. That was in 1892. Earl Douglass, working the area for the Carnegie Museum of Pittsburgh, found the rich main deposit in 1909, and Dinosaur is now one of the most famous of the world storehouses where there were strange mass deaths of the creatures and they were preserved under exactly the right conditions, so that we are now able to recover and re-create the skeletons of the nightmarish reptiles that swarmed in the semitropical Jurassic plains more than 100 million years ago.

By 1922 the Carnegie Museum had removed a score of dinosaurs. Afterward the U. S. National Museum obtained additional specimens, and still later the University of Utah continued the exploration. It was while the Carnegie Museum was active in the quarry, in 1915, that the original area of eighty acres was set aside by Presidential proclamation for perpetual protection by the National Park Service.

In 1938 the original monument was enlarged to include about 325 square miles of federal land in Utah and Colorado. The irregular boundaries were calculated to preserve not merely the dinosaur quarry but the classic canyons of the Green River—Lodore, Whirlpool, and Split Mountain—through which Major John Wesley Powell had twice been buffeted on his way to the un-

The bone is 135,000,000 years old. The girl is, say, 20? Dinosaur National Monument. [*Photo: M. Woodbridge Williams*]

charted waters of the Grand Canyon of Arizona; and included also were the canyons of the Yampa River from near Lily Park to the Green.

Now, the increase in the size of Dinosaur National Monument was no whim; nor was the National Park Service hungry for land, merely as such, to administer. With appropriations far from sufficient to do justice to the ever-growing desire of our mobile people to see their pristine America, it is hardly likely that the Service would invite additional custody of areas unrelated to its well-defined purposes. Nor was the extension due to any recent discovery of the profound beauty and significance of these river reaches. Adventurous souls had been thrilled, over the years, by the colossal examples of nature's forces to be seen there. It was merely that the country had just arrived at this point in its program of preservation.

It happened that this magnificent area was placed in safekeeping none too soon. We are in a period of dam building. It might be called our national "beaver period." Perhaps that is unjust to the beaver, who may have a prescience of which I know nothing. There is no doubt that many river dams are not only justified, but most necessary. Many are valuable, but less necessary. Some are of doubtful long-range value; some pose as being for one purpose when they are really for something else; some are just dams, resulting from the simple fact that if you are skilled in building dams, you like to build dams—in itself, if bridled, a very human and laudable trait. I admire these expert engineers no end. But I tremble for the day when they first see the trout brook behind my humble country box.

As for the extension of the boundaries of Dinosaur, it has been well said that errors in the creation of national parks have seldom been that too much land was taken but have often been that too little was taken. Let me see if I can present an analogy. It may limp a little, but I think it will do.

The reader of this chapter may be one of those who, each working day, passes through the entrance of some great office building whose portals are reared on blocks of polished granite. Perhaps you have paused beside one of those stone blocks for a moment and admired its texture. It might be, even, that you became curious about granite and got out your old geology textbook and relearned that those crystals in the stone, made brilliant by polishing, were quartz and feldspar and some kind of mica. Now, those things are good to know; but if you stop there, you really know very little about the story of granite and its place in this fascinating natural world.

The meaning of these rock pictures is unknown; but they surely had purpose. Dinosaur National Monument. [Photo: M. Woodbridge Williams]

Perhaps the quarry from which the granite block came is not very far from the place where it now rests. So one Saturday afternoon you go out to the quarry. Here, on a cliffside, is exposed the mighty jointed raw material from which the finished building blocks are broken and hewn, and there are the great cranes and derricks that swing them from their bed. Now you know more about granite, but you are still far from the whole story. How did the granite come to be there, on that spot, and not somewhere else?

So you go on a hike in the adjacent area. And soon you discover, maybe, that the outcropping rock you now find around you is not granite at all, but a kind of slaty rock, with the bedding planes turned up at a sharp angle; and in making a great circle around the dome of granite, you find that the inclination of the slate layers is such that they seem to have been thrust back by some force from the center. Thus you come to the fact that the big dome of granite was actually an intruder, which thrust up as molten rock under an older rock that had hardened from mud at the bottom of a shallow sea. It did not break through to the surface, this hardening granite, but bowed up the older rock above it.

You can get the same effect (with the housewife's permission) if you take a dozen dinner plates and slip them under the tablecloth to the center of the table. You make a dome, but the plates are not visible. In the case of the granite, it was exposed and ready for quarrying only when the surface rock had eroded away. But there is more yet to find out, and you need more travel. Your area must be extended.

Perhaps this country where the granite is quarried is mountainous. But the rivers do not flow as though they had first made their beds while coursing down steep declivities. They take meandering courses. How could that be? To determine the answer to that, you need a still wider range of observation.

Now, Dinosaur National Monument needed extension for reasons similar to those in this imperfect example I have given. To begin with, perhaps you have seen first the reconstructed skeleton of the colossal dinosaur called *Diplodocus* on exhibit at the U.S. National Museum. With infinite pains and scientific skill this skeleton was put together from the petrified bones taken from the quarry at Dinosaur National Monument. You gaze at the remains of a prodigious creature that has disappeared from earth. You are glad there are none of them to meet on the way home from work. Your imagination clothes those stony bones with flesh. But still, you know little about those reptiles and the conditions under which they throve.

When you visit the quarry at Dinosaur National Monument, you come nearer to that strange life form. You may see where the bones are adroitly taken from the rock—that rock of the "Morrison formation" which in this exact spot represents a former shifting river channel. Here the dinosaurs and other reptiles met death in a great group, for some reason not known. A museum near the quarry contains the fossilized bones of some of these reptiles, as well as explanatory maps, photographs, and paintings. Now the dinosaur becomes somewhat more real, and yet there is still much to observe on the road to knowing.

You are here in a mountainous country, but obviously these ungainly creatures were never built to climb hills. It is evident that they lumbered through lush vegetation in a region almost as flat as your hand, where the sluggish streams took winding courses through sandy or muddy plains. Here are the bones, then, of gigantic sauropods—but this is surely *not* the landscape that, alive, they saw!

Where Major John Wesley Powell had hardships, nowadays river-runners have thrills.
Dinosaur National Monument. [*Photo: M. Woodbridge Williams*]

The intervening millennia have brought mighty changes. To see what has happened, you must leave the bone quarry and look at the gorgeous canyons of the Green and the Yampa. There you will find not only beauty and the ferocity of swift-flowing rivers armed with abrasives, but also the explanation of what has occurred to the whole Rocky Mountain region since the dinosaurs floundered and fed there.

You will see that the Green River, instead of taking the easy way westward, has apparently plunged directly southward through the hard rocks of the Uinta uplift, creating the turbulent rapids of Split Mountain Canyon. You will see that the Yampa also has done things the impossible way. Like the Colorado at Grand Canyon, it is flowing along the flanking slope of a plateau. But a river cannot start in business that way; and so, by viewing the monument as a whole, the perception comes that this Rocky Mountain region was once a plain, or nearly so. Earth forces have raised it high above the sea and arched it into ranges. It has been crumpled, broken, deformed, and worn down. The Green and the Yampa have kept to the beds they made before the uplift came, and as a consequence are now flowing at the bottom of stupendous canyons; and the picture is considered by many even more revealing than that shown in the Grand Canyon.

The reconstructed skeletons in the great natural-history museums are the tickets to a long journey into the past; a visit to the dinosaur quarry has the thrill of approaching a little nearer to that faraway period. But it is the surrounding country—so extraordinary that it may someday gain the status of a national park—that enables us to imagine the conditions which made possible the reptilian life that once dominated the scene.

5. BADLANDS NATIONAL MONUMENT
[South Dakota]

TOURISTS WHO DRIVE through the Black Hills of South Dakota on their way to Yellowstone or other Western national parks will be richly rewarded by a visit to the School of Mines in Rapid City. They will be even more surprised and delighted if, coming from the east on U. S. 16, they do *not* rush blindly through the "Mauvaises Terres," or Badlands, intent only upon the principal objects of their tour. To do so is to miss some of the strangest as well as the most beautiful scenery of the West.

In the boiling river at Split Mountain. Dinosaur National Monument. [Photo: M. Woodbridge Williams]

The mineral collection of the School of Mines is outstanding. There are larger exhibits and greater curiosities than those shown here, but I know of no collection that is displayed with finer taste and museum skill than this one. Perhaps it is only natural that it should be so, for right at the door of the school is, for a start, one of the most variously mineralized regions in the world. In addition to those local specimens, there are precious trophies of crystals and ores from most of the best world sources.

What may interest the average visitor most, however, is the fine exhibit of extinct animals that once roamed in grassy swamps where, in the Badlands, now stands an almost barren labyrinth of pinnacles and bizarre shapes, washed into existence first from the high levels of the ancient Black Hills, and then carved by weathering. From Cedar Pass to Pinnacles, along the road through the monument, visitors may stop their cars and view billows and peaks and valleys of delicately banded colors—colors that shift in the sunshine, reds, grays, and a thousand tints that color charts do not show. In the early morning and in the evening, when shadows are cast upon the infinite number of peaks, or on a bright moonlight night when the whole region seems a part of another world than ours, the Badlands will be an experience not easily forgotten.

Now a country almost devoid of water, this region once must have had ample moisture. The three-toed horse, the camel, the rhinoceros, the saber-toothed tiger, and all the rest of those creatures whose artfully reconstructed skeletons are to be seen at the School of Mines were snuffed out of existence for the same reason that the people of Mesa Verde were finally forced to migrate. With the people, the cause was a short-term drought; with the extinct animals the gradual climatic change went on over a myriad of lifetimes. But the change from a moist condition to one of aridity did it; and the huge titanothere, king of the grass-eating animals, part elephant and part rhinoceros, literally starved to death, to be covered by silt and sand, and 40 million years later to be washed into the light of day again.

Little by little the Badlands are disappearing. The easily eroded volcanic cinders that were spewed over this region by volcanoes when the Rocky Mountain front was being raised and all nature was in labor pains are being carried to the sea—the destiny of all raised earth surfaces—through gullies and draws to the White River, thence to the Missouri and the Mississippi.

A mere glance at this wild, barren land might convince anyone that animal and plant life would be impossible. Yet a surprising number of small animals manage an existence; birds are not scarce, and the golden eagle is sometimes seen hovering over the peaks. As for flowers, they simply cannot be sup-

On the trail through the "open door." Badlands National Monument. [Photo: R. A. Grom]

pressed, it would seem. For here on these inhospitable clays the gumbo lily, or evening primrose, luxuriates. The prickly pear—great fields of it—bursts into its waxy red and yellow bloom, and the Spanish dagger—that same resolute plant which battles with the shifting gypsum sands in White Sands National Monument in New Mexico—finds the Badlands to its liking.

So do not hurry through the Badlands. The Dakota Indians found it hard to travel through, and called it *makosica* (bad land); but they had no surfaced highways and no speeding carriages that go without horses. They did, however, have plenty of time. In that respect let us emulate the Dakotas.

6. COLORADO NATIONAL MONUMENT
[*Colorado*]

AT A TIME when human beings were still in the blueprint stage—they were "on order," as the procurement division says—some very strange beasts were roaming the shallows and swamps that existed where the present Colorado National Monument is situated. Here in the sandstone—called by geologists the Morrison formation—are found the bones of five species of dinosaurs. They were lizards. I saw one of the modern representatives of the family the other day as I was walking a shady path in the damp woods. He was a bright-red eft, with black spots—about an inch long. The family has shrunk in size, but is probably just as happy.

These Morrison lizards were of tremendous bulk. About sixty-five of them, head to tail, in a circus parade, would stretch a mile. Brontosaurus—called the thunder-lizard because the earth might seem to have trembled under his tread—was at least sixty-seven feet long, as a well-articulated skeleton in a museum shows. Diplodocus may have reached the length of ninety feet. But Diplodocus had a brain that weighed fifteen ounces.

The ultimate in brainlessness seems to have been the Stegosaurus, the fellow with heavy armor plate over his neck. His brain weighed two and a half ounces, whereas his body weighed ten tons. It is something to speculate upon—why, at the period when these dinosaurs lived, there should have been such a tendency toward flesh and bone. Can it be that brain development keeps down one's weight? If this should be so, and your friends tell you that they are planning to reduce, you may look for some pretty handsome intellectual results.

One of the other saurians was a giraffelike wading creature, and there was a meat eater with short forelegs and long hind legs. Even in museums, stripped down to their bones, the dinosaurs have an unpleasant look, to most people; but this may be sheer prejudice. Certainly, in a world that has so many difficulties currently, we need not regret their extinction.

Colorado National Monument is an area of fantastically carved and highly colored highlands, with sheer-walled canyons, towering stone towers, and fluted columns. Weird formations come into view at every turn of the road that follows the rim of the canyons for most of its twenty-two miles. There are parking spots at particularly scenic outlooks. Devil's Kitchen, Coke Ovens, Monolith Parade, and Window Rock are a few of the examples of nature's handiwork. The monument road is open and passable all year.

7. BLACK CANYON OF THE GUNNISON NATIONAL MONUMENT
[Colorado]

GOVERNMENT PUBLICATIONS are commonly regarded as desiccated fodder circulated to everybody and read by nobody. There may be some truth in this, but there was a period when some of the most stirring narratives of adventure and courage poured fom the government printing presses. It was in the middle part of the nineteenth century, when the great westward march of Americans was attaining its swing. Army engineers, supported by meager detachments of troops, were surveying the states west of the Mississippi for practicable railroad routes to the Pacific. Geologists, botanists, topographers, accompanying the surveying parties, were furnishing the reports that, for the first time, acquainted the people with the potentials of their little-known territories.

And there were tragedies in those Senate and House documents, too. These explorations were no tea parties. The reports to the Secretary of War are replete with harrowing tales of hardship—soldiers who had straggled, lost in the desert; the loss of food and transport; attacks by seemingly friendly Indians who suddenly went on the warpath.

I have before me, as I write this, Volume II of a Senate Document, which opens with the day-by-day journal of Lieutenant E. G. Beckwith, Third Artillery—the narrative of the survey for a possible railroad along the 38th and 39th parallels. The first paragraph is severely formal:

Sir: In order that you may be put in possession . . . of the result of the investigations of the exploring party organized under your order of the 20th of May, 1853, by the lamented Captain J. W. Gunnison of the Corps of Topographical Engineers, who was barbarously massacred by the Pah Uta Indians on the Sevier River, in the Territory of Utah, I deem it my duty . . .

The account is more thrilling than any Wild Western fiction.

Captain Gunnison had encamped early in the afternoon. . . . It was known that a band of Indians was near him, but a recent quarrel had terminated, and an experienced citizen of the Territory, acting as guide, had considered a small escort sufficient. . . .

The sun had not yet risen when the surrounding quietness was broken by a volley of rifles and a shower of arrows. . . . Stepping from his tent Captain Gunnison called to his savage murderers that he was their friend; but this had no effect. . . . Only those escaped who succeeded in mounting on horseback, and even these were pursued for many miles. . . .

And there, near the Sevier, fell Captain Gunnison, for whom is named this Gunnison River; and the thrilling Black Canyon constitutes one of the most remarkable bits of scenery of the Rocky Mountain states. Within the boundaries of the national monument lies the deepest and most spectacular ten-mile section of the gorge of the Gunnison, cut through the heart of a great plateau; it is notable for its narrowness, its sheer walls, and the extraordinary depth, which ranges from 1,730 to 2,425 feet. So narrow are some places in the canyon that the channel of the river has only forty feet of space; so deep that only at midday does the sun light up the perpetual twilight on the bottom. It was partly because of this that the canyon was called "black," but also because of the nature of the rocks through which the river has cut. These are ancient dark schists, with many intrusions of dark granite; and where they are weathered and stained, the gloomy and forbidding aspect is heightened.

Both rims of the canyon within the monument are accessible by automobile in the late spring and in summer.

The trees of the monument are of unusual interest. On the highest point on the south rim, at an elevation of 8,300 feet, is a stand of piñon patriarchs. Borings taken from some of the trees showed ages of from 467 to 742 years.

8. CAPITOL REEF NATIONAL MONUMENT
[Utah]

INACCESSIBLE? Not to the prehistoric Indian, at first a "basketmaker." He seems to have lodged everywhere in the Southwestern country where there occurred a reliable trickle of water and a flat of soil that would provide sustenance. And meager though that sustenance was, he had the urge to make pictures on the surrounding rocks. The spirit of the artist budded in his soul: cornbread and snared rabbits were not all of life, and hands could do other than wield a wooden hoe. Some of these mystifying petroglyphs at Capital Reef were tinted with color obtained from minerals and the scant vegetation.

Inaccessible? Yes, so far as the white man was concerned, until very late in the exploration day. This great, brilliant escarpment, extending from Thousand Lake Mountain southeastward for 150 miles to the Colorado River, was uncharted domain until Colonel John C. Frémont looked down upon it one day in 1854. Later a band of Mormons came in and gazed at it, for they were ever seeking tillable land. But the first real study of the area waited for a member of the Powell survey of 1875.

Beautiful though the reef is—this edge of an earth-folding—it will never be described as an agricultural breadbasket. A sturdy pioneer managed a homestead here in 1880, but a few families was all it could support. Fortunate that there are places without the chance of exploitation for material ends! Visitors will come here to delight their eyes, and engage their wonder.

The present Rocky Mountains began their upheaval, rising from forces working within the earth crust. Swamps and shallow lagoons that had been the lush feeding grounds of giant reptiles (they have left footprints in the rippled shale along the base of the escarpment) were gradually elevated until it was no longer a place for such animal life. They went—or died; and finally they did both. This shale is a reddish brown; above it is another shale of many tints and shades, and then still higher the red sandstone is cut into strange pinnacles. Finally comes the capping of the white Navajo sandstone, whose domes (like those of many state capitols) give the reef its name.

From the visitor center, a road leads southward to Pleasant Creek. Off this road are spurs that can be followed into Grand Wash and Capitol Gorge. Richly rewarding is the short hike that is needed to find yourself in a narrow street with walls that tower a thousand feet on either side. Somewhat more than two miles into Capitol Gorge there is a trail that leads to the top of the reef.

The upper sections of the monument offer opportunities to do some exploring in wild country, but all except the initiated should stick closely to the trails, and should by all means tell the superintendent what they plan

In trolley-car days someone said, "Look! The Motorman!" The name stuck. Capitol Reef National Monument. [Photo: George Grant]

to do and report their return to him. It is better to be frankly prudent than to boast of a self-sufficiency that is likely to disappear when most required.

9. Arches National Monument
[*Utah*]

Not far from the old Mormon pioneer town of Moab, a great mass of buff-colored sandstone towers over the surrounding plain. Into this rock the weathering forces of nature have cut more natural stone arches, windows, spires, and pinnacles than are to be found anywhere else in the country. So far, eighty-eight openings large enough to be called arches have been discovered within the boundaries of this monument, but it is certain that others will be found hidden away in the less accessible rugged areas.

Landscape Arch, believed to be the longest natural stone span in the world, has a length of 291 feet. The lower end of Devil's Garden, a part of the monument known as the Fiery Furnace—a great jumble of vertical slabs of red rock that glows in the setting sun like a mighty fire—is such rough terrain that it has never yet been thoroughly explored. Another part that awaits full knowledge lies west of the Dark Angle portion of Devil's Garden. Tower Arch, a rock formation known as Joseph Smith and the Golden Plates, and the long rows of immense parallel sandstone fins can be seen at the end of a four-mile trail trip necessary to reach the Klondike Bluffs section.

The impressive grandeur of Delicate Arch, in its setting of precipitous cliffs and massive domes of "slickrock," with the gorge of the Colorado River beyond and the snow-capped peaks of the La Sal Mountains in the distance, may be enjoyed by taking a spur road to a point two miles away and then following a foot trail.

10. Natural Bridges National Monument
[*Utah*]

Formerly the three great natural bridges within this monument were known by the names of Edwin, Caroline, and Augusta. These are good wholesome names, fit to be embroidered on a bath towel. But they were no more in place in this kaleidoscope-cliffed San Juan County of Utah than a Paiute Boulevard would be in the city of Liverpool.

On a side gulch in Armstrong Canyon is Owachomo. Natural Bridges National Monument. [Photo: George Grant]

Hickman Natural Bridge. Capitol Reef National Monument. [Photo: George Grant]

It is true that the local Indians did not have individual names for the holes in the rocks. To them any kind of bridge was simply "under the horse's belly." Quite graphic, surely; but the visiting Indian (and some of those early redfolk were tourists traveling light) might well ask: "Which horse?" Well, somebody recalled that the prehistoric inhabitants of southern Utah were possibly the ancestors of the present Hopis. Whether or not this is so, the bridges now have Hopi names. Edwin became Owachomo; Caroline is now Kachina; Augusta is Sipapu. And for excellent reasons, which I leave you to discover when you rest at the bases of these colossal arches and peruse the park folder.

Though of great size, and each possessing a marked individuality, these natural bridges are surpassed in grandeur by Rainbow Bridge, which lies in a preserved area of the National Park System about sixty miles to the southwest. Yet they are among the world's greatest; and after all, our captivation by such superlatives as biggest, highest, or fastest is rather a juvenile trait. Do you *like* it? Does it *inspire* you, more than anything else of its kind? Do you *tune* to it? These are the important matters. Of all these natural arches I somehow like Landscape best. But don't ask me why. I can't explain. There is no disputing of taste.

You are here in a country of piñon and juniper forest, and in the canyons the bighorn find food and a pleasant place to ruminate in the winter midday sun. Coyotes and bobcats move around without undue noise—though occasionally the coyote practices his song at night. Once in a while a cougar prowls through. Maybe you already know this kind of country—vast, mystic, satisfying when you come partly to feel its allure.

You won't fail to interest yourself in the origin of such natural bridges as these, wherever they exist. How the studies of the geologist and naturalist have determined that they are of various stages of maturity—some young, some old, some on the road to departure and destined to leave behind only relic abutments on the canyon walls. How swift water erosion has mostly chiseled some of them; how others are more the work of frost and sand-laden winds and rain. How varying rock material and climatic conditions may govern the type of arch. All such things. Fascinating, and wonderful

Landscape Arch and Devils Garden. Arches National Monument. [Photo: Jack E. Boucher]

considerations to think of, to take your mind off your worry about a dis-
ordered world.

There are thousands of prehistoric ruins all through this painted canyon
world, too.

11. RAINBOW BRIDGE NATIONAL MONUMENT
[Utah]

PARTLY SPANNING BRIDGE CANYON, which extends from the western slope
of Navajo Mountain to the Colorado River near where that stream crosses
the Arizona-Utah boundary, Rainbow Bridge was long the least accessible
of all the natural wonders included in the National Park System.

If I know anything about Americans, this statement was always accepted
as a challenge. It is like telling the venturesome that a certain mountain peak
has never been climbed. Very well; if you knew how to make your way
through a desert country with no roads—unless you call *those things* roads—
or if you wanted to make a six-mile hike up Bridge Canyon after having
come down the Colorado River by boat, you were one of the small number
of Americans who saw this phenomenon of erosion.

Worn into the salmon-pink rock of the Navajo sandstone, Rainbow
Bridge is, so far as is known, the greatest natural bridge in the world. It not
only is a symmetrically curved arch below, but also presents a curved surface
above, thus suggesting a rainbow to the Navajos and the Paiutes, who had
names for it in their own languages. Both tribes had called it Rainbow Bridge
before the white man came.

The bridge is 309 feet in the clear from the bottom of the gorge, and the
horizontal span from pier to pier is 287 feet. If it could be arched over the
dome of the Capitol in Washington, there would still be space to spare.

Somewhere between Rainbow Bridge and Navajo National Monument
the car stalled. It had been raining, though the cart track across the desert
looked dried out. You never know. In a low spot, down went one of the
rear wheels, and it began to spin. Well, that is nothing. You get out and
look for sage or greasewood, and you finally rock the tire up on some brush
—it may take some time and some brush—and off you go. But this time it
didn't work. The wheel got deeper into the treacherous sand, and it looked
like a long sojourn on the spot.

An old Navajo came along. He couldn't speak English or Spanish, but
he was interested in the predicament. He squatted down and looked and
reflected. He knew what was needed: horses. Off to the right a flash flood

had left a wide, shallow "river." The Navajo peeled off his good trousers of civilization, waded across, and disappeared. More perspiring efforts with sagebrush under the wheel. No result, except to go deeper into the sand.

Then a young Navajo schoolboy came along. He knew English. He said he would try to get help, and he disappeared. Would either he or the old man bother to come back *¿Quien sabe?*—Spanish, which, in a case of growing despondency like this, means "probably not."

But after three long hours something appeared in the distance. It was a wagon. Sideless, drawn by two horses, with three passengers on the seat: the old man, the schoolboy, and another. Glory hallelujah! They had delivered their "message to Garcia." While the automobile was being dragged out, two more Navajos, gypsy-looking men, rode up and looked on.

A typical experience in the Navajo country. Something to talk over and laugh about when you get safely to port. But those incidents can be discouraging at the time!

12. CHIRICAHUA NATIONAL MONUMENT
[*Arizona*]

IN MANY of the Western parks and monuments the agencies of erosion have carved the rocks into strange and imitative shapes, but to see what Nature can do when she sets out really to create a museum of "the grotesque and arabesque" (as Edgar Allan Poe called one of his collections of stories), it will perhaps be necessary to visit Chiricahua National Monument, in the southeastern part of the state. Here is the domain of whim. Here, if you get fun from finding silhouettes in stone of humans you like or don't like, of animals and edifices, of historical and legendary characters, you will find endless material.

Pinnacles are not uncommon, but here are incredibly slender ones, delicate needles reaching far skyward. Giant beasts and men you may have seen elsewhere, but these in Chiricahua are out of nightmares. Seventeen square miles on the western slope of the Chiricahua Mountains are crowded with mad sculptures.

They come into being mainly from the nature of the rock. Old lava flows, layer on layer, varying in thickness, spread out over this area. The lava shrank in cooling and vertical cracks were created, and when later the earth was slowly lifted and tilted, the forces of erosion began to work. Some of the rock layers were undercut. The great fissures were developed along lines that dimly indicated the finished work the sculptor might produce.

Massive rocks are balanced on teetering points; sometimes other rocks on top of the balanced ones; jutting rocks maintain such precarious positions that the law of gravitation seems defied. There are Punch and Judy's, China-Boys, and—but you may have more amusement in choosing your own names. Whatever you look at now will someday not be there, because the forces that created them will demolish them; but there will be others just as curious in their places, and some of the squarish blocks you see are the raw material for the shapes to come.

This is historic ground, too, which with the fine wildlife habitat gave additional reason for its preservation in the National Park System. For centuries the Chiricahua Mountains in southeastern Arizona were the home of the warlike Apaches. Living on wild animals and native plants, these people were always on the move, following the game and the seasonal supply of food, and varying their activities by raids on agricultural Indians of the desert valley.

With the coming of the white man, who introduced cattle, horses, and new foodstuffs, the Apaches waxed even more prosperous. Here was new and bigger plunder. Nor were these nomads respecters of persons. The inoffensive farmer Indians or the mail-and-passenger stages of the old Butterfield Express route—all were one to the Apaches.

Fort Bowie was established in 1862, to command the strategic Apache Pass at the end of the Chiricahua Mountains, and a troop of U.S. Cavalry was stationed there. But under the leadership of the slippery Chief Cochise the Indians continued their raids. It was not until 1886 that the famous Geronimo and his band finally surrendered, and even then a small force of Apaches led by Big Foot Massai continued to give trouble.

Because the Chiricahuas rise as a cool refuge from the semidesert grasslands of Arizona and neighboring New Mexico, there is a surprising variety of wildlife and forest cover. Whitetail deer are numerous, and among the birds are those which come from their homes in the wooded highlands of Mexico—birds like the coppery-tailed trogon and the thick-billed parrot. Dense vegetation covers the shaded canyon bottoms and the cooler northerly slopes of the high elevations.

An excellent mountain road can be followed by automobile up the Bonita Canyon to Massai Point, where there is a splendid view of the monument and the valleys to the east and west. Fourteen miles of trails enable visitors

Lava rock was ideal for nature's sculptors. Chiricahua National Monument. [*Photo: Wayne Bryant*]

to reach all parts of the monument on foot or horseback. When personnel is available, visitors are accompanied by park rangers, who explain the natural and historic events that have created the need for preservation of this fascinating bit of Western America.

13. AGATE FOSSIL BEDS NATIONAL MONUMENT
[*Nebraska*]

IN THE MIOCENE EPOCH of the Tertiary Period (which is the geologic-clock division just before that in which modern man arrived to upset nature's applecart) there was a population explosion among the mammals. This evolutionary profusion has been referred to as the Golden Age of Mammals. How long ago? It isn't much use talking about millions of years, because we cannot readily comprehend the passage of even ten thousand. The geologist doesn't try. He contents himself with a scale of references governed by what he finds in the earth crust.

In these fossil beds in Sioux County, Nebraska, is a boneyard of strange creatures that came into being and passed into extinction without leaving more than the faintest characteristics associating them with the mammals of today. For example:

A two-horned rhinoceros, small but swift, about the size of a Shetland pony and presumably as numerous as later became the bison on our Western plains of the eighteenth century. A bizarre creature with a head like a horse, a suggestion of the giraffe, front legs rhinoceros-like, hind legs like a bear. Then there was the "terrible pig," a beast ten feet long and seven feet tall at the shoulder, with great tusks. Then a graceful little deerlike animal, no doubt in great numbers—some vague resemblance here to the South American guanaco.

This mammalian ossuary, called by Henry Fairfield Osborn the most remarkable deposit of the kind ever found, has long been known and studied by paleontologists, and the two grass-covered hills of the site are named University and Carnegie, for the work done in the field by parties from Nebraska University and the Carnegie Museum.

The find was on a ranch owned by Captain James H. Cook, a cattle-rancher who had been army scout, big-game hunter, and guide, and trusted friend of the Indians. He, and later his son Harold, fully understood the scientific importance of their fossil quarries, and they generously helped to preserve them for educational use and for ultimate possession by the public.

Though at the time of this description there are no exposed fossils to be seen at the two sites of the monument, the plan is that someday visitors will not only see the skeletons of these creatures of 15 million years ago, but also watch scientists working among them.

14. PINNACLES NATIONAL MONUMENT
[*California*]

ASSUREDLY, this is the place for the hiker. If only to exercise the legs and fill the lungs with dry pure air, this alone is worthwhile. To get away from urban rush and conformity is better. Best of all is to follow some of the fifteen miles of trails and see an aftermath of one of nature's moments of violence. For here one views the wreckage of a lava field. Out of fissures in the crust flowed molten rock, piling up until it stood in domelike form three times as high as what is seen today. Roaring explosions of steam and gas threw liquid and solid rock into the air. A pudding was stirred—the breccia that became the common landscape base seen along the trails.

The rainfall here is scant, and comes ordinarily in winter and early spring. Then come months of dry heat. But the clothing vegetation has found

The humble coreopsis becomes a giant on Anacapa Island. Channel Islands National Monument. [Photo: Ronald Mortimore]

a way to creep in and get established upon this naked rock. Not trees, though you could call it a forest. These are leathery-leaved shrubs—chamise, some manzanita, some buckbrush. Altogether, this miniature forest is known as chaparral. Here in Pinnacles is perhaps the finest example of this type of vegetative cover that exists within the National Park System.

It is a curious thing that this chaparral's continuity is a matter not merely of its defenses against desert drought, but is also controlled by natural wild-fire; that is to say, not fires set by man, but usually by lightning. Long before man ever came to the scene, these fires swept the chaparral at intervals. This regular burning could be borne only by a plant adapted to it—able to restore itself from a large root crown, or to produce seeds that germinate by the very heat that kills its mother plant. It follows that, in a case like this, when man protects the chaparral by extinguishing brush fires—ordinarily a prudent thing to do—species that are less resistant to natural fires may be introduced. So you will see, for instance, the digger pine gradually spreading within the monument, and it is possible that someday it may replace the "pygmy trees."

Nevertheless, it is better for us to be careful with our matches. Don't draw unfortunate conclusions from one interesting biological fact. Don't "play Nature!"

15. CHANNEL ISLANDS NATIONAL MONUMENT
[California]

SOMETIMES during the misty geological past the eight islands that lie off the southern California coast were part of the mainland. In relation to the land mass, the ocean level changed, so that what were the tops of mountains were alone left unsubmerged. Two of these former peaks, Santa Barbara and Anacapa—the smallest of the group—constitute the monument that was set aside in 1938 for the preservation of a plant and animal life which in the course of time has had to pursue its own special way. Whatever could adapt itself to new conditions survived, somewhat changing its form; all the rest was destined to extinction. Thus the story told here, of the results of geographical isolation by the forces of nature, is suggestive of what has happened everywhere in our world under like conditions.

Santa Barbara Island is about opposite San Pedro, thirty-eight miles away. Anacapa Island, forty miles to the north, is ten miles from the mainland. Visitors have been few in these wild domains, where the barking of sea lions is continuous and the voices of the gulls and other sea birds advertise the questing, nesting, and quarreling that goes on along the cliffs that face the sea. More frequent than human visitors are the cruising sea elephants, huge and fantastic in shape—the bull of the species has a foot-long snout that gives it its name. Occasionally one of the rare sea otters is seen. But the California sea lion, which learns circus tricks so readily, is the sure attraction.

The National Park Service has plans to provide ways for more Americans to know these interesting places which have hitherto been so near and yet so remote. Anacapa, in particular, will have means of access, camping accommodations, and the interpretive services so greatly needed for appreciation of the "way of life" in a community that is highly specialized.

For example, the giant coreopsis, seen to fullest perfection on the island of Santa Barbara, is a treelike sunflower whose thick, gray-barked "trunk" grows to a height of eight feet. It aspires to be a tree. In summer, which is rainless, coreopsis appears to be without life. It is only sleeping. With the rains, it puts forth a new growth of feathery leaves. Coreopsis reminds the botanist of the odd tendency, on islands, for the Compositae family to become shrubs and even trees. On Juan Fernández is seen an example of how even the lowly lettuce plant can be a lusty figure in the landscape.

The boatman approaching Santa Barbara Island sees from miles away the golden yellow flame of its full bloom of spring. But this is only one flower of a great number of plants that are as distinctly individual as those of the deserts of the mainland.

Sea elephants eye the photographer with sullen suspicion. Channel Islands National Monument. [Photo: Lowell Sumner]

[V]

The Underground World

By and by *somebody shouted:*
"Who's ready for the cave?"
Everybody was. Bundles of candles were procured, and straightway there
was a general scamper up the hill. The mouth of the cave was up
the hillside—an opening shaped like a letter A. . . . By and by the
procession went filing down the steep descent of the main avenue.

—MARK TWAIN, *Adventures of Tom Sawyer*

1. CARLSBAD CAVERNS NATIONAL PARK
[*New Mexico*]

WHEN the Spanish conquistadors forged their way northward from Mexico—a march of continuous reconnoitering in an unmapped wilderness—they probably skirted the foothills of the Guadalupe Mountains in what is now southeastern New Mexico. It is quite possible, as they searched everywhere for loot, that they saw the dragon-mouth entrance to Carlsbad Caverns.

Two and a half centuries later the Butterfield Trail, the first such route across the West, freighted more gold on one stage, from the California placers, than the Spaniards ever found in their fruitless quest; and the Butterfield wagons crossed the older trail not far from the caves. Behind the gold-rush wayfarers came the cattlemen and the permanent settlers. They knew the caverns, called them the Bat Caves, and found them rich in—what? Beauty? Mystery? Geological revelation?

Not at all. They found in them a new and valuable product: bat guano.

Temple of the Sun, in the "Big Room." Carlsbad Caverns National Park. [Photo: George Grant]

The occupancy of millions upon millions of bats, through at least fifteen centuries, had presented the eager exploiters of the nineteenth century with what seemed at first glance an inexhaustible supply of agricultural fertilizer, rich in nitrate, and easily mined. In twenty years, before the caverns were set aside as a national park, at least 100,000 tons of guano were taken out and mostly sold to growers of citrus fruits. Thus—and not for the qualities that attract so many visitors today—the great Carlsbad Caverns came into use.

Yearly visitors to Carlsbad Caverns are approaching the half-million mark annually, which, all things considered, is amazing. The Texan who confessed that he had never been in this great cave would be a Texan who might say that Texas was not the greatest state in the Union, and there is no such person.

But the white man was certainly not the first to see the caverns. In making trails through the caves, the Park Service men uncovered, a short distance inside the entrance, a sandal. This footgear was identified as belonging to the prehistoric Indian period of the Basketmakers who lived in the region four thousand years ago. The Indian was in such a hurry to leave that he did not stop to pick up his shoe. Somehow I feel I understand that. There were no electric lights in the caverns then.

Among the early explorers was a local cowboy, Jim White. Jim was deeply impressed by the wonders of the caverns. He saw more than guano and bats in them. He became a walking advertisement for these underground marvels, preaching them with almost religious devotion, and was an unofficial guide; and when the area was set aside by Congress for preservation, White finally became chief ranger. The name of Jim White is tied tightly to what is without prideful claim, the greatest of all known caves. And this is said without prejudice to the superlative qualities that other renowned caverns possess. A cave has an individuality, a personality almost. So, as with so many other natural wonders, you have your choice. As I have suggested before, the "best" national park is the one that is best for you.

Thoroughly to enjoy the stupendous work of engineering and artistry that nature has performed in Carlsbad Caverns, you need not have more than a smattering of the scientific facts. The history of Carlsbad goes back to a remote period. Call it 200 million years. We cannot grasp that retrospect, but it may do for vague comparison. It was perhaps in that period that the limestone, or the sediments that hardened into limestone, were laid down in a shallow sea. Later the uplifting and folding that produced the Rockies also elevated the Carlsbad country. This uplift occurred about the time the dinosaurs were taking their leave, and you may call that about 60 million years ago.

As the limy sediments settled and as the earth contortions later squeezed and bent them, cracks in the stone were made. The surface waters began to find their way along these cracks, increasing them in size, and keeping each chamber and corridor so created full of water, which hastened the dissolution. Later another series of uplifts, which brought the Guadalupes into being, allowed surface streams to cut canyons into the limestone, and this drained the caverns. Air entered the chambers and corridors, and then began the deposition by slow, evaporating seepage of the lovely sculptured decorations —the delicate mineral growth called helictites, the huge stalactites that hang from the ceilings, and the stalagmites that rise from the floors. The delicate colorings come from pigments of iron or other mineral matter.

This explanation is inadequate, but the study of caves is a complex specialty within the science of geology, and for most of us a general notion of cause and effect will suffice.

Huge as Carlsbad Caverns are known to be, nobody as yet has reached the limits. Seven miles of corridors and chambers are open to visitors, who go through in parties accompanied by a ranger guide, who explains the salient points and answers questions. But the truth is that the part of the caverns open to inspection by the public is only the 750-foot level. Below that level, at 900 feet, is another vast apartment; and below that still another at 1,320 feet. Nor is it known how far it may eventually be discovered that these passageways and rooms creep into the Guadalupe Mountains.

For the present, and for years to come, the display now offered in those seven miles will prove sufficient for visitors. Anyone in good health can make the trip, for it is not hurried, and there is a rest for lunch, just at the door of the Big Room. It may seem profane to sit down in a cafeteria and get hot coffee and a snack in such awe-inspiring surroundings, and perhaps it is; but mortals are weak, feet get tired, exercise means hunger, and I have not seen anyone decline the lunch on aesthetic grounds. We are naturally depraved. Why else would an overweight person nibble on a chocolate bar during a lecture on diet and reducing?

Am I requested to give a word picture of the architectural and sculptural masterpieces of Carlsbad? Respectfully, I decline. Even photographs, which better than words delineate these strange and charming forms, fall far short of revealing what you will see. Photography in caves is extremely difficult, as every expert knows: without artificial lighting, nothing; with it, dilution and distortion.

I once heard a lecturer trying to describe some beautiful primeval park— maybe it was Yosemite. Now and then he came to the end of his verbal rope and stammered: "It—it—*beggars* description!" He had to resort to this several times—"It *beggars* description"—and I came away with an amusing picture in my mind of a poverty-ridden *thing* known as Description, in mendicant rags, standing with a tin cup outstretched: a victim of too much natural perfection. Actually it was the lecturer who was reduced to want. I wish to avoid that fate.

The main corridor of the cavern, just beneath the yawning entrance, is enormous, but gives no indication of the beauties that will greet the journeyer as he passes through the corridors and chambers beyond. The trail through the main corridor extends for almost a mile, leading to the Green Lake Room, which gets its name from a small green pool beside the trail. Then into the King's Palace, a place of such surpassing loveliness that some cave lovers think it the finest display in all the world. A natural "keyhole" leads from the King's Palace to the Queen's Chamber; and then comes a charming little room called the Papoose Room.

After the stop for lunch, the Big Room is entered. Although not the most beautiful, this section is the most impressive chamber of the cavern. The trail around it is a mile and a quarter long, and at one place the ceiling arches 285 feet. Here the Giant Dome leans like the Tower of Pisa; the stalactites vary from delicate needles to huge chandeliers, and the stalagmites are equally of strange contour.

Carlsbad Caverns National Park is open all the year. Whether the summer temperature outside is more than 100 degrees or the winter temperature approaches zero, a constant 56 degrees always exists inside. Therefore visitors should wear clothes that suit the outside temperature, and in summer a light sweater will suffice for the walk through the cavern. For their comfort, it is recommended that women wear low-heeled shoes, though the trails and stairways make progress easy.

Thus far we have been concerned with the inanimate marvels of Carlsbad. But there is another spectacle visitors should not miss. This is the singular bat flight from the mouth of the caverns, which takes place about sundown in the summer. Pouring out from that part of the caverns known as the Bat Cave—a great chamber into which visitors do not go—these little creatures of the underground world swirl in a spiral stream through the entrance arch and over the rim toward the south. They are not in hundreds, not in thousands —they are literally in millions, when the night-flying insects on which they feed are in ample supply. The bats return before dawn the next day.

To give some notion of the incredible bat population at its height, naturalists have computed that, assuming the number to be three million, they would consume nearly twelve tons of moths, beetles, flies, and other insects during one night's foray. What a colossal amount of insect life, unseen and unsuspected, there must be in this New Mexico semidesert to support such a bat population as this!

There are five kinds of bats in the caverns, but the greater number belong to a species called Mexican free-tailed bats, the name being descriptive of a tail projecting beyond the skin that stretches between the hind legs.

Having witnessed this prodigy of massed animal flight, visitors may well ponder a little the queer, unreasonable superstitions that get indelibly fixed in the human mind and imagination over the years—notions that go un-challenged and seem to thrive on the very fact that they bear no relation to the truth.

Most people shudder even at the mention of bats. The impression is that they are unclean things, dangerous, and fit only to be present at a hellbroth-brewing ceremony conducted by witches, like that described by Shakespeare in *Macbeth*. And what is the truth about the poor little creatures who during the day hang by their hind legs, head downward, in dense clusters from the ceiling of their favorite caves? Do they suck blood? Do they get caught in people's hair, and scratch and bite their victims? Do they have a nauseating odor? All in all, are they creatures that the world would be better off without?

Poor little bat! Personally clean—though their apartment houses may have a disagreeable odor—with fragile little claws used only to hang with, the "flying mouse" is a timid thing with fine, soft fur, whose naked wings are not dry or parchmentlike, but really triumphs of silky, translucent structure, filled with those nerves which may explain their accuracy of flight. It is true there is a Southern American species that has bad manners. But the "vampire bat" is mostly a figment of the imagination and belongs with the werewolf and the basilisk. One of the tropical bats eats the bananas of the plantation owner. But what are bananas for?

The bat seems to be a leftover from some strange animal that lived in a warm and uniform climate in past ages. Unable to adapt itself to sharp climatic changes, the bat took to the uniform temperature of caves. This is what the cave bear of Europe did; and no doubt for the same reason; but the bat has made a go of it, whereas the bear died, probably of disease—arthritis, some of the European naturalists think.

The bat has been able to compromise with nature in several ways. The bats that remain in a cave all winter cluster together, head down, with their wings folded around them, and go into a sort of suspended animation. The lethargy cannot be continuous, for the bats have been found flying about the caves in midwinter. But some of the bats migrate instead of hibernating. It was long a subject of speculation where certain bats went when they disappeared from the caves of southern France. They were not seen anywhere in Europe. The answer was found after they were banded, as birds are banded. The bats spent their winters in Japan.

To witness the Carlsbad bat flight it is necessary for most visitors to stop overnight in the city of Carlsbad, after going through the caverns. There are no overnight accommodations in the park. But the whole district around Carlsbad richly deserves more time than tourists give it; and he who misses the bat flight is losing the chance of seeing one of the world's greatest sights associated with the mystery of caverns.

2. MAMMOTH CAVE NATIONAL PARK
[Kentucky]

SOMEWHERE AMONG the stalagmites on the floor of a great chamber in the Mammoth Cave of Kentucky, there is an English shilling, lawful money of Her Majesty Queen Victoria. How do I know? Well, I have it on the word of "An Officer of the Royal Artillery," who honored the cavern with his presence in 1850. This British military man was a sad wag. He roguishly wedged the shilling piece into a crevice to deceive the archaeologists of 2300 and, as he put it, "to throw fresh confusion into all the chronology of American History."

Just how it would bother the archaeologists I cannot quite see. The modern archaeologist is a hard man to hoax, and he becomes less gullible as the years pass. It was not always so, and perhaps the Briton had in mind the fact that up to a century ago it was a firm conviction in England that the great stones of Stonehenge were erected by the Romans, the "proof" being that Roman coins were dug out of the surrounding turf. It seems never to have occurred to anyone that when the Romans were in Britain they were as much puzzled about these slabs of stone as any later people. They went on weekend trips to see them, just as the British officer went to see Mammoth Cave. They lolled around on the grass and dropped coins out of their pockets.

So the archaeologist of the future, discovering the Queen's shilling in Mammoth Dome floor, will say: "Ah, how interesting! Sometime during the Victorian period a visitor here dropped a coin. No; on second thought, from the position in which we find it, it was probably deliberately placed. Possibly—but not certainly—he was an English visitor to the cave. He may have been the man who dropped the monocle we found near the Giant's

Coffin. The coin, judging by the usual rate of deposition, seems to date from the same decade of the nineteenth century." Do not waste time trying to outwit the modern specialist!

One day, as I was reading the artilleryman's account of his American cave experience, in the stained pages of an old *Fraser's Magazine*, the thought came to me that Mammoth Cave is not merely a cave; it is not alone a cavern of international geological distinction: even more it is one of our historic shrines. For, long before the imagination of American people went beyond the Mississippi River, this giant cave in a region dotted with caves and sink-holes had been at least partly explored, and had played a role in stirring events.

It was from Mammoth's bowels that the new Americans gathered saltpeter —in the form of what they called "petredirt"—to make their gunpowder for the War of 1812. The ruts of cartwheels and the hoofprints of oxen remained in the clay, leading to pipes and pumps and vats, from which Archibald Miller took the vital material to Philadelphia by wagon train. Venturesome marvel seekers from all along the seaboard and visitors from Europe were threading their way through these dark corridors in a day when the great Western parks were still to be discovered. And we make a great mistake

River of the blind fish. Mammoth Cave National Park. [*Photo: National Park Service*]

if we imagine that our ancestors did not get around. Within the limitations of their slow, hard means of travel, they were incorrigible rovers. When they could not find a road for wheels, they went on horseback; and where they could not go on a horse, they tramped.

Our early Americans challenged the physical country and made it give over. Their eyes were always searching for the metals and the earths they needed. Every outcrop of bull quartz had to be hammered: if they couldn't find gold or silver, it might be lead or graphite, or talc or soapstone, or something else they could use. But they were not wholly material. When they found Mammoth Cave, even if it contained nothing but adventure and beauty, they reveled in those qualities also.

Very early in the last century, as is apparent from the writings of that time, Mammoth Cave was one of the things the traveler had to see. Foreign visitors went inevitably to Niagara Falls; there they were told not to fail to go to Kentucky and see "the greatest cave that ever was." Then they could go back to Europe or die; and in the estimation of these heady, boastful, insular new Americans, one fate was the same as the other.

And what a country it must have been that the first visitors to Mammoth looked upon! It was virgin forest, most of it—broad-leaved trees, with a sprinkling of conifers. The Kentucky shrubs and wild flowers made a riot of color in spring and summer; the hillsides and ravines were painted with St.-John's-wort, with the butterfly weed and blazing stars, with May apple and Solomon's-seal and the puccoon. They still are. For what is now Mammoth Cave National Park is to be enjoyed not only for the cave, but for the forest cover, the flowers, the great variety of birds that either live or visit there, and the wildlife that is now under protection.

Truth to say, it was not easy to impress upon the independent, individualistic folk who lived in this hill country that casual trespass and free and easy gunnery had gone out and a preservation policy had come in. The hill folk have many virtues, like their counterparts in the Blue Ridge and the southern Alleghenies: self-reliance, courage, and hospitality. They are of ancient stock, and probably the most colorful and uninhibited Americans that now exist. And just because they are as they are, it has not been easy to steer them from their old-time ways. But the superintendents of the national parks are chosen as much for their patience and tact and understanding as for their technical ability. Force is always reserved for last resort. But when it must be force, the men who operate the parks can use it, and will. With every passing year, however, the local conditions are a little happier in areas like Mammoth. There is finally the dawn of appreciation of what is being preserved for all of us *by* all of us. As often happens, some of the natives who were toughest are now proudest.

As long ago as 1926 Congress had authorized the establishment of Mammoth Cave National Park, and years before that many ardent conservationists had been pressing for such an act. Finally, through the acquisition of land by Kentucky and by donations from the people of the state, and further by direct purchase by the federal government, the fifty thousand acres of forest and caves were put together, and the many objects of historic, prehistoric, and scientific value will be kept in their integrity.

In general, Mammoth Cave follows the typical development of all limestone caverns, but here the more than 150 miles of explored corridors were created by a chain of geological events that took a different turn from those which left Carlsbad, for instance, as it is today. There was the same original laying down of sediments on the floor of an ancient sea, the same story of percolating surface waters along the cracks and joints of the rock; but whereas the region of southeastern New Mexico turned gradually arid, the ample rainfall of the Kentucky country has kept a live river, the Green, as an attendant of the deepening of the caverns.

The five separate levels of the Mammoth corridors are explained as corresponding to five different levels of the Green River. Whenever the river deepened its channel, the water in the cave accommodated itself to this level, following horizontally through the limestone and emptying into the nearby stream. Today Echo River, 360 feet below the ground surface, flows slowly along the fifth, or lowest, level of the cave and drains into the Green. Visitors to Mammoth Cave may have the strange sensation of boating on an underground river that contains eyeless fish and other creatures that have adapted themselves to a life of perpetual darkness.

The water that trickles down the walls of the cavern forms sheets that hang like folded draperies, and masses that resemble fountains. The largest onyx formation in the cave is called Frozen Niagara, and while some of the names given to cave formations are, as Mark Twain dryly remarked, a bit "overdescriptive," this one is no misnomer. But even more impressive to me are those gypsum formations which take the shape of flowers and coils, pendants, and grotesque shapes; some of them look like Corinthian-column decorations, while others are gargoyles. Some are so fragile as to be mere spider webs.

It is not hard to grasp the idea of the creation of stalactites and stalagmites. Sometimes you can actually *hear* them—drip, drip—being brought into existence. But what of these fairylike forms, of the same or of like mineral composition, which may rise at an acute angle, fling out tentacles, grow upward and sidewise, with the facility of plantlife? They are called helictites, and, apparently defying the laws of gravity, they have invited the puzzled speculation of many a cave expert.

Mammoth is redolent of the memories of famous visitors. At a point about half a mile from the Historic Entrance, a place now called Booth's Amphitheater, there must have been a hushed and deeply affected audience one day in 1876 when the great Edwin Booth mounted the stage of rock and recited from Shakespeare's plays. Ole Bull, the famous violinist, likewise gave his name to one of the chambers.

It is said that Mammoth was originally sold by its earliest claimant for the sum of forty dollars. It sounds like a moderate price for so valuable a property. On the other hand, in those days there were no modern facilities for printing paper money, and what there was of it went farther. The royal artilleryman who secreted his shilling on the cave floor noted the fact, in his relation, that he traveled from Buffalo to Sandusky on one of the finest little steamers he had ever seen, with commodious staterooms and beds carved of rosewood, and the fare with meals was two dollars.

The early guides of Mammoth Cave were Negroes, and one of them, Stephen Bishop, became famous. He knew and loved the cave and for many years girded on his canteen of oil every day, supplied visitors with a lamp, and bade them follow him into the gloom. It was not an easy trip in the old days. I note with some amusement that there was some early conflict between the "improvers" and those who wished to keep the caverns as rude and primitive as possible. One visitor was already writing that "electric lights would gradually illuminate the large halls and domes. Telephones would be of advantage. Tramways might be laid through the main cave and the more accessible avenues. Shafts might be opened at certain terminal points, through which the visitors might be taken up by elevators and conveyed back to the hotel in hacks." Curiously enough, when this critic mentioned his suggestions to the proprietor of the cave, he was rebuffed with the blunt remark that "it would take away the feeling of adventure, and it would be flying in the face of Nature." Possibly the proprietor was not so idealistic as the words would seem to imply; he may not have wanted to risk the expense. But nowadays when there are suggestions for more and more "facilities" and "improvements" in the national parks, more ease for visitors and more interference with the natural scene, this evidence of a former conflict in the conception of management has an enlightening touch.

3. WIND CAVE NATIONAL PARK
[*South Dakota*]

IN A THIRSTY MIDSUMMER DRIVE across the high plains, bound westward toward Yellowstone and the great national parks beyond, the Black Hills of South Dakota constitute an island of refuge and a pause of soothing delight. Just as the jaded wayfarer has concluded that his world has flattened to a dusty plane, scorching under a pitiless sun, just then the great bubble of granite, worn down and clothed with trees, green and refreshing, appears.

Well I remember the day when, leaving Mitchell after a night of little sleep and no restoration, we skidded along upon a road surface made slick by the crushed remains of grasshopper armies that had been on their march for several days; we threaded our course through the bare pastel-colored forms of the badlands and finally came to rest in a shady campground beside a little pond on the outskirts of Rapid City. Then we knew how Xenophon's tired Greeks felt when they had finally fought their way back from Persia and staggered to a height from which they could discern the waters of the Euxine. "The men embraced one another, wept, and cried: '*Thalatta! Thalatta!* The sea! The sea!'" We were not so dramatic. We merely pointed at the pond and feebly murmured: "It looks like real water!"

These satisfying Black Hills, upon the southeast flank of which is Wind Cave National Park, seem to have everything necessary to make them a popular resort. They present a geological phenomenon so compact and evident that it can be readily appreciated without any special knowledge of the science. It is one of the most richly mineralized spots in the United States. Custer State Park, operated according to policies that closely approximate those of the National Park Service, is adjacent to the national park and has excellent accommodations for those who want to spend some time there. It is within easy distance of a group of highly interesting national monuments—Devils Tower and Badlands.

The Black Hills came into existence as a result of one of those strange but not uncommon occurrences in the drama of mountain-building whereby the molten material below the earth crust thrusts up under the overlying rocks in the form of a great dome. It does not, when it ceases to rise, appear at the surface. It simply bows back the upper crust, just the way your tablecloth

---

Overleaf: As our pioneers saw these Dakota lands. Wind Cave National Park. [Photo: Wayne Bryant]

would be disturbed if you slipped an orange underneath it. Only when the overlying layers have been broken up and taken away by time, wind, and rain can what took place be seen. Then you find, as in the Black Hills, tilted remains of the former cover, encircling the core in concentric ridges.

Electrically lighted Wind Cave presents a formation quite unlike that of any other cave in the National Park System. Instead of stalactitic and stalagmitic growths, here was developed a series of passages, known to be at least ten miles in extent, covered with a delicately beautiful boxwork, on which newer and even more fragile crystals have been deposited. It appears that when the original limestone was cracked by earth movement, the fissures were tiny ones, just large enough to permit the calcite fillings to make finlike, interlacing shapes. The calcite was less soluble than the limestone rock. Consequently as more dissolution went on, through percolating waters, the "boxes" were left projecting, in lacy compartments.

The cave is easily accessible and both dry and clean, and anyone in reasonably good physical condition can make the trip with little fatigue. The entrance door has been artificially constructed, and for an excellent reason. You could hardly expect to get in by the passageway that Tom Bingham, an old Black Hills pioneer, discovered. It was only ten inches in diameter, and Bingham did not find it by seeing it; he found it by *hearing* it. He was deer hunting one day when he heard a strange whistling sound coming from the underbrush. No other natural opening to the cave has ever been found. The strong currents of wind that alternately blow in and out of the cave mouth are responsible for the whistling.

When the barometer is falling outside, the air from the cave is likely to blow outward; when it rises, the air rushes in, and the small size of the opening causes the sound. Many visitors like to stop at the cave entrance and post themselves on weather probabilities. Having found out, their next reflection is that they can do nothing about it anyway.

But Wind Cave National Park is much more than a cave. Here, in the 28,000 acres of range and forest land, is one of the most engaging of wildlife pictures. There is a herd of four hundred buffaloes living under—I was going to say natural conditions. No; not quite that. Their boundaries are fenced. That, of course, is artificial. Still, as visitors are never likely to see much of the fence, the impression of the primitive grazing of one of our noblest native mammals is strong. I have sat in an automobile on one of the park roadways and watched a band of fifty or sixty of the big creatures quietly feeding or lying down only a few hundred yards from me, and I had the definite sense of looking upon an unspoiled frontier scene. It was a delightful picture. Once in a while a big bull would lift up his head to scowl in my direction; then, convinced that he had me disciplined, he would go back to grazing.

By all means, see these fine animals at Wind Cave; and by all means do not disregard the signs that the Park Service has posted along the roads, warning visitors not to leave their cars and approach these herds. The buffalo is not a safe mammal to trifle with. Even if you try to flatter him by calling him a bison, which is of course his true name, you will get nowhere, or worse. Every bull buffalo believes that human visitors to the park are blood relatives of the late William F. Cody, known as Buffalo Bill, and there was an unfortunate feud between the Cody and Buffalo families many years ago, which nearly resulted in the disappearance of the bison. To avoid being involved in a recrudescence of that quarrel, be sure to obey the warnings.

The Wind Cave buffaloes prosper so well that at times they have really exceeded the capacity of their range. Custer State Park also has a fine showing of bison. Elk are numerous in the park, and there are some antelope. Deer are there too, but they usually remain in the wooded parts and are seen only when crossing the grasslands on their way from shelter to shelter.

There are two colonies of prairie dogs. And here is a queer incident that happened in the park recently, which illustrates, more forcibly than preachment, in what danger we always stand of wholly losing some of our native fauna and how vital it is to preserve enough of them to make our wilderness picture a true one. One of the Park Service men was standing beside a visitor, who had just left his car to watch the antics of the prairie dogs. There were buffaloes not far away, but the visitor was more interested in the smaller animals. He turned to the man at his side and said: "I never saw any of those before. What are those funny little critters, anyway?"

The answer was: "Those are prairie dogs."

The man went on watching, and the park official walked away. But before he left he observed the registration plate on the visitor's automobile. *Kansas.* Of all places in the world—Kansas! The state that once had prairie dogs by millions upon millions. Yet it was entirely possible. No doubt the man was a late settler in a region where the little creatures had been poisoned out of existence years before.

4. JEWEL CAVE NATIONAL MONUMENT
[*South Dakota*]

YOUR TRUE SPELUNKER is a bibliophile who collects books with stone pages, set in crystal type and rubricated with initials of iron salts. He snorts at the cheap editions of caves run off on rotary presses for the millions. He wants the real Gutenberg—no electric lights, no elevators, and everything achieved the hard way. If you are going to make it as easy as that, he says, why not engineer a four-lane highway through the cave and set the speed limit at about fifty?

Very well: this time I give you Jewel Cave, also of the Black Hills, and not far from Wind Cave. Here the cave adventurer will not be pampered. Though perfectly safe, Jewel Cave means gasoline lanterns instead of electricity, and old clothes instead of fastidious attire. There are ladders and steps at certain points, but that is about all the modernization.

In the cave are crystals of dogtooth spar—calcite crystals which, as they grow, take on the shape of longish, slender pyramids, resembling the teeth of dogs. It is this mineral that accounts for the name Jewel Cave, for many of the chambers are solidly coated with calcite in this glittering form. Box-like cavities along the walls and ceilings are covered with minute crystals that stand in bold and dazzling relief from the mass behind them. There is an attractive color range from light brown to a deep chocolate. Some of the rooms have a peculiar light-green tint; others are darker green, or bronze.

Jewel Cave, like Wind Cave, was discovered by the whistle of wind coming from a small hole in the cliffs on the east side of Hell Canyon. Two prospectors, the Michaud brothers, found the cave opening and enlarged it in the hope of finding valuable minerals. By "valuable minerals" they would have meant, of course, gold or silver, or at least a lode of tin, which would be even better, since nature seems to have forgotten the United States when tin was parceled out. What they found was a rich jewelry display of dogtooth spar. Is that a valuable mineral? It is for the visitor to look and say.

Anyway, the Michaud brothers had found something they felt sure would attract tourists. They built a log house nearby to accommodate visitors. And though they did not prosper at this, at least their efforts made the lovely little cave known and hastened the time when it came into the preserves of the National Park System.

Within this monument is a forest of virgin ponderosa pine, one of the last remaining such stands in the Black Hills. Besides the ordinary cave bat and Say's bat, there is found in Jewel Cave the so-called pallid lump-nosed bat. With all due respect to the naturalists, no bat deserves a name like that. It sounds to me like unprovoked vituperation. After all, bats may be sensitive.

5. TIMPANOGOS CAVE NATIONAL MONUMENT
[*Utah*]

FROM THE HEADQUARTERS of Timpanogos Cave National Monument a trail winds for a mile and a half up the steep side of Mount Timpanogos to the cave entrance. Along this trail are the most stirring and stimulating views of the Wasatch Mountains, Utah Valley, and American Fork Canyon. To turn from these brilliant scenes, etched against a blue sky and flooded with sunlight, and enter the cavern is to go into a strange world of the underground, not less beautiful, but so different!

Mount Timpanogos is a snow-capped giant that raises its head 12,000 feet above sea level, one of a group of peaks of the Wasatch Mountains that tower above the Great Salt Basin. The monument covers an area of 250 acres in American Fork Canyon. The cave entrance is about 1,000 feet above the canyon floor.

Much of the cave interior is covered by a filigree of pink and white translucent crystals, which glow and sparkle like an array of jewels. Feathery boas, braided wreaths, and needle stalactites are among the many smaller features, which culminate in larger forms such as the fantastic Chocolate Falls, the Jewel Box, and the Great Heart of Timpanogos. The formation of these wonders is still going on. Tiny pools of water reflect the magic of the dazzling beauties overhead.

From the tips of countless stalactites hang gleaming drops of water, each of which leaves behind its tiniest layer of lime before it drops to the floor to build up a corresponding form. So slow is this action that hundreds of years may be required to add one inch of the mineral.

At monument headquarters is a picnic ground, with water, tables, and stoves. Meals and supplies can be had from the nearby store. The cave is only a few miles from Provo or Pleasant Grove, on a paved road, which is normally free from snow between April and November.

6. LEHMAN CAVES NATIONAL MONUMENT
[*Nevada*]

THE EARTH FORCES were experimenting when the caves discovered by Ab Lehman, the Nevada pioneer homesteader, were in course of construction. No two rooms in these caverns are alike. Strange stone faces, animals, and figurines line the paths of the easy trails. A rippled curtain of stone here, gracefully tapered stalactites there; and high-arched, multicolored ceilings over all. The great artist tried almost every device that was later to bewilder the human eye.

Pools of water on the floors have built tiny, beautifully terraced dikes, or dams, around their edges, and have deposited a white, spongy, nodular growth in the pool itself. Huge fluted columns reach from floor to ceiling. Tiny needle crystals, peculiar mushroom effects, frosty incrustations in infinitely varied forms, grow on the larger shapes, or cover the walls and ceilings where the others do not occur.

Some stalactites here grew laterally in one plane, forming graceful draperies of dripstone, or translucent ribbon like partitions, or "bacon-strips." Thin round disks of dripstone were deposited on the flat bedrock ceilings, and as the lengthening stalactites that hung from them grew heavier, these plates were slowly peeled away. These strange structures, called tom-toms, because when struck they give a drum sound, are abundant throughout the caves.

The Lehman Caves are in the heart of a region of wide basins and towering mountain ranges, five miles west of Baker. The mighty Snake Range, on the eastern edge of the state, is topped by Wheeler Peak, over thirteen thousand feet high, one of the higher mountains of the Great Basin. On the eastern side of this peak the monument, one square mile in area, is found in the belt of piñon and juniper. There are mule deer in the meadows and higher forests of pine, spruce, and mountain mahogany. Cougars are not uncommon in this wilderness, but casual visitors are not likely to see them, for they have learned that the combination of man, dog, and rifle is catastrophic even to big and ferocious predators.

In a deep deposit just adjacent to the natural entrance of the caves the skeleton remains of prehistoric Indians have been found, indicating that many thousands of years ago it was used as a burial chamber.

The National Park Service maintains attractive overnight camp and picnic facilities in the headquarters area of the monument. Refreshments, limited food service, and overnight cabins are maintained near headquarters by a concessioner operating under contract with the government. There are also many beautifully situated campsites in the nearby Nevada National Forest.

7. OREGON CAVES NATIONAL MONUMENT
[Oregon]

IT IS INTERESTING to note the variety of accidents that led to the discovery by modern man of those caves which are now included in the primitive areas of the National Park System. There is no doubt that prehistoric men of North America knew about most of them and used them for refuge, burial, or other purposes. The presumption is that the flight of bats from the cave entrance may have attracted the attention of the first white men to Carlsbad Caverns; but of the others, the two in South Dakota attracted notice by the whistling of the wind that rushed in and out of their small apertures. Mammoth Cave was discovered by a pioneer hunter pursuing a wounded bear; Ab Lehman was driving cattle when his horse stumbled into an opening in the ground, which thus revealed the Nevada caverns; and, finally, another hunter, pursuing another bear, is said to have found Oregon Caves.

The only natural openings of many of the great caves seem to have been so small as to escape attention. A slight rockslide or growth of brush would hide these openings effectively. This has been true in the Pyrenees, where cave hunters resort to an ingenious method of discovery. Through field glasses they watch the flight of jackdaws—birds that resemble our American grackle—on a mountainside. The jackdaw is one of the few birds known to nest and rear its young in caves, and the French speleologist Casteret tells of observing the flight of the fledglings in the chambers of a cave, where they spend an apprenticeship in lateral flying before they attempt to ascend to the mouth of the cavern.

One wonders whether in the United States there may not be vast limestone caverns as yet unknown, either because the small openings have been unobserved or because they have no visible outlets.

While the Oregon Caves are not in limestone, they are in a marble rock that represents a former limestone which became changed under terrific heat and pressure and later was raised above the sea as part of a mountain range. Marble is dissolved out by the action of surface water charged with carbonic acid from decaying vegetation, so the Oregon caves were formed in much the typical way.

The deposits in these caves assume grotesque shapes as well as pleasing forms. Here and there are miniatures of lakes or waterfalls, done in stone. Among the early visitors here was Joaquin Miller, the Poet of the Sierra, who celebrated "the Marble Hills of Oregon" in many of his writings.

There is guide service through the electrically lighted caves throughout the year, and in summer there are accommodations and meals in a mountain chateau and in cabins. There is also a picnic area, but no camping is permitted in the monument, though there are adequate facilities at the Greyback Campground, eight miles away on the approach highway.

[VI]

The Ice Moves Down

THE LONG SUMMER *was over. For ages a tropical climate had prevailed over a great part of the earth, and animals whose home is now beneath the equator roamed over the world to the very borders of the arctics. . . . But their reign was over. A sudden intense winter, that was also to last for ages, fell upon the globe; it spread over the very countries where the tropical animals had their homes, and so suddenly did it come upon them that they were embalmed beneath masses of snow and ice, without time even for the decay which follows death.*

—LOUIS AGASSIZ, *Geological Sketches*

1. ACADIA NATIONAL PARK
[*Maine*]

SOME YEARS AGO a minor poet, having visited Mount Desert Island, in Maine, upon which the greater part of Acadia National Park is situated, referred to it as "the most beautiful island in the world." This sort of statement, I confess, always irritates me. It is a double impertinence, a discharge of both barrels of egotism at once. It assumes that the writer has seen all the islands of the world—an impossibility—and it also conveys the assumption that whatever the writer considers most beautiful the reader must tamely accept as his own standard. Let us have done with such nonsense.

Besides, even if Mount Desert Island is actually the most beautiful island in the world, the description utterly fails to do justice to this rock-built natural fortress which thrusts forward into the Atlantic and challenges its

Climbers meet a great crevasse on Sperry Glacier. Glacier National Park. [Photo: Jack E. Boucher]

power. You may have affecting beauty in a meadow sprinkled with daisies and paint-flowers; in any glen where dryads frisk in the evening hours; but where can you find anything in our country to match these mountains that come down to the ocean, these granite cliffs alongside which the biggest ship could ride, these bays dotted with lovely islets clothed in hardwood and hemlock, altogether such a sweep of rugged coastline as has no parallel from Florida to the Canadian provinces?

This is the theme of Acadia—the final expression of a strange act of nature by which the ocean flooded in upon an ancient, worn-down land surface and turned its high hills into islands, its rivers into slender arms of the sea, and its wider valleys into bays and gulfs. And having done this, then all was dressed at last, in the greenest of green vegetation, soothing to the eye, hospitable to migrating birds, a kind shelter to browsing animals. Everything is here to rejoice the soul of the human visitor—the combination of summer warmth from the mainland, the fresh salt tang from the sea, cool sleepful nights, silvery dawns and the reddest of sunsets, and unforgettable pictures from any height of granite rock. Beauty, certainly, but far more. Visitors to Acadia take their place with the long line of Maine homefolk, part farmer, part sailor and fisherman, and with their summer guests, who discovered long ago that this is a place where you can stand with one foot in the brine and one on the blossomy land, fish with one hand and pick blueberries with the other—in short, be a Janus and look two ways at once.

Strange forces of nature have worked to contrive a landscape that makes Mount Desert and Acadia National Park unique. If you look at the map of Maine, you will see something very strange about its coast. From Portland across to St. Croix, drawing a straight line, is less than 200 miles. But between the two places, if you were to follow the tortuous line where the ocean touches the land, you would travel 2,500 miles, or about the distance by sea from New York City to a Venezuelan port. Good hikers, who usually carry in their pockets a topographic map, will guess what happened to produce the astonishing result. In any hilly country, if you set yourself to follow that brown contour line on your topographic map which shows a height of, say, 300 feet, you would expect to ramble a long distance, as opposed to cutting straight across country, up hill and down. The present Maine coast is precisely a contour line drawn on an upland surface by an ocean which drowned everything up to that level.

An ancient valley, then, is now the Gulf of Maine; the little valleys and rivers and smaller streams that once flowed into the big valley are now arms and fingers of the sea. Somes Sound, which nearly divides the island into two

From the top of Cadillac the seascape writes indelibly on the memory. Acadia National Park. [*Photo: Jack E. Boucher*]

parts, is probably one of the deeper-cut valleys that existed long before the coastline was depressed; and so sheer is the drop from mountains to the floor of the sound that the greatest ocean liner could find plenty of water near shore. And when you see the lobster-trap buoys sometimes so near the edge of the rocky promontories that you could hit them with a pebble, you realize how for ages the sea has been attacking the hard stone, undercutting the cliffs, and dropping their upper parts into the hungering maw. Brave the rocks are, and grand in their defiance of the sea, but the end is foreseen. The ocean always wins. But as a visitor, you will have ample time to enjoy the present duel.

What caused this Maine coast to sink and the sea to rush in? That goes back to another story, and the evidences of that story are everywhere you look in Acadia and on the mainland behind the park. The great ice sheet is supposed to have depressed Mount Desert Island as much as 600 feet. The

solid rocks are not so inflexible as they appear, and the outer crust of the earth will give and rebound; for after the final surge of ice from the north had melted away, the land rose again. But it never came back to the previous level, as is shown by the old sea cliffs and beaches on the mountains 250 feet above the present ocean shore. As you go along the road beneath the two smaller peaks known as The Bubbles, you will see one of the great erratic boulders dropped by the glacial ice almost on the very top. It looks precariously perched, but actually it would be hard to move.

Although the skilled geologist will laugh at my simplicity, I cannot help feeling a likeness between this great granite intrusion of the Mount Desert country and the granite that came up beneath the covering rocks of the Black Hills in South Dakota. Superficially the weathered exposures are entirely different. In the Black Hills the granite is worn down into towering pinnacles; here in Acadia all is smoothed and rounded by glacial ice, and you may see places where scratches and crescents were made by the rocks the glacier used for tools. But standing on the mushroom summit of Cadillac Mountain, and looking about on one of the greatest land-and-ocean scenes of America—so different from anything in the West—I cannot help considering how Mount Harney and its surrounding peaks would look if they had been subjected to seaboard forces like those that molded Acadia. A road winds around Cadillac till you reach the very top, with ample parking space there. And what a view is this!

Frenchman Bay on one side, with the little Porcupine Islands, which resemble amphibians swimming out to sea; Great Cranberry and Little Cranberry to the south, with the blue Atlantic behind them; and on the horizon still more islands that were once mainland mountaintops. Eastward the eye traces the jagged coast on its way to New Brunswick, and on the land side, on a clear day, Mount Katahdin and the White Hills of New Hampshire can be distinguished. And even if the day is not perfectly clear, it is a grand thing to look upon. For myself, I do not mind if a bit of fog comes wreathing in, curling among the estuaries, blotting out one marine view only to reveal another. Indeed, you may well ask for a little fog—not too much!—to complete the picture, for the fog patches here are like the clouds for which the outdoor photographer lies in wait.

If you look at a map of Acadia National Park, you will see that the boundary is very vagrant: a big block of the park east of Somes Sound, an area across Frenchman Bay on the Schoodic Peninsula, and other segments

The cliffs fall sheer to deep water. Acadia National Park. [Photo: Jack E. Boucher]

scattered about among private lands, not forgetting fractions on the islands. There is a reason. The Western national parks have mainly grown, you may say, from the inside out: they were federal lands diverted to the high park uses, and they try to exclude, when the money is available, sections that are still privately owned. Acadia is the opposite. It has grown from the outside in. There were no federal lands to be diverted; the park has come into existence through the generosity of heart and purse of idealists who, having tasted the beauties and joys of the region, longed to make it the protected, preserved haven of all the people. It will continue to expand that way. Meanwhile, what there is of it is superb.

Land and sea, woodland, lake, and mountain are all contained in a neat package in Acadia National Park. This, added to the fact that Mount Desert is exactly where the northern and the temperate zones meet and overlap, results in a land-and-sea bird congregation that will delight the amateur naturalist. The number of warblers that either nest on the island or visit it when migrating is exceptional. Among them are the flashing redstart, the myrtle, the black-and-white, the magnolia, the yellow palm, and the brilliant yellow.

The osprey, that expert but victimized fisherman, is always to be seen along the shore and over the lakes. Also, you may have the luck to see the bald eagle executing his airway robbery at the expense of the osprey. The black ducks, goldeneyes, and scaups and the eiders and old squaws are conspicuous in winter and spring.

Those who come from inland to see this land-and-sea national park will always be most interested in the sights of the rocky coastline. The harbor seal is frequently observed along the shore of the island and on the ledges that lie outside. The fishermen who depend on their nets and weirs for a livelihood are not so enthusiastic about the sportive harbor seal as are the rest of us. The seal refuses to admit that any fish is private property. The most he will admit is that a net may be.

At certain times of the year whales may be seen spouting close to shore or lying near the surface. Porpoises are commonly seen by those who make boat trips to the outlying islands or in the waters of Frenchman Bay. The smaller marine forms—mussels, crabs, and occasionally a lobster that gets entangled in the seaweed and washes ashore—and the sea anemones and other creatures of the changing tides are of unfailing interest to those who for the first time get the tang of the ocean in their nostrils.

I am in Acadia National Park on an afternoon in late June. One of the many sylvan footpaths and fire-control roads passes a swampy pond, a glacial

Retreat of the ice sheet left this boulder perched on the edge of South Bubble. Acadia National Park. [Photo: M. Woodbridge Williams]

remnant on its way to becoming dry land in time, but there still is plenty of shallow water with lush vegetation. Somebody has dumped gravel to make a dry-shod approach to the water's edge. The round-leaf sundew has come up through the gravel and, with its sticky leaves, sets a snare for tiny insects. Over at one side of the footway a single pitcher plant, the Jedediah Smith of the plant-trappers, rears its head from the water. Behind it a pair of inquiring eyes is fixed on me—those of a frog that has just dunked in.

The air is bland, but a faint breeze has zest in it, and in the open spaces among the reedy growth the sky-blue reflections are rippled. The stickwork of a beaver dam is out just in front of me. I watch awhile for a beaver to appear, but none comes. Behind me in a natural plantation of poplar, I have already seen where these tireless and inventive woodsmen have been at work. Dozens of trees as big through as my upper arm show the neat chiseling of the teeth. The bottom end of the felled trees is a cone; and where the beaver has left his felling job unfinished, the cut is in the shape of an hourglass. I wonder at just which point in the cutting the animal dodges and gets from under.

[263]

Something comes swimming straight toward me: a muskrat, making good time, half out of water, with easy strokes. He finally sees me standing there, jams his rudder hard aport, and without too much concern sets a course straight back again. There are plenty of birds flitting about, but they are unusually quiet—a chip here and a twitter there.

Nothing exciting happens. The surrounding hills shimmer a little in a filmy haze. I come away from the spot with a pleasant feeling of partnership in all the small business transactions of the wild. Several thousands of eyes have been looking at me all the while—little lives I could not see with mine. I am not a naturalist. My perception misses a good deal. I do not flatter myself that any of the creatures has overrated me; not even that they had any keen interest in me. Yet I do have the agreeable sensation that I have not, as a guest, been unwelcome.

It is now three days since I saw a newspaper headline. I feel relaxed. A little swampy pond in a national park can be a healing thing, I find.

The history of the white man on Mount Desert goes back into the earliest days of the exploration of North America. Champlain came in 1604, and nearly a century later Louis XIV gave the island to the Sieur de la Mothe Cadillac, who signed himself Seigneur des Monts Deserts. The French word did not imply what we now call a desert; it described a wild uninhabited land. It was, indeed, heavily forested.

In the early part of the nineteenth century the only settlers were fisherman farmers who sold off the virgin timber and lived an austere but healthy and self-reliant life. But about the middle of the century, Mount Desert began to be discovered. New York and Boston people—the venturesome sort for that day—came in and "roughed it," finding the native people hospitable, ungreedy, intelligent. Then, naturally, came summer homes, boardinghouses, and finally large hotels and "development." That part of the island which is outside the park is still a vacationland, for people of modest incomes as well as for the rich.

I have seen the journal kept by a New York paterfamilias who spent about six weeks on the island in the summer of 1855. It was a family of ten, with friends also; and they journeyed into what then seemed like the utter northern frontier, with some misgivings. As they felt they would need a tie to conventions and culture, they ordered a grand piano sent up from Boston, and installed it in the home of the sturdy Mr. Somes, one of the earliest natives to accept boarders. After the piano had brought unusual pleasure to the islanders, who were generously invited for miles to enjoy it, the instrument went back to Boston by schooner, being reverently loaded at Southwest Harbor.

The New York family was enraptured. The writer of the diary galloped into dithyrambs over such beauty and wildness and inspiring scenes as he had never experienced. They kept Sundays faithfully. Some Boston ladies came up to Bar Harbor for a few days. They "appeared like superior persons; but we were willing to let them go by without acquaintance because of their slack notions of Sunday-keeping." What Papa would have said if the Boston ladies had appeared in shorts and halters one shudders to consider. The schooner would have called for the grand piano at once.

Papa of the large family, back in New York, ended his diary: "The expedition has been interesting and often exciting, in a very high degree. It will be the fund of story and conversation for years to come. The children come back broader, browner and stronger than they went."

I will wager that Papa went back the following year, bought a piece of land, and built a cottage on Mount Desert; and perhaps his heirs have been among those generous souls who later gave their land to help establish Acadia National Park.

Fog shuts down on a lobsterman. Acadia National Park. [Photo: Paul M. Tilden]

2. GRAND TETON NATIONAL PARK
[*Wyoming*]

THE IMPRESSION made by the Teton Range is indelible. No matter how many years afterward, if one were shown a photograph of these Wyoming mountains, just south of Yellowstone National Park, there would be not a moment's hesitation. "I know those peaks. Those are the Tetons. And *that* peak is the Grand Teton."

This is not because of their beauty, though their beauty is ravishing. Other mountains and other ranges are beautiful too. It is partly because from any point where you are likely to come to rest to look at them, the eye involuntarily puts a frame around them. Close your eyes, you who have seen the Tetons, and bring them back to mind as you saw them. Is it not a framed picture? But this surpassing individuality arises even more from the way they were created and from the forces that later worked upon them to create their aspiring peaks.

Once upon a time (perhaps all references to geological periods should have that fairy-tale beginning), when the Rockies were heaving and straining in their orogenic labor, the earth crust cracked along this forty-mile line, the "Teton fault." There came a time when the rocks on both sides of the fault began to slip, one along the other; one rising, the other going down. It was not a sharp catastrophe. How long the movement went on is not known and is really not important. But when the slip had ended and the rocks had come to rest, the Tetons were towering seven thousand feet above the basin now called Jackson Hole. In the ensuing centuries, as the Tetons were being torn down, Jackson Hole was filling up with the debris; so perhaps the relationship, in height and depth, has not greatly changed.

So you see that the Tetons, as you view them from Jackson Hole, are mountains without foothills. They rise impetuously from almost level land on the Wyoming side. On the Idaho side of the range it is different. The mountain block was tilted to the west as it rose, just as was the greater uplift of the Sierra, where it accounts for those foothills through which you wind on your way to the sequoia country. One may imagine that before the tearing-down processes began, the eastern side of the Teton block presented a colossal sheer escarpment of crystalline rocks, frowning bluntly upon the depression below. Actually such a stark wall never existed, because erosion and uplift were working in unison; but I think it aids comprehension if one pictures it that way.

Grand Teton National Park

The wondrous jagged outline, the cirques and horns and knife-edged ridges, the headlong slopes and pinnacles that characterize the Tetons as you see them from the perfect observation point provided by Jackson Hole, were to be the later work of storm and frost, wind and sun, and chiefly of that master carver, ice. There came an age when at high elevations the snow accumulated faster than it could melt, piling up such depths that rivers of ice began to move and pluck and tear, bringing down burdens of broken rock to the lowlands. There are still impressive glaciers and snowfields in the Tetons.

Where the ancient and much greater glaciers stopped and began to retreat, embankments of debris were left, called moraines, and behind these were formed lakes. Thus came into being Jackson, Jenny, Phelps, Taggart, and Leigh Lakes, and the other bodies of water, without whose enchantment the Teton picture would be incomplete. To see the Tetons mirrored in Jackson Lake early on a clear summer morning when not a breath of wind is stirring and the image of the range is so sharply defined that its identical twin lives in the water—this is an experience never to be forgotten in discovering the real America.

The tent is not yet secured, but little sister sends a message to someone. Acadia National Park. [Photo: M. Woodbridge Williams]

Just as it is easy to understand the lure of this Rocky Mountain retreat for present-day Americans, so it is not hard to believe that the aesthetic quality of the surroundings was fully appreciated by the Indians in their time and by the fur traders who so well knew this ground. Can anyone suppose that the red man could look upon such a scene without a thrill, and an inner impulse of devotion? Or even that the Colters and Sublettes, Smiths and Bridgers and Fitzpatricks, though their tough muscles and iron wills were bent upon their trade, could come back to Jackson Hole after long journeys without a similar feeling? Other holes these men used for rendezvous, truly, but there was only one like Jackson Hole, which Sublette named for a fellow trapper, David E. Jackson, who was said to be especially enamored of the basin.

The winters were savage in this region then, as they usually are now. It was no place for a weakling when the first white settlers came there to home-stead, in the mid-1880's. Less stubborn men and women than those first settlers would not have remained a second year, despite the beauty of the spot. Early in 1949 three or four approaches to Jackson Hole were closed for months by continuous storms. Yet, interestingly enough, in March of that year, three men—all skillful and seasoned climbers—made the ascent of the Grand Teton, a challenging feat at any time.

Exactly here is a good place to speak of climbing 13,766-foot Grand Teton and other peaks of the range. This range is ranked by practiced moun-taineers all over the world as among the most delightfully defiant. Every year sees increasing numbers of alpinists coming from abroad to test their skill against the Tetons. There are those who regard such difficult and dangerous ventures as foolhardy. I am not one of these, though personally I shall choose easier delights. My own notion of excessive temerity goes no farther than pre-empting the favorite window chair of the oldest member of some club like the Union or the Somerset. That is danger enough for me. But I seem to see that these rugged fellows in the hobnailed boots, with their ice axes and rope, risking their necks to say no to the impossible, may after all be inheri-tors of the spirit of those undaunted primates who insisted on rearing up and walking on their hind legs at a time when swinging from branch to branch was accepted as positively a permanent condition. If Prometheus had not challenged invincible Zeus, we should have no steam heat.

It does not follow that the mere wish to scale the Teton peaks will end happily. Those who have not served the hard apprenticeship of this sport will be well advised to get the services of experienced guides who are author-ized to serve in this capacity. Of course, the tyro may find some good climb-ers to accompany, but the chances are that before the end of the bout the

The Tetons seen from the Idaho side. Grand Teton National Park. [Photo: William Henry Jackson, 1879]

adepts will wish they had left their companion at home. Under all circumstances rangers and guides should be consulted before any attempt at climbing is made, and each expedition is required to report at park headquarters or at Jenny Museum before and after the trip. Climbing alone is absolutely prohibited.

The usual climbing season embraces July, August, and September, though weather and snow conditions are uncertain, naturally. Usually two days are allowed for an ascent of Grand Teton, Moran, or Owen. For other peaks, one day may suffice.

The trails of Grand Teton National Park are truly magnificent, and most visitors will be well satisfied to leave the alpinists to their special thrill and go afoot or on saddle horses over these ninety miles of adventure, constructed to give the very best experiences for the least possible physical exertion. For those who wish to ride these trails, a concessioner, with a fine string of saddle horses and with equipment for long or short trips, will be found at the south end of Jenny Lake.

The lakes trail parallels the mountains, following closely the base of the Tetons and skirting the shore of each large lake from Leigh to Phelps. Leigh and Jenny Lakes are completely circled by trails.

Teton Glacier Trail goes up the east slope of Grand Teton to Surprise and Amphitheater Lakes. The end of this trail is at Amphitheater Lake, which is the starting point for the climb to Teton Glacier. All along this trail are superb views of the surrounding country.

On the Indian Paintbrush Trail, which begins near the outlet of Leigh Lake, not only is there a profusion of wild flowers for gay company, but the chances are good for seeing some of the park's large animals, especially Shiras moose. What this creature lacks in beauty he duly compensates for in bulk, and, unlike some of the others of the deer family, he is not timid about being watched. You will probably see mule deer along this trail, too. This trail connects with the Cascade Canyon Trail by way of the small but exquisite Lake Solitude, and one of the finest views of the looming Tetons is to be had across this body of water.

Cascade Canyon and Death Canyon Trails pass through deep and impressive chasms, whose walls rise sheer. Death Canyon Trail, as awesome as its name, emerges finally into broad meadows. Cascade Canyon Trail leads into the deepest recesses of the mountains, along the bases of the great peaks.

Skyline Trail, from the head of South Cascade Canyon to the head of the north fork of Death Canyon, passes through a part of Alaska Basin and to the west of the Limestone Wall at the head of Avalanche Canyon.

In isolated parts of Grand Teton National Park there are small herds of Rocky Mountain sheep, or bighorn, and there are bears in the mountains and canyons, but these are not numerous, and until visitors learn not to fraternize with this animal, perhaps it is just as well. Cheerful ground squirrels and chipmunks are everywhere, and there are beavers, martens, minks, coyotes, and other small animals. More than one hundred species of birds have been identified. In a park where movement of humans is practically restricted to Mr. Shanks' or somebody else's mare, the relationship between people and wildlife tends to be on a fine basis.

The botanists tell us that the plantlife of the Tetons is in some respects unique. The high mountains have proved to be a barrier that many forms could not cross. The region is the range limit for many plants deriving from

The classic fault: uplifted range seen from Jackson Hole. Grand Teton National Park. [Photo: George Grant]

all four points of the compass, and there are a few known only to the Tetons. The flowering period begins in the park as soon as the ridges and flats are free from snow, usually in May, and continues until about mid-August in the higher places, so there is bloom of some sort continuously in spring and summer. Though much of the Teton Range is above timberline, the usual Rocky Mountain evergreens clothe the lower parts of the mountains and fringe the many lakes.

Jackson Hole is in every respect the complement, the fulfilling adjunct, to the Teton Range. Historically it completes the scene of discovery and pioneering. Geologically it is the other half of a story. And it supplies the sloping stadium seats, so to speak, from which the majestic mountains are witnessed in their glory. All this was understood many years ago, and among those who realized the importance of Jackson Hole to the park was John D. Rockefeller, Jr., whose keen and generous understanding had already done so much to ensure the integrity of many of the finest examples of American scenery.

Rockefeller's interest, once enlisted, went to work in the usual practical way. It was asked then, and unthinking people still ask in similar cases, why it was necessary to make a part of the National Park System an area that nobody could ever carry away and that would always provide a site for viewing the Tetons. What harm could there be in leaving it in private hands? Any sensitive visitor to the national parks can give the answer to that. One of the joys of being in these preserved spots is the consciousness and the observation that there is at least a brave attempt to keep the scenery free from the ugliness of commercial exploitation. One comes to look at the beauties of nature, not to gaze on intruding claimants for attention, some tawdry, some impudent, and even when least offensive, still out of place.

Over many years, Rockefeller, through a corporation set up for the purpose, acquired 33,562 acres of land in Jackson Hole, with the intention of presenting it to the American people at such a time as he could feel assured that the lands would be administered by the National Park Service. On March 15, 1943, President Roosevelt proclaimed an area of about 223,000 acres, 173,000 of which were already owned by the government, as Jackson Hole National Monument. This child of the National Park System, however, came into the world with a birthmark in the form of angry litigation.

It is all settled now. Today there is no Jackson Hole National Monument. The Tetons and Jackson Hole are what they should have been many years ago: one national park. There is no possible good in rehashing the sorry story of verbal violence and political maneuvering that followed upon the Presidential proclamation of 1943. Most of the participants in the outcry, in Wyoming and elsewhere, are sufficiently ashamed of having been so easily drifted across the legal landscape ahead of a small group of interested persons who were afraid of the loss of long-enjoyed benefits accruing from the use of public lands. The clamor long ago died down and was kept alive only by poking. In September 1950 President Truman signed an act of Congress that established the enlarged park.

The compromise—it had to be somewhat of a compromise—was not altogether satisfactory from the viewpoint of those who would like to see fewer rather than more management problems in the national park. For example, ever since the white man came to the Teton and Jackson Hole region the elk, or wapiti, one of our finest big-game animals, has been of the greatest impor-

But you must know how. Grand Teton National Park. [Photo: Herb Pownall]

tance and interest. In spring it leaves the low country and the Elk Refuge near the town of Jackson and moves into the higher lands north and east. Some small bands go into the Teton Range for the summer. When the snow falls, the elk return to the refuge.

It is on this return, in crossing open country, that the elk herd is usually thinned by a great assemblage of sportsmen, curiously and variously armed, in all stages of emotional elevation. But sometimes the elk do not come down on schedule, or they perform a quick migration before the armament can be assembled. If this occurs and the thinning does not take place, the elk tend further to outrun their natural feed.

The fishing in Grand Teton is considered very good. During most of the summer fish may be taken with artificial fly, but in Jackson and Jenny Lakes the mackinaws must be taken with heavy tackle by trolling. Cutthroats (locally known as blackspotted trout) and Eastern brooks are in the park waters.

Among the many reasons for visiting the museum at Jenny Lake is the collection devoted to mountaineering. There are also exhibits showing the history and geology and the plants and wildlife of the area. Adjacent to the museum is an open-air amphitheater where campfire talks are given. Nature walks, all-day hikes, and auto caravans are conducted regularly by naturalist guides.

3. ROCKY MOUNTAIN NATIONAL PARK
[Colorado]

"THIS CITADEL OF EARTH; this outpost of heaven."

As a description of the Colorado Rockies, you might think this a trifle perfervid—a little on the hysterical side. But pause. Let us consider the manner of man who uttered the words. Samuel Bowles, the founder and publisher of the Springfield (Massachusetts) *Republican*, a newspaper that carried the flag of literacy to all the Eastern seaboard in the middle of the last century, was a great economist of praise. Some thought him a severe, metallic person. He had attained the reputation with himself of never being wrong about anything; therefore his newspaper could not be in error.

Tell me whether you would quarrel with the dictum of a man like that. Not I. And besides, the recollection of my own first sight of the Rockies and the journey into their magnificence is so vivid to this very day that I am not disposed to weigh any poetic flight.

Far out on the plains, east of Denver, clouds appear to be gathering in the

Camping with elbow room. Rocky Mountain National Park. [*Photo: M. Wood-bridge Williams*]

west. They are not clouds. Drive only a little more on your westward trend to a point, say, thirty-five miles out from the city, on what was called the Smoky Hill road, and you no longer doubt your eyes. The great Barrier Wall confronts you. You are already a mile above sea level, or somewhere near it, but on the landscape on three sides of you there is nothing to indicate it. On the remaining side, the Front Range of the Rockies, drawing a horizon line far up the sky, seems to warn you that you shall go no farther. There is more United States beyond, you know; indeed, the San Franciscan making a trip to Salt Lake City says that he is going "back east"; and you are not so naive as not to know that there are passes through the mountains that will take you into the Great Basin. Still, the impact of the first sight of the Great Barrier is stunning.

You do go on. You do find shrewdly engineered roads of fine quality, and you do easily find yourself before long in the very heart of the Front Range of the Rockies, marveling at what is one of the greatest mountain masses in

"I took a few pictures of the park. Would you like to see some of them?" Courtesy requires a warm affirmative. Rocky Mountain National Park. [Photo: M. Woodbridge Williams]

the world. For *mass* is the word. There are higher peaks elsewhere. The eastern escarpment of the Sierra may be even more precipitous. But for sheer sense of towering density, of closely packed mountaintops, I know of nothing like this. And today your course will probably be steered toward one of the entrances to Rocky Mountain National Park, for, of all the national parks, this one is perhaps the most accessible to the greatest number of populous states, being but a short distance from Denver and an overnight trip from most of the Midwest. But the accessibility reaches farther than this. Nowhere else can the tourist so easily attain the high mountains and achieve familiarity with them.

These majestic mountains are amiable. Even Longs Peak, 14,255 feet above sea level, is not difficult to climb for those who are properly equipped and in good condition and take the advice of a park ranger. But within the four hundred square miles of park there are sixty-five other named peaks more than ten thousand feet high; and of these, fifteen are more than thirteen thousand feet high. True, one starts from an elevation of eight thousand feet; but the real reason why these might be called the Intimate Rockies, aside from the peculiar incident of their formation by nature, is that roads and trails have been so constructed that visitors can view with ease sights that almost anywhere else would cost great physical effort.

Think of a fine, transcontinental road, of which eleven miles are above the timberline of eleven thousand feet, and four miles are above twelve thousand feet! This is Trail Ridge Road. Bear Lake Road leads to a network of trails where hikers can go on to mountain peaks or into lake-studded gorges. Old Fall River Road is narrow and one-way-controlled, the sort of challenge to good driving and the kind of path to adventure well remembered by many a motorist who navigated in the mountain country only a few years ago.

Good morning, Miss! Yes, I'll join you in a snack. Rocky Mountain National Park.
[Photo: M. Woodbridge Williams]

After winding along its steep, forest-bordered course, the one-way road joins the modern Trail Ridge Road.

Although Rocky Mountain National Park is open all year, Trail Ridge Road is normally closed to trans-mountain travel by snow about the end of October, opening again about the first of June. But, as in other primeval parks, those who can arrange to enjoy them before and after the great rush of summer travel have a real reward. A friend of mine who lives not more than seventy miles from several beautiful sea beaches said to me not long ago: "I never go down to the beaches in summer. I wait till the winy, sunny days in the fall, when the hotels and boardinghouses and cottages are closed. I have the beach to myself—along with a few others who feel as I do. It isn't that I don't like people; it's just that the things I go for are not there for me when there are crowds."

All the wild animals you expect to find in the high country are in Rocky Mountain; but the elk and the mule deer are especially abundant. Outstanding, naturally, is that noble old-time resident the Rocky Mountain bighorn. These animals are not to be seen, except accidentally, without going up into the high places where they feed and have protection from their enemies, the cat family. But those hikers who see them on Specimen Mountain or at Sheep Lake have something to tell about. The beavers are everywhere, logging and constructing. They are the army engineers of the animal world; they never see a running stream without having thoughts of a dam. But beavers are shy, and you must be patient and quiet before you can see them at their business locations.

Here, too, if you love birds, even if you are not an expert, you may meet some old friends and some new ones. Above timberline, pipits, rosy finches, horned larks, and ptarmigans are often seen, and anywhere you can strike up an expensive acquaintance with the Rocky Mountain jay, known as the camp robber, who will filch any article not weighted down. John Muir tells of his taking a cake of soap and a towel down to a brook one morning for a wash. He lathered himself, laid the soap on a rock at his feet, made one pass across his face with the towel, and saw one of these feathered kleptomaniacs swooping off with his soap, all in a split second.

Looking back through the years, it is interesting to note that this Colorado mountain fastness was one of the first to be appreciated by holiday-makers. A party from the East went into what is now part of Rocky Mountain National Park long before Yellowstone was revealed, and came to a deserted mining village. "Here we found welcome. Half the place was *pre-occupied* by a large party of men and women, some 20 to 30 in all, from the villages

Where beavers abandoned their house. Rocky Mountain National Park. [*Photo: Roger Contor*]

in the lower country . . . they had ox teams for their baggage, saddle animals to carry themselves, and a cow to furnish fresh milk. Thus generously equipped, they were jollily entering upon camp life for ten days or a fortnight up among the mountain tops."

Think of that! These were pioneers, already living no delicate life in the lower altitudes. But the lure of the higher places drew them; they wanted that "distinctive charm of the atmosphere, so clear and dry and pure all the while, as to be a perpetual *feeling*, rather than a vision, of beauty."

There were even forerunners of the concessioners who now serve the public in the national parks. Here were a man and wife and daughter who had driven a herd of forty or fifty milch cows up from southern Colorado and were making 150 pounds of butter a week, selling it to eager campers at seventy-five cents a pound, and paying all their expenses with the increase in their herd. And this was back in the middle part of last century, in a period when the Utes were killing four thousand antelope in a grand hunt of three weeks.

No doubt the keynote of this park is the rugged uplift picture as a whole, with its gorges, its glacial carvings and moraines; its alpine lakes, profuse and of sumptuous beauty; the flattops on which even a soft and sedentary tourist can feel himself on the world's roof; hanging valleys and plunging streams, eternal snows, even small glaciers. That is the impact on the visual sense. But against this mighty background is the loveliness and imaginative appeal of the second look. There are the flowers. All through the Rockies, it is true, you are constantly delighted with the bloom that begins when the snow has hardly begun to retreat and ends only when all is frozen and blanketed. But here in Rocky Mountain, with such a wide range of elevations, the variety of plantlife is remarkable. In the park are more than seven hundred species of flowering plants. Perhaps the best known is the blue columbine, the Colorado state flower. But the gentians and lilies, the paintbrushes and primroses are ever with you in your ascent from zone to zone, till finally, above timberline, mats of flowers spread everywhere. In June on the north slope of Twin Sisters the alpine moss campion, clinging to every space where there is nourishment between the rocks, makes a crazy quilt wonderful to look upon; and later in the season the sight is repeated on Fall River Pass, Flattop, and Longs Peak.

To many, the great dramatic moment of a visit to Rocky Mountain will be witnessing the struggle at timberline. Timberline is a mountain climatic zone, which varies, partly, according to the latitude. In the White Mountains of New Hampshire, timberline is only a few thousand feet. Here it is very high—about 11,500 feet. Timberline is the place where plantlife says: "I *will* live. I shall bend. I shall creep on hands and knees. I shall dodge, devise, join hands, and compromise; but I *will* live. Let the cruel gales blow; let the snow and ice pile up; if I cannot grow as I would like, I shall still grow."

Below that timberline you see fair-growing, luxuriant yellow pine, lodgepole and Douglas fir, Engelmann spruce and aspens, with the fine Colorado blue spruce, alder, and birch along the streams. But once at the deadline, how different! Aged trees, lacking symmetry and bent like staggering crones under a heavy burden, sometimes stand out alone; again the dwarfed trees have grown so closely packed, for mutual protection, that they appear as a woven mat in which the strands of differing trees can hardly be distinguished. In places snowdrifts mulch the creeping trees; the shoots emerging above the snow are promptly nipped, but those beneath the protecting blanket grow outward defiantly. If the ice tears and strips the bark upon the windward

Wild sheep on McGregor Mountain. Rocky Mountain National Park. [*Photo: Merlin K. Potts*]

side, no matter. Half a bark is better than none: the tree will make do. Little caves of scrub growth are formed, where the hiker, caught in one of those storms which blow so suddenly at the alpine level, can take shelter. But thrashed unmercifully though these insistent plants are, they cannot be subdued. For every one that, beaten or dying of old age, gives up the struggle, another is ready to take its place.

Above the timberline, where it would seem impossible for any vegetation to exist, much less to produce a lovely carpet of bloom, is the Alpine tundra. We associate such a meadow of grasses, lichens, mosses, and stunted plants with the Arctic regions. Indeed, to see anything resembling what is shown on the mountaintops of Rocky Mountain National Park, one would have to go, in our own country, to Alaska. There is a nature trail, beginning at the Rock Cut parking area more than twelve thousand feet above sea level, where visitors, advisedly at a slow pace, may observe this phenomenon of pygmy vegetation not merely existing, but thriving, in a mantle of moist wet soil— plants that have needed perhaps several hundred years to attain the growth one now observes. Yet these indomitable little dwarfs—forgetmenots, avens, harebells, and other species—put forth their gay flowers in July, invite the pollinating insects, and go to seed in a season that cannot be more than six weeks and is usually less. Do not tread on the plants when you walk this strange trail. Can you imagine a more delicate growth than one which may require five years to grow a quarter of an inch?

4. GLACIER NATIONAL PARK
[*Montana*]

IF YOUR VACATION TRIP should happen to take you from the range of the Tetons northward through Yellowstone National Park—not hurriedly, if later you wish to tell the precious beads of reminiscence—and then on to Glacier National Park, in northwestern Montana, you would find yourself translated into what, at first glance, seems to be an entirely different scenic world. Yet there are interesting points of similarity between the Tetons and the mountains of Glacier, and the chief one is their "personality."

As, once having seen them, you will never mistake the Tetons for any other range, just so the marked characteristics of the mountains of Glacier will remain in your memory. You have gone from the vertical to the horizontal, as the eye receives it, even though you are among mountains that top ten thousand feet. Granted, such a statement has the flaw of all attempts to simplify. But as you journey through Glacier, your impression will be of mountains that are on the march. The explanation is found in the different nature of the two rock masses, and though your interest in geology may ordinarily be mild, here you are certain to be fascinated by the story revealed. As the cowboy said of Grand Canyon, "Something has happened here!" Later we shall see what it was.

First, though, another point of likeness between the Grand Teton and Glacier. The mountain part of the Wyoming park provides a thrilling trail

The pure gothic architecture of nature. Glacier National Park. [Photo: George Grant]

experience. Glacier National Park is a trail park on a much vaster plan. It is true that you can see gorgeous scenery in Glacier, traversing one of the most spectacular roads of the world, without ever getting out of your car. You can enter the park in the morning on the eastern side at St. Mary, cross the Continental Divide at Logan Pass, look out of the rock windows of the famous Going-to-the-Sun Road, follow the shore of Lake McDonald down to Belton, and by driving in your safe but fast way you could play canasta in Spokane that night, arriving a little late, with apologies for having loitered to look at the scenery.

There is a story current in Park Service circles about two young men who chugged into Yellowstone on a motorcycle one evening at dusk. One of them had evidently been there before. This conversation was overheard:

"Is there a good night club here?"

"I don't think they have 'em here."

"Well, we'll go and see a good picture."

"I don't believe they have any, except maybe some fillums of animals and flowers and that kind of stuff."

"No kiddin'? What do you know? Well, what the hell *do* they expect a feller to do here—look at *scenery*?"

Although mountain-and-forest-and-lake wilderness can never be savored to the full except by those who leave their automobiles and take to the trails, a great degree of compensation has been provided for those who must get their enjoyment from the roads. If the Going-to-the-Sun Road is not the finest and most spectacular road in the world—which individual taste must decide—nobody will question that it is one of the best. It is both an engineering and a planning triumph. Where it was necessary, in order to present the magnificent vistas, the roadway bores through rock cliffs, and the outside wall of the west tunnel has two picture windows that constitute framing in the grandest imaginable manner. The transition from the quiet loveliness of lakeside into the rock fastnesses of the Continental Divide and then down again to the limpid and tree-fringed glacial waters will remain always in your memory. Yet this trip is no stencil, for when you drive back again over the same road, as you should do, there is no sameness of impression. The wonder is not how much was seen on the first journey, but how much was missed.

Although there is but this one road that traverses Glacier National Park,

Hikers on the knife-edge slope of Mount Lincoln. Glacier National Park. [Photo: Jack E. Boucher]

there is another that, coasting along the Front Range of the Rockies, has its own strong attractions. At Kennedy Creek still another road leaves the Blackfeet Road, swings round the base of Chief Mountain, and crosses the international boundary to Waterton Lakes National Park.

Even if this trip were not a glorious adventure on its own natural account, it would be well worth taking for its historical significance. Here are two nations that can not only live in amity, but actually pool their scenic treasures in an International Peace Park. If someday Mexico creates a national park adjoining our own in Big Bend, we shall have on our two borders a pulsating gage of friendship such as has no counterpart in the story of nations.

Waterton-Glacier International Peace Park was established in 1932, authorized by the U.S. Congress and by the Canadian Parliament to be "forever a symbol of permanent peace and friendship." And if when you are at Waterton Park you should take the launch that goes to the southern end of the lake, you will have again crossed an invisible boundary between the two countries, and no ferocious gendarme will have held you up and demanded to see your visa, your wallet, and the lining of your briefcase.

Outside the park but much worth seeing is the Museum of the Plains Indian in the town of Browning, twelve miles east of Glacier Park Station. Here are exhibits that interpret the life and arts of the Indians of the Plains, who once roamed at large among the buffalo herds in the grasslands or hunted in the mountains where your trail trips will presently lead you.

The only other well-surfaced roads inside the park are the short spurs that lead to Many Glacier and Swiftcurrent Lake, and from Glacier Park Station to Two Medicine. From those centers, where varied overnight accommodations are available, and where visitors who are out to taste the joys of roving the wild country may get horses and guides as well as what equipment they may need, the trails take off in many directions. For horseback riders and hikers, the many trips are made as convenient as anyone would wish. Those who crave to rough it may certainly do so, but those who want the prospect of a good meal and a bed at the regular hours will be satisfied. After all, the greater number of people who visit the parks are not muscle-hard and are not saddle-wise. Unfortunately a good many thousands who would really like to follow the trails are deterred by the fear that they may fall by the wayside for lack of skill.

The truth about this is that all you have to do is be frank with yourself and with others. The first rule is that, afoot, you do not attempt more than you should, do not wander off the trails, do not try to climb peaks or go into uncharted country alone, do not attempt other kinds of stunting. As for the saddle trips, if, when you engage a mount you tell the wrangler frankly that you have not ridden or are years out of practice, if that is the case, you will make a friend of him at once. You will get special attention and end by having a better time than some dude who has been pretending to be an equestrian adept. It would be well, though, to make a few short trips and limber up before going on one of the longer jaunts.

Especially attractive in Glacier National Park are the profusion of wild flowers and the abundant wildlife. In both respects hikers and horseback riders will have the best of it, though on the Blackfeet Road there is usually an opportunity to see elk, deer, moose, and bears as well as the smaller animals; and on the Going-to-the-Sun Road, especially between Mount Cannon and Logan Pass, the automobilist will probably see, besides the ubiquitous black bear, plenty of the deer family and mountain goats and bighorn, which can be made out on the cliffs on either side of the highway or on the "fishbone" known as the Garden Wall.

These bighorn, or mountain sheep, are characteristic of the Rocky Mountain parks generally, but the goats are the distinguishing wildlife feature of Glacier. All visitors look for them and feel triumphant when they see a group close at hand, or decide through field glasses that the white spots on the side of a sheer cliff are really animals and not patches of snow.

No one can consider the story of man's ruthless attitude toward the wild game in pioneer days without a feeling of thankfulness that the creatures in Glacier, among other parks, are now protected and allowed to go their own way according to the natural law of tooth and claw. In saying this I am in no way reflecting upon those mountain men who lived on the country and shot game for their food. They were doing a logical and proper thing.

As to sport hunting, I am not a Nimrod myself, but I know many excellent people who love to try their skill with the gun, and I trust they are all as good sportsmen as was Henry Cuyler Bunner, once editor of the comic weekly *Puck*. An aspiring poet sent Bunner a sheaf of verses with a terse note asking: "What do I get for these?" The editor sent back the poems and scribbled on the contributor's letter just three words: "Ten yards start."

I merely ask that my hunting friends give as much start to their game as the editor was willing to grant a poet. But what is the truth about the hunting of animals that once went on in these delectable mountains? From the early 1880's until the establishment of the park in 1910 the wildlife must have been extraordinarily plentiful. A visitor to the region in 1895 was told by the trappers themselves that at least five hundred elk and moose, to say nothing of mountain sheep, goats, and deer, were killed every year for—what would you think! For bear bait! The trapping of grizzly bears for their furry hides was then at a peak, and the traps were baited with carcasses of these splendid animals.

Over the entrance to the Nairobi National Park in East Africa is a sign: "The wildlife of today is not ours to dispose of as we please. We have it in trust." Whenever I think of that African-refuge admonition, I somehow instantly recall the grizzly traps of Glacier in the days before it was a national park, and I feel a sense of deep satisfaction and relief that somewhere the animals have havens of trust.

As to the flowers of Glacier National Park, the showiest is undoubtedly the bear grass, which blooms almost everywhere, beginning on the valley floors and rising to the alpine meadows as the summer warmth comes. With its tall head of tiny white lily blooms, it dominates the scene, somewhat at the expense of many others of the lily family which follow the retreating snow and fill the eye with their color. There are more than a thousand species of wild flowers in Glacier, and though many of them are not advertisers of themselves, a considerable number of them are exceptionally brilliant when they form their dazzling carpets.

Then, too, one must take to the trails to see the living glaciers. There are many of these in the park, and some of them are accessible with very little trouble. Though these glaciers are not large, there are few in our country that can be visited so readily. These glaciers, in common with others in Western America, have been diminishing in recent years, making meteorologists wonder if we are entering a warm cycle that may have some far-reaching effects. Whatever may be the truth about that, the glaciers of this park should certainly be visited, for most of them display the curious features that distinguish such moving ice—tables, cones, moulins, crevasses, cirques, and all the rest. Even if the living glaciers should disappear wholly from this park— a matter of guesswork, because a series of colder and snowier winters could set the ice building up and flowing again—Glacier National Park still would be well named. Almost all of what the eye now sees, in the sculpture of these mountains and valleys and the creation of more than two hundred lovely lakes, is referable to the work of mighty glaciers of the past.

And this brings us back at last to the fascinating geological explanation of why the mountains of Glacier National Park strike the eye as they do—the reason for that uncompromising selfhood which I have compared with that

Near the summit of Logan Pass, Lake McDonald side. Glacier National Park. [*Photo: George Grant*]

of the Tetons. I remarked that they seem to be marching; or, rather, they seem to have been checked and frozen in the midst of a lateral movement. I suppose my thought in this respect is in some degree directed by the fact that I happen to know something of the geology of the region. But nearly every visitor has some comment on the peculiar Mayan-temple shape that characterizes so much of the mountain mass, and also on a certain dark arrow-band, with two light arrow-bands on each side of it, which is seen on the sides of so many of the peaks. And there are other horizontal layering lines that carry out the feeling of the lateral movement.

Glacier National Park records a colossal event in our earth history. The same thing has happened elsewhere, but nowhere in this country is there such a perfectly graphic example. First, it must be understood that all this region was under a shallow sea, not once but many times, and each time erosion brought down to the sea floor mud and sand—mostly mud. Layer upon layer, as the sea level rose and subsided, these deposits were later to be hardened into shales, sandstones, and limestones, of varying hardness. These are known as sedimentary rocks, and it is said that here in Glacier are the oldest *unaltered* rocks of this kind known on earth. Some of them retain in perfect delineation the mud cracks, ripples, raindrop dents, and casts of salt crystals that were in the original drying muds.

Then came the uplift, which strained the crust and broke it in many places; and some great force, little understood even by the experts, began to thrust a whole huge mass to the northeastward for a distance of fifteen to eighteen miles. Perhaps in that great thrust the soft rock of the Plains refused to give way before this moving mass, and as the force from behind was terrific, the rocks wrinkled just as a sheet of paper would be wrinkled by shoving it along a table against a hard object. At the finish of the movement some of the oldest rocks in the region were lying *above* the youngest rocks of the Plains. At Chief Mountain this may be seen clearly.

The identifying arrow-band of which I have spoken came from a different source. It is a sill, or intrusion of molten rock, which found its way between layers of limestone, just as the Palisades of the Hudson River on the New Jersey side once intruded horizontally into such established rocks, finally to remain the surface rock itself, in our time.

Finally came the series of glacial periods which set ice flowing down the valleys that streams of water had already cut, to gnaw on the rock cliffs, to tear and pluck and grind, build moraines, impound the lakes behind them, and at last produce the physical Glacier National Park we see today. Such a sketchy account as this is almost impudent, but the naturalist guides in Glacier will be delighted to explain fully and correctly all these things to visitors who are interested.

Identical forces working on the Teton Range produced mostly spire forms, with sides that tend to be concave. In Glacier the ice carved the rock, generally speaking, into rectangular forms, and even the horns are those of the pyramid rather than the cone. It makes a difference, you see, whether the ice is working upon sedimentary rocks or upon the crystalline kind. The great carver knows the material, and fashions accordingly.

5. YOSEMITE NATIONAL PARK
[*California*]

[1]

AT A TIME when Yellowstone could record but a scant five hundred visitors, Yosemite Valley was already a thriving tourist resort. There is doubt that any scenic locality ever enjoyed such a quick publicity and growth. Within a year from the day when the Mariposa *Gazette* published the account of the Hutchings tourist party's expedition into the area, a camp for travelers had been built on the south fork of the Merced, and trails for saddle parties were being pushed toward the valley floor. The Hutchings account was reproduced all over the country and found its way to Europe. On to Yosemite!

Horace Greeley was an early visitor. He arrived in August, when the falls, especially those of the Yosemite Creek, had almost suspended operations, according to habit. Greeley, who had come specially to see the longest leap of water, felt that he had been swindled. Besides, his riding boots hurt his feet, and his saddle chafed him. There are people today who arrive at the same time of year as did the journalist and wish the Park Service to install hydrants of some sort above the valley, so that they may see exactly what the June visitors do. It is a modest request, it would seem: like asking for the postponement of an eclipse of the moon because it coincides with an evening when one usually bowls.

But Greeley, recovering from his tantrum, became a captive of Yosemite's special beauty. He sent back to his newspaper an account that did the tourist business no harm. It was said that Editor Greeley's handwriting could be read by only one typesetter on the *Tribune*. That typesetter deciphered his employer's measured opinion that Yosemite was "the greatest marvel of the continent," that the "grandeur and sublimity" of the wondrous chasm were "overwhelming," and that it was to be hoped that California would immediately provide for the perpetual safety of the Mariposa Grove of Big Trees. The appeal was to the state because at that time the area had been so entrusted by the federal government.

Considering the fact that for twenty-three years after the Hutchings party described what they had seen, the only access to the valley was by means of horses and guides, the number of visitors in that period was remarkable. But when the wagon roads were built and it became possible for soft and timid people to make the journey in a less arduous way, then the influx really began. There was great competition among the travel agencies in San Francisco for this increasing business. One traveler of the period remarked that he was advised by a stagecoach agent to be sure to go to Yosemite by way of Mariposa. If he ventured by the Calaveras route he would be "traveling steerage."

No city was more excited by the photographs and writeups of the new place to see than was Boston. Bostonians had always been great travelers, but they had usually gone to Europe to see the Alps, or to the White Mountains, or to Mount Desert (where Acadia National Park is now) or to favorite Eastern watering places. Transcontinental travel had now become relatively easy and safe, so they turned to Yosemite, and exposed its wonders to the home folks with an infinite deluge of letters to the *Transcript*. For those accustomed to the graceful amenities of the Parker House and Young's Hotel, the hotel accommodations and cuisine of Yosemite were a trifle rugged. The first-comers especially were shocked to find that a "room" might be a space with a bed in it, surrounded by cloth curtains; and besides split infinitives there were other and more serious errors in California locution; but when all was done, and they had looked upon the valley from old Inspiration Point and seen Half Dome and Mirror Lake and the Mariposa sequoias and all the rest then accessible, there was nothing stingy in their enthusiasm. They agreed with Horace Greeley—it was grandeur and sublimity.

It was never, and is not now, "the greatest marvel of the continent," however. There is not an area among all the parks and monuments which merits that title. Each has its own kind of beauty, its own charm, its own story to tell. But it is true that Yosemite has a gemlike luster, a sort of fulfilling completeness, which makes its devotees cling to it as a first and last affection. They are lovesick swains and proud of it; and they will fight a duel with you over their superlatives.

Not all the Bostonians were weak in the muscles. Soon after the State

Monolith. Yosemite National Park. [Photo: Ansel Adams]

Geological Survey Corps had declared that Mount Lyell was impossible to climb, John Boies Tileston, of Beacon Street, was at the top of the highest pinnacle in two days. Tileston left his engraved card on the summit, where it was picked up by later alpinists. The card, of course, was not to be construed as an opening of social relations with the finder.

One party that journeyed from the East in the early seventies was attracted as much by the reports of the Big Trees of Mariposa Grove as by the waterfalls and towering cliffs. In this party, which entered the area by the old road to Wawona and consequently visited the sequoias first, was a man named Isaac Bromley. He recorded the experience for a magazine of the period, and it is worth passing notice for two reasons. It was, first, an uncommon bit of intellectual honesty. But, better than that, it stands as a warning to those who approach such natural phenomena as the national parks have to offer in an artificial and self-conscious spirit.

"I was in a sort prepared for the big trees," wrote Isaac, "and had worked, up pretty carefully what I should probably think about them. I think I had fixed pretty nearly upon the emotions I should take down and spread out, and had arranged judiciously the profound impressions they were to convey to me. I was dismally disappointed. I supposed the spectacle of the Grizzly Giant would inspire me, and that I should think of a great many things to put down in a note book and preserve. I confess I was not inspired at all."

The truth was that Bromley had come a long way, and the end of his trip, in a coach, was irksome. He had not eaten since noon, his pampered stomach was in rebellion, and he was suddenly plumped down at the foot of a sequoia with the remark: "Well, here we are. Now go ahead and enjoy it!" He was fully prepared to attitudinize heavily. Nature does not tolerate any such posing. It was not a matter of the slightest importance to the giant trees what Bromley thought about them or felt about them, nor are the trees concerned today with what the millions of Bromleys think. A tree that was already a sturdy forest specimen when Julius Caesar was crossing the Rubicon is not to be flattered by the condescension of a few small bipeds in trousers who cannot, from its lofty top, be very well distinguished from beetles. The Grizzly Giant had been overadvertised to Bromley by those who had not the slightest conception of its deeper meaning.

Just as soon as Bromley put away his vanity and made a respectful approach to the sequoias, he began to enjoy the privilege of being near them, walking around them, looking up at their lightning-riven heads, feeling their bark, noting their fire scars, forgetting himself in the contemplation of the trees. Then, in a humbled state, he was able to say:

"And though one looks with profoundest wonder at the vast size of these monsters, it is, after all, the suggestion they give of their far reach backward into time that most impresses the beholder."

The early exploiters of the resources of the region had no such awe of the historical significance of the Big Trees. Without compunction they would have logged them all and carted them away. Curiously enough, the very thing that made them most desirable to the lumber hunters was what constituted their best defense. The Big Trees were too big. Especially were the biggest Big Trees almost invulnerable to attack. The Lafayette Tree is thirty and a half feet in diameter at the base and has a girth of ninety-six feet. Archimedes said that if he was given a fulcrum and a place to stand he would pry the earth off its foundation. A skilled axman, or two good men with a crosscut saw, have talents that cannot be laughed away; but the saw was not yet made that would not disappear before the bark of a Big Tree was penetrated; and if the assault was made with axes, where would the choppers stand?

Ingenious little man did fell at least one of the giants with pump augers. Hardly anyone nowadays knows what a pump auger was. It goes back to the time when water pipes were made from the trunks of trees; it was used to make the hole. By literally boring the tree down, the end was finally achieved. Having demonstrated the power of steel over wood, the men went away, and the prostrate tree remained to be the wonder of visitors. Other good reasons protected the sequoias from slaughter. Their weight was so great that they checked or broke when they came to earth, and the cost of transporting the logs was such that Maine pine and spruce could be brought to San Francisco by ship at no greater expense.

This is not the place to discuss the sequoias, because far more extensive groves were later to be found in the Sierra, and were to be protected in what are now Sequoia and Kings Canyon National Parks. But if you should wish the refined pleasure of driving *through* a Big Tree, you should do it while at Yosemite. The Wawona Tunnel Tree, twenty-seven and a half feet through at the base, has a hole eight feet wide cut through it. This operation, a touching tribute to age and dignity and beauty, was performed in 1881, and the tree is still alive. On the Big Oak Flat road, about seventeen miles from the Valley, there is another sequoia, of even greater diameter, through which automobiles can glide.

Eight feet cut from nearly thirty leaves ample wood for a tree to stand on and bring up its sap. The health of the giants seems not to have been prejudiced. Still, the sequoias must have wondered, if they have time for dealing with such affairs, why it would not have been possible to detour around them. For it could not possibly occur to them that anyone would want to drive through a tree just to be able to say that he had driven through a tree.

[2]

SEAMING AND GROOVING the western flank of the Sierra Nevada range are many yosemites, but there is only one Yosemite. It is difficult to say why this is. The ingredients are not different, and some of the other rock sculpturings are on just as grand a scale. You would find the same thing true of the mellow, serene landscape of the Berkshire Hills, or the Shenandoah Valley of Virginia. The ingredients that make up the scenery are the same in various spots in those places, too; yet one spot pleases the eye more than another. Perhaps it is a matter of proportion. Perhaps in Yosemite the combination of grassy floor, of trees and rocks, of dome and cliff and pinnacle, in just that relationship, under a faultless sky, fills exactly the outer and inner eye, with nothing in excess. Add one of the greatest spectacles of leaping water in the entire world—it is no wonder that yosemite means *this* Yosemite, this one of the seven falls, the Three Brothers, Cathedral Spires, and Glacier Point.

Behind all this which can be so readily seen lies the rest of Yosemite, the part of Yosemite Park that makes clear the meaning of what is commonly viewed; and just as he who remains on the rims of the Grand Canyon of the Colorado is staggered, delighted, but only half informed, so the Yosemite visitor who remains on the beaten track or with the crowds must miss the great adventure. Not everyone, certainly, has either the time or the physical equipment to take the knapsack and bedroll paths, but some access to the back country has been made available for almost everyone. For Yosemite National Park extends from El Portal to the perpetual snows of the crest of the Sierra, from the Tuolumne Grove on one side to Tioga Pass on the other, and in that great sweep of dissected rock are hundreds of icy streams, hundreds of lakes where the snow water pauses and gathers volume, again to renew its turbulent way toward the Great Valley of California. There is much more than a thousand square miles of it, and many hundreds of miles of well-built trail invite those who wish the fullest pleasure.

There is nothing in human experience that would enable us to comprehend the reaches of time in which nature works. The scientist, using observable differences connected with rock material and the evidences of life found

For real sport, ski the Tuolumne Meadows! Yosemite National Park. [Photo: William C. Bradley]

in it, may construct a table of periods, but they are after all only bookmarks in a volume so ponderous that nobody could read much of it. So most of us, standing on the valley floor of Yosemite and staring up at granite walls that tower three to four thousand feet above us, sometimes almost sheer, can only gasp and wonder. It was all done by water, after the uplift and tilting of the Sierra Nevada block gave the existing streams their impetus. By a flow of glacial ice later, yes; but ice is merely the mineral form of water.

The Sierra Nevada is carved out of a single "fault block," as the geologists call it, mostly composed of a granite that welled up from below the earth crust. The fissuring or fracturing to be expected when a molten mineral mass hardens and shrinks may be observed by anyone who lives where a highway has been cut through rocks. But sometimes, when the earth movement is intense, the rocks move along the fracture, the movement being greater on one side than on the other. This happened here. A block four hundred miles long and eighty miles wide moved upward and tilted toward the west. On the eastern side of the block, as you see it from Owens Valley, for instance, is a towering escarpment two miles high; it looks like a final barrier in that direction.

Probably there was a first uplift of a few thousand feet and then a long rest, one of those rests of a duration no one can imagine. Then followed another movement, which tilted the block still more westerly and sent the edge a mile higher. There were streams already established, possibly running sluggishly through a fairly flat country, when the uplift began. It is not hard to imagine what happened. The sluggish streams began to run faster, and then faster as their heads gained slope, and the increasing elevation meant increased rainfall to feed the streams. Having cut down through softer rock, which has long since disappeared, the raging torrents went to work on the granite. The result, after long enough, was a V-shaped canyon where Yosemite Valley now lies.

Afterward came the period of glaciation, when ice moved down from the highlands to finish the job water had begun. The V became a U. The glaciers are supposed to have deepened the valley 1,500 feet opposite Glacier Point, and 500 feet at the lower end; then widened the valley 1,000 feet at the lower end, and 3,600 feet in the upper part.

But how could water and ice carve their way through one of the toughest rocks? Half Dome looks as neatly cleft as though it had been machined. Tap any of the rocks with a hammer, and the sound they give forth makes them seem anything but victims of water or ice. The answer, of course, is that the water and ice used tools to do the work. Ice has a hardness, at the freezing point, of about the same as graphite, and all graphite would do in collision with granite would be to leave a smear. Well, all a granite cutter in Barre, Vermont, could do with his bare hands, too, would be less than a smear; but give him an edged tool and a mallet, and he will make the chips fly.

The mountain glaciers found their edged tools in the form of loose rock masses, breaking away on natural joints and loosened out of place by frosts and sun. Once gripped by the ice, these were tools enough, and the mallet was gravity and the push of the ice masses that lay behind. The water torrents used the same device: abrasive material, from quartz sand and pebbles to boulders, with an irresistible corroding force behind them. The tough Vishnu schist of the Grand Canyon, and many another resistant canyon bed, are being gouged out in the same way today. It is the story of earth-building and earth-tearing-down that we look at everywhere, no matter where we live; but the most startling evidences of the process, past and present, are seen in those areas set apart as national parks.

Then the visitor asks: "How about the waterfalls? What of the Yosemite Fall, which leaps first a sheer 1,430 feet, and then, after a series of cascades, another 320? What of the lovely Bridal Veil and Nevada Falls, one 620 feet and the other 594? And Vernal and Ililouette; and the Ribbon Fall, 1,612 feet straight down, a distance ten times as great as that of Niagara?" Unforgettable are these falls when the snows are melting fast in the upper Yosemite, when the Yosemite Creek is pouring such volumes of water that the ground seems to shake, and the Merced is a leaping, whirling mad thing, breathtaking to see and not to be trifled with. But how did it happen that Yosemite Creek and Bridal Veil Creek and the rest of the streams that suddenly leap into the valley from such heights—why did not these cut their way down through the granite as did the stream that carved the canyon?

Because the tributaries of the main stream were not traveling west, perhaps. They did not acquire the speed and power of the Merced because they got no benefit from the tilting of the Sierra Nevada block. They were left as "hanging valleys"—stranded far above, even higher after the glacier had plowed the canyon deeper. They flow as streams as far as they can go, and end their careers by jumping. And these prodigious leaps are known wherever photography has gone.

[3]

NOBODY NEED WONDER, after visiting Yosemite, that Chief Tenaya and his tribe wanted no competition in their occupancy of the place. Even if their food was mostly acorns, they had one of the noblest all-year resorts to be found. Tenaya bragged on one occasion that "a small party of white men once crossed the mountains on the north side of the valley," but were deliberately prevented by the Indian guides from seeing Ahwahnee, the place of the deep grass. The comment may have referred to the Joseph Walker expedition of 1833. Walker could have been the first white man to come at least to the brink of the valley.

In this stronghold Tenaya and his people enjoyed, besides a good natural fortification, a nearly perfect climate. Not too hot in summer, not too cold in winter, and when the temperature fell lower than desirable on the southern side of the great chasm, they could bask in the sunshine by crossing over to the northern side. So it is today, and that is why winter visitors may take a choice of skiing on Glacier Point Road, near Badger Pass, or hiking in perfect comfort where the sun shines in and the towering cliffs cut off the chill winds.

Whether Joseph Walker ever saw the valley remains a little vague, but there is no doubt that Major James D. Savage did, some years later. Major Savage went out to California in 1846 with one of the overland groups from the Middle West and remained to become an almost legendary figure in the San Joaquin country. What his life lacked in duration was compensated for by high variety. Possessed of a great fund of animal courage, quick wit, ability to pick up the Indian tongues, and a cheerful pawnbroker's outlook on life, Savage was a soldier, a trader, and a professional husband. Having discovered that by taking to wife one of the squaws of the San Joaquin tribes he established a business and social alliance with the whole group, Savage married five of them in easy succession and would have gone further if he had not run out of tribes. He thus became a sort of feudal baron, with half a thousand retainers, who rendered fee by bringing him gold nuggets and dust, for which they received beads. It was not as unfair an exchange as it sounds. The Indians could not understand what anybody wanted of gold, which could be picked up anywhere, whereas bright-colored bits of glass were rare in the region and highly desirable as ornaments.

Early in 1850, after Savage had established a trading post on the south fork of the Merced, not more than fifteen miles below Yosemite Valley, a band of Indians attacked his place and plundered it. This act led to the actual discovery of the Yosemite and the revelation of its astonishing scenic

In spring the Merced River floods. Yosemite National Park. [Photo: M. Woodbridge Williams]

qualities. When, in the following year, Major Savage went in command of a punitive expedition against the Yosemite tribe, he took three companies of trained men, among them an impressionable youngster named Lafayette Bunnell. Savage's purpose was not to kill Indians but to force them to come out of their stronghold and give themselves up to the Indian commissioners. Tenaya and some of his followers did come into the white man's camp, but as Savage suspected that others were recalcitrant, he set off over the old Wawona Trail and went into camp near the waterfall now called Bridal Veil.

Next day the military party began exploring the Yosemite. They went above Mirror Lake and into Tanaya Canyon and up the Merced Canyon beyond Nevada Fall. The young Bunnell was ravished by the beauties and the majesty of the place. The streams above were coming into flood, and Yosemite Falls was at its wildest. The granite walls rose out of a floor lush with grasses and bordered by inviting shade. The sky was azure, except that clouds were massing for what might well be a late snowstorm. Bunnell took side trips, with full knowledge of the danger that Indians might appear from behind any pinnacle of rock and hurl stones at his head. He came into camp breathless with admiration and said to Major Savage: "Yosemite must be beautifully grand when the foliage and flowers are at their prime, and the rush of waters has subsided a little. Such cliffs and waterfalls I never saw before, and I doubt if they exist elsewhere."

The young man was horrified in the evening, around the campfire, by the party's indulging—in the presence of so much natural loveliness and mystery and the display of nature's power and craftsmanship—in coarse jokes and raucous laughter. It seemed to him like sacrilege.

But Major Savage did not share these elevated thoughts. He sat moodily considering that it was likely many Indians were still around and defiant. He thought of his trading posts, which had been sacked, and realized that, baron though he was, and generous as was his supply of wives, he was a man beset by enemies, of whom the worst were jealous white business devils. It looked like a storm.

Major Savage gazed up at the granite walls and growled. He said to Bunnell: "It looks to me just as I expected it would look. It's a hell of a place!"

[4]

FROM AMONG all the large-souled men and women who from the very first days have devoted themselves to the preservation of the integrity of Yosemite, it seems partial and ungrateful to single out one alone. Yet they all, without hesitation, would testify to the pre-eminence as an impresario of John Muir. Muir was the understanding, untiring, articulate press agent of the Sierra.

Arriving in San Francisco as a youth, Muir tarried not a needless moment in that mushroom municipality. He wanted nothing to do with cities, crowds, and marketing. He struck out for the mountains, of whose hugeness he had been hearing, and he came to Yosemite in 1868.

Soon after, he was herding sheep on the mountain meadows and spending a shepherd's leisure by exploring, botanizing, climbing, speculating, and scribbling. Nimble, observant far beyond the average man, educated in the truest sense, with much shrewdness and a pawky humor, Muir was something more than all that. He was a possessed man. He copyrighted the Sierras, all rights reserved, including those of translation. He made his way through canyon, up peak, across rivers, through woods, all alone, not foolhardy but with supreme confidence. Caught in a snowstorm, he could burrow a hole and wait it out. He was a born naturalist, always doing fieldwork for the love of it.

Muir was the Western Thoreau. They had much in common, though there were sharp differences, too. They were most alike in their capacity for incorporating themselves into any primitive natural scene—no fuss, no attitude, no tinge of strangeness, simply becoming instantly a part of what they saw. Muir was expansive—couldn't wait to tell the world about it. Thoreau chewed the end of his pencil wondering whether anybody was worthy to know, finally setting down some gnarly paragraphs on a chance. Both men wrote two languages. One language was the identic gossip of field mice and squirrels, unstudied and expressed with obvious fun. The other language was for company, for publication.

It was when John Muir was writing for the joy of setting himself down in homely particular that he could write delightfully. In 1875 he made a trip, alone, into the Sierra, and took with him a "little Brownie mule." Now listen to this:

> Many a time in the course of our journey, when he was jaded and hungry, wedged fast in rocks, or struggling in chaparral like a fly in a spiderweb, his troubles were sad to see, and I wished he would leave me and find his way home.

What a picture in those homespun strokes: of the poor beast, and of John Muir's perfect self-reliance; his instinctive humanity and tenderness; the twinkle in his eye as he thought the thoughts of a tired mule—and, over all, the tough going of a ramble in the Sierra's vastness!

Yosemite National Park

When Muir was writing for the *Century*, to arouse in the minds of a nation of readers an enthusiasm and solicitude for these Sierra treasures, he was not so artless. He frequently opened the word faucet and let the flood loose—two adjectives for every noun, a verbal phalanx in which every clause was trained to march straight ahead, fire a tremendous salvo at the end, and disperse the enemy, galvanize the unappreciative, spread the good news of conservation to the world. It came out of the goodness of his great heart and from his passion to have these precious places understood and protected. Still, it is a question whether understatement and a lower temperature will not go farther. After all, the national parks, insofar as they may lack anything, do not want for rhapsodies. You can turn *Roget's Thesaurus* loose upon them, epithet on eulogy, but they will offer their deepest satisfactions when they are recognized for what they are. They are not merely scenic places in America. They are America.

[5]

JOHN MUIR HAD READ the essays and poems of Ralph Waldo Emerson and felt that here was the one man who could "interpret the sayings of these noble mountains and trees." He wrote letters to the Concord philosopher urging him to visit Yosemite and testify that justice might be done the beloved Sierra. Though Emerson was sixty-seven, and not vigorous, he came. The result was not what the impetuous Muir had wished, but at least it gave him an opportunity for one of the most charming and touching passages of auto-biography ever penned.

The scene has its humor, and it has its pathos. Here was the indefatigable, wiry, youthful Scot who could start out with a handful of rice, sleep in hollow logs, frisk up a rock-strewn canyon, camp on a glacier, and return the following week fresh as you please. He was now asking an elderly gentleman—who had, to be sure, climbed Wachusett in his youth and had been rowed up the gentle Concord by Henry David Thoreau, but had never been a physical rival of the mountain goats—to join him "in an immeasurable camping trip back in the mountains." Those are John's own words, and when he said mountains, he did not mean foothills. Said John to Emerson: "The mountains are calling! Run away, and let plans and parties and dragging low-land duties all gang tapsal-teerie. We'll go up a canyon singing your own song, 'Good-bye, proud world! I'm going home.' "

After many years, this remains one of the noblest pictures ever taken in the parks. Yosemite National Park. [Photo: Ralph Anderson]

Emerson—such is the power of honest enthusiasm—might have gone up a canyon, in which case it would unquestionably have been "Good-bye, proud world," for him. But Emerson was with a party of devoted friends, who had come along to see that he did not take cold or overexert himself. They sized up young Muir as a man who made overexertion a life design. So they said, as affably as possible, *no*.

John was cast down, but he made one more attempt. He proposed that the Boston gentlemen remain in a hotel while he and Emerson camped for the night in a sequoia grove. Muir promised his friend "at least one good wild memorable night"—a promise that would have been easy to keep; but again the conventional friends intervened with a *no*. Finally:

> The party mounted and rode away. . . . I followed, to the edge of the grove. Emerson lingered in the rear of the train, and when he reached the top of the ridge, after all the party were over and out of sight, took off his hat and waved me a last goodby.
>
> I felt lonely, so sure had I been that Emerson of all men would be the quickest to see the mountains and sing them. Gazing a while on the spot where he vanished, I . . . made a bed of sequoia plumes and ferns by the side of the stream, gathered a store of firewood, and then walked about till sundown. The birds, robins, thrushes, warblers, that had kept out of sight, came about me, now that all was quiet, and made cheer. After sundown, I made a great fire . . . and though lonesome for the first time in these forests, I quickly took heart again. . . . Emerson was still with me in spirit, though I never saw him again in the flesh.

The curious thing about all this is that the romantic Muir had created for himself an Emerson that did not exist.

In the presence of nature Emerson was uneasy and distrustful of himself. He revered beauty, more especially the inner beauty, which is harmony and unity. He was never unmoved; rather, he was made silent and deeply meditative in the presence of wilderness life. Muir noted that among the sequoias Emerson "hardly spoke a word . . . yet it was a great pleasure to be near him, warming in the light of his face." Again: ". . . he gazed in devout admiration, saying but little, *while his fine smile faded away*." And, truly, the *Essays* are sprinkled with pithy comments on Nature, showing how shrewdly he had appraised its aspects.

The deer are unconcerned with landscape beauty—or are they? How do we know? Yosemite National Park. [Photo: Ralph Anderson]

Nevertheless, Emerson feared Nature; and for the reason that he expounds, by indirection: he believed that man had such capacities that, if only they could be developed, Nature would not then seem so grand by comparison. Instead of marveling at a beautiful waterfall, or at the miracle of spring, he wished that someday the onlooker would almost swoon at the sight of a perfect human. So, not loving Nature less, but man more, Emerson heartily wished that the dice were not so loaded. *That* is why his fine smile faded.

When Muir said to Emerson: "You are yourself a sequoia. Stop and get acquainted with your big brethren," he meant exactly what he said. It was no flattering turn of phrase. But Emerson saw mankind as something special and removed. Perhaps lazy eons may prove him to have been right, but meanwhile many of us who visit Yosemite and the other primeval parks will conclude that John Muir, on this point, had the better part.

6. Devils Postpile National Monument
[*California*]

THE DEVILS POSTPILE is a remnant of a basaltic lava flow that originated in what is now known as Mammoth Pass and extended approximately six miles down the canyon of the Middle Fork of the San Joaquin River, to a point just beyond Rainbow Fall. This outpouring took place during the later interglacial periods in the Sierra Nevada—at least 915,000 years ago. The basalt cracked into columns as it cooled.

During the thousands of years that the ice held sway, the bulk of this basaltic flow was removed, with only the more resistant parts left standing. Of these, the largest is the Devils Postpile, which is about nine hundred feet long and two hundred feet high. The top of the formation presents an unusual sight. Here the cross section of the three- to seven-sided columns has been worn smooth by the grinding action of the glacier, and the exposed surface has the appearance of a mosaic or tile inlay.

Two miles down the river trail from the Postpile, the Middle Fork of the San Joaquin makes a sheer drop of 140 feet into a deep-green pool. The dark basaltic cliffs contrast strikingly with the white water, and during the middle of the day many rainbows add to the beauty of the scene.

7. Mount Rainier National Park
[*Washington*]

SOMEWHAT LIKE a retired business executive, Mount Rainier, after many years of close application to its volcanic activity, once upon a time ceased

The *"Alpine Specialist." A mountain is about to be climbed. Mount Rainier National Park.* [Photo: Bob and Ira Spring]

operations and contemplated a pleasurable idleness. Prudently, it kept its physical plant intact and left a few fires burning, in case of a change of mind. Such impulsive retirements are always questionable. Mount Rainier, in the course of centuries, had worked itself up to a height of possibly 16,000 feet, all solid growth of rock material. It had more than a local reputation. Any eruption from this mountain was guaranteed up to standard, or lava refunded.

Also like many a tired business executive, Mount Rainier as a loafer was uneasy, fretful, undecided. Many times it quit repose and went back into active business, even with new branch operating units. There is some reason to think that, seized by a fit of renewed energy and delighted to be back at work, it once put on so much steam that it blew about two thousand feet off its top. But it was really tired. And there was competition, too. New and

At 11,000 feet, climbers rest at an overhanging "serac." Mount Rainier National Park.
[Photo: Bob and Ira Spring]

well-furnaced volcanoes, circling the Pacific Ocean like a ring of beacons, had gone into production.

So finally Mount Rainier definitely retired. This time it did a wise thing. It acquired two hobbies. One of them was flower arrangement. The other was rock carving, with glacial ice as a tool. In both respects the mountain became pre-eminent in conterminous United States, and so remains today.

There is still fire in the old factory. In the crater at the very highest of three summits, Columbia Crest, steam vents still melt the snow. There are hot springs at the foot of the mountain. But today Mount Rainier tends its flower gardens, weaves the blooms into glorious rugs and other displays, and maintains the finest single-peak glacier system this side of the Arctic chill, with twenty-six active glaciers that radiate from a lofty white center and cover forty square miles with their slow-moving tongues.

It may seem strange, in dealing with Mount Rainier National Park, to begin with its flowers. Flowers are such small and fragile things, and the mountain is such a giant! It is the fourth-highest mountain of the continental United States, if we except Alaska. Only Mount Whitney and two peaks in Colorado top it. Its height is so great and its bulk so enormous that when one views the mountain from Puget Sound, it seems to rise abruptly from the ocean. Yet the truth is that there are ridges and crests around Rainier's base that would be considered lofty in many other regions.

This national park covers about 380 square miles, and the mountain itself occupies more than one fourth of the whole. *That* is mass! No wonder the native Indians always felt that it dominated their every puny human endeavor!

Lovers of flowers are, of all people, very sure of what they like best. It would be rash indeed to proclaim the flowers of Rainier foremost in an assembly of national parks, where the show of bloom is one of the usual great attractions. Besides, there must always be considered the mood, the moment, and the associated incidents, all three being most important in weighing our pleasures afield. But at least it can be said that the display of wild flowers in Rainier is superb, soul-satisfying, memorable; we may leave it that way.

Centuries ago the philosopher Theophrastus made a few comments about flowers and trees. He noted that "all trees grow fairer and more vigorous in their proper positions . . . some love wet and marshy ground . . . some love exposed and sunny positions, some prefer a shady place." The severe botanist shies away in professional alarm from that word *love*. "No *love* about it," says he, "it is a matter of adaptation. The plant has no choice." Of course he is right, but let us be erringly romantic and insist that plants *love* Mount Rainier and the country around it. And then we can explain the reason. It is due to the peculiar combination of climate, of soil, of topography. The flower display of Rainier is what it is because it is where it is.

You begin, for instance, with the flowering plants that grow in the forest zone from the two-thousand-foot elevation up to about four thousand feet. Here you observe some queer species—plants that live on decaying vegetation. Ghostlike plants that manufacture no green coloring matter, like the Indian pipe. But there are many others that provide their own living—the clintonia, the trillium, and the forest anemone. And here the ferns luxuriate. Many trails take you along the shaded, quiet places where you will see this sort of plant at its best.

Then you go upstairs. I cannot help thinking of this display as being like a horticultural show held upon several floors of a building. Up one flight you will find the squaw grass, the coralroot, pyrola, and salal, and the twinflowers, graceful and fragrant, draping the road embankments.

Another flight, and you will be in the glacial valleys, forest-bordered, clad in their season with the devil's-club and salmon flower, with the mertensias and stonecrops. Do not expect any arbitrary divisions, however. The flowers, according to their special situations, blend easily, variety into variety. Often in late summer where it has been shady and the melting of the snow has been tardy, a group of the "early" flowers will be found crowded by a surrounding ring of the later ones.

The grassy meadows begin at an elevation of about 4,500 feet. First we cross meadows that are moist, even swampy, and the typical plants here will be the spiraeas, cotton grass, monkey flowers, and arnicas. But a little higher up is drier ground, and interspersed with lovely tree groups the greatest floral display comes into view. This is the "subalpine garden" that John Muir described as the greatest he had ever found. "A perfect flower elysium," he said. We all make reservations about an enthusiasm like that; we want to judge for ourselves. But if any man was able to discriminate, it was that tireless tramper of the mountain wildernesses John Muir. I, for one, will take his word for it.

Winter comes early in these gorgeous "parks"—Yakima and Paradise and Van Trump and the rest—and the snow lingers late. But during June, July, and August the flowers hasten into beauty and fulfillment. There are two peaks of bloom, one coming late in June, when the avalanche lilies, the heathers and pasqueflowers arrive, and another late in July, continuing for a month or more, when the slopes are radiant with lupine, paintbrush, valerian, and bistort. These parks, between ice and dense forest, circle the great Rainier "like a wreath," as John Muir said.

Visitors who revel in color and form amidst these flower fields should bear in mind a fact that may at first seem odd. This soft volcanic soil on which the enchanting flower rugs are laid is extremely delicate. Picking the flowers without a permit is generally known to be forbidden, but what is not so well understood is that wandering off the established trails sets up tiny channels of erosion that may result in deep gullies. And tramping among the flowers is injurious to the plants, too. By all means, remain upon the provided trails. They afford as fine a view of the display as you could possibly want.

The splendid forests of Rainier follow much the same pattern in distribution as that of the flowers. The dense evergreen growths characteristic of the lower western slopes of the Cascades extend into the park in the valleys of the Nisqually, the Carbon, the Mowich, and the Ohanapecosh. These are mainly Douglas firs, red cedars, and Western hemlocks, many of them of

Pack oufit on the trail: Tatoosh Range in the background. Mount Ranier National Park. [*Photo: National Park Service*]

great size and age. Other species of fir occur higher up, and above 5,200 feet the dense forest growth gives way to charming tree groups.

Since the summer season is so short, one would not think that Mount Rainier forests would be especially subject to fire hazard. The truth is that, in the higher altitudes especially, there is always great susceptibility; many burns in the subalpine growth, where recovery is painfully slow, testify to the carelessness of men years before the region became a park. At lower elevations restoration after a fire is more rapid, but everywhere constant vigilance and care are imperative.

There are twenty-six active glaciers remaining on Mount Rainier. Twelve of these are major glaciers originating either in large cirques at about ten thousand feet, or in six of them possibly at the very summit. As in Glacier National Park, the glaciers have diminished rapidly in the past quarter century, and the Nisqually, on the south side, which is one of the most accessible and can be reached over a good trail a short distance from the surfaced road, has been retreating as much as seventy feet a year. The Emmons Glacier, on the northeast side of Rainier, can be best seen from Yakima Park. Of the fourteen minor glaciers, the Paradise is the easiest to inspect. It is comparatively small, but presents all the features connected with such flowing mineral masses, and at times fine ice caves can be seen where the outlet flows from beneath the snout.

In a park where the snow covers the mountainsides in winter to a depth of fifteen to twenty feet, and where large centers of population with eager ski enthusiasts are so near, you would expect a heavy use of Rainier for this rapidly growing sport. You would be right. From December until May the conditions are usually ideal for both the expert and the duffer. The annual snowfall at Paradise Valley averages about fifty feet, and the slopes provide wide-open and safe courses. Unlike skiers in the Eastern states, with their "January thaws" and eccentric winter weather, the Seattle or Tacoma folk never have to wonder whether snow conditions will be good when they start out with the boards atop their automobiles.

When Captain George Vancouver of the British Navy first glimpsed Mount Rainier, in 1792, and named it for his friend Admiral Peter Rainier, it is not recorded that he had any desire to climb the mountain. But the day was certain to come when mountaineers could not resist the challenge to their endurance and skill and their will to conquer. In 1857 Lieutenant A. V. Kautz and four companions made the first recorded attempt to achieve the summit, but the party was forced to turn back. Thirteen years later Gen. Hazard Stevens and P. B. Van Trump attacked the volcano over what is now known as the Gibraltar Route, and it is a testimony to the judgment and preparation of these men that this attack has since proved to be the safest and most convenient.

Rainier is a difficult climb. Whether it is more arduous than the Grand Teton is a matter for the experts to decide. It is certainly very different. A large portion of the mountain flanks is covered by dangerously crevassed ice, and the sharp ridges among the ring of glaciers give a precarious footing of crumbling lava and pumice. The rock climbing of the Cowlitz Glacier and Gibraltar Rock is not for the unguided amateur. Consequently all aspirants for the conquest of the volcano must prove to the park rangers that they have the requisite stamina and experience, as well as proper equipment.

The eighty miles of paved roads in the park provide a satisfactory range of representative scenic views. In Rainier, as in so many other parks, the trails take the hiker and the horseman into a real wilderness area, with alpine meadows, waterfalls, and constantly shifting volcano prospects. There are many short trails, but the Wonderland Trail, completely encircling the mountain, with shelter cabins spaced not more than a dozen miles apart, offers a packing trip of a week or more for those who want to taste the ultimate joys of the primitive.

There is something else at Mount Rainier National Park that every visitor should see—and not only see but ask about and think about. It is a dramatic example of the inexorable law of nature by which the earth's surface—all that we see and all that we think we see—is constantly undergoing change by upbuilding and demolition. It is also, when understood, a graphic interpretation of the concept of land management that governs the setting aside of national parks for *preservation* "in their natural condition."

In October 1947, after several days of moderately heavy rains, the sky really opened and dropped nearly six inches in a few hours. At park headquarters at Longmire the ground shivered for many hours as great boulders hurtled down the Nisqually River. But to the west of the Nisqually, in the broad valley of Kautz Creek, a melodrama of the highland wilderness was in the making. High up on the slopes of Mount Rainier a part of the Kautz Glacier was being undermined and broken up by the streams of water that were pouring down upon it from the sides. Loose rock and debris of all kinds began to move down into the streambed, first creating a dam, then breaking the barrier with deafening roars and sweeping down upon the heavily wooded country below.

Trees five feet in diameter and hundreds of years old were pounded and sawed till they went down as helplessly as the ferns and other undergrowth. In building Hoover Dam, the engineers figured that they had removed eight million cubic yards of earth and rock. In about fifteen hours the waters coming down from the upper Kautz Valley moved more than six times as much material as was moved at Hoover Dam in three years with the finest modern machinery!

After the flood there were all kinds of suggestions for dealing with the situation. Some people recommended that the felled trees be salvaged for lumber, and the scarred area near the road be nicely landscaped. The standing trees, many of them partly cut through by the abrasive waters, should surely be converted into boards and planks, because they would die anyway!

Such proposals were no doubt very well meant, but how obvious it is that they could come only from people who have never realized the under-

---

Overleaf: "The Mountain" from Marmot Point on Paradise Valley Road. Mount Rainier National Park. [Photo: C. Frank Brockman]

lying meaning of the parks! In the life of the wilderness a flood like this one is the merest incident. It has, of course, some local importance to the plants and animals involved. For eons these petty "catastrophes" have happened and will happen. The aim of the Park Service is to preserve natural phenomena, wherever humanly possible—not to repair and reconstruct and refashion them. Whatever nature does is right. It is only the dilapidations and changes brought about by human occupation and use that have to be curbed and managed.

8. ALASKAN WILDERNESS

A. MOUNT MCKINLEY NATIONAL PARK
[*Alaska*]

CAME MY WAY, just before I sat down to begin this chapter, the notice that John Rumohr was dead, in Anchorage, Alaska. Have you ever heard of John Rumohr? It is not likely. He was just another of those unsung rangers of the wilderness whose lives have been mainly spent in preserving the precious preserves known as national parks. He fitted into the Alaskan wilderness readily, for he came from the mountains of Norway. Stubborn of opinion was John, but a loyal public servant, if there ever was one.

From 1931, for ten years, Rumohr made the winter rounds of the park boundaries by dog sled. Some of the patrols kept him absent from his winter quarters on the Lower Toklat for six weeks at a time, carrying enough provisions for himself and team. One day he and his sled broke through the ice while crossing a deep river. His lead dog, Tige, rallied the strength of the other dogs to pull their master from the water. He was a good dog man, as they say in the north. There is plenty of courage, of a sort, left in our country, but it takes a special kind of self-reliance and relationship with nature to do this kind of job. In the early days of our history such men were so numerous that they were not remarked. There has been a softening.

And, thinking of the late chief ranger, I remembered Adolph Murie, too. Many years ago I came into possession of his book *The Wolves of Mount McKinley*, and reveled in it. Published as a government document and written in the line of duty, it is modest, professional, and purely factual; yet it has a breath of romance in it that for me is far beyond any literary confections.

Alpine firs, Yakima Park. Mount Rainier National Park. [Photo: Joseph Dixon]

This is real wilderness. Even the dogs feel the call. Mount McKinley National Park.
[*Photo: Bob and Ira Spring*]

When I feel the need of getting away from myself, and wonder what book will do it, *The Wolves* never fails me. I find myself interested even in the naturalist's close-up examination of animal droppings.

> In 1939 I was requested to make a study of the relationships between the timber wolf and the Dall sheep in Mount McKinley National Park, Alaska. I arrived in the Park on April 14, and three days later was taken 22 miles by dog team and left at a cabin on Sanctuary River where I started my field work.

Thus, in the way of a businesslike report, Murie begins the account of studies made over a period including most of three spring and summer seasons, two autumns, and one winter. Much of the time he worked alone, afoot or on skis, and he must often have been dog-tired, hungry, frustrated; but I cannot remember that he ever said so. Aside from furthering research, his patient work emphasized that the predatory wolf has a right to live (my phrasing, not his) and to be part of the wildlife community in areas governed by such a land-use concept as that of preservation in national parks—subject, of course, to considered judgment and constantly renewed appraisal of wildlife conditions.

Of course the Dall or white Alaska mountain sheep, sometimes prey of the timber wolf, must be preserved too. One of the handsomest of our park animals, the heavily horned ram may weigh two hundred pounds. Against any but a snow background the Dall sheep looks perfectly white; only against the snow is its slightly yellowish tinge apparent. During the tourist season at McKinley, the best places to see the sheep are on the slopes of Igloo Creek and the East Fork and Toklat Rivers. The lambs, since their birth in May, have been scampering about on grassy mountain slopes in little bands under the watchful eye of an old ewe, playing the game of follow-the-leader, which gives them sureness of foot and almost incredible agility later on the rocks. It is said that even a lamb can make a vertical jump of six feet, and easily.

The principal scenic feature of the park is Mount McKinley itself. Not only is it the highest peak on the North American continent, rising to 20,300 feet, with snow two thirds of the way down from the summit all the year, but it is probably the tallest mountain in the whole world *from its base.*

Harmony at Camp Denali, just outside the park. Mount McKinley National Park.
[Photo: Bob and Ira Spring]

Everest and the peaks of the South American cordilleras thrust up from what are already very high levels. McKinley is naturally a challenge to the very toughest of the alpinists, but those who should attempt the climb are very few, and even experts have sometimes had to give up when success was close to their grasp because of weather conditions. Permission to try an ascent must always be obtained from the park superintendent.

The northward-flowing glaciers of the Alaska Range rise on the slopes of Mount McKinley and Mount Foraker. The largest of these glaciers are the Herron, the Peters, and the Muldrow, the last with a front of fifteen miles and a source in the unsurveyed heart of the range. But the greatest are those on the southern slope, which gets the moisture-laden winds of the Pacific, piling up the snow that is to become a river of ice. A strange thing is ice—so brittle, so rigid under ordinary conditions, yet, under pressure, plastic and almost fluid. The southern-slope glaciers have their sources high up in the range and extend south far beyond the boundaries of the park.

The wildlife of this national park is second only to the great mountain peak in interest; some will rate it first. Here are thousands of caribou. Or, rather, there may be and there may not. They may be grazing in the park or they may be many miles away, for they are rovers, at home equally on the high ridges and on the barrens. Almost anywhere in the park there are caribou trails through the tundra and battered trees where the animals have rubbed the velvet off their antlers.

The Alaska moose is the largest animal in McKinley. The biggest bulls weigh as much as seventeen hundred pounds with an antler spread of more than five feet. The moose is no Apollo among the ungulates. His shoulders may be nearly eight feet from the ground, and his hindquarters much less, so that, with his overhanging muzzle, he looks as though he had pushed against something so hard that he flattened his face and buckled his front end. In summer, moose will be met along the willow thickets and the margins of spruce timber growths.

The other large mammal is the grizzly bear. The most conspicuous evidence that the grizzlies have been in the vicinity is the presence of little craterlike holes on the tundra. The bears have been there digging out ground squirrels. Adolph Murie found the grizzlies unusually well behaved. "One day my companion and I met a female with three cubs. We were about 100 yards from her, far from any trees, and unarmed. . . . She stood placidly

"Barren ground" caribou move across the tundra. Mount McKinley National Park. [*Photo: Charles Ott*]

What the well-dressed ptarmigan wears. Mount McKinley National Park. [*Photo: Steve McCutcheon*]

watching us and soon resumed her grazing." So much for the tradition that a bear with cubs is invariably dangerous. Naturally, discretion is indicated. Murie did not press any nearer acquaintance.

The white spruce is the characteristic evergreen of Mount McKinley National Park. There are white birches in the lower valleys, and cottonwoods along the streams. The willow is common, ranging from the small trees of favored locations to the matlike growths on the mountain slopes. These willows, insistent upon survival, hide their woody stems underground, putting above the surface only the catkins of their flowers and a few leaves.

Denali Highway, the only road to the park, connects with the Richardson Highway at Paxson, about 160 miles from the park entrance. The Denali Highway is passable from about June 1 to September 15. The Alaska Railroad provides daily passenger service in summer to McKinley Park from Fairbanks and Anchorage. It is a four-hour trip from Fairbanks, an eight-hour trip from Anchorage. A three-thousand-foot airstrip, within easy walking distance of the hotel, is available for small private and nonscheduled aircraft.

B. GLACIER BAY NATIONAL MONUMENT
[*Alaska*]

IT WAS JOHN MUIR, the sure-footed pedestrian of the Sierra, who let the world know about the wonders and beauties of Glacier Bay. "I decided," said John, telling of his 1879 travels, "to turn westward and go in search of the 'ice mountain' that Sitka Charley had been telling us about. Charley said that when he was a boy he had gone with his father to hunt seals in a large bay full of ice . . . he thought he could find his way to it." And Sitka Charley, Muir's guide, did find it.

At length the clouds lifted a little, and beneath their gray fringes I saw the berg-filled expanse of the bay, and the feet of the mountains that stand about it, and the imposing fronts of five huge glaciers, the nearest being immediately beneath me. This was my first general view of Glacier Bay, a solitude of ice and snow and newborn rocks, dim, dreary, mysterious . . . breasting the snow again, crossing the shifting avalanche slopes and torrents, I reached camp about dark, wet and weary . . . and glad.

It was a sight that Muir never forgot. Passionately loyal as he was to his Sierra country, he had to share his passion with this newfound place of primitive beauty. Visitors who see it today will understand.

As late as 1700, Glacier Bay was covered with an icecap at least three thousand feet thick. It doesn't seem possible, yet we know that there is never rest in the advance or retreat of mountain glacial ice. The snowfall increases, piling up the feeding heads, and the mean temperature lowers; or the climate turns a little warmer, the air grows drier, and the front begins a retreat. The John Muir system of glaciers, originating in the southerly part of the Mount St. Elias cap, is one of the most active groups. The so-named Muir glacier has retreated approximately thirty miles since John was there with Sitka Charley, a rate of more than two fifths of a mile a year.

Here on the coast of southeastern Alaska is the unrivaled place to see the life of the glacial ice on our continent. The glaciers of Mount Rainier

---

Overleaf, left: An ice-fall from Margerie Glacier, Tarr Inlet. [Photo: Steve McCutcheon] Right: Margerie Glacier snout. Glacier Bay National Monument. [Photo: John Kauffmann]

The clouds lift and there is His Majesty! Mount McKinley National Park. [Photo: John Kauffmann]

and Glacier National Parks are impressive, but it is in Alaska that they may be studied and enjoyed on the grandest scale. For these glaciers come down to the sea, and when the great cliffs, some as tall as a twenty-five-story building, are broken off and sent crashing into the ocean, they put out a circle of immense waves and fill the tidal inlets with thousands of drifting bergs. Here, in the twenty tremendous glaciers and others of lesser but still great size, may be viewed all stages of activity—the fast-moving ice, the slow-moving ice, the slowly dying glacier.

The famous Muir Glacier is distinctly a lively one, moving at the rate of twenty or thirty feet a day, a rare speed indeed. It has a sheer face that rises 265 feet above the water and is nearly two miles wide. Most of the eight fiordlike inlets of Glacier Bay terminate at similar ice cliffs.

In 1899 an earthquake speeded up the downhill flows of ice. Glacier Bay became choked with floating ice, which put an end to the steamship excursions that for a number of years had brought sightseers close to the cliffs.

Following this speeding up, the ice receded rapidly. Between 1899 and 1913 Muir Glacier retreated eight miles. Tarr Inlet emerged as open water. In the following thirty-three years Muir Glacier went back another five miles, leaving the old John Muir cabin, which had formerly been near the terminus of his day, more than thirteen miles from the present face.

Wherever the glaciers recede, vegetation is not long in seizing the exposed land. It may be only mosses and lichens at first, but they prepare the way for flowers and shrubs. Then when there is sufficient soil, the trees move in: spruce and hemlock forests. The climate changes again, and again the ice is on the move down the mountain slopes. Ancient tree stumps, showing where giant trees once flourished and were overwhelmed, are being revealed by the glacial streams, which wash away the gravel that covered them. Yet still the forest moves in when it can. The retreat of the ice from stage to stage can be plainly seen in the kind of plants and trees that appear as soon as the land is unlocked.

Toward the mouth of Glacier Bay these forests are now heavy. Here visitors can go ashore, push through the dense thickets of alder near the beach, and emerge into a luxuriant mossy growth of old trees.

Fishermen dream of a situation like this. Katmai National Monument. [*Photo: Bob and Ira Spring*]

At present, transportation facilities to this monument are limited. It is certain that someday it will be a favorite objective of the millions who visit the national parks annually. The enthusiastic report on this Alaska coast written forty years ago by Dr. Henry Gannett and circulated by the Smithsonian Institution is heartily echoed by all those who have had the joy of making this visit. The Alaskan coast, said Dr. Gannett,

is to become the showplace of the earth, and pilgrims not only from the United States but from far beyond the seas, will throng in endless procession to see it.

There is one word of advice and caution to be given those intending to visit Alaska for pleasure, for sight-seeing. If you are old, go by all means; but if you are young, wait. The scenery of Alaska is much grander than anything else of the kind in the world, and it is not well to dull one's capacity for enjoyment by seeing the finest first.

The wildlife of the monument includes a number of bears—the Alaskan brown, the grizzly, the black, and the rare bluish-colored glacier bear. Then there are mink, marten, beaver, red fox, wolverine, Sitka black-tailed deer, mountain goat, and smaller land mammals, while the waters of Glacier Bay are frequented by the porpoise, whale and hair seal. Various waterfowl inhabit the coves and inlets of the bay—loons, ducks, geese, king eiders, many gulls and shorebirds, cormorants, puffins, murrelets, and guillemots. In spring and summer, during the spawning season, salmon crowd the streams.

C. KATMAI NATIONAL MONUMENT
[Alaska]

BEFORE THE FIRST WEEK of June 1912, no one would have thought of creating a national monument of 2,700,000 acres in the Alaska Peninsula. Except for one valley the whole region was an unexplored wilderness. For ages there had been a trail between a village of natives at Katmai, on the Pacific side, to Sabanoski, at the head of Naknek Lake, whence there was easy passage to the Bering Sea. Adventurous white men, Russian and American, knew the valley as a dense forest of spruce, poplar, and birch, with low spots of tundra. Herds of caribou, as well as moose and the great brown bear, added their footprints to the trail. But it was farther from New York than the moon, which is an object of interest in that city only during an electric-power failure.

In that June week Vulcan called attention to this significant and beautiful Alaskan wilderness with one of the most violent exertions of subterranean power of which we have any record. When it was over, Katmai Valley had become the Valley of Ten Thousand Smokes, and Mount Katmai, disemboweled, had collapsed with a roar that was heard hundreds of miles away. So far as is known not a single human life was lost, but the disaster to wildlife must have been pitiable. Earth shocks that preceded the eruption sent the few natives in the vicinity scurrying for safety.

A lake thought by some to be an impact crater, but not yet so proved. Katmai National Monument. [*Photo: John Kauffmann*]

Kukak Bay. Katmai National Monument. [*Photo: John Kauffmann*]

In 1918 a member of the National Geographic expedition interviewed "American Pete," the chief of the Sabanoski villagers, who was the last person to quit the valley before all organic life was blotted out. After six years Pete was still frightened. All he could recall was that, as he had been on the trail from Ukak,

the Katmai mountain blow up with lots of fire, and fire come down trail from Katmai with lot of smoke. Me go fast Sabanoski. Everybody get in bidarka [skin boat]. Helluva job! We come Naknek one day. Dark. No could see. Hot ash fall. Work like hell. Now, I go back every year, one month maybe, after fish all dry, and kill bear. Too bad! Never can go back to Sabanoski to lib. Everything ash. Good place, too, you bet! Lot moose, bear, deer; lot fish. No many mosquitoes. *Naknek no good.*

As Pete was living in Naknek when he made this final remark, it must have annoyed the local Chamber of Commerce.

The final gigantic explosion of Katmai Volcano, which blanketed the neighboring island of Kodiak with a foot of fine ash and sent eye-smarting sulfurous-acid rain for 360 miles around, actually was not quite as strange as what happened in the once placid valley. The human mind is not capable of imagining the inferno there, when innumerable holes were suddenly blown through the floor, to hurl forth ash and pumice in unthinkable quantity. The "ten thousand smokes"—seen by the first expedition to enter the area—have dwindled with the passage of years, but seven years after the eruption scientists reported a number of fumaroles sending forth heat that melted zinc (784 degrees F.) and one record of a temperature of almost 1,200 degrees F. It is estimated that a *cubic mile* of incandescent sand was spewn into the valley—a sand similar to granite dust. One cubic mile! Someone has tried to adjust our minds to that figure by imagining that all the stonecrushers in the United States were pulverizing that mass of granite. It would take them one hundred years. Vulcan did it in a week or less.

The jagged-rimmed bowl of collapsed Katmai, with its jade-green lake, is cradling a number of glaciers upon its cliffed walls. They hang below the rim, separate from the regional snowline. All of us who have seen and trodden upon glaciers have many times wondered how old they were. When fell

Katmai Crater. Katmai National Monument. [*Photo: Lowell Sumner*]

Alaskan brown bear at lunch. Katmai National Monument. [Photo: Steve Mc-Cutcheon]

those first snows that compacted into the ice that began to flow? Many North American glaciers are supposed to be more than four thousand years old. A five-thousand-foot core driven through the icecap in Greenland reflects nearly ten thousand years of Arctic history. But there is a more-or-less quality about these figures. Not so with the glaciers formed on the walls of Katmai. They are the youngest glaciers in the world, no doubt, and we know their birthdate. Into this crater lake, which is warmed by volcanic heat, the immaculate ice cows are already calving.

Ever since the National Geographic expeditions "opened up" the Katmai country, the ardent fisherman's mouth has watered from stories of the size, number, and hungriness of the rainbow trout, grayling, and mackinaws. During World War II military personnel came to Katmai to fish. It was a heavy drain on the supply, but there are still plenty. The great brown bear —largest of the world's carnivorous animals—has been fishing the streams there since time out of mind. When the salmon are migrating in summer, bears may be seen wading into the water and seizing fish with their front paws. In drifting down the Sabanoski River for a distance of ten miles, a park ranger from Mount McKinley saw twenty-three fishing bears. My friend Lowell Sumner, a Park Service biologist, who knows and loves the monument, reports that on one occasion a party of human fishermen came back to Brooks Camp with the story (greeted with lifted eyebrows) that they had seen bears swimming in the streams with their noses just out of water, submerging like submarines, and surfacing up with their prey. It may be that some bears do this while others do not, but this "yarn" has now been well substantiated. After all, not all human fishermen are snorkelers, either.

The elusive wolverine, the beaver, and other fur-bearing creatures are here in Katmai. In such a country of swampy forestlands, unexplored and without trails, who can say what the number of beaver may be? In the forest near the mouth of the Brooks River is a small lake formed by a beaver dam three quarters of a mile long, eight feet high, and twelve feet wide at the base. Large cottonwoods growing up through this house indicate that it is old and has been undisturbed.

Eagles are numerous along the Katmai coastline, and the second enlargement of the monument in 1942 added the coastal islets—not merely for their landscape beauty but to secure them as refuges for an ample and varied wildlife.

D. SITKA NATIONAL MONUMENT
[*Alaska*]

WE COMMONLY THINK of the romantic fur-trading era as exclusively a matter of British-American competition. But the Russians, too, were early arrivals in the field. There was a Russian-American Fur Company, and in 1790 Alexander Baranof, as chief manager, set up headquarters on Kodiak Island, beginning the slaughter of sea otter. Later he moved over to Sitka Sound and called a post New Archangel.

The neighboring Tlingit Indians, who wanted no white neighbors, promptly attacked the settlement and killed most of the inhabitants, ending "Old Sitka." But the Tlingit were gradually forced back by the cannon of a small warship. These Indians were not the ones who carved the classic totem poles to be seen in the monument. Most of them were made by the Haida Indians, who lived farther south. These bright-colored totem poles depict family or tribal histories and the familiar wildlife.

The Russian colonial outpost was once a busy place. In the foundries were cast some of the bells of Padre Serra's California missions. Yankee sea captains spoke of Sitka in its heyday as "the Paris of the Pacific." A replica of one of the spruce-log blockhouses tells the story of defense from the Kik-Siti Indians, who proved no friendlier than the Tlingit.

[VII]

Savor of the Tropics

THE WISDOME *of God receives small honour from those Vulgar Heads that*
rudely stare about, and with a gross rusticity admire His works: those
highly magnifie Him whose judicious inquiry into His Acts,
and deliberate research into His Creatures, returne the duty
of a devout and learned admiration.

—SIR THOMAS BROWNE

1. EVERGLADES NATIONAL PARK
[*Florida*]

WHENEVER I visit Everglades National Park I am reminded of these words of a seventeenth-century doctor and antiquarian. I must explain that by "Vulgar Heads" Sir Thomas did not mean stupid or unpleasant people. He had in mind those (a larger majority in his day) who are content merely to gaze at natural or man-made wonders without inquiring into the manner in which they came about. What he was extolling is exactly what we are nowadays suggesting when we use the words "research" and "interpretation."

Of all our great national parks, none stands more in need of interpretation than this land-and-water ecological gem of southern Florida. As Dr. William B. Robertson, park biologist, has written: "Everglades is a prisoner of its notoriety . . . many find the real thing pale and unsatisfactory beside the synthetic Everglades they built"—whether from overdone advertisement or passionate romance. It is true, in my own experience, that I have heard more expressions of disappointment from day-visitors in this park than in any other.

A fast getaway just ahead of a cruising shark. Everglades National Park. [*Photo:* *M. Woodbridge Williams*]

It is not that this preserved subtropical area has lacked for in-park inter-pretation. On the contrary it has had consistently fine naturalists or other communicators, who tell the story of this intricate natural order with the enthusiasm of those who themselves find new wonders every day. Nor does the park lack beauty. It is not of the spectacular kind; it is timid, subtle. Yet it has its great moments: the winter sunset, painting the Southeast, viewed across a sea of sawgrass, dotted with tree-islands, on one of which may rise a single palm, flagging down the speeding wildfowl. But truly the beauties of Everglades are chiefly of another kind, appealing to what Darwin called "the eye of the mind."

Far more beautiful than what the senses perceive is the never ending adventure of organic life itself: the creation of communities adapted for survival in whatever earthform they find existence. He who comes into such a life community with some knowledge of what he is about to find will not demand the stunning landscape. His pleasure will come from the recognition of complex relationships, from lower to higher forms, and not excluding his own position of triumphant but risky dominance.

Seen from this point of view, Everglades, one of the largest of the national parks in area, is also one of our most significant preservations of the natural scene—preservation at least insofar as possible. Here are just such complex relationships, life with life, from plankton to panther: a food chain of prey and predator in which the only incongruous link is the intrusion of a man-aging predator, the human.

The present park is the southernmost segment of what was, in nature, a great self-sustaining unit. Southern Florida is a flat plain, rising so little above sea level that it is nearly awash by the tides. It resembles a great pie plate, with low edge, and with a nick upon the Gulf of Mexico side. From central Florida the high annual rainfall, and streams like the Kissimmee, have been held in the Lake Okeechobee reservoir until floodtimes, and then spilled southward as a mighty marshy river moving almost imperceptibly for 120 miles to the ocean. The Seminole Indians, relative latecomers to the region, called it a river of grass—pa-hay-okee.

A flat, flat land, where a few inches of elevation make all the difference in the nature of the plant cover and the kind of animate creatures! Visitors to the park who are familiar with the mountain areas of the Western states are amused by the sign on the road to Flamingo: "Rock Reef Pass—elevation

Young spoonbill "playing with sticks." Everglades National Park. [Photo: M. Wood-bridge Williams]

3.1 feet." At this point, where the highway eases over a gentle hump of limestone ridge, the sign is a reminder that inches, not thousands of feet, may create a zone of sharp variance. The plants and animals of the elevated or submerged parts of the Everglades—the sawgrass, hammocks, bayheads, pineland, and mangrove swamps—are all dependent on these existing or missing inches.

The self-sufficing unit, which the Seminoles and the early white explorers of this wilderness saw, no longer exists. The drainage canals that made possible the agricultural development to the north of the park and the creation of almost continuous cities of leaping population upon the coastal strips have diverted the flow of fresh water that formerly moved into what is now Everglades National Park. Of course, there had always been minor catastrophes, so far as plant and animal life were concerned. Hurricanes, natural fires, and periodic droughts and flooding were part of the order. The healing, or restoration of equilibrium, was not difficult.

The man-made threat to the continued existence of the park—to the conditions which were intended to be preserved—is entirely different. Much, in recent years, has been published on this threat, and since the study of the possibilities is in process, I shall not go farther into the matter here, except to say that competent biological opinion holds that in the long run the park cannot continue to function upon its local rainfall alone. The terra firma would still be there. The bland, inviting winter climate, yes. Much of what the visitor comes to see would finally disappear. Even the sport fishermen and the commercial shrimpers of the Gulf, might get a shock. The primitive glades were creative even beyond present knowledge.

If your idea of the tropics is that of frost-free lowlands, then south Florida is not tropical. It can be described accurately as almost but not quite. In fact there is an extraordinary mingling here of two zones. It is nearly the southern limit of certain plants and animals and the northern limit of others. The crocodile and the sea cow are here, but so is the black bear, the raccoon, and the panther, the latter making his last stand east of the Mississippi. Here are the palms, the mahogany, and the strange strangler fig, but also the hackberry and the persimmon. Willows, too; but that family feels at home almost anywhere. Where the channels of the Shark River empty into the Gulf of Mexico is a mangrove forest that is possibly the greatest in the world. But the "feel" of the region is that of the tropics, despite the cold winter winds that sometimes descend.

Nesting time in the mangroves. Everglades National Park. [Photo: M. Woodbridge Williams]

The alligator claims a larger share of the visitor's attention; perhaps more than he should, for you can find him much farther north than this. But your chances of seeing him in the Everglades, without going into a swamp, are excellent. There are usually numbers of them below you in the Pa-hay-okee when you go to the top of the elevated platform that has been built to permit a wide-sweeping view of the island-dotted, grassy ocean, a true wilderness.

But it is for its birds that southern Florida has been most famous over the years since white men came. These flooded glades with their shallow water heated by an almost tropical sun are a biological marvel of productivity of aquatic life. When the early summer flooding comes, the lower end of a long food chain sets to work with vigor. The freshwater plankton, crayfish larvae, and tadpoles quickly build up a population of small fishes, which are eaten by larger fishes, and by the end of the rainy season, when lowered water levels concentrate this supply of food, the birds, especially the waders, move to their dinner. But on this point, biologist Robertson has a word of warning to the enthusiastic bird watcher. No matter what their numbers, the birds are still "where you find them." The birds go where food is in abundance. You may find a location in a slough where the show is fantastic— waders and waterfowl of many species, including the roseate spoonbills "sweeping" in their odd fashion; and ten days later in the same spot there will be merely a few come-late janitors cleaning up.

The bird population of the Everglades is still impressive; only careful research can reveal the fluctuations and their identic causes. But if visitors now thrill at the sight of so many water birds of so many kinds—the herons and egrets and wood ibises (so-called, but really storks), spoonbills and limp-kins, cormorants and anhingas—we can only wonder what were the numbers when, for instance, William Bartram was on the lower St. Johns River in 1774, and reported that "sleep was almost impossible because of the continuous noise and restlessness of the seafowl." In 1832 Audubon wrote of Sandy Key that "the flocks of birds that covered the shelly beaches and those hovering overhead so astonished us that we could for a while scarcely believe our eyes."

Even more impressive than these quotations, I think, is an extract from the diary of Charles William Pierce, who as a young lad accompanied "the old Frenchman," Chevalier—a collector and feather hunter—on a long voyage in the glades. Pierce described one nesting place as "the biggest I ever saw . . . as we went along the birds kept flying up, all kind mixed together, . . . Mr. Chevalier just sat there, pointed his gun first one way, and then another . . . at last laid down his gun and said 'Mine God, 'tis too much bird on this countrie, I cannot shoot.'"

Everglades National Park

Pierce's trip was of that lamentable period when women had discovered that good taste required them to wear bird feathers on their bonnets. The slaughter was pitiless, especially of those birds so unlucky as to have exceptional plumage. Pierce says that Chevalier got ten dollars for the great white heron and twenty-five dollars for a flamingo, though the pelican brought only fifty cents and the least tern twenty-five. A "plume hunter," named Batty at Big Gasparilla Pass had sixty men killing birds for him on the Gulf Coast.

When I first visited the Everglades, which was not long after the park was established, there were no commodious visitor centers and only a few rough trails. Flamingo, now with its fleet of powerboats, lodge, cabins, and campgrounds, was just a collection of framehouses, rude piers, and fishermen who took fish seriously. Mahogany Hammock, to be treated so brutally by Hurricane Donna in 1960, was a dark and tropically forbidden jungle, at the door of which a group of paurotis palms invited visitors, like Chamber of Commerce professional greeters. I knew nothing then, by personal experience, of the Cuthbert Lake rookery, Whitewater Bay, and the maze of channels among the mangrove islands of the Shark River Basin.

From the "river of grass" rise the forested "hammocks." Everglades National Park.
[Photo: M. Woodbridge Williams]

But I came away from that first visit with a vivid realization, somehow like an answer to long wondering, of what the word "ecology" means, for I spent several entranced hours on Paradise Key, with its then homemade platform walk which extended a short distance out into the waters of Taylor Slough. Then, as now, it was called Anhinga Trail, but since that time, to accommodate the vastly increased number of visitors, it has been modernized and greatly enlarged. I think it will ever be one of the high spots of our park system for those who suspect their implicit kinship with all the other forms of life. I also recall that I acquired, from brushing against the shrubs on the trailside, a dozen or more "redbugs," whose chumminess made itself violently apparent next day, when I reached Fort Jefferson. Also, the mosquitoes wolfed me. But it was worth it.

I had seen many of the birds and fish and reptiles that assembled for me at Anhinga Trail, though as I recall the showy purple gallinule and the water turkey were new. But it was to be able to view, so clearly and easily, the relationship chain! I saw the spearfisherman, the anhinga, who easily runs short of oil for his feathers, leave the water and hang himself out to dry in a tree, and here was the cormorant, who dives and hooks his fish—each bird being expert in its profession. The poet Sidney Lanier, a Georgian who visited the Everglades a century ago, wrote of this "water-turkey":

The anhinga . . . is the most preposterous bird within the range of ornithology. He is not just a bird; he is a neck . . . he has just enough stomach to arrange nourishment for his neck; just enough wings to fly painfully along with his neck; and just enough legs to keep his neck from dragging on the ground.

This is good fun, albeit a shade on the heavy side. But the fact is that the anhinga, thus insulted, might have retorted that to him Lanier was a comical-looking biped with a loose outer skin and a nose ill adapted for spearing fish.

I hope that those of my readers who leave the Everglades to go north along the Gulf Coast may be able to visit the superb Corkscrew Swamp Sanctuary, maintained by the National Audubon Society. Here are more than six thousand acres of the last of the virgin bald cypress forest—the oldest trees in eastern North America—that once covered millions of acres of swamplands. Cores taken from some of these giants suggest that they were ancient trees when Columbus came ashore.

The mangrove trees build land, and the birds build nests. Everglades National Park. [*Photo: M. Woodbridge Williams*]

2. Virgin Islands National Park
[*Virgin Islands*]

During World War I the Danes maintained a nervous neutrality; but the United States, anxiously viewing its sea approaches in the Caribbean, thought it wise to acquire the Danish holdings in the Virgin Islands, notably the three larger ones known as St. Thomas, St. Croix, and St. John. The price was 25 million dollars, and after the war ended there was considerable doubt as to the value of this real estate situated on the summits of a submerged mountain chain. There was no doubt about the delightful quality of the climate, where the northeast trade winds temper the sun's daytime heat, and the nights are blissfully cool—only a mean temperature difference of about six degrees between winter and summer.

But, 25 million dollars! One of the government civil servants wrote to his home folks in the mid-twenties that the United States had been horn-swoggled. He was wrong, just as those jeerers were mistaken when they referred to Seward's purchase of Alaska as an investment in icebergs. It did take some years to demonstrate that it was a bargain.

In the early thirties there was a minor government functionary on St. Thomas, a peppery sort of chap, who likewise took the dim view. He wrote that "the enchantment of distance turns into a commonplace reality," refer-ring to both the capitals of St. Thomas and St. Croix. But Hamilton Cochran raved about the island of St. John. He called it "a paradise of solitude." He was a lover of unspoiled nature, with a pair of legs that he used for walking. He got around; there was little he didn't see and enjoy. I quote him:

Three miles westward from St. Thomas, across the flashing blue waters of Pillsbury Sound, lies St. John, the smallest, most romantic and best-beloved of the Virgin Isles. Best-loved, that is, by those few happy mortals whom destiny had privileged to know its charms. Strangers are rare. Occasionally some white people go over for short holidays to refresh their souls . . . aside from these the island slumbers through the years, happy, forgotten, serene in its own for-getfulness. It is as wild, detached and primitive as if it were lost somewhere on the rim of an unknown sea.

The white population of St. John in Cochran's time could be counted on the fingers of one hand. Cruz Bay was the "capital," where were ten or fif-teen board shacks, a frame cottage or two, a tiny barracks on stilts that once housed a squad of U.S. marines, and, the "White House," residence of the

Ruins at Annaberg tell the story of sugar-cane days. Virgin Islands National Park.
[Photo: M. Woodbridge Williams]

dispatching secretary. One wonders what the dispatching secretary dispatched. The five white residents were: the dispatcher and his wife, an ex-construction foreman and his wife "trying to carve an estate out of the bush," and "a lonely Dane over on Lovango Cay." About five hundred "ebony and chocolate faces" were sparsely sprinkled through the bush.

St. John was a sweet, verdant tropical isle when the Danes began sugar-cane culture there in the early part of the eighteenth century. In truth, considering the great extent of lands suitable for cane, it was not highly adaptable even for that crop. The hillsides were steep and stony. But slave labor made the competitive difference. All through the reviving landscape of today are the old boundary walls of stones, piled when the black folk from Africa cleared the slopes. It is doubtful if the Danes brought their hearts with them into these islands. Rather, they hoped to carve out a competency and go home to the Baltic and spend the money. Even with slaves, the profits were for the big operators: still, for poorer white men it was, at least, an easy life. There was, however, always the fear of an outbreak by the slaves, who so greatly outnumbered the proprietors.

The servile insurrection came in 1733, with a great loss of life on both sides. Those planters were lucky who got refuge at Durlieu's Caneel Bay plantation. A tough soldier, imported from Martinique with the consent of France, ended the rebellion mercilessly, and the few remaining mutineers rafted themselves over to British Tortola. But a letter sent to Copenhagen by Governor Gardelin of the Danish West India Company in that black year sufficiently describes the tragedy:

> Most of the planters and their families are dead. I cannot tell how many. No work is being done on the estates. The cattle are running wild . . . I myself have been ill with fever these two days. Nor have we a priest to say a burial service. He, too, is dead . . . send us a ship!

Denmark forbade any further importation of African slaves to the islands in 1802, and in 1848 slavery was abolished. In the intervening years, since the insurrection, the planters had become more prosperous than before. In 1789 the population consisted of 167 whites, 16 free Negroes, and 2,200 slaves. But the termination of slave labor sent the island back to bush. It had been gutted of most of its original beauty; now it could begin the long job of restoration. The restoration, as visitors to the park see today, is still proceeding. This, in itself, should be of great interest to observers of nature, who need not be biologists to enjoy the processes at work on a ravaged landscape. Within the boundaries of the park, nature will be allowed to proceed in her own way, except that certain exotic nuisances, like the mongoose, might be expelled.

This animal, very worthy where it belonged, which was in India, was brought to the West Indies to cope with the rat population that had escaped from shipboard. It was a typical instance of do-it-yourself treatment without consulting a doctor, who would, in this case, have been a biologist. The mongoose eats rats in India, but on these isles his range of taste expands to include a menu of delicacies we prefer to keep for ourselves.

Virgin Islands National Park was dedicated in December 1956. On the first of that month, Laurance Rockefeller, as President of Jackson Hole Preserve, Inc., presented more than five thousand acres of the island land, accumulated by purchase over a number of years, to the Secretary of the Interior, then Fred A. Seaton.

It was a happy and generous inspiration to set aside so much of this relatively unsophisticated island of St. John. Modern technology will make it possible for the other West Indian islands to become suburbs of the Atlantic coastal cities. I have a friend, an art editor, who for several years has been commuting regularly from his home on St. Thomas to his New York office, where his presence is required only one week a month. But faster planes, with an assist from helicopters, will do far better than that. It should be possible, for those in the upper income brackets, to breakfast on a veranda overlooking the tropical sea, have luncheon in the neighborhood of Madison Avenue, and arrive home with the evening newspaper in time for a cocktail—maybe even for a brief swim—before dinner. The newspaper could even be that day's London *Times,* or the Paris *Figaro.* Each of the smaller isles that were thrown in with the purchase from the Danes should bring a pretty front-foot price.

At such a time, the suburbanites of the islands will look forward to a trip over to St. John on weekends, where they can experience a tropical wilderness. Instead of the cement pavement at their front door, they can enjoy a jeep trip over the unimproved road from Cruz Bay to the Bordeaux Mountain overlook, or the Annaberg ruins. In time, the renewed native forest of mahogany, breadfruit, cinnamon bay, and the palms and mangroves and soursops, will be a relief from the nursery-stock flowering shrubs of their own front lawns. There will always be a limited number willing to walk, so a park ranger will lead groups and tell the story of the old plantations and sugar mills. At the Trunk Bay underwater trail, the snorkeling swimmer will follow a series of submerged labels describing the marine world he is invading with his fabricated fins.

This is partly a view of tomorrow, but it is not fanciful. However, if I were able to choose, I would visit St. John differently. I would leave a northern city, say New York, on some blustery winter day, preferably during a frigid spell when cakes of ice are floating down the Hudson. I would have a pardonable thrill of pleasure, having stowed myself on board ship, that there might be a blizzard next day that would tie up traffic horribly. It should be a slow boat. Six days to St. Thomas would be all right; but slow boats are hard to find nowadays, at least ones that take passengers.

The first day out would be cold: too cold for a deck chair. Walk the deck! Second day, a warming trend would come into the air. And the ocean would begin to look bluer. Lafcadio Hearn—who could have been one of our best writers, but who decided to go to Japan, marry a Japanese girl, and become a naturalized subject of the emperor—made a trip on a slow boat like

Overleaf: A marine garden of corals. The undersea growths strangely resemble a desert scene. Virgin Islands National Park. [Photo: M. Woodbridge Williams]

this on a journalistic assignment from *Harpers Weekly* back in 1887. He noticed, two days out from New York, that the water was becoming bluer. He said as much to a fellow passenger, an elderly French gentleman going home to Guadeloupe. "Blue?" was the reply, with a snort. "*This* isn't blue!"

Two days later, Hearn ventured to intimate that now the water looked blue. His French gentleman admitted that it "was *becoming* slightly blue." But not blue. Hearn resorted to the ship surgeon. "Wouldn't you say this ocean looks very blue?" "No sir, not yet. Not really blue." But there came an hour when "over the verge of the sea there is something strange growing visible, looming up like a beautiful golden-yellow cloud. It is an island, so lofty, so luminous, so phantom-like, that it seems a vision of the Island of the Seven Cities."

It was, indeed, St. Vincent, but it might have been any island in that Caribbean. The man of Guadeloupe came to Hearn and touched him on the shoulder and pointed down at the water. "That, monsieur," he said with satisfaction, "is *blue*." And surely, those tropical waters such as in. the Virgins, are blue—an indescribable blue—as distinctive in their blueness as is the blueness of Crater Lake, also not imitable on the color chart. Lafcadio Hearn put it this way: "the sea is absurdly, impossibly blue. The painter who should try to paint it would be denounced as a lunatic."

That blue, which on the coraled fringes of the islands becomes an equally incredible aquamarine, is one thing. The tropic night is another. "The Caribbean night falls with a weight and density from which it is difficult to believe that day will ever re-emerge," is the way Peter Quennell put it. It has to be experienced—that feeling of finality. You can't tell anyone about it. It is not like cave darkness. It is, at first, a disturbing feeling that you are being *left alone*. You become used to it, of course. On St. John the bats like it. Maybe their sonar equipment works better than up north, where night has a dallying, indecisive way. There are six species of bats in this national park. They are, in fact, the only native land mammals. One of them is red, and eats figs, and has been rediscovered only recently. And, incidentally, though the bird watcher may see here a great variety of land birds, there is no such show of waterfowl as one finds in Everglades. The food chain which makes possible the vast numbers of waders and shore birds of the shallow glades river does not exist here.

But to come back for a moment to the definiteness of the Antillean night: I have asked many of my friends who have taken passage on one of these cruise ships (nine fun-packed days, six ports, $395.50 and UP, go now and pay later) what they thought of the quality of night in the islands. I was at first surprised that they didn't know what I was talking about. Then it occurred to me that, of course, they had never known it was night; they had been aboard a navigable night club—a sort of Manhattan Times Square with propellers, blazing with incandescent lamps. Don't misunderstand me on this point: I not only have no objection to people having fun-packed days and nights, touching at duty-free ports and defeating inflation by getting perfume at half price; bringing triumphantly home a quart of rum free of duty—I think it a charming adventure for young, buoyant people in no need of rest. I merely say that one doesn't get intimately acquainted with the tropical isle that way. A leisurely fortnight in a cottage, or at the guest facility at Caneel Bay, or at the campground at Hawksnest Bay (equipment can be rented), is something greatly to be coveted, and will not be forgotten.

Paradise? I have before me a picture of smooth sailing water, a sloop in the foreground, waving palm fronds, and the island hills giving invitation across the blue expanse. "Island Paradise," the picture is captioned. So seductive is this that I am nearly deceived. Would it not be a joyous forever? But then I recall that Paradise is like the mirage of cool lake seen by the traveler in the desert: when you reach it, it is not there; it is farther on. People have to live with themselves, and this is as difficult in the tropics as in Norway. This sour statement out of the way, I suggest that if you shall be so lucky as to have a chance to live with the realities of St. John Island for a while, you are by no means to miss it.

3. BUCK ISLAND REEF NATIONAL MONUMENT
[*Virgin Islands*]

WE FEEL *surprised when travelers tell us of the vast dimensions of the*
Pyramids and other great ruins, but how utterly insignificant are the
greatest of these when compared with these mountains of stone
accumulated by the agency of various minute and tender animals! This
is a wonder which does not at first strike the eye of the body but,
after reflection, the eye of reason.

—CHARLES DARWIN, *Voyage of the Beagle*

THE SNORKELER has a fine field for underwater adventure in the coral shrubbery at Trunk Bay, Hawksnest, Annaberg, and Lameshur on the island of St. John, but I suppose the high point of this modern educational sport will always be found on Buck Island, a mile and a half off the northeast coast of

St. Croix. For here, on an islet that looks no different from hundreds of others in the dotted West Indies, exists an unusual barrier reef which surrounds the eastern shore. The resultant lagoon is protected from the waves of the open sea by a wall of elkhorns, staghorns, and other cone forms erected by the unconscious cooperation of the countless tiny marine animals that colonize to produce a stony structure often in treelike form. It is cause for wonder, this unthinking cooperative effort. The coral polyps are architects of an undersea beauty that rivals anything of the land surface.

Each of the three main islands of the American Virgin group has its nearby "Buck" satellite. The one off St. John, to be sure, is labeled "Le Duck" on most maps, but that name is not common locally. The Buck Island that is now a national monument of our National Park System was set aside in 1961 from the rest of the island authority because of its precious natural features. It has a length of only a mile, a width of a third of a mile, and the highest point is but little more than three hundred feet above sea level, but that small package holds a world of the highest enjoyment for visitors of future years.

Deliciously clear is this lagoon which lies between the barrier reef and the shore. Even when there is a fifteen-knot wind curling the surface outside, the ocean gently laps over the barrier into this placid pool that some see as emerald green. Color is a tricky thing, even for the color-sharp. *Some* green surely is. No fresh water drains into the lagoon to discolor it or dilute its salinity. Indeed, the underwater photographer, I am told, must stir the plankton or limy cloud, lest the clarity of the undersea gardens be too much like that of a land view.

Frigate birds hover continually over Buck Island. These gliders are unrivaled in the world of wings. Circling, circling, hour after hour with no apparent expenditure of energy, they are a challenge to the technologist. With a similar rate of fuel expenditure, the fare from New York to Los Angeles should be about one dollar. But these magnificent gliders do not seem to nest now on Buck Island. If once they did, they may have changed their habits because of that "infamous mongoose," as the delinquent rat-catcher has been called. The mongoose certainly raids the sand nests of the turtles, as the raccoon does in Everglades, and also preys upon the pelican. The mongoose should be returned to India, with thanks for the loan.

I am not a skin diver or snorkeler myself, for a reason which I may explain at some opportune time, but I am quite willing to believe that it is a royal diversion, with more than mere entertainment value. Of course, it represents an impudent human invasion of marine-life sovereignty, and I am surprised that the sharks do not resent it more than they seem to do. It has its hazards,

A spanking wind heels a pleasure craft off St. Croix. Buck Island Reef National Monument. [*Photo: M. Woodbridge Williams*]

but they are not great, and it is a little gamier for that. Of course the snorkeler should know his equipment and should not go alone, but the latter injunction applies as well to the surface swimmer. In fact, with snorkel equipment you don't even need to be a good swimmer. My old friend "honest John" Lewis, who used to be superintendent of Virgin Islands National Park, said that dog-paddling would suffice. But then, John was a very accomplished dog-paddler. The main thing for the initiate is not to panic. This cautionary advice is not from me; it is from those who know. My acquaintance with the under-sea wonders comes to me secondhand, through "Woody" Williams and George Schesventer, snorkeling photographers, who went down to the Virgins for me to make some pictures for this book. I asked Woody to make some notes for me describing his operations and his sensations. He felt self-conscious about this assignment, and started in with something like this:

A rim of tossing silver split my vision of land and sea: above rose the tawny slopes of Buck Island, spotted by weird cactus; below spread diaphanous scenes of blue and green through which strange shapes drifted.

Snorkel diver watches a school of grunts. Buck Island Reef National Monument.
[Photo: George F. Schesventer]

Now *that*, Woody, is purple prose, and you know it, who are not only my favorite photographer, but my sensitive and perceptive philosopher! You weren't thinking of anything diaphanous below. Nor weird cactus above. You were quite properly thinking about your camera and your diving equipment, and wondering whether you and George Schesventer had brought enough film along, and other un-purple thoughts. And then overboard you went, like the professionals you are.

But when you tell me about the closeup experiences in that lagoon, about the dark-skinned form that suddenly came down, with cheeks puffed, hands clenched over a supply of bread-crumb chum, and how the gaily colored wrasse swarmed in like butterflies in migration, and how when the Negro's lungs could sustain him no longer he swam to the surface with the blue and yellow wrasse in hot pursuit: well, then, Woody, I am with you; I am down there underwater.

Some of the snorkelers went along above me clinging to cork rings towed by a guide. Others hung to the arms of stronger swimmers. Some gave me a wave of the hand as they passed overhead. They looked like nothing else but giant, clumsy frogs. George was watching out for sharks, and keeping an eye on me to see that my preoccupation didn't keep me under too long, and switching cameras when my film ran out.

Yes, I can see all that. I am there.

And I can see, through Woody's eyes, among the coral patches, the schools of tang—surgeonfish they are sometimes called, because of the razor blade they carry at the base of the tail—and the trunkfish that came along, black-polka-dotted on a white background and with "a snout pursed in a big sneer at me."

We can expect that the bird watchers will have a rival host, one of these

Yellowtail and parrot fish in the antler coral. Buck Island Reef National Monument. [*Photo: M. Woodbridge Williams*]

days: the fish watcher. Buck Island Reef will be one of the prime locations for the hobby.

4. CHRISTIANSTED NATIONAL HISTORIC SITE
[*Virgin Islands*]

THE SPANISH CONQUERORS who followed Columbus into the New World regarded the islands of the Lesser Antilles with slight esteem; but with an eye to the safety of the golden galleons, and the loot from the mainland, they wanted no other European settlements either. Thus for many years these islands, including St. Croix, were a sort of no man's land which the French, the Dutch, or the English could claim and try to make good the claim. Actually, we know little enough about the history of St. Croix from 1493 to 1733, when the Danish Guinea Company bought it from France. We do know, however, that it was a romantic frontier in which the pirate, the freebooter, or the buccaneer was often top dog. Interestingly enough, the word "freebooter" is from the Dutch *vrij-bueter*.

National Park Service headquarters are in Fort Christiansvaern, and guided tours are available from there every day except Saturday and Sunday; or visitors may stroll around and see Government House and the Landmarks Society Museum in the Steeple Building on their own. In any case, what is represented here is a period of prosperous Danish occupation, when, with slave labor and good prices for sugar, island plantation owners were able to build luxurious homes and public buildings, and indulge in other refinements that stemmed from a fictitious well-being.

Fictitious? Yes, because a one-crop economy, slave-worked or with free labor, has never offered true prosperity. Sugar was king for many years, but even at the best of times the cane production was running a losing race with debt. Agriculture is a good ambling nag, but compound interest is a racehorse. The Danes found it out. Better cane lands were opened up elsewhere; the slaves of St. Croix got their freedom; production costs increased; finally the Danish state took over. When the United States bought the Virgin Islands in 1917, St. Croix was on its way toward a new crop that the slave-owning planters could never have imagined: an influx of tourists eager to enjoy the climate and learn the history of the West Indies.

PART

THREE

[I]

The Seashores

1. Cape Cod National Seashore
[*Massachusetts*]

THOREAU'S NEAT DESCRIPTION of the topography of Cape Cod could not be bettered. "Cape Cod is the bared and bended arm of Massachusetts; the shoulder is at Buzzard's Bay; the elbow, or crazy-bone, at Cape Malle-barre; the wrist at Truro; and the sandy fist at Provincetown."

In 1849, when the great migration to the California gold fields was getting under way, Thoreau and the younger William Ellery Channing packed their bags and left Concord on a treasure hunt of their own. Neither one was greedy for mineral riches; both preferred the companionship of forest and stream, of birds and animals, and both had stout and willing legs. What was this Cape like? As flew the crow, it was not very far from their homes, yet to them it was unknown land. At Orleans they stopped at Higgins' Tavern. "The inhabitants of Orleans measured their crops not only by bushels of corn but by barrels of clams." With that introduction to the fresh salty air, they began a long walk over marsh, dune, and strand.

From this first visit, followed by two other expeditions, in one of which Thoreau walked alone, emerged the book which should be in the baggage of every visitor to what is now a national seashore. There have been great changes, of course, since the Concord naturalist ventured his volume. Yet much remains the same as when the two explorers spent a memorable night with the Wellfleet oysterman, who took them for tinkers or peddlers—and was the more certain of this when Thoreau's nimble fingers set going a stubborn clock.

Already, far more than a century ago, Henry Thoreau was worried about

The cliffs reminded Sir Francis Drake of home. Point Reyes National Seashore. [Photo: M. Woodbridge Williams]

The fishhook of the Pilgrim fathers: Cape Cod. Cape Cod National Seashore. [Photo: M. Woodbridge Williams]

the kind of people who would sometime "discover" the Cape. He had a large contempt for the gentry who went to Newport and Saratoga Springs to be noticed by their peers and waited upon by varlets. "The time must come," said he, "when this coast will be a place of resort for those New Englanders who really wish to visit the seaside." He hoped that "fashionable people" would "always be disappointed here."

True, it was not many years before summer saw a great influx of visitors. At Eastham a vast camp-meeting ground was the scene of revivals that brought 5,000 hearers of 150 ministers, who, to the delight of the Cape Codder, as well as visitors, gave religion "in earnest," in a loud voice, plenty of swinging gesture, and no clipped syllables. The Eastham people themselves were not mumblers. They didn't say "Eastum." They said "East-ham," and you knew the word ended in h-a-m.

No, the fashionable world never did come to the Cape, but the population billows were ever coming shoreward, and more people who loved the place were seeking summer homes. The Cape Codder had shunned the ocean front: he built his house in the shelter of an inland hollow, out of the galloping winds. Folks who intended only ten weeks of occupancy could feel differently. They were not farmer-fishermen.

The wonder is not that so many mobile millions flow down the highways into the Cape nowadays: the wonder is that four wonderful sections of this alluring land could so lately have been thus redeemed from private holding and placed in the hands of the National Park Service for the pleasure of all Americans. For some years, although ardently desired by conservationists, it just didn't seem possible. But the effort proved not too tardy. Congress authorized the establishment of this national seashore in 1961.

Snug in the palm of the "sandy fist" lies old Provincetown. In the peak of the summer season the place is sufficiently frantic. It offers a humorous study of human swarming, apparently for the purpose of watching people watching other people. The dementia is highly profitable to the professional oddball, who is nobody's fool, and puts on a pretty good show. This is fun— for a while; and when you get satiated you can go up to the Ocean View lookout and see some real history.

Browsing deer leave their footprints on the dunes. Cape Cod National Seashore.
[Photo: M. Woodbridge Williams]

Cape Cod National Seashore

All Cape Cod, of course, is the creature of the great continental glacier of recent age, but the miles of dunes on this windswept front are truly impressive. Ocean currents have furnished the material and the winds have piled them; and still they do, where the sands are not anchored by vegetation. You are here within those "province lands" set aside by Plymouth Colony folks who fondly remember the "commons" of old England. You will have good protected swimming at Race Point; and this is the strip of coast where in the old days so many brave ships were torn apart by the furious sea—Cape Codders on the shore watching the fatality, usually unable to offer more help than a prayer.

The Pilgrim Heights area is just a little farther up the "arm." What a page of our history is here! The *Mayflower* reached the Cape the second week in November. The provisions of the Pilgrims were scanty; it was an unfavorable time of year to arrive. They found a spring of pure, sweet water. They had agreed, one remembers, upon setting up a government of pure communism—from each according to his ability and to each according to his need, as the Essene Christians had attempted centuries before. It failed, naturally: people are not like that, yet. The married women refused to do the laundering for bachelors, especially if they seemed shiftless. Four days the Pilgrims spent here; then they went to the mainland and hewed the timbers for their first building.

This hallowed spot, marking the first timid explorations of the immigrants, was formerly a Massachusetts state park. The nature trails present essentially the scene as the fathers viewed it: the pines on the higher ground, the heath of bearberry and shrub sloping down to the Pilgrim Lake, a "kettle" that was formed in glacial times, salt meadow and swamp. There will be surf fishermen all along Great Beach, hoping to hook one of the big, fighting striped bass.

More acres of the seashore surround the Marconi Wireless Station, where the first wireless message went out from the United States to England in 1903. The sea has moved in upon the old station, but a part of it still remains. Inland there was formerly a military reservation with its consequent disruption of the natural scene, but this area is being restored. But what was never much disturbed, thanks be, is the precious white cedar swamp. You do not look for this rare island of tree life on Cape Cod; indeed it is not usual anywhere in the latitude. A boardwalk trail leads into the very heart of it. On a

Today's Huck Finn on Herring River. Cape Cod National Seashore. [Photo: M. Woodbridge Williams]

*You can have company without being crowded . . .
or you can be alone with the sea and your thoughts.
Cape Cod National Seashore.
[Photos: M. Woodbridge Williams]*

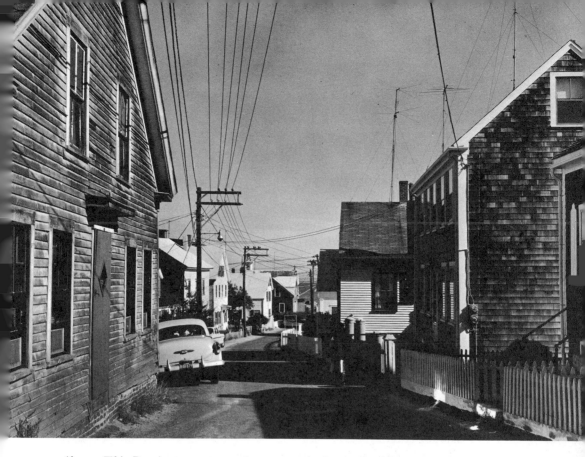

Above: This Provincetown street in summer is thronged with tourists. Cape Cod National Seashore. [Photo: M. Woodbridge Williams]

summer day this is a cool spot. The swamp soil is cold: that's why the trees are here.

Thoreau remarked that "to an inlander" the Cape landscape is a constant mirage. He gave the instance of seeing a solitary traveler on the plains of Nauset who at a distance loomed like a giant. I wonder if this is a common phenomenon, or whether it occurs only on certain days? I had this experience on an October day, when a distant automobile loomed like a bus.

Charles S. Olcott, in 1914, wrote an introduction to a new edition of Thoreau's *Cape Cod*. He said, "The visitor who goes to Cape Cod today in the spirit of Thoreau may still avoid, as he did, most of the signs of habitation . . . observing the birds and flowers and trees, the sands and the shellfish in very much the same way Thoreau did." Well, not quite true today, for the most part; yet there are nooks: and as for the restless Atlantic and the sandy

Left: Fresh-water ponds, legacies of the ice age. Cape Cod National Seashore. [Photo: M. Woodbridge Williams]

beaches, after Labor Day there are long stretches where you may walk alone.

One of the first trails in the National Park System specifically built for bicycling was opened at Cape Cod National Seashore while this volume was being prepared. One such trail, in the Province Lands, will run about eight miles. Another, in the Pilgrim Springs area, will be two and a half miles. Later, the two trails will be joined.

2. CAPE HATTERAS NATIONAL SEASHORE
[North Carolina]

ATLANTIC SEABOARD WEATHER, in general, is full of sudden surprises. Hatteras weather is only a little more brusque and whimsical, perhaps. For example, I once spent the first three weeks in November in a cottage just south of Nags Head. November is a month when the prudent visitor does not set his hopes too high. Yet those three weeks, except for one two-day northeaster, gave me as perfect a run of Indian summer as I have ever known. Day after day of delight for the beachcomber, the surf fisherman, even the stout bather. And every evening the sun dropped below the Roanoke Sound horizon and left an incredible riot of color in which red was merely the major theme.

But while it lasted, that northeaster was an experience I would not have missed. Like the sedentary idiot that I was, with muscles softened by sitting at a desk, I ventured out upon the beach of the Outer Banks and plunged against that gale. It was like pushing against one of the great bronze doors of the Interior Building in the Washington I had just left. I hadn't staggered far before I was glad I had moved against the wind. With the raincoat as a sail, I could easily blow back, provided I could keep erect. In the misty rain the skittering sand hit my goggles with a force that I could hear. I had the miles to myself. There was a queer, exultant feeling about that. Just myself, a mere flyspeck between dunes and waves, facing a gale! No surf fishermen today. Not even sanderlings dancing along the margin of the ebb. Alone, but with no sense of loneliness.

No; not quite alone, because when I paused to wipe the mist from my goggles, I saw at my feet a shipwrecked loon, lying on his side in the sand. It was obvious why he was where he ought not be. He had somehow swum, or risen into, a patch of oil sludge dumped from a lawless steamship passing

---

Right, above: Schooner Kohler *high and dry on Hatteras sands in 1933.* [*Photo: Roger A. Toll*] *Below: All that was left of the* Kohler *in 1956. Cape Hatteras National Seashore.* [*Photo: W. Verde Watson*]

coastwise. He had life enough left to challenge me with an open bill. He naturally regarded me as the author of his disaster. I could do nothing for him but wish him a miracle. The patch of bones and feathers I saw at about that spot, after the storm cleared, were probably his. If it was a raccoon that found him, I wondered how the prowler liked the petroleum flavor.

But next day all was Indian summer again on the Outer Banks, and black clouds of boattail grackles were feeding on the sea oats, lighting deftly atop the straws and bending them to the dune tops, holding them down till they were stripped of seed. And a few surf fishermen were back, because the channel bass had been running well. There is wonderful fishing on the Hatteras Seashore, but of course the summer season is the time for the deep-sea trolling for marlin and tuna or less spectacular mackerel and bluefish. From Oregon Inlet and Hatteras and Ocracoke villages the charter boats go out.

This barrier bank, broken by inlets at only two places in the seventy-mile reach between Whalebone Junction and the tip of Ocracoke Island, has none of the boulder and moraine and kettle aspects of the Cape Cod Seashore of Massachusetts. Yet really it is a child of the same glacial stage, for when the melting of the polar ice loosed a vast addition into the Atlantic bowl, a former shoreline that stood some miles to the eastward of the present one was submerged, flooding the low tidewater areas and creating the "sounds," like Pamlico, that now lie between the open ocean and the mainland.

These shoals that once lay to east, together with ocean currents driving alongshore, have supplied the material for this great bow-shaped barrier, erratically widening and narrowing. Winds have created the dunes, and where feebler plantlife has been able to hold the sands for long enough, the shrubs and trees have marched in. Instead of a bare landscape, then, we have here well-carpeted flats behind the dunes—wild flowers blooming almost into winter, bright-berried yaupons, even pines and lusty live oaks. When the ponies that now roam wild on Ocracoke first came to the Banks there must have been plenty of good grazing.

Just as the shore, dunes, and ponds of Cape Cod are on the fringe of a folkway, and as the Blue Ridge Parkway pictures something of the secluded life story of the southern Appalachian people, so the Hatteras Seashore brings visitors to the doorstep of a unique human habitation. The Outer Banker came here in colonial days, recruited mainly from Virginia and Maryland. It was not what we now call the abundant life, though the sea

---

Its beacon warns that these shoals are "the graveyard of ships." Cape Hatteras National Seashore. [Photo: Ralph Anderson]

offered ample food, there was plenty of game on the mainland, and a limited amount of stock could be raised. Fishermen they became naturally, and pilots and sailors.

The villages, you will observe, are all on the Pamlico Sound shore, Rodanthe, Avon, Buxton, Ocracoke, and the four others. From time to time, as the dreaded Diamond Shoals claimed its maritime victims, a good harvest of necessaries and luxuries came ashore, or could be salvaged. Not without reason was this coastal strip called "the graveyard of the Atlantic." Buried beneath the sands are hulks that appear after a great storm, to remain in sight until the next tempest covers them again.

Blackbeard the pirate maintained a lair on Ocracoke Island. Coast Guard stations were once maintained at locations seven miles apart, and the narrative of the heroic exploits of these brave men forms one of the inspiring chapters of marine history. What a strange story is that of the five-masted *Carroll A. Deering*, which went ashore on Diamond Shoals in 1921! When the Bankers boarded her, there was not a soul on the schooner, though the ship's cat was there. The crew? They have never been heard from. And, as an instance of

Morning plunge of the Ocracoke wild ponies. Cape Hatteras National Seashore.

what the restless power of the sea can do, after the wreck was dynamited the bow drifted over to Ocracoke, where it remains—sometimes beneath the sands, sometimes uncovered by the storms. The story of the "men against the sea" is graphically revealed at the visitor center, situated about two miles from the Cape.

When I first went down to the Hatteras shore, the crossing of Oregon Inlet was made by automobile ferry. I boarded the good ship *Conrad L. Wirth*, and to my amazement the pilot headed straight out to sea—or so it appeared. He knew his business: he knew where the bars lay that day, and he had to keep up with his homework, because on some other crossing they might be otherwhere. There is a bridge there now. It is not so romantic, but the waxing needs of tourism will not be denied. I suppose Hatteras Inlet will be bridged too, in time, and finally the wild ponies of Ocracoke will approach visitors for handouts, like Great Smoky Mountain bears. But the need for more seashore space for the millions is imperative, and something has to give, even if conformity is the result.

One of the never-failing attractions, at the upper end of Hatteras Island,

[*Photo: H. Raymond Gregg*]

is Pea Island National Wildlife Refuge. Undisturbed, and quite aware that they are in sanctuary, here every year arrive the thousands of snowgeese and Canada geese, and all the species of ducks which favor this bit of coast. There are whistling swans; gadwall, too. Altogether, within the seashore limits, you may see forty species of shorebirds, and the area around Bodie Lighthouse is a favorite haunt of bird watchers.

At Coquina Beach, not far from park headquarters, is a day-use area for surf bathing and picnicking, and campgrounds are at Pea Island, Salvo, Frisco, and Ocracoke. The nature trail at Buxton Woods should not be missed.

3. POINT REYES NATIONAL SEASHORE
[California]

WHEN I FIRST FREQUENTED SAN FRANCISCO, my Golden Gate friends assured me that the afternoon fogs never came down Market Street farther than Van Ness Avenue. Therefore, when I met this invigorating fleece in the neighborhood of Grant Avenue I had my choice of believing my friends or believing my eyes. Naturally I put the thing down as due to my poor vision.

This "Bay" climate, where the mean temperatures of January and July are so phenomenally near each other, extends up the coast to this new seashore of the National Park System. Sir Francis Drake and his men simply couldn't understand this weather where, on the 38th parallel (about the same as Lisbon), they "felt cold in midsummer." They could not know that one day the people who lived inland in Alta California would flock to Point Reyes Peninsula to get away from the cloudless sky and its shimmering heat. Anyone who has come in from Sacramento on a summer day knows the galvanic effect of the whiff of air as you drop down from the rise at Pinole. (I am thinking of the "old road" as I used to drive it.)

There is history here at Point Reyes—and landscape beauty, and a botanical meeting of northern and southern California plants, and beaches and cliffed headlands, and always the reviving air that pours out of the Pacific waters. What more can the day-user and the camper wish?

Drake's *Golden Hind* was leaking badly when he put in here in 1579, at the bay that now bears his name; and from here he continued on his epic circumnavigation of the globe. He met the Indians and looked over the

Right, above: The upland meadows are famous grazing lands. Below: Gathering succulent oysters. Point Reyes National Seashore. [Photos: M. Woodbridge Williams]

adjacent country, seeing "hordes of Deere by 1000 in a company, being large and fat of body." On the wooded uplands today, deer can still be seen. But what were these "conies" seen by the English sailors, "with the tail of a rat, of great length?" Is it possible that they were the unique "mountain beavers" of which a few colonies are now found in the thickets?

Drake was reminded of the chalk cliffs of Dover, which come down abruptly to the English Channel just in the manner of these highlands at Point Reyes, so he called the country Nova Albion and claimed it for his mistress, the Queen; and he "set up a monument of our being there . . . namely, a plate, nailed upon a fair great post, whereupon was engraven her Majesty's name . . . together with her Highness's picture and arms in a piece of sixpence current money. . . . It seemeth that the Spaniards had never been in this part of the country."

Drake's narrator was wrong. Cabrillo had preceded the Englishmen, but had attempted no settlement. Later, Vizcaino came and gave the place its name—"Port of the Kings." In the nineteenth century the whalers out of · Cape Cod and Nantucket were to know the peninsula as a resting and trading station.

Much of the land to be included in this national seashore, at present under development for outdoor recreation, is still in private ownership and likely to remain so. But the 25,000 acres of cattle and dairy ranchland offer in themselves a beautiful pastoral scene. Visitors are asked to respect the rights of these landowners.

The gradual recreational development will provide for both freshwater and ocean swimming, fishing, campgrounds, picnic sites, and interpretive trails, with campfire programs. At any time one of the great attractions will be the sea lions who gather on the rocky beach at the end of the point. Several California state parks are nearby.

4. PADRE ISLAND NATIONAL SEASHORE
[Texas]

MORE THAN A CENTURY AND A HALF HAS PASSED since Padre Nicolas Balli pastured his horses and cattle on this barrier island, reaching almost to the Mexican border (as it now is) from the bay of Corpus Christi. As cattle range, there were lusher pastures. The beef animals were long on horn and short on fat, but for those who had good teeth they developed real flavor.

Later, for generations, this was a seashore wilderness visited by few. There was no bulging population in southern Texas to move in upon the

Gulf front and speckle it with cottages. Sport gunners and fishermen and adventurers came across the shallow Laguna Madre that lay between the island and mainland, but the squirrels and coyotes and rabbits had the flatland behind the dunes as mostly an undisturbed reservation. Long before Father Balli ever saw it, the island was the refuge of brown and white pelicans, innumerable gulls, and herons and egrets. The ghost crabs scratched their burrows in the glistening white sand, ignorant of what a man looked like—something for which perhaps they had reason to be thankful. For man is the Great Predator, and it is only when he suddenly becomes alarmed at what he has done to the natural scene of which he is a part that he hurries to preserve the remnant and create a sanctuary which may curb his own rapacity.

   Still later, when Texas reached the point where its people began to look around for places of public recreation that would be beyond the whim of private owners, a county park was set aside at the northern end of Padre Island, and another at the southern tip. In addition, some of the 113 miles of this seashore will remain long in private ownership. But as a gift of Texas, the federal government has come into possession of the submerged lands

Underwater tidal life. Point Reyes National Seashore. [*Photo: M. Woodbridge Williams*]

What shall I do when I retire? A suggestion. Padre Island National Seashore. [*Photo: M. Woodbridge Williams*]

within the boundary of this superb National Seashore, and the resulting wilderness strip of coast, eighty miles long and about as wide as the island itself, constitutes the largest of the seashores administered by the National Park Service.

This is a year-round place of outdoor recreation. The climate, winter and summer, is what you would expect of a shoreside park on about the same latitude as southern Florida. The great orange and grapefruit groves of the lower Rio Grande are nearby, and even if a biting, northerly wind comes down occasionally, it does not remain long.

Most visitors will come to fish, to swim, to watch the seabirds; perhaps just for a day's picnicking, perhaps for a camping week. The surf fishermen will be rewarded with redfish, trout, drum; and boat fishermen will find sailfish, tarpon, and other gamefish in the deeper Gulf waters.

But whatever reason we give for coming down to the sea, there may lie behind this lure of the strand a vaguer impulse: hard to define, but by most people keenly felt. It may go back to our very beginnings as human beings. Of the origin of mankind, it is believed that it was "riparian"—that is, beside either fresh or salt water. If this is true, in most of us the homing instinct is strong. Carl Sauer, in his *Land and Life*, says that "when all the land will be filled with people and machines perhaps the last need and observance will be, as it was at his beginning, to come down to experience the sea."

5. FIRE ISLAND NATIONAL SEASHORE
[*New York*]

IT SO HAPPENED that I was in New York City on that September day in 1938 when a West Indian hurricane, taking an eccentric course, struck the Long Island and Rhode Island coasts with lethal fury and continued through New England, even across the Canadian border. The rain in metropolitan New York was torrential, but that was all. We did not know for some hours what had happened at Fire Island and Great South Bay, at New London and at Newport. A member of my club who owned a cottage on Fire Island told me several days later that he had not only been unable to find a remnant of his structure; he couldn't even locate exactly the spot where it had stood. Had the storm come before Labor Day, when recreation was at peak, the loss of life would have been ghastly.

Some time afterward I went down there to view the shambles. I felt convinced that few persons, even of the sort that loved the relatively isolated thirty-mile stretch of delightful beach, dune, and marshland, would ever risk an investment there again. How shortsighted of me! I had forgotten that after each outpouring from Vesuvius, the Italians have always returned with vine and flock. It is a prime factor perhaps in man's advance that he will take a chance, if it looks at least fifty-fifty.

And sure enough the "developments" came back; not merely villages of summer residents, but state, county, and town parks. Nature "came back," too, healing the battered dunes, filling the breaches, planting new seed for stabilizing grasses. But meanwhile, at the edge of the greatest population concentration in the nation, the very people who loved the place because of its somewhat isolated location were faced with proposals that would make the whole of the island a Sunday edition of Jones Beach. This is no sneer at Jones Beach. For what it is, and what it must necessarily be, it is a masterpiece of devoted and brilliant management. But among ardent conservationists, and even among many Fire Island owners, the question was: cannot Fire

Island remain something different, looking forward to future years, when a seashore retaining a virgin quality will be such a precious possession? In September 1964, the President signed an act establishing Fire Island National Seashore "for the purpose of conserving and preserving for the use of future generations" its beaches as examples of unspoiled areas near urban centers.

Here is perhaps the greatest challenge to the Department of the Interior and to the National Park Service that has yet to be faced in the acquisition of seashores for the public use. For the congressional act, properly protecting individual rights, especially where ownership is in favor of maintaining the beautiful primitive scene, the vegetation, and the wildlife, implies that the process of entire restoration will be a slow one. Toward the ideal end, however, the job has already begun. It will be expensive; it will mean a program of conservation education; but it will be worth all it costs.

It must have been a halcyon day—that day when Fire Island National Seashore became a fact—for the ardent local group of preservationists who since 1960 have been wardens of the unusual "sunken forest," financing its protection and inviting to it those who can appreciate its beauty and strangeness. Who would expect to find these large hollies and sassafras trees, or black gums or maples, springing from the sands of a barrier reef? Yet, unique as it is, it is only a part of a beautiful plant cover that can be saved to delight generations to come.

6. ASSATEAGUE ISLAND NATIONAL SEASHORE
[Maryland–Virginia]

ANNE MORROW LINDBERGH, writing in her lapidary prose style, some years ago offered a little book called *Gift from the Sea*. She had herself received from the ocean and beach an experience of the spirit, and she wished to share it with others. But she had a note of warning: "The sea does not reward those who are too anxious, too greedy, or too impatient. To dig for treasures shows not only impatience and greed, but lack of faith. Patience, patience, patience, is what the sea teaches. Patience and faith. One should lie empty, open, choiceless as a beach—waiting for a gift from the sea."

Perhaps it was not exactly in Mrs. Lindbergh's sense; yet in March 1962, the people of America received a gift from the sea. It was unexpected. The sea has no publicity department. The gift came in the form of a hurricane.

Vegetation clothes the dunes and ties them down. Fire Island National Seashore.
[Photo: M. Woodbridge Williams]

Let us go back a little. In 1935 the National Park Service had surveyed the coastline of the Atlantic and Gulf states, searching for unspoiled seashore that could be preserved for public enjoyment. Assateague Island, off the eastern shore of Maryland, was one of the strands that possessed all the desirable natural features. But the survey party did not recommend it. Private development had reached the point where acquisition seemed impossible. A fifteen-mile stretch south of the Sinepuxent Neck Bridge had already been subdivided, and there were already three thousand private owners, and many houses built. Too late!

Then came the hurricane. When the winds died down all but the sturdiest homes were overturned, and many were driftwood. The beautiful barrier reef, thirty-three miles along the Maryland and Virginia coasts and within easy reach of 34 million people, again became a possible reservation for outdoor recreation, federally owned and administered. A gift from the sea, was it not? On August 25, 1965, President Johnson signed the congressional act by which this precious bit of shoreline became a national seashore.

The sea gives, and the sea takes. These barrier beaches, so nearly on the level of the ocean, are subject to erosion of wind and wave. Indeed, that hurricane of 1962 was but one attack in a constant recession of the shore, especially at the northern tip of the island. A cedar forest that once grew on the shore and was overwhelmed by rising waters was revealed by the great storm. The tree stumps now dot a stretch of beach as mute testimony to the changing shoreline of Assateague, and the power of the elements.

As you near the southern end of the island—the final nine miles are within the Chincoteague National Wildlife Refuge—the vegetation becomes a notable feature, and here are the marshes where the famous wild ponies fatten on the grasses and the wildfowl gather in prodigious numbers. Occasionally a sika deer is seen. A difference of a few inches in elevation determines whether the loblolly and Virginia pines can have their feet out of brackish water.

All kinds of outdoor activity will be provided for at Assateague—boating and surf fishing, swimming, and even crabbing and digging for clams. But the recreative value will always be determined not by the activities available but by the place itself. To quote Anne Lindbergh again:

Rollers on the beach, wind in the pines, the slow flapping of herons across sand dunes, drown out the hectic rhythms of city and suburb, time tables and

---

White pelicans winter luxuriously. Padre Island National Seashore. [Photo: M. Woodbridge Williams]

schedules. One falls under their spell, relaxes, stretches out prone. One becomes, in fact, like the element on which one lies, flattened by the sea; bare, open, empty as the beach, erased by today's tides of all yesterday's scribblings.

That is the consolation of the sea. A gift to the needy.

7. CAPE LOOKOUT NATIONAL SEASHORE
[*North Carolina*]

SEVENTH, AND LATEST, of the seashores that have been set aside for the physical and spiritual comfort of the nation's people (not forgetting our foreign friends, of course!) is this barrier bank of nearly sixty miles that extends down the North Carolina coastline from Ocracoke Island to the hook of Cape Lookout, then turns westward to Beaufort Inlet. This barrier reef is a primitive one, and its existence is unsuspected even by the millions who visit the three island "banks" that constitute the seashore styled "Hatteras."

In all, nearly sixty thousand acres are involved in this acquisition—but the word "acres," in relation to a barrier reef, hardly suffices to describe. Continually widening and indenting as the natural wave and wind action has been speeded or retarded by the storms that sweep it, Core Banks especially —the stretch that lies below Portsmouth Island—stands in need of restoration. Fortunately this is something that man's skill can do almost as easily—but not quite—as it can destroy. It takes time and labor to tie the bare dunes down with vegetation; but given a chance, nature gladly takes over. North Carolina, which acted with such prudent generosity in the case of Hatteras, has already acquired four fifths of the desirable recreational area and given it to the federal government.

Unlike Fire Island, this new seashore did not pose problems of redemption from private ownership. There is a little village at Portsmouth, on the island just across Ocracoke Inlet; and at the other end the Shackleford Banks have some holly, oak, myrtle, and red cedar. But otherwise the sand bar, broken across by a number of inlets, is just dune and flat and marsh. And who wants better than that, when it is stabilized? What more does one come to do and to see and to enjoy? I understand that the director of the National Park Service, on his inspection trip to the area, kicked off his shoes, climbed barefoot over the dunes, and declared the place "simply terrific." Well, why not?

Old Coast Guard station. Assateague Island National Seashore. [*Photo: M. Woodbridge Williams*]

Think forward to the millions of Americans who will be able to do the same, with no signs that say, "Private Property—Keep Off."

All the delights of seashore recreation, which do not require mechanization, are here in prospect. The sea birds will come in great numbers, the sport fisherman will take part of the harvest that now goes to commerce. Such development for public use as is necessary can be confined to a hundred or more acres on the mainland, with perhaps a ferry or causeway to take visitors to a day-use area on Shackleford Banks. Core Banks and Portsmouth Island could well remain roadless, with access by boat and simple facilities for hikers and campers. It is all in the planning stage so far; but the main point is that

Where the tides creep into the land. Assateague Island National Seashore. [*Photo: M. Woodbridge Williams*]

this *is* the newest seashore, and preserved against all enemies but the sea. If the sea, in partnership with the wind, makes an occasional foray—well, that is a part of the natural history we really aim to keep alive.

Nor, in spite of its remoteness today, does this strip of seashore lack historical interest. The huts of whale fishermen once were frequent along Core Banks, built not only by the hardy men who made homes here on the Carolina coast, but by eager New Bedford and Nantucket sea hunters, too. Portsmouth was once a place of more than five hundred "frontier" folks. Now it has more houses than people. In the mid-18th century, corsairs, sniffing loot, cruised along these lower banks.

An overwhelmed cedar grove once grew here. Assateague Island National Seashore.
[Photo: Robert K. Bergman]

[I I]

The Parkways

1. BLUE RIDGE PARKWAY
[*Virginia–North Carolina*]

A COMPUTER IS . . . A COMPUTER. Far be it from me to let myself become involved in a discussion of the qualities and possibilities of a mechanism which I do not understand, or to venture into a field where I have no place. Some of my friends have told me, in a kind of awed ecstasy, that this truly wonderful device "almost thinks." It may be so. That makes me want to defend mankind against the menace of a potential monster; and thus I reply that the difference between almost-thinking and thinking is so great that it can be expressed only in terms of light-years. It seems to me akin to the difference between a contract and a quasi-contract. The latter isn't a contract. It is just a quasi, as has been frequently and annoyingly revealed.

The computer, I hazard to assume, makes no decisions. It does not declare war; it does not get married; it does not go into debt. It ponders no abstractions: justice, beauty, good. If you want those parameters in, put them in if you think you can. What comes out will supply the basis on which somebody can make a decision. The speed with which the output pours forth is the amazing, the revolutionary, thing. Already commerce is a changed affair, and the politician views the computer with fearful respect.

These modest reflections come to me because I lately heard that a certain Western municipality, planning a highway, used the computer to lighten the chores. Relative cost of land acquisition, exit roads, population factors, traffic considerations: all those engineering details that had formerly exhausted so much time and patience. The machine did a fine job. It is inherent in it that it should. It was not the computer's fault that when the highway was completed, it had cut right through the city's finest park. That vital parameter,

Tidewater creeps up through the marshes along the way to Yorktown. Colonial Parkway. [Photo: M. Woodbridge Williams]

Mabry Mill—the word "photogenic" could have originated here. Blue Ridge Parkway. [Photo: M. Woodbridge Williams]

of the value of the preservation of beauty, had not been part of the input. Almost-thinking proved an illusion. Thinking will remain, for some time at least, the activity of persons. And, more than thinking, feeling.

I had such thoughts in mind on an April day, going down the Blue Ridge Parkway, when I stopped at one of the overlooks where a self-guided trail takes off into the forest. The wind was northerly and chill, but I found a place where I could beg a backrest from a matronly tulip poplar, shielded from the breeze. "Pardon me, madam; may I recline against your warm back?"

My mind went back a good many years, to the day when I first drove a section of this Appalachian avenue. I don't remember how many miles of it had then been opened. I do recall that about 1950 I wrote that about two thirds of it could be traversed. Now, as I write again, only a few miles of the total project remain to be completed. I said formerly that it would be one of the great scenic highways of the world. It is. Four hundred and sixty-nine miles of ribbon park.

The thought came to me that for most of the years of construction the engineers must have had to do a tremendous amount of time-consuming figuring. The only computer in those earlier days was an adding machine. I suppose, in a sense, the modern marvel is still an adding machine, but with an incredible extension of powers.

But it seemed good to realize that those landscape architects and other planners and doers of this parkway had in their minds primarily that though this was to be recreation, this journey into human and natural history, it was never to be forgotten that it was also to be a sojourn in an outdoor museum where all that was beautiful could remain so, and that nothing of disharmony should creep in. To what an astonishing degree this ideal has been achieved!

I wonder how many people had used any part of the Blue Ridge Parkway when I was writing about it in 1950? My statistical computer-user tells me that "approximately *eight million* visits were made to it in 1965." It led all

Tranquil resting spot near the Peaks of Otter. Blue Ridge Parkway. [Photo: W. E. Dutton]

but the numerous attractions offered by the great National Capital Parks complex.

Again I look back to what I wrote. "Connecting Great Smoky Mountains National Park, which sits astride the Tennessee and North Carolina boundary, with Shenandoah National Park, in Virginia, is the Blue Ridge Parkway." Very crisply said, sir; go on from there!

Distinctly, this is not a highway for anyone who wishes to go somewhere in a hurry. It is not like the highways that have been advantageously built as access roads to our great cities. This is a road the holiday-maker will browse upon, like a booklover among rare and beautiful volumes, stopping every little while to look upon a scene that has no counterpart in America. These are the Southern Highlands, and for miles upon miles you pass the fences of split rails, the weathered cabins, the livestock, and the barns of the people who have lived here so long.

Where the road has been engineered to offer as much interest and beauty as possible, the cuts and fills have been and are being planted with the native shrubs and trees—the white pine, azaleas, rhododendrons. This is one road where, because the highway is protected by a buffer strip, the traveler will not be importuned to use any particular shaving cream, dentifrice, or chewing gum. There are no signs suggesting that you come in just as you are and eat at a restaurant that went out of business several years ago. If you wish advice on what pills to take for your special misery, you will have to leave the Blue Ridge Parkway and use one of the older routes.

Well, retrospectively, I believe this wasn't bad. It had a good measure of enthusiasm. But as I now see it, and now go up or down the parkway, that chapter sounds a bit stingy. I suppose I may have felt cramped for space. That is a ready escape hatch for an author. I certainly didn't give Linnville Falls—the gift of a lover of beauty, John D. Rockefeller, Jr.—their due notice. I did not mention the Moses H. Cone Memorial Park, mile 292 on the log, with its twenty-five miles of horse and carriage trails. And Mabry Mill! How could I have neglected that masterpiece, so photogenic that the worst duffer with a camera has been unable to make a failure of it, unless he superimposed it on a picture of Uncle James?

Forgivable was the lack of mention of certain other features of the parkway, because they hadn't then come into existence; at least as part of the present scene. Well, the Blue Ridge Parkway is so well known (eight million visitors in one year!) now that it doesn't need the advertising I rather skimpily gave it in 1950 or thereabouts.

2. NATCHEZ TRACE PARKWAY
[*Mississippi–Tennessee–Alabama*]

NASHVILLE WAS THE POINT to which the footsore or muleback travelers of the old Natchez Trace were used to look with eager expectation. My friend and I, one early spring day when the redbud and the dogwood were blended upon the hillsides, were also following the Trace, but we were going in the opposite direction. They had it hard; we were pampered wayfarers with benefit of rubber tires. Yet, even in an automobile you may encounter discomfort; it looked like rain after we had left Cunningham's Ridge, just south of Leiper's Fork, and county roads, though good enough when dry, can become well greased under a drizzle.

At Cunningham's Ridge, not far from the home of Thomas Hart Benton, statesman and historian, we had left the car and footed it with great joy along a stretch of the very ground where so many thousands of pioneer travelers had slogged. That, my friends, is a real thrill, for American history is walking with you. You bunt your booted toes against the stones of the ancient trail just as did the Kentucky boatmen when they toiled, cursing their pedestrian fate, toward home. The French traders went along this ancient path; so did the missionaries whose zeal to bring the Light to the Indians led them to become bedfellows of roisterers and thieves; and long, long before all these the ancestors of our historic Indians went bartering for the exotic things they craved from far-off tribes. No road is fuller of romance than this—the Natchez Trace.

When the French first explored and mapped this land they saw a trail running from the home of the Natchez Indians to the villages of the Choctaws and the Chickasaws in northeast Mississippi. And horrible was the vengeance taken by the armed French against these Natchez in 1729, following the massacre of their compatriots who had settled on the river bluffs and in the St. Catherine Creek valley. The Indians had grievances and struck with blind rage, killing men, women, and children. The French replied in kind, and when it was over, all who were left of the Natchez nation were sold into slavery or managed to escape to the Chickasaw people, who received them with a hospitality that was to make trouble for the hosts in later time.

Before we go forward toward Natchez, let us pause a moment to consider what this Natchez Trace Parkway really is, or will be when it is completed. You may call it, if you like, an elongated National Park. For about 450 miles it will be a motor road with ample space upon either side to preserve

Sunken road near the southern end of the trail. Natchez Trace Parkway. [Photo: M. Woodbridge Williams]

the natural scenery of the route. Here it will show a meadow; there a copse of native trees, some perhaps dating from Indian-treaty time; over there a hillside farm, its natural operations undisturbed.

The parkway does not, of course, follow the identical ancient trail. It crosses and recrosses it, giving easy access to the historic spots along the route —the "stands" where travelers got bed and board at the end of their day, the ferry sites, the Indian mounds, and many spots where the native plantlife may be studied and enjoyed. Now and again the parkway traveler will see the Trace where it moves furtively off into the underbrush—always unmistakably the old Trace, however, even though nobody pursues it today.

Distinctly this is not a parkway for speeding or for local convenience in going places. In its finest aspect, it will endure for future generations as an outdoor museum of human history, of quietly beautiful scenery and of the

The plodding "Kaintuck" boatmen were near home at this part of the trail. Natchez Trace Parkway. [Photo: Tennessee Conservation Department]

ways of nature. Happiest, to my mind, of all the visitors to the region will be those who leave their automobiles at some proper point and follow a piece of the Trace afoot. That is the ideal journey into the past, and in some shaded spot, on a genial day, thoughtful ones will sit on a fallen tree and meditate upon the ways of men, weaving their own short experience into the tapestry of time and change.

So, at some point along the Natchez Trace, we re-create the motley procession passing by, following the ridges, even though steep and stony, to avoid the swamps and streams. First the aboriginal people, the excavations of whose ceremonial and burial mounds telling us how they lived; then their descendants, either on the warpath or on a peaceful trading journey; next the hardy explorers—Spanish, French, English; and after them our own colonials, engaged in that westward push which so many of our National Monuments commemorate. We see the boatmen of Kaintuck, who floated their rude boats down the Ohio and Mississippi into New Orleans and there broke them up for the lumber they contained. The steamboat had not come to the Great River, and against its current they could not return home the way they came. This Trace they took.

First, after leaving Natchez, they made their way upon the soft, loose, easily eroded soil; and that is why, today, if you leave your car and tramp awhile, you will go along sunken roads with high vertical sides, walking on a level below even the tree roots of the forest. Not at all like the thin, stony path the Trace becomes farther north, when sometimes it goes upon a limestone outcrop supporting only scrubby growth.

And here, as we watch, comes "Old Hickory," Andrew Jackson, indignantly marching his stalwart followers back from Natchez when he was ordered to disband them; and again we see Jackson's men returning victorious from the Battle of New Orleans; and with Jackson comes a circuit rider, a government official, and sundry vagrants who have attached themselves to the troop for security and the chance to mooch their rations. And then there is the ill-starred Meriwether Lewis, friend of Thomas Jefferson and co-leader with Clark on the epic journey to the Pacific Northwest. His violent death, for many years thought to have been a murder, occurred at Grinder's Stand— one of the rough taverns of the Trace, in Tennessee.

Not least among the shadowy figures that haunt the Trace are those vigorous missionaries, either sent forth by established churches to carry the gospel to the benighted or evangelizing by personal inspiration: James Hall, the Presbyterian on horseback in 1801; the eccentric Methodist Lorenzo Dow, the "crazy preacher" from Connecticut, sallow, lean and hard, holding forth to the sinners of the grogshops; Jacob Young with his band of five, undeterred by reports from the white tavernkeepers that the Indians "would be unimpressed by preaching."

The American settlers were moving in, meanwhile, and so came demands for regular mail service along the Trace. At first the Washington authorities were doubtful; the Postmaster General complained that the Natchez Trace was only "an Indian footpath, very devious and narrow." Well, so it was, until the United States troops were called upon to clear a wagon road and bridge the creeks, finally shortening the distance from the Mississippi terminus to Nashville by at least a hundred miles.

One thing remains of the Choctaw culture. Perhaps because their language was more adaptable than that of the neighboring tribes and so became in a modified form a sort of trading tongue along the lower Mississippi region,

A ruin can be beautiful. Tower of the brick church at Jamestown. Colonial Parkway.
[Photo: M. Woodbridge Williams]

this country along the Natchez Trace abounds with a delightful and racy nomenclature. Bogue Chitto, so common in Mississippi, is Big Creek. Shocka-loo Creek is really Cypress Creek. And that Dancing Rabbit Creek, the scene of an Indian treaty, was Chukfi Ahihla Bok, and in the words you can almost see what the Choctaw observer one day saw there—an Uncle Remus rabbit doing a jig.

But the whites, after they took possession were also quite able to give challenging names. By-wy Creek, Sugar-tree Hollow, Coon Box, Buzzard's Roost, Crippled Deer Creek, Many Panther Creek, Trimcane Creek (the

kind of cane growing here was woven into baskets by the Choctaw women)
—these are a few of the names that delighted my companion and me as we
went across, around, and along the Natchez Trace on those delightful April
days.

3. COLONIAL PARKWAY AND COLONIAL NATIONAL HISTORICAL PARK
[*Virginia*]

IN COMPARISON WITH THE BLUE RIDGE PARKWAY and Natchez Trace Parkway, this one is short indeed. But its twenty-two miles represent a gentle
conspiracy between the historian and the landscape architect to the end that
the traveler in the classic triangle that includes Jamestown, Colonial Williamsburg, and Yorktown shall have the fairest possible experience with the beauty
of the Tidewater Virginia into which Englishmen first came for permanent
settlement. From planning to execution to maintenance this highroad has
always been a labor of love. It follows no pathways of early days. Rather, it
traverses an unspoiled ribbon of countryside and brings one to the gates of
cherished historic memorials.

Jamestown, Williamsburg, Yorktown—one chapter of our national story
led inevitably to the next. So we begin the journey into the past at Jamestown
Island. It was close to the shore of the James River that the newcomers built
their stockaded fort. For health it was not the wisest choice. But at their
backs were an uncharted wilderness and a savage people. They were unweaned
from their homeland; and so long as they were at the waterside they were
assured that the way back to the white cliffs of Dover was open.

The parkway runs across Powhatan Creek and eastward along the James
for a few miles, then turns off into the woods. The forest is not spectacular,
but soothing. Of course there will be no billboards. You will not miss them.
Then a tunnel lets you pass under Williamsburg: an excellent idea because
the restored city does not need more traffic, and you will do best to see it
afoot.

The Williamsburg Information Center is just beyond the tunnel. Williamsburg advertises itself. You may have seen the advertising—restrained yet
alluring, messages that make one want to march for a moment in this procession of people and events. Thanks to the generosity and wisdom of John D.
Rockefeller, Jr., this restoration is not for profit. It therefore advertises not
for customers but for beneficiaries. The interpretation of life as it was lived
in this second provincial capital is here admirably done, and of course the

felicity with which the restoration work was accomplished is known wherever taste and talent exist.

Your destination is Yorktown. From the woodsy surroundings the way comes out on blue water—the York River, really an estuary at this point. Six miles, along which there are pleasant overlooks and instructive historical markers, and then you are at the city, which in the eighteenth century was a busy mart and port, and where the American Revolution came virtually to its close in 1781. In this famous spot where Cornwallis surrendered to Washington and his French allies, a self-guided motor trip will take you from the visitor center (where Washington's actual military tents can be seen) to the Siege Line and the redoubts with old cannon in place. Thence you will wish to go about the present-day Yorktown, where there is not much that is of Washington's day, but that little remainder is precious.

Preserved as a part of Colonial National Historical Park is Cape Henry Memorial, where the emigrant Englishmen saw the "Land of Virginia," "about foure o'clock in the morning" of April 26, 1607, and rejoiced that their voyage in their three small ships had been fortunate. Here they remained for four days, after claiming the country for God and king. It was 174 years before one of these proprietors was eliminated.

[III]

National Recreation Areas

1. Lake Mead National Recreation Area
[*Arizona–Nevada*]

Within the vast area, land and water, where two lakes were created by the damming of the scouring Colorado River, visitors may swim, boat, fish, water ski, skin dive, camp, hike, or just drive the hundreds of miles of road. But, also, they may observe and study extraordinary rock formations; delight their eyes with the red and yellow splendor such as that in Iceberg Canyon; or watch the great variety of birds from hummingbirds to eagles. Wild burros, desert bighorn, and a number of smaller mammals make their homes here; the great forest of Joshua trees is found on the Pierce Ferry road; on the high plateaus of Shivwits and Hualpai is piñon and juniper wilderness.

With these facts in mind the reader may well ask, "How does this differ from a national park? Why do you call it a national recreation area?" Good questions; and since we fortunate Americans should not only know our parks, but also have awareness of the management policies that govern them in preservation and use, this seems a favorable moment for explanation.

In midsummer of 1964 a Secretary of the Interior sent to the director of the National Park Service a memorandum titled "Management of the National Park System." It was not a revolutionary document, but it was a highly important one. It was based upon long and careful studies of the great changes that had taken place in American life since the Park Service came into being half a century before. This means the phenomenal mobility, the increase of leisure, the greatly increased take-home income, and the consequent urgent need for more and more opportunities for outdoor recreation for the exploding population growth.

Lake life: aquatic forms. Lake Mead National Recreation Area. [*Photo: Fred Mang, Jr.*]

The memorandum was a study within a study. It sought not only a reassessment with a view toward necessary changes; it studied the older principles and policies to see how much could be retained and even emphasized. And much remains as it was. The natural areas will be, as was stated by Secretary Lane in 1918, "maintained in absolutely unimpaired form for the use of future generations." In historical areas the memorial purpose is paramount, but use of natural resources can be made when it offers no detriment. But in the recreational areas the emphasis will be upon "outdoor recreation." The area has a "recreation mission." There may be other values within the area, and these may be utilized for public enjoyment. But they are a plus. Outdoor recreation is the dominant resource.

Also you find another plus, not mentioned in the memorandum but inherent, that will apply in cases where dams like Hoover and Davis have created these manmade places of outdoor recreation. The dam itself becomes part of the enjoyment offered. Man cannot hope to rival nature's wonders, but he can produce a work of gigantic skill. Though built in the period 1931–5, Hoover Dam remains the tallest dam in the western hemisphere. From the road across the top visitors look down 726 feet to the base rock. The entire flow of the Colorado River for two whole years can be stored behind this wall. Davis Dam, behind which Lake Mohave forms, is not so high, but has a longer span. Indeed, these dams are memorials of American technology. So it is three-way: physical recreation, history, the grand natural scene.

Nobody has yet found a satisfactory definition for the word *recreation*. However, it isn't necessary to define it. Observing the way visitors to these two manmade lakes find and constantly change their diversions would provide a better definition than any word. For example, the fisherman comes here. He may think he is interested only in fishing. But he finds himself using a boat for water adventuring. The tourist, perhaps on his way to Grand Canyon or Yosemite, stops to have a look at the dams. The clear, clean, and buoyant nature of the surroundings exercise their allure, and you find him back as a camper, in one of the many designated campgrounds or even in an isolated spot on the lakeside.

Or the weekender, usually from one of the adjoining states, who comes in "just to have a look" finds so much to interest him that when the summer heat has subsided he returns with a trailer. Just to relax and forget the naughty, irritating world? That is what he tells himself, but he hears a campground slide talk, or sees an exhibit at a visitor center, and decides he wants to know more about the wildlife, the geology, or the prehistoric people who

Uncrowded spaces for the fisherman. Lake Mead National Recreation Area. [Photo: R. C. Middleton, Bureau of Reclamation]

left their picture stories on the canyon walls along the shore of Lake Mohave.

Without a doubt, it is the great area of water surface which forms the primary attraction. "Our folks down this way have a hunger for water," a park director told me once in Oklahoma. "Or maybe I should say 'thirst.' " I replied that I thought his word *hunger* was the better, because it really wasn't that they lacked water to drink. Their craving was for the feeling, the eye-soothing presence of a hill-bordered lake, an invitation to swim in it, or skim over it. Yes, *hunger* is the word. Even those of us who come from the regions of glacier-formed lakes feel the ceaseless urge to return and refresh.

It was within the Lake Mead–Lake Mohave area that some of the signifi-cant events of the famous expeditions of Major John Wesley Powell occurred. Much has been learned of the geology of the country through which this river takes its winding course. Yet there are still baffling mysteries. My favorite geologist tells me that it is in the Lake Mead region and below that answers to questions about the Colorado River will be found.

2. COULEE DAM NATIONAL RECREATION AREA
[*Washington*]

FROM MAY THROUGH OCTOBER this is a region of almost continuous sunshine. There may be morning mists, but they burn off just as the unaccustomed visitor had resigned himself to a cloudy day. A wind begins to blow down over Lake Roosevelt from the surrounding hills and fills the sails of those who regard this kind of boating as the sport of kings. But there are other kinds of craft, too; and there is no restriction on the size of them, though they must be handled with respect for the rights of others. Swimming, of course, is the favorite sport on the twelve developed beaches along the shore of the lake and in many other places.

Fishing, yes; and improving each year. At the mouths of the creeks you may get trout, though the Kamloops breed will be found farther out in the colder waters. Up the creeks and in Banks Lake are rainbows, bass, pike, and crappies.

A good way to begin acquaintance with this huge manmade body of water, created by halting and harnessing the Columbia River, is to see the dam and the impoundment from the lookout point about two miles from the town of Coulee Dam. Here is the dam from above; on one side the immense concrete face and on the other the blue waters of the lake. The Bureau of Reclamation, which operates the dam, offers free sightseeing tours on a self-guiding basis. During the long summer season, lights play a variety of color combinations upon the water that curtains down the face of the massive structure.

Even though the emphasis may be on the various kinds of physical recreation, visitors can hardly fail to be aware that the natural surroundings are most unusual. What is the meaning of this prodigious gorge, with its columnar cliffs that so plainly indicate that they were built up a little at a time? The many layers are clearly delineated from any point in the bottom of the canyon. To the geologist it is all relatively simple. With a little interpretation, the whole story is not hard for the layman to grasp. And in terms of

---

On the Trinity Division. Whiskeytown-Shasta-Trinity National Recreation Area. [*Photo: L. K. Noonan, Bureau of Reclamation*]

geologic time it all took place just a short time ago. In all the western hemisphere there is nothing comparable in magnitude to the flows of lava out of which the present scene was created.

The lava squeezed out of earth rifts that developed in the regions to the south. Not as one great flow—there were long inactive periods. But the lava kept coming until it piled up a plateau that in places reached a height of four thousand feet. That was the first chapter. As the lava surface rose, it naturally blocked the rivers in its path, and the great Columbia was forced out of its course.

The latest advance of the ice age arrived, and thousand-foot sheets moved southwesterly out of the Canadian mountains. This time, the new blocking created a glacial lake about where Franklin D. Roosevelt Lake now spreads, though it was much larger. The cutting of the coulee was done by the immense volume of water, made abrasive with sand and pebbles, which spilled over the edge of this glacial lake.

A short distance south of Banks Lake is Dry Falls State Park. Visitors who wish to understand the geological story will do well to visit that area. One could call it a preface to the recreation area.

3. GLEN CANYON NATIONAL RECREATION AREA
[*Arizona–Utah*]

CONSIDERING THE VAST EXTENT and variety of the areas included under the administration of the National Park Service, visitors encounter surprisingly few "don'ts" in their recreational enjoyments. Wherever such warnings appear, they relate either to normal good social conduct with a regard for the rights and welfare of all, or to the safety of the individual.

Here is an example of what I mean. The folder that invites us to make use of the recreational facilities which have been created by the Glen Canyon Dam and its resultant Lake Powell has a word of caution. "The water of the lake is deep, right to the shoreline in most places, and—especially in side canyons—the smooth vertical cliff walls offer a swimmer no handholds . . . swimming in Lake Powell is not for the beginner . . . taking these warnings into account you will find some delightful coves such as those in Last Chance Canyon."

One incidentally gets from this warning a pretty clear picture of what

---

Major John Wesley Powell gave the canyon its name. Glen Canyon National Recreation Area. [Photo: W. L. Rusho, Bureau of Reclamation]

this part of the Colorado River looked like before the waters were impounded: the deep, sheer walls of the brick-red Navajo sandstone that represent wind-blown sand dunes, and the sedimentary rocks at Wahweap that
tell of an ancient sea which once covered the region. With Major Powell on
his second trip down the great river was Frederick S. Dellenbaugh. It was in
October, he said, that Powell came to this labyrinth, then called Mound, but
later consolidated with the part below called Monument, and "altogether
now standing as Glen Canyon."

"The walls," said Dellenbaugh, "were strangely cut up by narrow side
canyons, some not more than twenty feet wide, and twisting back a quarter
of a mile where they expanded into huge amphitheaters, domes and cave-
like." Now, deeply covered by the water of the lake (and obviously with no
handholds for a swimmer), these side canyons form mystically beautiful
avenues of adventure for the prudent man with a boat.

The Navajo Reservation forms the southern boundary of Glen Canyon
National Recreation Area. The Indians, conservation-minded, with tribal
parks of their own, invite all visitors to see their way of life, their flocks of
sheep and goats, and their round houses called hogans.

For fishermen there have been plantings in the lake of rainbow trout,
kokanee salmon, and largemouth bass. Catfish needed no introduction. They
have ruled the river over the centuries; and speaking only for himself, the
present writer finds them the best eating of all. Perhaps a plebeian taste, but
my own.

Just as the catfish has so long called this entrancingly lovely country his
own, so did the beaver. It is hoped that this competent rodent will adapt to
the fluctuations of a manmade lake, and return to build his houses.

From Wahweap Campground, where there are campsites for both tents
and trailers, it is now less than sixty miles by boat and trail to Rainbow Bridge
National Monument.

4. WHISKEYTOWN-SHASTA-TRINITY NATIONAL RECREATION AREA
[California]

IF THE NAME Whiskeytown brings into your mind an image of the bearded
and wool-shirted miners of the California gold rush, you will not be in error.

The breeze is 'long shore. Shadow Mountain National Recreation Area. [*Photo:
L. C. Axthelme, Bureau of Reclamation*]

It was not long after the strike at Sutter's Mill that Clear Creek began to yield its placer wealth. Whiskey Creek flows into one side of the recreation area and Brandy Creek on the other. The strength of the stimulant reflected, perhaps, the relative size of the nuggets that were panned from the gravel in those feverish days.

The coarse gold played out. You could still get a "showing" in any of those creekbeds, but it would be a tough way to make a living. Instead, people are now coming here from San Francisco, Portland, and Sacramento to make use of the golden opportunities to camp and picnic and fish, surrounded by some of the most charming scenery in northern California.

The dam and reservoir are features of the Trinity River section of the Bureau of Reclamation's Central Valley project, making multiple use of the excess waters of a stream that formerly raced to the ocean. First stored behind Trinity Dam for a powerplant, later carried in a tunnel through the Hadley Peaks and down to another source of electric energy, the water finally enters Whiskeytown Lake to create a surface area of 3,600 acres. Before the needs of man are satisfied, the same water will have joined the Sacramento River for irrigation and other purposes. Altogether an elaborate and carefully studied engineering project!

The movement of earth incident to the building of a huge dam—this one is 272 feet above the streambed—necessarily effects a disturbing change upon the local landscape. As restoration gradually takes place, however, some of the working trails of the constructors will be maintained for hiking and horse-back riding, leading through thickets of toyon and manzanita and offering fine views of the lake.

Not the least interesting thing about the Whiskeytown Dam is the fact that the water is released through two outlets of different levels, blending the warmer and cold waters of the impoundment, just as you would turn on both faucets in your washbowl. The reason is (as you may have guessed already) that the salmon and steelhead trout which use Clear Creek as a spawning ground require a certain water temperature for their reproductory process. Since fish are not notably communicative to man, they have only one way to signal whether the temperature is right or wrong: they either spawn or they don't. Here is where preliminary research pays off. We don't have to find out the hard way.

5. SHADOW MOUNTAIN NATIONAL RECREATION AREA
[*Colorado*]

IT HAS GENERALLY BEEN TAUGHT that the Continental Divide decides whether the precipitation that falls in the Rocky Mountains shall wend toward the Pacific or the Atlantic Ocean. This information remains accurate, but with the addition of the clause: "provided man's applied scientific ability does not rule otherwise." The Colorado–Big Thompson reclamation project takes surplus water from the Colorado River Valley west of the Divide, flows it through a thirteen-mile tunnel underneath the towering peaks, and turns it into the valley of the South Platte in eastern Colorado.

Apparently nature is not hastily vengeful, even though this impertinence comes close to being the unforgivable pride which the ancient Greeks called *hubris*. Nothing serious has happened yet. On the contrary, in the progress of this water diversion several other diversions have come into existence: ample facilities for boating and fishing, picnicking, camping, and hiking in the recreational area thus created. Grand Lake is, of course, a natural body of water, long known and enjoyed; but now there are two manmade lakes, Shadow Mountain and Granby, both of them much larger than the glacial one. Intensive use of the area, which even at present offers many possibilities for the vacationer, is planned by the National Park Service by agreement with the Bureau of Reclamation and Bureau of Land Management.

These three lakes in the valley of the Colorado are in the high region that was torn and reshaped during the most recent period of geologic history when ice covered much of the North American continent. Many of the islands in the lakes are the tops of hills which represent the accumulation of rock and sand plucked and milled by the irresistibly flowing ice sheet. The forest is not varied, being for the most part lodgepole pine and aspen— quaking aspen, the tree that flutters its leaves when there is not a noticeable breath of wind. Curious lovers of trees—I don't mean professional botanists but just outdoor folks—have discovered by examining the leaf stem just how the quaking comes about.

The lakes are open to fishing all the year, but regulations and permits are those of Colorado. There are brook trout as well as cutthroat, rainbow, and brown; in the manmade lakes the kokanee, or landlock sockeye, salmon is caught.

Visitors have a choice of several fine campgrounds, where housetrailers are accommodated. Picnic anywhere you like in the areas open to public use—

With a dog as pilot. Flaming Gorge National Recreation Area. [*Photo: Stan Rasmussen, Bureau of Reclamation*]

but be a good housekeeper! Riding horses may be rented in the town of Grand Lake. As to hunting, the laws of Colorado apply.

There are many privately owned boat docks where rentals can be arranged, or if you bring your own you can launch it at no cost.

6. FLAMING GORGE NATIONAL RECREATION AREA
[*Utah–Wyoming*]

THE IMPOUNDED WATERS of the Colorado River at Flaming Gorge have created a lake that extends upstream for ninety miles, almost reaching the city of Green River, Wyoming. You are in truly historic country here. It was about at this point that Major John Wesley Powell put his boats in the stream in 1869. The hardy one-armed Civil War veteran began his voyage into the unknown, literally betting his life upon a generalization he had made from his knowledge of geological processes. Many intelligent men avowed that there *must* be great falls in the Colorado. They said it was inevitable. If there were, Powell and his companions would not have a chance. They could not retreat, once they entered the canyon.

Powell said no; there were no falls. Rough waters, undoubtedly; not falls. He later told Dr. William H. Brewer of Yale that he was perfectly convinced that a river so loaded with silt and abrasive material would have long since scoured its bed down to almost an even grade. But he felt sure also that it would be a wild journey.

Again, two years later, and better equipped, Powell essayed the second conquest of the river. Dellenbaugh, who was with him this time and who wrote the story of the expedition, says that when they left Green River

there was a gale . . . filling the eyes with sharp sand. But we could see high up before us some bright red rocks, making the first canyon of the wonderful series that separates this river from the common world.

From these bright rocks, glowing in the sunlight like a flame above the grey-green of the ridge, the major [Powell] had bestowed on this place the name of Flaming Gorge. We were now at the beginning of the battle with the "sunken river."

This recreational area is under the joint administration of the National Park Service and the Forest Service. The southern part, the most scenic canyon sector, is within Ashley National Forest. To the north, centering around Green River city, the rolling rangelands with their typical wildlife are bulging with memories of the pioneers like Jim Bridger—the roguish trader who invented fantastic fables to tell the tenderfeet in revenge for their disbelief in his true stories of the wilderness marvels. Jim was here, and many other mountain men ranged this territory where Indians fished, trapped, and hunted.

[IV]

Wild Rivers

Toward the end of the eighteenth century Samuel Taylor Coleridge, the English poet-philosopher, went to Germany. He has left us a bitter epigram in verse, descriptive of what humans achieve when they congregate in large numbers upon a river that nature offered as a clean, sparkling, and free-flowing stream:

> In Köln, a town of monks and bones,
> And pavements fanged with murderous stones,
> And rags, and hags and hideous wenches
> I counted two-and-seventy stenches,
> All well-defined and separate stinks!
> Ye nymphs that reign o'er sewers and sinks
> The river Rhine, it is well known,
> Doth wash your city of Cologne,
> But tell me, nymphs, what power divine
> Shall henceforth wash the river Rhine?

Yet, at about the time that Coleridge was venting his disgust, a substantial citizen of the young American republic, living in New Hampshire just south of Concord, was noting in his diary that "three of us went down to the river today and catched a good lot of fish which is just now helpful and the Lord continue his mercy." And what were these helpful fish? They were the delectable Atlantic salmon, running up the Merrimack River toward its headwaters. Not only up the Merrimack they swam, but the Maine rivers,

---

Unpolluted, serene, a river preserved for the delight of posterity. Ozark National Scenic Riverways. [Photo: Gerald R. Massie]

and the Connecticut, and even the Hudson. And now? What self-respecting salmon would be found in those nauseous corrupted streams?

The story is old; it repeats itself with the insistence of a whippoorwill. When Caesar was in Gaul the Rhine was one of those unpolluted rivers, and so was the Seine, and the Loire and the Thames and the Danube. Still, nobody today would wish to return to the age of the Roman republic, when the life expectancy was about thirty-five years and the luxuries of the rich were less in quantity and quality than what the modern man now considers a minimum requirement. Every technical advance in the creation of economic welfare, save perhaps the use of the oceans as highroads, is necessarily an attack upon the landscape and upon nonrenewable resources. The diminution of natural beauty, and the effect of that aesthetic loss on humans, is the price paid for easier labor, for conveniences, for longer if less placid lives, for mobility and its various rewards. It becomes a question of preserving the benefits of exploitation while curbing the losses. A fast-growing nation is not likely to make much effort toward a discreet balance in this respect. "Take the cash and let the credit go." There are always a few farsighted thinkers, like Dr. George P. Marsh, who in 1874 published a warning book with the clumsy title: "The Earth as Modified by Human Action." The volume had few readers. But within the past few years more and more people have realized the importance of checking the prodigal and dangerous pollution and abuse of those precious resources, the American rivers.

In early 1961 the Senate Select Committee on National Water Resources recommended that "certain streams be preserved in their free-flowing condition because their natural scenic, scientific, aesthetic and recreational value outweigh their value for water development and control purposes now and in the future." The Secretary of the Interior and Secretary of Agriculture joined to appoint a study team to determine what rivers might be suitable in a nationwide system. Such a study was made. It was a fine start, but like all such innovations, it needed the voice of the highest authority. When President Johnson, on February 8, 1965, transmitted to the Congress his message "On Natural Beauty of Our Country," he said in blunt terms ". . . the time has come to identify and preserve free-flowing stretches of our great scenic rivers before growth and development make the beauty of the unspoiled waterway a memory. To this end I will shortly send to Congress a bill to establish a *national wild rivers system.*" The hour had struck.

Where the layman becomes interested in geology. Flaming Gorge National Recreation Area. [Photo: Stan Rasmussen, Bureau of Reclamation]

Whether these wild river preserves are administered by the National Park Service or by the Forest Service is not important. They would be well served by either agency. It is true, as Interior Secretary Udall said in his letter to the Chief Executive, that "a truly wild river is a rare thing today in the United States. But there are still many free-flowing rivers, or parts of such, that retain much of their original character and beauty." They speak to the spirit. They can even cure melancholy, according to the old Oxford vicar Richard Burton, who wrote: "Fishing is good . . . and if so be the angler catch no fish, yet he hath a wholesome walk and pleasant shade by the sweet silver streams."

Theodora Kroeber, in her "Story of Ishi," goes deeper into that yearning of urbanized man for an association with the waters of an unspoiled stream. "Perhaps," she comments, "creek and river continue to draw old and young to their quiet pools, to fish, because it is restful and healing to re-enact an age-old craft. No other occupation today brings modern man so close to his stone-age ancestors."

1. OZARK NATIONAL SCENIC RIVERWAYS
[*Missouri*]

As a PROTOTYPE of the elongated parks that are planned to preserve the un-stained wild river, no better location could be found than the Ozarks, and no finer free-flowing streams than the Current and the Jacks Fork of south-eastern Missouri. Much of this country has the aspect of being unpeopled. I recall that, driving down from St. Louis, I felt that I had never been over so long a stretch of forest where so few habitations could be glimpsed along the highway. Not virgin, to be sure. Much of this was once pine-clad, and lum-bered off; but the succeeding oak-hickory growth is dense and appealing, and dogwood and redbud announce themselves boldly in the spring, and then modestly withdraw into forest anonymity.

This is a country of extraordinary variety in its plantlife. The Ozarks saw nothing of the ice of the period of continental glaciation, but they felt the effect of it; and here you have an amazing mingling of northern plants that migrated southward away from the arctic breath; of southern species that moved north when a warm stage renewed; and finally of plants that have moved in from both east and west. With such forest cover it is no wonder

---

From a ledge of limestone Big Spring boils out its vast supply of water. Ozark National Scenic Riverways. [Photo: Don Wooldridge]

that the wide variety of animals has persisted, despite constant hunting. Even the rare red wolf is here. Birdlife is abundant. This must once have been a great ground for the wild turkey which Ben Franklin thought should be our national bird instead of the eagle. The species has been exterminated here, but has been reintroduced and is making a good comeback.

But of course the most notable feature of this Ozark region is what is known to the geologist as the "karst" topography, quite like the type of formation on the eastern side of the Adriatic Sea. That sounds pretty special and scientific. But no; the delight of visitors in this scenic riverway will spring wholly from the fact that the region *is* karst. How else the fascinating caves, with their dripstone creations, like Round Spring Cavern? How else the rugged limestone bluffs, and the clear cold springs with their phenomenal output of water? Big Spring, four miles south of Van Buren, alone could supply the needs of the city of St. Louis. It has had years when it could do far more than that; 840 million gallons in one day, if the figures mean anything to you. Other springs, like Welch and Blue Springs on the Current River and Alley Spring on the Jacks Fork, may seem small in comparison, but they would be sensational almost anywhere else.

All this adds up to fishing—the Current and Jacks Fork are famous for their bass—and for boating, swimming, and camping. The National Park Service has plans for a comprehensive program of outdoor recreation, but the natural and human history that make the region unique will definitely be preserved.

Other riverways on the list presently discussed for legislative action that will preserve them in their wilderness state are the Salmon and Clearwater in Idaho; the Rogue in Oregon; the Rio Grande in New Mexico; the Eleven Point in Missouri; and the Capacon and Shenandoah in West Virginia.

PART

FOUR

[I]

Americans Before Columbus

1. CHACO CANYON NATIONAL MONUMENT
[*New Mexico*]

THE ENGLISH ARCHAEOLOGIST GEOFFREY BIBBY, in his book *The Testimony of the Spade*, asserts that archaeology is meaningless without asking the question: "What did it *feel like* to be prehistoric?"

As stated, the question is rather absurd, because one may as well ask the question: "What does it feel like to be a human being?" We are all descendants and progenitors of people. Did anyone ever think of himself as a prehistoric person? And if not, how could he have any feelings about it?

But I think I know what Bibby had in mind. He probably meant, and justly, that in viewing what was left behind by a vanished people such as those who lived at Chaco Canyon for so many centuries before Columbus sailed, we are not to consider them as exhibits like the showcase of animal bones, charcoal, weapons, and pottery dug from ruins, but as working, wondering, striving, loving, quarreling, progressing human beings with basic emotions and problems not essentially different from our own. Were it not for the printed word our latest generation would find it hard to conjecture a world without the electric lamp. Equally, the late Basketmakers must have put the question: "How do you suppose our ancestors got along before (as some of our old folks say) there weren't any bows and arrows?" There *was* just such a time. And there was a Golden Age, to be sure—to which a grandfather in the *kiva* looked back sorrowfully. "In my time the teenagers were disciplined; now look at them!"

Probably about 600 A.D., about the time Pope Gregory was sending Augustine into England to carry the word of God to its pagan inhabitants, a farming people known to the archaeologist as Basketmakers were planting

---

From mesa top to the ancient dwellings is sheer fall. Canyon de Chelly National Monument. [*Photo: Fred E. Mang, Jr.*]

maize and squash on the floor of Chaco Canyon, watering their gardens with carefully hoarded summer rainstorms, and eking out a subsistence with edible wild plants and such small animals as they could trap or shoot.

The early Basketmakers, living in pit houses and thinking themselves pretty well off—possibly pitying those who lacked nice pithouses like theirs —developed thinkers and visionaries who said: "We can do even better than a hole in the ground!" Thus developed the laying up of blocks of sandstone, mortared to create structures to house many families under one roof. Other innovators began to weave from the fibers of the plentiful yucca around them, and not only to make pottery but to decorate it so that the eye might be pleased as well as the stomach. The aesthetic urge had arrived. And then, in that transition period when Basketmaker became pueblo dweller, we find that it became modish to flatten the heads of infants by laying them on their backs on hard cradleboards. If your children did not have flattened skulls, they were not "in." From that sort of thing to the society pages of the newspaper is not, after all, too long a jump.

This desirable luxury and modernity of the Chaco people would attract immigration—a human flow toward the affluent society. So they began really to build. Pueblo Bonito (Spanish for "beautiful village") went up to a height of five stories on a floor plan that covered three acres. Eight hundred or more rooms could shelter twelve hundred persons; and the developers of this high-rise included thirty-two *kivas* which served as ceremonial chambers or men's clubrooms. Perhaps the *kivas* were a sentimental memory of the days when the earliest Basketmakers burrowed into the ground for shelter.

And then? The Chaco people began to leave for parts unknown. Why? Also unknown. Drought, internal politics, enemies—perhaps a combination of these factors. Before the fourteenth century, rabbits and other game stared at tenantless dwellings and wondered at the stillness.

2. CANYON DE CHELLY NATIONAL MONUMENT
[*Arizona*]

ACCORDING TO THE TIME OF DAY, the color of these canyon walls changes, but always there is redness of some sort. In some places there is a sheer drop of a thousand feet from the mesa to the river—a meandering stream which has come out of the mountains to the east and ends in the Chinle Wash. The water that was so precious to the prehistoric Indians who lived here for a thousand years still is at the whim of stingy rainfall or snow-melt. It is a land in which primitive people simply must have a rain god to be propitiated.

Some years ago I started out over the mesa with a Navajo who, because he apparently had conceived a liking for me, said that he was going to take me to a spot where we could see some ruins of ancient dwellings that "even the folks at headquarters don't know about." Alas, I never saw them. Just as we neared the edge of the canyon one of those blizzardy late-spring snow-storms came down upon us. Visibility dropped almost to zero. So we sat in the truck and tried to wait the weather out. And we talked—of many things.

"No," said Tom, in answer to a question, "I don't feel any closer to those old people than you do. They were not Diné [Navajo]. Some ways, I think, they were smarter than we are today; some ways not."

We discussed the pictographs that are seen on the cliff faces. When I told Tom that some people think they were just "doodling," to while the time away, he snorted. "That's foolish. I don't know what they mean, but they mean something."

R. J. C. Atkinson, an English archaeologist, would agree. He thought there was too strict an appeal to the canons of archaeological evidence, which in fact may "merely serve to conceal a lack of imagination."

3. RUSSELL CAVE NATIONAL MONUMENT
[*Alabama*]

UNTIL A FEW YEARS AGO, Russell Cave was just another cave; and the United States has no paucity of caves. In 1953 a group of members of the Tennessee Archaeological Society began digging here, not far west of Bridgeport, Alabama, and uncovered the evidence that archaic man was an occupant nine thousand years before our time. It was an exciting discovery. If indeed our first immigrants came from Asia across Bering Straits "ten thousand years ago," a view commonly held, they must have moved fast across North America at a period when motion would presumably be slow.

But they were here; and curiously enough they began to take refuge in Russell Cave rather soon after it became habitable, for there had been a stream running through it, and only a fall of rock from the roof had created a dry flooring. On this slabby foundation the firstcomers camped and began to leave for the archaeologist the tell-tale charcoal from which the time clock can be approximately read by measuring the radioactive carbon.

The first occupants were "hunters and gatherers." Nuts and seeds were plentiful, and so were game animals—deer, turkey, squirrel, fox, and skunk—and then even the porcupine, now found only much farther north. The tough chert that occurred in the surrounding limestone was the perfect material from which to fashion spearpoints. We can see them in the colder weather, well protected from the elements, sitting beside their fires smithing a good supply of weaponry against the coming hunts. They fished with hooks made from bone. The nearby great river furnished a pleasant diet-variety item of fish and mollusk.

Ornaments they seem not to have had. Was time for leisure not sufficient? Nor did they make pottery. That appears only at the much later period when the Woodland Indian began his occupancy of the cave. Maybe the early ones were conservatives—even reactionaries.

4. MONTEZUMA CASTLE NATIONAL MONUMENT
[*Arizona*]

EXCEPT FOR TWO BOTHERSOME FACTS, Montezuma Castle was aptly named. It never was a castle, and Montezuma's Aztecs had nothing to do with it. The information of the early settlers who christened it was outpaced by their enthusiasm. Still, should we cavil too strongly at a touch of romanticism in a too-drab world?

Called by any name, this ancient tenement house, built into a naturally eroded hollow of the northside cliff of Beaver Creek, will delight those who have interest in our prehistoric Americans. In almost pristine condition, a few miles up a tributary from the Verde Valley, it gives to visitors an impression of a relatively happy life lived by the folks who occupied its twenty rooms, in five stories. Farming the valley by day for their corn and squash, coming back in the evening to climb the ladders and enjoy happy security from raiding enemies, these cliff dwellers should have been envied by the other inhabitants of the region, who had to cluster for protection.

Part of this monument preserves Montezuma Well, about seven miles by road northeast of the "castle." Out of this sink in the limestone flows the great quantity of water that was used by the aboriginal farmer for his irrigated land below. The ditches are still to be seen.

5. TONTO NATIONAL MONUMENT
[*Arizona*]

BEFORE THE ROOSEVELT DAM WAS BUILT, the irrigation ditches of the Salado people could still be seen in the valley of the Salt River, though the pre-

---

They chose a safe location for their apartment house. Montezuma Castle National Monument. [Photo: Bob Bradshaw]

historic Indians who built them left their cave-shelter homes six centuries ago. Why did these early farming folk live so far from their croplands, toiling with their burdens several miles, and climbing uphill a thousand feet of elevation? Certainly for protection against the incursion of freebooters hovering on their flanks, ready to seize the opportunity to loot and enslave. From the visitor center, a trail winds up the steep hillside through the plant cover, which thrives now, as it did then, in desert conditions—the cholla and other cactuses, jojoba, ocotillo, yucca, and sotol—to the "lower ruin." Familiar enough to those who live in the Southwest, this is a plant world strange indeed to all who come from regions where the rainfall is more generous.

Apparently these Salado people were not only well advanced potters and weavers, but they traded widely. Since they could not raise cotton the fibers they wove so artfully must have come from farmers farther south; and in the ruins were found ornaments—pendants, bracelets, and beads—made from shells brought in from the Gulf of California.

6. Pipestone National Monument
[*Minnesota*]

WELL ETCHED IN MY RECOLLECTIONS is my first visit to this monument in southwestern Minnesota. Looking across the grassy plain that stretches endlessly toward a straight-line horizon, I saw a single tepee, and beside it seated on a campstool an Indian. As I approached, I saw that the Sioux was working on a piece of the clay rock called catlinite, rough-shaping it into what might be a pipe bowl. His remote ancestors would have done it with stone tools; he had saw and knife of steel.

The scene was idyllic—except for one detail. At his side the Indian had a battery radio, which was blurting forth a nauseating cacophony. Thus the white man's technology was completing the job that the white man's bad whiskey had failed to finish.

Yet, as I remained in this preservation of prehistoric and historic Indian life and habit, the place became ever more satisfying. What a story is told here! The odd lithogenetic puzzle of this bed of red indurated clay between two layers of sandstone that became quartzite. The decision of primitive man that this was the superlative material from which to fashion ceremonial smoking bowls and sculptured ornaments. The trading of this most-esteemed rock

Standing Eagle, a Chippewa, shapes a peace pipe of "catlinite" rock. Pipestone National Monument. [Photo: Thomas Roll]

wherever calumets or figurines were shaped. (A beautiful piece of art by the hand of a Rodin of ancient days, unquestionably made from this very Pipe-stone catlinite, was found in a mound on Shiloh battlefield.)

7. MOUND CITY GROUP NATIONAL MONUMENT
[Ohio]

THESE SO-CALLED "HOPEWELL" PEOPLE lived for at least a thousand years in the Middle West. Here, in the valley of the Scioto, in southern Ohio, early explorers had observed a group of mounds that they perhaps thought to be merely a feature of the local landscape. But in 1846 the two pioneer archaeologists Squier and Davis began excavating the prehistoric earthworks. Out of them they took a surprising collection of artifacts, including stone tobacco pipes artistically carved in the shapes of human heads, birds, and animals. The British Museum now has these first trophies.

It seems certain that these primitive Americans, laboring with rude picks and shovels and baskets, reared the mounds as memorials for their high-ranking dead. Borrow pits from which the earth was gathered can still be seen within the monument. From far and wide this vanished people, who developed the arts to such a high point, obtained the materials with which they worked. They had obsidian (from Yellowstone?), mica from North Carolina, native copper that could have come down only from Lake Superior, shells gathered from the Mexican Gulf, and the teeth of grizzly bears. Fine objects taken from these and similar mounds throughout southern Ohio are to be seen at Chilicothe and at the State Museum in Columbus.

8. EFFIGY MOUNDS NATIONAL MONUMENT
[Iowa]

THERE IS A BONUS for those who come here to see the unusual work of a mound-building people who had novel ideas as to the way in which their distinguished dead should be honored. In scenic quality, the monument, situated on the high bluffs across the Mississippi River from Prairie du Chien, Wisconsin, is outstanding. Even if there were no important prehistoric evidences here, the forests, wild-flower displays, and interesting animal community would still qualify the place as a delightful parkland. You have the feeling that the first primitive occupants of this region were in a well-chosen spot where game-food abounded.

Within the boundaries, enclosing about two square miles, there are known to be 183 burial mounds. Most of them, like those seen in other areas, are conical or linear. But twenty-seven of the mounds are an astonishing departure from the rule. Working with the crudest of instruments, this group of people created barrows in the shapes of birds and animals—the hawk, the eagle, the bear, the fox, the deer, and the dog. One of these mounds—the Great Bear—is 137 feet long and 70 feet across the shoulders. The persistence of these low mounds of pictorial earthworks over the centuries is hardly less remarkable than their ethnic origin.

9. Ocmulgee National Monument
[*Georgia*]

A FAITHFUL DIORAMA, to be seen in the museum, reconstructs for visitors a council of the religious and governing elders of the farming Indians who lived here more than ten centuries ago on the outskirts of what is now the city of Macon. Here, over the original clay floor, is a reconstruction of one of the earth lodges of these mound-building people.

In the center is the sunken pit where the town's sacred flame was kept alight. Around the red-clay walls is a bench containing forty-seven seats. Opposite the door is a platform shaped like an eagle, and three seats are here—for the bigwigs. To purify the body, to cleanse it for the reception of advice from supernatural powers, the leaders first drank cassina, an emetic made from stewing the leaves of the yaupon shrub. The Egyptians had the same idea, but they used castor oil. Those of us who have been dosed with castor oil will prefer cassina—provided we have never tasted cassina.

Such an earthlodge was probably used in winter. Just north of this reconstruction is the Cornfield Mound, perhaps built in a field of holy maize seed. The prehistoric town was protected by two big ditches, indicating, perhaps, that successful farmers in those days had frequently to fight to keep what they raised.

10. Bandelier National Monument
[*New Mexico*]

LIFE WAS NOT ALL ROSES for the prehistoric peoples of North America, especially among the farming folk, with whom maize was a staple of diet. They had trouble with their teeth—they had toothache—and we wonder what they did about it. Did the shaman, or medicine man, offer anything better than consolatory words?

You might happen to be one of a group at Bandelier someday when the ranger is demonstrating, with the very utensils the ancients used, how the corn was ground in a *metate* (hollowed stone) with a stone *mano* (literally, a hand, in Spanish). Nothing more flavorful than this fresh-ground grain, and nothing worse for the teeth, for in the grinding, particles of grit are rubbed off the stones into the meal.

This monument was named for the Swiss-American ethnologist Adolph F. A. Bandelier, who studied these ruins, and entered into the life of the Pueblo Indians around Santa Fe, in the early 1880's. Bandelier set the scene of his novel *The Delight Makers*, in this Frijoles Canyon, where cliff ruins extend along the base of the northern wall for two miles. The Pajarito Plateau, in the tuff canyons of which the dwellers cut their houses, is of great geological interest. At any given spot in the Jemez Mountains it is hard to realize that you are on the rim of one of the world's greatest calderas—a gigantic saucer created by the collapsed summit of a volcano.

11. Tuzigoot National Monument
[*Arizona*]

When the Spanish adventurer Espejo came into the Verde Valley in 1583 he found Yavapai Indians living in thatched shelters amid the many ruins of old pueblo masonry houses. Actually it was an instance of a settlement "reverting to type," although the Yavapais did not know it, and probably cared less. Long before those crumbled stone dwellings had been built, there had been another people here in the valley, also living in pole-and-brush huts. These first settlers were related to a group that farmed the irrigated terraces near what is now the city of Phoenix.

The Tuzigoot settlers had been here somewhat more than a century when they were visited by Indians from the north, who liked the region and decided to stay. Perhaps the union of the two was peaceful—we cannot know that; but as always happened, new customs came in with the immigrants. The archaeologist finds that cremation of the dead gave way to burials: adults on the hillsides below the dwellings that were now built of stone; young children beneath the house floors.

In 1933 and 1934 the University of Arizona began to work upon the heaps of scattered rock, revealing enough of the original town so that, with

---

The Indians ground their corn this way, with mano *and* metate. *Bandelier National Monument.* [*Photo: Robert W. Gage*]

a partial reconstruction, visitors receive a good idea of what it looked like in its flourishing days.

12. GILA CLIFF DWELLINGS NATIONAL MONUMENT
[*New Mexico*]

IN THE FACE of a high cliff on a stream that flows into the west fork of the Gila River, some prehistoric Indians, looking for a home easily defended against marauders, found one ready-made by nature. The year-round water in the canyon, though not of great volume, was treasure-trove, too. More than thirty-five rooms, some of them large, were built into the cavities of the rock. From the largest shelter, natural archways led into two other sites suitable for rooms, separated by walls built of flat stones and adobe. The adobe is in such a good state of preservation that fingerprints can still be seen.

These ruins are in a rough country to which the only access is through Silver City to the Sapillo on the Forest Service road, and up Copperas Canyon truck trail to the head of Copperas. The last fourteen miles of the road are passable only to trucks with four-wheel drive, or to jeeps. The trip from Silver City to the ruins, by trail, takes about three hours. Therefore, anyone wishing to visit this area should get in touch, at least two or three weeks in advance, with the National Park Service superintendent, Box 1320, Silver City, New Mexico 88061.

13. WALNUT CANYON NATIONAL MONUMENT
[*Arizona*]

IMAGINE YOURSELF to be one of a band wandering across the semiarid lands of our Southwest looking for a likely place to create a community. Perhaps your group has swarmed out of a home which could no longer contain so many people, as bees leave the hive under a new leader. The place you are looking for must have, above all things, a dependable supply of water. It should have fuel—if not for warmth, surely for cooking. There are unfriendly nomads not far away; you seek a place not too hard to defend. Finally, since you are peaceable farming people, there must be fertile soil for your beans and corn and pumpkins. If the spot should be pleasing to the eye, so much the better.

Tyuonyi Ruins. Bandelier National Monument. [*Photo: John V. Young*]

Eureka! Happy discovery! Here is the place of your dreams. A canyon with sufficient all-year water; farmland on the rim above. Not being geologists you do not know how it happened, but there are ready-made shelters in the rock, where the top of the cliff projects over the lower part. What a roof over which to build a series of one-room homes! Good hunting here, too—almost every game creature from pack rat to cougar. You have only stone tools to work with, but these will suffice.

You and your descendants live here for many years. The time comes when for some reason your people decide to go. But you leave behind the testimony that you were there: your walls, your refuse dump, your pots and trinkets. Centuries later a people who call themselves American will come to look and to wonder. They will call the place Walnut Canyon.

14. CASA GRANDE RUINS NATIONAL MONUMENT
[Arizona]

IF YOU LIVED in a flat country, subject to raids from your enemies, and if you had the wit and skill, you would build yourself a watchtower high enough to see the invaders before they came too close. This is precisely what these Gila Valley pueblo people did. From the top of Casa Grande's four stories the watchmen could look far out over the desertland.

The archaeologists found here a fascinating story of prehistoric building methods. The lime clay found on the scene was good material for the purpose. Since they had not been intended to house anyone, after the walls had gone up seven feet above ground level, the first rooms that had been formed were filled in. That made a stout foundation for the next two stories and furnished a brace for the inner walls. As the archaeologist interprets: "They built an artificial seven-foot hill, then constructed a three-story house upon it." The upstairs apartments probably accommodated eleven families, and if the pueblo folk were like later Americans, those apartments were reserved for the elite. "I live in the Tower Apartments; my father has an official position."

It was the Jesuit missionary Father Kino who provided the name Casa Grande—"Big House." Did these pueblo people waterlog their lands by excessive irrigation? Why did they drift off—some of them to become, as is thought, ancestors of the present Pima Indians? The Pimas speak of them as the Hohokam, meaning "ancient ones."

The "sheltered life" in one respect. Navajo National Monument. [*Photo: Fred Mang, Jr.*]

15. Navajo National Monument
[*Arizona*]

Just as the Pima Indians refer to their supposed ancestors as "the ancient ones," so do the Navajos called the vanished pueblo people of the San Juan River region Anasazi—which means the same thing. Actually the tie of kinship is vague. The Navajo people are almost as awed by the ruins of Betatakin and Keet Seel as were Byron Cummings and the Wetherills when they stumbled upon them and gazed in astonishment.

In time three prehistoric cultural centers developed in this Four Corners region where the boundaries of Colorado, Utah, New Mexico, and Arizona meet: the Mesa Verde of southwestern Colorado, the Chaco Canyon people of northwestern New Mexico, and the Kayenta in northeastern Arizona. The three cliff dwellings of this monument represent the life and arts of the Kayenta.

Betatakin was built on the floor of a great cave, the roof of which projected far out over the dwellings. It once had nearly 150 rooms, and tree-ring dating indicates that it was occupied between 1242 and 1300 A.D. Keet Seel, which can be reached from Betatakin on horseback over a primitive trail, is the largest cliff ruin in Arizona, and was the last one to be abandoned in the Segi Canyon region. Visitors are not allowed to enter those two ruins unless accompanied by a guide. But you are free to make an unannounced journey to Inscription House, the smallest of the three communities.

16. Aztec Ruins National Monument
[*New Mexico*]

The "ancient ones" here built large stone houses and farmed on nearby lands which are still in cultivation, irrigated with water from the Animas River. Situated as these people were, between Chaco Canyon to the south and Mesa Verde to the north, it was natural that they should, at different periods, be influenced by the culture of both. For instance, the large pueblo, built during the time of Chaco dominance, reflects the pattern and large size characteristic of those builders. Later came a change to the thin walls and low ceilings of smaller structures similar to those of Mesa Verde.

It must have been hard going at first for the settlers at Aztec. With only stone and wooden tools the irrigation ditches were dug. They hauled sand-

Only a pile of stones, where a people once lived. Hovenweep National Monument.
[Photo: Fred Mang, Jr.]

stone blocks for a considerable distance without benefit of wheeled vehicles or beasts of burden. Their roof timbers, too, had to be brought in. Yet the time came when they touched a high level in the arts and crafts. Their intricately woven cotton cloth was noteworthy, though they cultivated no cotton themselves. The Great Kiva, excavated and restored by Earl H.

Morris and similar to those at Chaco Canyon, has an inside diameter of forty-eight feet.

17. HOVENWEEP NATIONAL MONUMENT
[*Utah–Colorado*]

IT WAS WILLIAM HENRY JACKSON, the pioneer "wet-plate" photographer accompanying the Hayden Survey party into Yellowstone, who gave Hovenweep its name. He was here in 1874, and used the Ute Indian word meaning "the deserted valley."

This is the off-beat adventure for those who find a satisfaction in following the fortunes of the pre-Columbian inhabitants of our country. To explore the vast, lonely region which lies north of the San Juan, and to see the extraordinary groups of defensive towers—square, oval, circular and D-shaped —is a delight reserved only for the hardy, those who thrill at overcoming difficulties. Hovenweep is almost off the map. You don't approach it over paved roads. Timid souls will think they have gone out of the world. There are no sleeping or eating accommodations, no gas stations, no food stores nearby. No wood for fires, and no water that you can wisely drink. And yet—of course you can get there. If it hasn't been storming recently, the approach roads are not so bad. And when you do arrive at the monument, and when you do see some or all of the ruins clustered at the heads of wild canyons—what a feeling of triumph!

The reason for so many defensive rock-towers? The people here had a vital water supply to protect.

18. PECOS NATIONAL MONUMENT
[*New Mexico*]

THE TALL TALES about the wondrously rich Seven Cities, which had led Francisco de Coronado north from Mexico, were proving to be a complete hoax. But there was one liar who had not yet had his inning—an Indian called by the Spaniards El Turco. The Turk peddled a yarn of new marvels "a long distance to the east." He told of the wonderful golden bracelets of which he had been robbed by the natives of Cicuyé.

This Cicuyé was in the valley of the upper Pecos River and at the foot of the Santa Fe Mountains. Coronado sent Hernando de Alvarado back to the Indian village, where shortly before he had been treated with hospitality, to demand the Turk's bracelets. The Indians replied that there were no such bracelets. Alvarado put the head chief in chains; other abuses followed; finally there was insurrection. The Spaniards were able to put down the Indians, but Pecos, or Cicuyé, was to be an important milestone in the advance of the conquistadors. Wherever Coronado or his lieutenants went thereafter, their promises of peace were jeered. The pueblos could be "pacified"; the Indians could be plundered; but implacable enmity had been established.

Pecos National Monument, twenty-six miles southeast of Santa Fe, has been a site administered by the Museum of New Mexico and known as Pecos State Monument. The area embraces the remains of two Indian villages dating from the thirteenth century, and two mission churches established by the Spaniards—one early in the seventeenth century, the other, about a hundred years later. On June 28, 1965, the National Park Service was authorized to assume administration of the area.

[11]

Struggle for the Continent

1. SAN JUAN NATIONAL HISTORIC SITE
[*Puerto Rico*]

"THREE THINGS SAN JUAN HAS, that Madrid has not: El Morro, San Cristóbal, and the sight of the ships coming in from sea." Thus speaks the Puerto Rican with pardonable satisfaction, not esteeming Madrid less, but loving San Juan more.

Historic ground, indeed. And if there comes into the voice of the interpreter at this historic site something different of fervor and flavor, it is somewhat like the effect of the illuminated initial on the page of an ancient manuscript. For here was an outpost and a fortification that had to exist, if the convoys of Spain, laden with silver from Mexico and treasure from Cartagena and Puerto Bello, were to reach their destination. Without this keeper of the gate on one side and St. Augustine on the other, the pirates and privateers (it was not easy to distinguish) would have had Spain in the position of a gull fishing for the profit of a man-of-war bird: the plunderer plundered.

Nor was it only that. Puerto Rico, in the hands of another European power, would have been a fatal menace. Juan Ponce de León saw this when he made a settlement at Caparra in 1508. From here he went to explore the North American mainland—not, you may be sure, because he indulged in any silly notion of a "fountain of youth," but because the glowing picture of new treasures was in his eyes.

To protect the sea route something better than Caparra was required, and something much stronger than the Casa Blanca of Ponce de León, or even the Fortaleza (fortress), of which Gonzalo de Oviedo remarked that

---

"Queen of the Spanish Missions." San José Mission National Historic Site. [Photo: Harvey Patteson]

Señor Morales tells the story of the "Castle." San Juan National Historic Site. [Photo: M. Woodbridge Williams]

"only blind men could have chosen such a site for a fort." There was certainly a better site. At the west end of San Juan was a *morro*, or headland, rising from the sea 120 feet. Here Morro Castle was reared, and it was none too soon. Havana had been sacked by corsairs, who were becoming even bolder. It was a time of conflict among European powers, too, and hardy mariners of many nations hungered for prize money as jackals eye a lion feasting on his kill. El Morro was still young when the English adventurer Drake came with a fleet of ships and three thousand men to test its worth. He very nearly succeeded in taking the town, but at the last moment, fortune deserted him. But then came George Clifford, Earl of Cumberland. Rather strangely, in this time of war, San Juan had been left with a mere skeleton force. An English warship proved too well armored for the shore guns at the point of attack, and its siege guns smashed the landward wall of El Morro. His Britannic Majesty's flag flew triumphantly over Puerto Rico, and Spain's domination in the New World seemed near an end. But San Juan was harder to hold than to gain. The Earl of Cumberland, his men weakened by disease, finally set sail for home.

But now Spain and the Netherlands were at each other's throats, and in 1625, after San Juan's defenses had been strengthened, the Dutchman Hendrick confidently entered the harbor, seemingly undisturbed by fire from the fort. For more than a month there were attacks and counterattacks.

El Morro, Cristóbal, La Casa Blanca, El Cañuelo—magic names with music in them. The last scene of all: Admiral Sampson with an American flotilla exchanging fire with the batteries of El Morro, without great damage on either side. Four centuries of Spain in the New World: the last page of this volume of Puerto Rican history was turned.

2. Fort Raleigh National Historic Site
[*North Carolina*]

"A most pleasant and fertile ground" was Roanoke Island in the eyes of Sir Walter Raleigh's agents, who explored the coast of what is now North Carolina when England was seeking a foothold in the New World. The year was 1584. The following spring, Sir Richard Grenville, Raleigh's cousin, brought more than a hundred colonists to these shores and set up "the new fort in Virginia," the land being named in honor of the so-called virgin queen, Elizabeth. But these transplanted hopefuls were homesick and discouraged, and when Sir Francis Drake anchored nearby, bringing them supplies in 1586, they had had enough of the wilderness.

Raleigh, wedded to his dream of an English empire in North America, was persistent. A second colony, with 150 men, women, and children, was begun in the summer of 1587, under sounder auspices. The fort was improved, the old houses repaired and new ones constructed. Manteo, the nearby Indian chief, welcomed the settlers. In return, he was baptized and created Lord of Roanoke. John White was governor, and one of his assistants, Ananias Dare, who had apparently overcome the handicap of his Christian name, was his son-in-law. The Dare's daughter, born soon after their arrival, was named "Virginia"—the first English child born in the new colony. But again there was dissension. Supplies ran short; Indian rations did not take the place of the good things of the old country. So White returned to England to arrange for the colonials' return.

But England was now at war with Spain and feared an invasion by a mighty hostile fleet. Two small ships were all that were sent out, and these

---

Overleaf: The "Castle" guarded the sealanes for Spain. San Juan National Historic Site. [*Photo: M. Woodbridge Williams*]

never arrived. It was not until 1590 that the governor could return to Roanoke Island. To his consternation, the colony had utterly disappeared. The houses had been dismantled, and high palisades had been erected. On a tree, of which the bark had been peeled, was written a single word: CROATAN. Croatan Island (part of what are now Ocracoke Island and Hatteras Island) was searched, and the Croatan Indian village visited. Never a trace of the colonists was found. The mystery has never been solved. Every summer, at this historic site, a pageant, *The Lost Colony*, is performed under the auspices of the Roanoke Island Historical Association.

3. JAMESTOWN NATIONAL HISTORIC SITE
[*Virginia*]

BY THE HAPPIEST of arrangements, the scene of the first permanent English settlement in America is preserved jointly by the National Park Service and the Association for the Preservation of Virginia Antiquities. Except for the historic site, the island where the colonists disembarked from three small ships in May 1607 is preserved as part of Colonial National Historical Park, with headquarters at Yorktown, Virginia. Inquiries relating to the work of the association should be addressed to it at Jamestown.

The day came, of course, when its distinction passed to Williamsburg, but for nearly a century Jamestown held its place as the political as well as the social and economic center of Virginia Colony. From the viewpoint of health there could have been far better locations. As in Raleigh's colonies, there were loneliness and inexperience, and here was added inevitable sickness coming out of the Pitch and Tar Swamp that lay behind. Only the will and resourcefulness of the redoubtable Captain John Smith and a few others held it together. And when Smith, disabled, sailed for England, there were threats of desertion. With the coming of Lord Delaware and a competent governor, Sir Thomas Dale, and not least with the arrival of English lasses to soften the rigors of bachelor life on the edge of a wild continent, a degree of prosperity came.

Admirably interpreted, the life of early Jamestown comes clearly to visitors today. It was never more than a country town, really, however important, and its appearance constantly changed according to needs and taste. Of seventeenth-century Jamestown nothing remains standing except the ivy-covered Old Tower, presumably part of the brick church of 1639. The landing place and the site of that "James Fort," which in the first years was the whole town, were long ago devoured by river floods.

"Happy are the painters, for they shall not be lonely."—Sir Winston Churchill. Fort Caroline National Memorial. [Photo: Barry Mackintosh]

There is no more charming self-guiding tour than this, which takes visitors around a colonial capital which not only ceased to exist at the time of the American Revolution, but actually became plowed ground. Yet the historian and the archaeologist have worked together to bring Jamestown back to the imagination. Not to be missed is a visit to the working glass furnace, where glassblowing is done as the colonists, with similar equipment, did it three and a half centuries ago.

4. FORT CAROLINE NATIONAL MEMORIAL
[*Florida*]

ON A JUNE DAY in 1564 the Timucua Indians who lived along the St. Johns River, in what the Spaniards had vaguely termed "Florida," saw three small ships put down their anchors at a point about five miles from the mouth. About three hundred white men came ashore. The Indians could not suspect it, but it was an important day in the story of fluctuating empires. France was knocking at the door of this treasure house, the New World, intending

[451]

to claim a share in the vast riches that had been pouring into Spain from Mexico and tropical America.

Gold! Silver! Pearls! Loot from thousands of "savage" towns and cities. Spain's monopoly in middle America was fairly secure. But to the north was a great expanse untouched.

René de Laudonnière, commander of this expedition, built an earth fort and named it Caroline, in honor of his king. In truth, though it might not seem to be in competition, this was a sword pointed at Spain. The treasure ships would have to pass the mouth of the St. Johns when they followed the Gulf Stream on their way home. Menéndez, the Spanish admiral, got orders to drive out such settlers "by what means you see fit."

The clash came without delay. The French were willing to fight, and decided to attack. But Ribaut's fleet was caught in a hurricane and wrecked. This was the chance for Menéndez. He marched straight for Fort Caroline, most of whose fighting men were in the wrecked fleet. In one hour it was over; the men in the garrison were slaughtered and the women and children taken prisoner.

What of the Frenchmen on the wrecked ships? That part of the story is told at another area of the National Park System—Fort Matanzas.

5. FORT MATANZAS NATIONAL MONUMENT
[Florida]

THE WORD *matanza*, in Spanish, means "slaughter." It is a befitting name for what took place on September 29, 1565, at this spot where visitors today come to the inlet south of Anastasia Island, just below St. Augustine.

The shipwrecked men of Jean Ribaut, more than 500, managed to scramble and swim ashore through the surf. In two groups they began a march up the coast back to Fort Caroline, not knowing its fate. The swift waters of Matanzas Inlet halted them. Menéndez, with a small force artfully deployed, trapped the first group into a surrender. Ten at a time they were taken across the inlet, herded together as though to be marched, and then pitilessly butchered. Of 208 men, only 8 were spared.

Part of the second group of Frenchmen, perhaps 350 in all, met the same fate when, about a week later, they straggled up to the inlet. After a talk between Menéndez and Ribaut, and in sight of the unburied bodies of their compatriots, more than half the Frenchmen turned and trusted themselves to the wilderness rather than to the Spaniard. The others were led across the inlet, where another cold-blooded butchery took place. And gradually

Menéndez rounded up the remaining enemies. France's first attempt to share New World riches had failed. But she was to have better fortune at a later time far to the north—in Canada.

6. CASTILLO DE SAN MARCOS NATIONAL MONUMENT
[*Florida*]

GRIM, VITAL, defiant of time, this monument of Spain's hours of greatness seems still to be peering defensively out upon the Gulf Stream, seems still to be guarding the homegoing galleons from the corsair. To touch its gray outer walls, to wander among its rooms, to climb its ramp and to look out upon the blue waters of Matanzas Bay, is to wish to know the story of Spain in America; and here a part of it is beautifully told.

The short-lived colony of France at Fort Caroline was a warning to the Spanish realm. Hungry predators had their eyes upon the prosperous sheepfold. Hardly more than two decades after the Spanish colonized at St. Augustine, England, in the person of Sir Francis Drake, was ready to test supremacy. Piracy? Official policy? In those stirring times the difference was not always apparent. In 1670 England was moving closer, with a settlement at Charleston.

The Castillo you see now was begun in 1672, and it required almost twenty-five years to complete. The walls were thirty feet high and, in places, twelve feet thick, built of the shellrock called coquina, conveniently quarried on Anastasia Island nearby. St. Augustine was raided and sacked many times, but the Castillo was impregnable against any cannon of the period. The British general James Oglethorpe set out from Fort Frederica in 1740 swearing to take this outpost "or leave his bones before its walls." Oglethorpe returned to Frederica discomfited, but still in possession of his bones.

7. FORT FREDERICA NATIONAL MONUMENT
[*Georgia*]

IF YOU WILL COMPARE the Spanish settlement at Fort Caroline with that of Oglethorpe's Britishers on St. Simon's Island in Georgia, you will perceive at least one important reason why England finally dominated North America, instead of France or Spain. Of the three hundred persons who landed with de Laudonnière, all but seventy were soldiers or sailors. There was not a farmer among them. The artisans were mainly chosen for their ability to construct defenses.

Outpost of Spain at St. Augustine, Florida. Castillo de San Marcos National Monument. [Photo: M. Woodbridge Williams]

Although Oglethorpe's Frederica, for reasons of state, lasted only thirteen years, it was a true settlement. It was designed with the greatest care by an intelligent group who actually aimed at reproducing a typical English village in the New World. Tailor, weaver, tanner, shoemaker . . . all the important trades were represented in that roster. There were doctor, preacher, midwife, also. They were not adventurers for gold and pearls. They came over the ocean to *live*.

They needed a fort, of course, and hurriedly built one; and they needed soldiers, because Spain did not want them there. Built of tabby (a mortar made of sand, lime, and oystershells), Frederica was soon a well-designed and prosperous town, with shops lining the principal street. After an attack by the Spaniards, Oglethorpe planned a full-scale invasion of Florida by taking the Castillo at St. Augustine. When this failed, Spain made the inevitable reprisal. Three thousand men in fifty-one ships got past the batteries of Fort St. Simons, but after being routed in a land fight they returned to St. Augustine. It was Spain's last attempt to control Georgia.

8. DE SOTO NATIONAL MEMORIAL
[*Florida*]

CRUEL, RAPACIOUS, UNSCRUPULOUS—call them any unpleasant adjective you please; but there was one word these conquistadors of Spain did not seem to have in their vocabulary: fear. In 1528, Narváez landed upon the west coast of Florida—and was swallowed up by the wilderness. True, the incredible Cabeza de Vaca and a few others of that party survived, to appear years later. Did such a mischance deter Don Hernando de Soto, Knight of Santiago, when he was commissioned by King Charles to conquer, pacify, and populate the great unknown North America, supposed to contain riches far beyond those of Mexico and Peru?

No whit. We see him in 1539 landing somewhere on Florida's coast between Tampa and Estero Bays, and with six hundred or more stout warriors and a dozen equally fearless priests plunging into an unknown land. Up through Georgia and Carolina, across the Great Smokies, down almost to the Gulf of Mexico, up north again nearly to Tennessee, then to the Mississippi River, a stream so wide that "if a man stood still on the other side, it could not be discerned whether he were a man or no."

There, on the bank of the "Father of Waters," De Soto fevered and died, and his followers, sorrowing mostly for the loss of his leadership, sank his coffin in the river. Doña Isabel de Soto, who was in Havana awaiting the return of her husband with news of the discovery of vast riches, received news indeed, months later. But it was that the Don was not returning to her.

9. CORONADO NATIONAL MEMORIAL
[*Arizona*]

AT THE VERY MOMENT when De Soto was in his winter camp near Apalachee Bay in Florida, surrounded by hostile Indians, another Spanish worthy was moving out of Compostela in Mexico into unmapped wilds. Francisco Vásquez de Coronado, with a strong force, aimed to search out and conquer the Seven Cities of Cíbola, reported to be richer by far than anything Peru had yielded. Here, according to a credulous investigator, Fray Marcos de Niza, were great populations with such wealth in gold and silver that they studded their doorways with turquoise and emeralds. It was the first exploration into what is now our American Southwest.

From Coronado Peak, visitors today look out over the great Sonoran Plain of Mexico. The borderline between Mexico and the United States lies just beneath him. It requires no great stretch of the imagination to see those lusting armed soldiers of the advance party coming into view, riding or walking beside their horses, mules heavily loaded with supplies. They come to a spot where two cuts in the mountain barrier indicate valleys. They choose one and press forward.

It is a thrilling story, this mad rush for wealth into a country where there were only poor Indian pueblo folk getting a meager subsistence by farming desert patches. Lured on and on by an artistic Plains Indian liar they called El Turco, they probably got as far as what is now Kansas. The finest thing they discovered was the Grand Canyon of the Colorado. But they were not looking for beauty; it halted them, and they were annoyed.

10. San José Mission National Historic Site
[Texas]

In 1777, Father Morfi came up from Mexico to San Antonio to report on the condition of Mission San José y Miguel de Aguayo. He was ravished both by the beauty of its structures and by its success as a converter of savage souls. In his eyes, it was "the Queen of all the missions in New Spain . . . a symbol of the faith, courage and vigor of the Franciscan Fathers." This noble mission is still queenly, for in spite of years of neglect, when parts of it became ruin and the cut stone was requarried by unsentimental settlers, there were those who would, a century later, restore the church and other structures to much of their former condition.

The administration of the mission today is rather unusual. On the operations board are representatives of the Texas State Parks, the Archdiocese of San Antonio, and the San Antonio Conservation Society. The Advisory Board also includes representatives of the National Park Service and the county of Bexar. Its welfare and future are in good hands.

In the old days what delighted the resident Indians and the mission folk were the bright colors that decorated the plastered walls of the church on three sides. The lovely rose windows were the work of Pedro Huizar, whose ancestors had chiseled the delicate tracery of the Alhambra in Spain.

11. EL MORRO NATIONAL MONUMENT
[*New Mexico*]

OÑATE WAS HERE. And lest ensuing generations should forget the fact, he incised upon a rocky bluff, rising two hundred feet above the plain, the record of his passage. "Passed by here the Adelantado Don Juan de Oñate, from the discovery of the Sea of the South, the 16th of April of 1605." The "Sea of the South" was the Gulf of California. As other explorers passed this same "Inscription Rock" they too left their names and sentiments. There is even a verse in praise of Governor Don Francisco Manuel de Silva Nieto, who "made it possible to carry the Christian faith to the Zuñi Indians." The Zuñis had their own ideas about this reported achievement.

The courageous and devoted padres had a stormy time of it for many years among the pueblo people. Often, when the neophytes seemed on the way to conversion and discipline, they suddenly reconsidered. At Acoma they slew fifteen Spanish soldiers. Many priests suffered martyrdom. We read today on the face of El Morro that one party passed the rock on the mission to "avenge the death of Father Letrado."

Many years after the Spanish had engraved their names, a camel train, conducted by Lieutenant Edward Beale, camped overnight at the rock. Of course his men duly added their signatures.

No further names, addresses, or telephone numbers, either on El Morro or an any other natural or manmade feature in the National Park System, are desired. This may seem odd to today's aspirants for immortality. They must remember that they are not Don Oñates, and the year is not 1605. Requirements and values shift with the years.

12. GRAN QUIVIRA NATIONAL MONUMENT
[*New Mexico*]

AS EARLY AS A.D. 800 in the territory that lay between the Chupadera Mesa of central New Mexico and about the present Mexican border, there were a people known as Mogollons (pronounced Mug-ee-yowns), gaining a sparse subsistence by farming the dry country as best they could and adding wild plants and game to their food supply. Three hundred years later their early crude brown pottery changed to one of black-on-white, because they had been influenced by contact with the pueblo people farther west, and the kiva, or underground ceremonial chamber, had been adopted.

By the early part of the seventeenth century this people had achieved the largest pueblo village in the region, the *pueblo de las Humanas,* as it was called by the visiting Spanish.

The Franciscan fathers arrived with the Cross and the Spanish language, to replace the way of life with one that would weld the Mogollons into loyal subjects of the Crown, besides endowing them with the unquestioned superiority of European civilization. Very discerning, as well as wonderfully effective, were these missionaries. They built churches, but they did not try to expel the kivas. If the natives believed that the forces of nature could be propitiated by old-time rituals, they were gently led to see that this was not necessarily inconsistent with the worship of Catholic saints.

But the Apache Indians, with whom the Mogollon people had traded for generations, were raiders, and warlike beyond the nature of pueblo folk. Sometime between 1672 and 1675 the pueblo was abandoned.

13. TUMACACORI NATIONAL MONUMENT

[*Arizona*]

WHAT MORE CONSOLING SPOT, where one can rest in a shaded patio, surrounded by cactus and other native plants, can possibly exist? Never oppressively hot nor bitingly cold, and bathed in sunshine, Father Eusebio Kino must have loved this place when he came in 1691 and said the first Christian mass under a shelter of brush in a little Pima Indian village. The Jesuit father was a man of practical good sense. No doubt the Pimas invited him to visit them because they wondered how these people of Spain had been able to acquire so many of the material good things of existence. Father Kino showed them. In a few years Tumacacori had fields of wheat, cattle, sheep, and goats.

The church we see here, however, dates from a later period. The Jesuits were expelled from all Spanish dominions in 1767, and the Franciscans took over the Sonoran chain of missions that had once been the charge of Father Kino. Although it was never wholly completed, as the unfinished bell tower shows, it had a period of prosperity and a body of Indian converts more than ordinarily devout. In the museum of the monument is a charming diorama which brings to the visitor the very spirit of the mission in its flourishing day.

14. CABRILLO NATIONAL MONUMENT

[*California*]

THE INDIANS of North America had their news services, though the transmission facilities may have been slow. The people of the Zuñi pueblo were well aware that there was a great ocean far to their east, over which the sun rose. And the Indians on Point Loma in San Diego Bay, when Juan Cabrillo went ashore, had already heard about white men of great strength but bad manners, who had mistreated pueblo folks in their search for precious metals. So, on the principle that the best defense is to shoot first, they shot a few arrows into the strangers.

Only fifty years had passed since Columbus had stumbled across a world new to Europe. But events had been swift in following. Balboa had found the "South Sea" in 1513. Cortes had gone from Mexico City to the Pacific. Lower California had been well explored. In 1542 the question remained: What lay to the north? What peoples? What vast riches?

Cabrillo was of Portugal, but he sailed for Spain. His two small ships came out of Navidad, on Mexico's west coast, went cautiously up the shoreline, asking questions of the natives along the way, and on September 28, 1542, saw the fires of Indian camps. Cabrillo National Monument marks the spot where they landed, remained a few days, and then continued northward until they had passed Point Reyes, above present-day San Francisco. At the death of Cabrillo, his successor got as far as Oregon.

Inscription Rock, where history was written by many hands. El Morro National Monument. [Photo: George Grant]

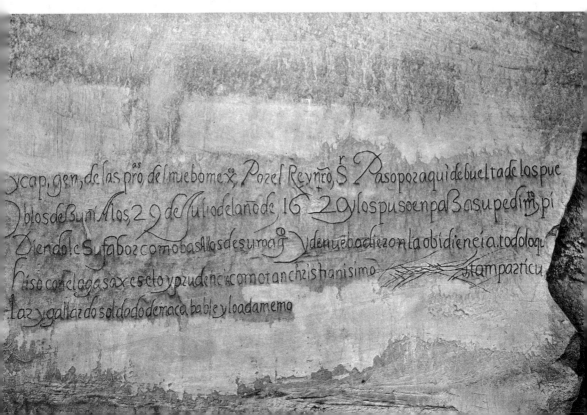

[I I I]

Our Early Days

1. INDEPENDENCE NATIONAL HISTORICAL PARK
[*Pennsylvania*]

Abraham Lincoln, speaking in Baltimore in 1864, remarked that "the world has never had a good definition of the word 'liberty'." So true it is: there are emotions and ideas for which the revealing word is not in language. But here in Philadelphia, lovingly preserved not only for Americans but for the world's peoples, you come into the presence of liberty itself. Independence Hall, Carpenters' Hall, the Liberty Bell: these are superior to definition. You see; you touch; you understand.

The colonial delegates who met at Carpenters' Hall in 1774 had all been schooled by Montesquieu. From him, and from their own keen observation, they well knew this truth: that "in constitutional states liberty is but a compensation for the heaviness of taxation; in despotic states the equivalent liberty is the lightness of taxation." The taxes levied on the American colonies by the Crown were not onerous, but they were the tokens of vassalage when political voice was denied. The colonials decided to pay the heavier taxes of independence.

And the bell. What an odd life it has had! "Life" is a permissible word, for in the course of years this metal has become nearly animate. From the first it "proclaimed liberty," but this was merely a reference to the charter of William Penn. One suspects that they got a cut-rate price from the London bell founders, for when it was tested, it cracked. Two "ingenious local workmen" recast it, and then it tintinnabulated hoarsely. Again it was recast, this time by workmen perhaps less ingenious, but more skillful. Now it had a

---

The bell called the Indians (sometimes reluctant) to prayer. Tumacacori National Monument. [Photo: George Grant]

pleasing tone and rang on proper occasions, and this is the very bell we so reverence today. The British having occupied Philadelphia, the bell was in hiding for a year, then returned to Independence Hall. Perhaps it was when it tolled for the funeral of Chief Justice John Marshall that it once more cracked. In silence it speaks with more meaning as years pass. Generations of Americans say: "I have seen the Liberty Bell." And still schoolchildren swarm to be near it and go home with that something the schoolroom and book cannot impart.

All that brilliant planning and skilled craftsmanship can perform, all that patriotic and generous cooperation can achieve, has been contributed to the end of placing this choice memorial of the nation's birth and infancy into safe deposit. In 1818 the city of Philadelphia bought Independence Hall from the Commonwealth of Pennsylvania, which now is developing a mall in the three blocks just north. Congress provided that with the agreement of the three groups which own the surrounding historic buildings, and with added sites to the east, all this should be preserved and interpreted for posterity. A lesson in history: not to be forgotten.

And to what end is recorded history? Emerson has given us the sufficient reason: "The world exists for the education of each man. There is no age, or state of society, or mode of action in history, to which there is not somewhat corresponding in *his* life." The study of history is not a deterrent of mass error: that is plain. It satisfies curiosity; but that is a meaner use. Not merely at Independence National Historical Park, but in every other historic or prehistoric unit of the great National Park System, the thinking visitor is revealed to himself. His ideals, his fears, his hopes, his loves. He asks himself the questions: "What would *I* have done? How, there and then, wherever and whenever, would *I* have measured up to need and opportunity?"

2. MINUTE MAN NATIONAL HISTORICAL PARK
[*Massachusetts*]

SUBURBAN BOSTON now lumbers out over the old Battle Road where, on April 19, 1775, Gage's British troopers marched to teach a lesson to defiant provincials. The precipitate return of the punitive expedition is one of the large facts of history. Today, embattled non-farmers struggle over crowded

The word "liberty" defines itself here for all Americans. Independence National Historical Park. [Photo: Ralph Anderson]

roads to get to work and back again without having the fenders of their motor cars bashed. East of where Mass. 128 makes its arc from the South Shore to the North Shore, there is no hope of restoring the original scene, though interpretive markers will identify the way taken by the threatening drums. But a considerable acreage in Lexington and Concord is still restorable, and by order of Congress this is being done. The interested visitor, however, need not wait till the long job is completed. This is ingratiating countryside at any time.

General Gage, you remember, had been stationed in Boston to quell a spreading "sedition." Through his spies (and there was no lack of them, for loyalists were many) he heard that military stores were being collected in Concord. What he did not know was that Paul Revere and his "patriot patrol" were hawk-eyed and keen of ear. The moment the redcoats crossed the Charles River the alarm was spread.

When the British soldiers come into Lexington Green they face Captain John Parker's unshowy muster of Minute Men. "Stand your ground," Parker tells his men. "Don't fire unless fired upon. But if they mean to have a war, let it begin here!" It began there.

The British did very well to get back to the shelter of Boston without greater discomfort than they suffered. It was unlike a European battlefield. From behind trees and stone walls came shots that speeded the quickstep. The minutemen were untrained but indignant.

3. YORKTOWN BATTLEFIELD, COLONIAL NATIONAL HISTORICAL PARK
[*Virginia*]

THE YEARS have been kinder to Yorktown and Gloucester on the lower Chesapeake than to the farmlands that surrounded Boston in the days of the minutemen. Indeed, Yorktown is not as populous today as when Lord Cornwallis surrendered there in 1781. This is fortunate for the lover of historic places, for still to be seen are structures of colonial times—the Customhouse, the Nelson House, two Digges homes, and the Somerwell and Sessions houses. Grace Episcopal Church originated in 1697. There are others.

The Moore House! In this historic home of a Yorktown merchant the

---

"*By the rude bridge that arched the flood . . .*" Minute Man National Historical Park. [*Photo: M. Woodbridge Williams*]

Revolutionary War came, virtually, to a close. The house has been restored to its original condition and furnished in period style by patriotic groups. It is easy to picture the agents of the British, French, and American commanders sitting here, debating the articles of capitulation. One wonders about the thoughts of Washington, who awaited the results in camp, and the Right Honorable Earl Cornwallis, who rested in a Yorktown residence. For Washington, it was the end of his long service as commander in chief, during which he had coped with treachery and ingratitude within his ranks. For Cornwallis, it was naturally humiliating, but, in truth, few of the English people, and not many of the British generals, had any great bitterness against their transplanted cousins. They frowned on this passion for freedom and felt that revolutions had to be scotched, but some felt that if His Majesty George III had been wisely advised, it wouldn't have happened anyway. At least, not at that epoch.

4. MORRISTOWN NATIONAL HISTORICAL PARK
[New Jersey]

AT A CERTAIN DESK in the Ford Mansion visitors today may feel the very presence of General George Washington, writing his letters and military orders during that bitter winter of 1779–80, when the British command had possession of New York City. For the Continentals, Morristown was a shrewdly chosen site. Only thirty miles from the enemy lines, it was behind the barrier Watchung Hills. This historical park is beautifully maintained, with a high degree of the original appearance, and is one of the gems of National Park Service preservation.

In lovely Jockey Hollow there were sometimes ten thousand patriot soldiers encamped in log huts. Go into one of these reconstructed shelters; meditate. Had you been one of these soldiers, you would often have been ill fed, homesick, cold, ailing, with only confidence in your devoted commander in chief to buoy your sinking spirit. Would help come from France, as Ben Franklin deemed possible? Yes; on a May day in 1780 Lafayette arrived with the cheering news of a second French expedition on its way.

Go into the Historical Museum and view the carefully prepared exhibits that tell the story of the Morristown winter and its relation to what went before in our Revolutionary period—and to what followed as a result of the stubborn courage and wise strategy displayed. An unforgettable page in the American story!

5. MOORES CREEK NATIONAL MILITARY PARK
[*North Carolina*]

WHEN NEWS of the clash of arms at Lexington and Concord came belatedly to North Carolina, there was rejoicing among the provincials there, at least among those who had become convinced that only separation from the mother country would end their subjection to royal whim. But in numbers these insurgents were not an easy majority. Martin, the Crown's governor, though opposed by the provincial legislature and later forced to flee, yet held strong cards against this "most daring, horrid and unnatural rebellion." He gathered a formidable well-armed force of Highland Scots and other loyalists and set about to reconquer the province.

About twenty miles above Wilmington there was a bridge across "Widow Moore's Creek." The creek, as you see it today in this military park, is not wide, but it runs deep and dark. Martin's troops had to cross it to get to the

The winter of 1776–7 was a bitter one in Jockey Hollow. Morristown National Historical Park. [Photo: M. Woodbridge Williams]

coast and provisions. The surrounding land was swamp. Who would get first to that vital crossing?

The loyalists lost this race, and when they camped six miles away, Lillington and Caswell were ready for them. They took up the bridge floor, applied a coat of grease to the girders, and covered the approach with their guns. When the attack came, it took three minutes to cut the King's forces down and send them flying. The "rebels" lost one man. Perhaps he had carelessly exposed himself.

6. KINGS MOUNTAIN NATIONAL MILITARY PARK
[South Carolina]

MAJOR PATRICK FERGUSON, head of a scouting force for Lord Cornwallis in South Carolina, was a doughty marksman and the inventor, in 1776, of the first breech-loading rifle carried by warring troops. But his invention was better than his judgment, for he potshotted a wasps' nest. When he threatened the Appalachian mountaineers, mostly Scotch-Irish, that he would "march an army over the mountains, hang their leaders and lay their country waste," they replied that they would see about that. So they took their hunting rifles, knapsacks, and blankets, mounted their horses (those who had horses), and went after Ferguson.

It was 1780. For two years the Crown had had doubtful success in the Northern colonies, but now a new plan, to conquer the South, seemed likely to succeed. It was a gloomy prospect for the patriots. An American army under Benjamin Lincoln had surrendered Charleston; Gates had been badly thrashed at Camden. Cornwallis had occupied Charlotte, North Carolina.

In the heavily wooded and rocky battlefield ridge of Kings Mountain, still possessing a wilderness quality, Major Ferguson's force was surrounded by the angry mountaineers and either captured or killed. Ferguson himself was a game one. The shrill note of his whistle, urging his men, could be heard above the shouting and crack of rifles. It took at least eight bullets from the backwoods sharpshooters to eliminate him. The tablet over his grave in the park does him justice.

7. COWPENS NATIONAL BATTLEFIELD SITE
[South Carolina]

ANOTHER VICTORY for the Americans followed the Moores Creek engagement. The numbers engaged were not great, but the effect was to depress the loyalists, to enhearten the colonial revolutionaries, and to move Cornwallis northward toward his ultimate surrender at Yorktown.

There was a new commander of the Americans in the South—General Nathanael Greene. Hearing that Greene had divided his forces, the British general sent a force to defeat Daniel Morgan in northwestern South Carolina, while he moved out of Winnsboro to get between Greene and Morgan. Learning that his pursuers were near, Morgan picked a spot near the North Carolina line to stand and fight, and his leadership and quick thinking were mainly responsible for the signal rout and capture of most of the troopers of his opponent, Banastre Tarleton.

8. SARATOGA NATIONAL HISTORICAL PARK
[*New York*]

THE FRENCH KING, eager enough to humiliate Great Britain, had been hesitant about intervention in this revolution of British subjects in America. In 1777, when Burgoyne's army moved down from Canada to unite with forces moving from the west and south, even the rebellious colonists were far from confident of their chances of success. The battle of Saratoga was a turning point in both respects.

The threat of Burgoyne was formidable. He had 4,200 British regulars and 4,000 German mercenaries, besides some Canadians and Indians. Fort Ticonderoga stood in his way only a few days. After that, the going was rougher. Some small engagements left him in the air; but instead of pulling back to Canada, he decided to risk all to reach Albany. September 13, 1777, found him moving down the west bank of the Hudson at Saratoga to a point four miles from Stillwater Village, where General Horatio Gates, newly selected commander of the American army, was entrenched and ready to receive him.

Kosciuszko, the Polish engineer who had come to assist the colonies in their fight for liberty, had selected this narrow defile where the road squeezed between river and hills. In the notable fighting that led to the final surrender of Burgoyne, Benedict Arnold, later to become villain rather than hero in Revolutionary annals, was one of the most brilliant figures.

All this is charming countryside in and around the battlefield area, and there is much to be seen, besides the famous Schuyler House, that recreates the time and occasion.

9. GEORGE WASHINGTON BIRTHPLACE NATIONAL MONUMENT
[*Virginia*]

IN A CODICIL to his last will and testament Benjamin Franklin wrote: "My fine crabtree walking stick, with a gold head curiously wrought in the form of the cap of Liberty, I give to my friend, and the friend of mankind, *General Washington*. If it were a sceptre he has merited it; and would become it."

The estimation of George Washington as one of the world's greatest men came early. The shock of the loss of the American colonies was scarcely over when perceptive Englishmen were ready to claim this man as an illustrious transplant from home soil. When Ralph Waldo Emerson, in 1833, visited Walter Savage Landor, he heard from that stout Briton the opinion that "three of the greatest men were Washington, Phocion, and Timoleon"— no hesitation in placing Washington first. The few paltry attempts to diminish the stature of this Virginia planter have merely served to enlarge him.

There is no pretense that the tidewater mansion called Wakefield, on Pope's Creek in Westmoreland County, is the identical house in which Washington was born. It is merely a memorial building that represents the eighteenth-century home of a plantation owner such as was Augustine, the father of George. But here, on the high bank of the creek, and near the sandy Potomac shore, a little boy of destiny spun his top and romped, and later, as a youth, returned to take his lessons. Here he learned surveying. At eighteen, he mapped the Bridges Creek area. And before his death, he was to survey a vast political area.

10. FORT NECESSITY NATIONAL BATTLEFIELD
[*Pennsylvania*]

AT THE AGE of twenty-one, George Washington, surveyor and officer of the Virginia militia, was sent with a small force to warn the French to withdraw from the upper Ohio Valley, to which Colonial Governor Dinwiddie and a Virginia corporation laid claim. The French, operating out of Fort Niagara, were harassing English traders on that side of the Alleghenies. The mission failed, and at the place which is now Pittsburgh, where Dinwiddie planned an English stronghold, the French hurriedly built Fort Duquesne.

In April 1754, Washington, now a lieutenant colonel, went out again, and became commander of the Virginia force when his colonel died at Wills Creek. After a skirmish in which a French camp was taken, Washington built a palisaded fort at a spot known as Great Meadows. In his diary he spoke of it as Fort Necessity. But the position could not be held. Coming down from Fort Duquesne, the French, with Indian allies, forced a capitulation. It was the first and last time Washington ever surrendered. The terms were honorable—the colonials gave up only their swivel guns and withdrew with honors. There is now a replica of the palisaded fort on Great Meadows, well worth visiting, and the nearby museum contains relics of the subsequent Braddock defeat.

11. PERRY'S VICTORY AND INTERNATIONAL PEACE MEMORIAL NATIONAL MONUMENT
[*Ohio*]

IN LAKE ERIE, a few miles from the mainland of Ohio, is South Bass Island. During the summer holidays, ferries are busy transporting visitors to this resort, where one of the "musts" is to ascend the memorial shaft and look out over the lake, the shore, and the nearby islands. About ten miles out in the lake is the spot where Oliver Hazard Perry scored a victory over a British naval squadron during the War of 1812. From the deck of the brig *Niagara*, 110 feet long, Perry wrote to William Henry Harrison, commander of the land forces, the famous message: "We have met the enemy and they are ours. Two ships, two brigs, one schooner & one sloop."

The pink granite of the memorial was brought from Milford, Massachusetts. The shaft, a Doric fluted column 352 feet high, has a rotunda made of marble, limestone, and granite. Besides commemorating the naval engagement, this national monument also serves to announce a cheerful fact: that the long boundary between the United States and Canada requires no armed forces to maintain; that the two nations are good friends and intend to remain so.

12. FORT McHENRY NATIONAL MONUMENT AND HISTORIC SHRINE
[*Maryland*]

WHEN ONE of our National Park Service Historians wrote that "on land, during the first part of the war [of 1812] American military operations left much to be desired," he achieved a nice piece of understatement. It was really messier than that. There was a baddish lot of running away by the young republic's troops. Still it must be said that the Americans didn't claim to be a military people, and the British army had the advantage that, after Waterloo, they could detach some of their best veterans from the European sphere. Besides, they had experts at arson among them, as shown by the burning of the White House in Washington—an incident that now makes English gentlemen blush and turn the conversation to the weather.

After an easy victory at Bladensburg the British took the capital city and then turned toward Baltimore—commercially much more important. Fort McHenry had to be reduced, of course. So sixteen warships anchored about two miles down river and started a bombardment that lasted more than a full day and night. Francis Scott Key was a witness of the action. Thrilled, after such a cannonade, to see the "star-spangled banner" still flying, he wrote the words of the song, fitted to the music of the English "To Anacreon in Heaven." Nearly all Americans know the first verse, though singing it has pitfalls for the unskilled.

13. CHALMETTE NATIONAL HISTORICAL PARK
[*Louisiana*]

THE TREATY OF PEACE, to end the War of 1812, had been signed the day before Christmas, 1814. It had not been ratified. A battle took place on a plantation near New Orleans, on the following 8th of January, that may have hurried a laggard British decision. More than five thousand crack troops, commanded by no less a personage than Sir Edward Pakenham, the Duke of Wellington's brother-in-law, met an incredible motley of volunteer riflemen from adjoining states, some regular soldiers, Creoles, Negroes, Indians, sailors, pirates, and disorderlies just released from jail. The result was astonishing. The British casualties were more than two thousand; American losses, seven killed and six wounded. It sounds like a myth, but it actually happened. How? Why?

Perhaps because Wellington's distinguished brother-in-law had a contempt for these overseas cousins. Perhaps because he was of the old school: you don't hide behind a mud rampart like a cowardly blighter; you form in a solid line, step forward three paces and fire, then repeat. Pakenham's troopers, nothing lacking in courage, so trained and led, came across canefield stubble against a murderous fire and were mowed down. Pakenham himself died of wounds; but the star of Andrew Jackson, credited with this stunning victory, was ascendant. He was on the road to the White House.

14. Horseshoe Bend National Military Park
[*Alabama*]

Nine months before Andrew Jackson defeated the British army at Chalmette, he had acquired a reputation for grim determination in his campaign against the "Red Sticks"—that part of the Indian Creek nation which warred upon the white colonial Americans during the War of 1812. The Creeks were divided by a sort of civil war among themselves. Jackson was one of five volunteer generals defending the Southern frontier.

At Horseshoe Bend, a hundred-acre peninsula in the Tallapoosa River in Alabama, the Red Sticks were completely crushed by the army led by our vigorous Tennesseean, who followed his success with a hard peace. More than 20 million acres—half the territory of the Creeks—were ceded to the whites, opening for peaceable settlement a rich country extending from

Where the Star-Spangled Banner yet waved. Fort McHenry National Monument and Historic Shrine. [Photo: M. Woodbridge Williams]

Georgia to Mobile. The natural features of the battlefield look about the same as in Jackson's time, but the log barricade and the Indian huts were destroyed after the battle. A stone monument records the victory.

15. ADAMS NATIONAL HISTORIC SITE
[*Massachusetts*]

MANY CUSTODIANS of historic ancient houses have remarked to me that there is one question almost invariably asked by visitors: "Is this place still in the hands of the *same* family?" May this thought somehow be a reflection of a longing to discover some sign, even if a pale one, of a *continuity* which each life may hope to share? Whether or not, this Adams house in Quincy, Massachusetts, is a satisfying memorial to four generations of a family famous in American history. The very walls breathe the Adams rugged individuality: intellectual, unspectacular, nonconformist, and, to be truthful, with something of the acidity of the crab apple. What a breed!

True, the oldest part of this home was not built by an Adams. But when John Adams bought it in 1787, he named it Peacefield, and he and his successors built additions as needs arose. The remarkable Abigail Adams, wife of one President and mother of another, was its first mistress, and her housekeeping eye was no doubt as sharp as her descriptive pen. Then came John Quincy Adams, who served one term as President and later went to the House of Representatives for seventeen years. His son, Charles Francis Adams, as Minister to Great Britain during the Civil War, had the delicate job of preventing a recognition of the Confederacy. Finally, all four of his sons were men of great ability, three of them distinguished in the world of literature. Henry Adams, in his *Education*, has left us fragrant memories of "The Old House."

16. SALEM MARITIME NATIONAL HISTORIC SITE
[*Massachusetts*]

THOSE SALEM SHIPMASTERS went everywhere upon the seven seas. In the earliest days of the port it was usually to the West Indian islands for sugar and molasses, from which the good rum was made, which buoyed the spirits of colonial men. Then, during the Revolution and the War of 1812, they built and manned swift privateers, roaming like killer whales in the lanes of enemy shipping. Salem was the one important American port that never fell into British hands in those wars, perhaps because of the shallowness of the water in her snugly placed harbor; but the time came, in peace, when bigger ships of deeper draft could not be accommodated, and then Derby Wharf, which visitors walk today, went slowly to seed.

But what great days those were when the Derbys, father and son, were building such rovers as the *Light Horse* and the *Grand Turk* and sending them on voyages to the East Indies and China Seas! Eager buyers of the cargoes gathered among the Derby warehouses, and the Custom House, opposite the long wharf, was a busy and exciting place. Here in later years sat, at a desk you may still inspect, a young aspirant for literary fame, Nathaniel Hawthorne. He was Surveyor of the Port from 1846 to 1849. Surveying the port was not then exacting, but he wandered much in the vicinity and developed plot and scene for *The Scarlet Letter*, a novel that has weathered well.

17. HOPEWELL VILLAGE NATIONAL HISTORIC SITE
[*Pennsylvania*]

IN THE EARLY DAYS of colonial development the need for iron increased rapidly—more rapidly than the colonists could accumulate the money necessary to import the metal from Europe. It was no wonder, then, that especially in the Northeastern states the ruins of old furnaces are plentiful, and many place names on the map end with "Furnace." Good sources of the ore, and of limestone, were not hard to find, and the plentiful hardwood forests were nearby to furnish the charcoal fuel to create the "bloom" of wrought iron. For nearly a century these small enterprises, requiring little capital and no year-round operation, supplied the demands.

When Mark Bird built Hopewell Furnace in 1770, to furnish cast iron for his forges, the industry had become big business, requiring ample capital, mines of high-grade ore, and a shrewdly directed organization of skilled workers. The ironmaster had arrived. In Hopewell Village, beautifully preserved within the National Park System, visitors learn what a self-sufficient operation this Hopewell Furnace was. An easy walking tour leads along historic village roads, past charcoal sheds, water-wheel and blast machinery, the casting house, the blacksmith shop, and other relics, to the house of the ironmaster, where may be seen the very furnishings that were there when the freshly baked bread was brought to hungry workers in the Big House.

18. HAMPTON NATIONAL HISTORIC SITE
[*Maryland*]

IT WAS FROM THE PROFITS of an iron furnace that Charles Ridgely, "Charles the Builder," constructed the elegant Georgian mansion known as Hampton. Who was the architect of this stately stone pile, with its wide porticoes set off by balanced wings, its big cupola and fancy dormers, and its urnlike roof decorations? It may have been a local carpenter, one Jehu Howell, for there were artisans in those days who could respond to the order of a rich man: "Build me the finest house that money can buy."

Furnishing this mansion with the proper pieces to display such a center of social life of that Maryland period was aided by the fact that much of the Ridgely furniture had never been alienated. A nephew of Charles the Builder, who became Governor of Maryland in 1816, added the formal gardens described at the time as "an object of beauty and renown." The Governor was said to keep the best table in America; fast horses munched their oats in his stables; and Charles Carroll spoke of a party there when three hundred of the county notables were entertained.

The daughter of Governor Ridgely played the harp, as visitors see from the copy of Sully's *Lady with the Harp* that hangs over the piano in the Great Hall. In the midst of all this beauty, it is impossible to believe that the lady handled the instrument other than well. Next best thing to having received a dinner invitation from the master of Hampton is to visit the place today.

19. FEDERAL HALL NATIONAL MEMORIAL
[New York]

BY 1840 THE ANCIENT NEW YORK CITY HALL, which had housed the convention of our first Congress under the Constitution, was in a ruinous condition. It had known great events. On its balcony George Washington had been inaugurated as our first President. Here was adopted the Bill of Rights. It was the first Capitol of the Republic, though not for long. Here Andrew Hamilton defended Peter Zenger in the famous trial that led to a free press in America.

The present Federal Hall, on the site of the older, is an outstanding example of Greek Revival architecture. Here visitors will find themselves in the presence of many historic objects and documents associated with the people and events of our nation's first days. The presentation of the Peter Zenger story has always seemed to me one of the chief gems turned out by those talented artists, unknown to the public, who produce the dioramas and other interpretive displays for National Park Service museums.

"Send these, the homeless, tempest-tost, to me, I lift my lamp beside the golden door!"
Statue of Liberty National Monument. [Photo: M. Woodbridge Williams]

20. STATUE OF LIBERTY NATIONAL MONUMENT
[New York–New Jersey]

WHAT AMERICAN, returning from abroad and coming into New York harbor, has not felt a quickening of pulse at the sight of this great lady of Liberty with the beckoning torch? A monument designed to commemorate the alliance of France and the United States during the War for Independence, the statue has over the years taken a meaning far beyond its original one. To generations of people, fleeing oppression from other parts of the world, it has been a beacon of welcome and promise.

The French historian Edouard de Laboulaye conceived the idea of this pledge of friendship, and he found an imaginative Alsatian sculptor, Frederic Auguste Bartholdi, to put it into this bold and classic form. The French people, notably frugal, raised by popular subscription the money to defray the cost of the gift; the cost of the pedestal on which the colossal figure stands was met by American subscribers. The security of the statue in a position where high winds often sweep was a great engineering accomplishment.

As modern lighting systems have improved since the torch first shone, its illumination has increased, so that now, if you multiply the light of the full moon by 2,500, you arrive at the gleam that goes out to sea from the little island of Bedloe—now known as Liberty Island.

21. ST. PAUL'S CHURCH NATIONAL HISTORIC SITE
[New York]

ANNE HUTCHINSON BELIEVED that we are saved by our personal intuition of God's grace rather than by obedience to church laws. It wouldn't make much of a ripple now, but in Puritan Boston of 1637 it was a scandal: besides, Anne's velvet tongue was corrupting even some of the ministers. So she was banished and asked not to come back. First she went to Rhode Island, then to the north side of Long Island Sound, near Pelham Bay, where she founded the church body of which the present edifice, built of brick and stone in 1760 and ensuing years, is her memorial. Its Freedom Bell is the twin of the one at Independence Hall—cast by the same founders in England.

22. TOURO SYNAGOGUE NATIONAL HISTORIC SITE
[Rhode Island]

GEORGE WASHINGTON, when President, told the members of the Newport Congregation that his government "gives to bigotry no sanction, to persecution no assistance." For nearly two centuries the small synagogue on a Newport street has "testified that men may seek eternal truths in their own particular ways without hindrance from the civil government that embraces them all." In December 1763, four years after laying of the cornerstone, the synagogue was dedicated, Isaac Touro then being the spiritual leader. Peter Harrison, the dean of colonial architects, was the designer—in the Georgian style, but modified to accommodate the Sephardic ritual. A plain brick exterior; no hint of the riches within.

23. Gloria Dei (Old Swedes') Church National Historic Site
[*Pennsylvania*]

There were Swedish settlers in the Philadelphia region before the arrival of William Penn with his land grant. Gloria Dei (Old Swedes') was founded in 1677, but the present structure dates from about 1700. The Swedish origins are apparent in the steep gable roof, the square belfry, and the small spire. The church still operates in the section of South Philadelphia that was early known to settlers as Wicaco, but in the pressure of modern life and commerce the surroundings have lost a good deal of their primitive charm. An ironic understatement, visitors will perceive.

24. Dorchester Heights National Historic Site
[*Massachusetts*]

The British commander General Howe looked out upon the fortifications that toiling patriots had created on the night of March 4, 1776, on the two highest hilltops of Dorchester Heights, and sourly remarked: "The rebels have done more in one night than my whole army would have done in a month." Well, he should not have been surprised. The provincials were working for their independence.

Washington's strategy paid off. The British were forced to evacuate Boston. The heights are now solidly built up with residences, but a white marble shaft at the summit is evidence that this spot was a formidable position.

[IV]

Westward Expansion

1. JEFFERSON NATIONAL EXPANSION MEMORIAL NATIONAL HISTORIC SITE
[*Missouri*]

HARDLY HAD PIERRE LACLÈDE of New Orleans received a patent from Louis XV of France granting a monopoly of the fur trade "between the Missouri and St. Peter's Rivers" when a secret treaty ceded the whole Colony of Louisiana to Spain. It was two years before Laclède knew he had a dead contract. But by that time he had picked a strategic location on the Mississippi sixteen miles below the junction with the Missouri, built a house, and made the brash prediction that this place would "become one of the finest cities in America." From Fort Chartres he sent a thirteen-year-old youth, Auguste Chouteau, to clear a way for the settlement. Thirteen years old! Maturity came early then.

A band of Missouri Indians arrived, when the house foundations were being laid, to help and to stay to dinner. The warriors restricted their help to giving advice, but the squaws actually shoveled. When Chouteau politely asked his guests to go home, they laughed and replied blithely, "We are like the ducks and the geese. When we see quiet water, we light on it, rest, feast and enjoy life." A poetic garment for a happy philosophy!

On a bluff above the river floods and convenient to other river approaches, St. Louis was to become truly the Gateway of the American West. Wise Napoleon knew that France could not hold this unmapped inland empire and sold it to an even wiser buyer, Thomas Jefferson. The mighty stainless-steel arch of Eero Saarinen, rising 630 feet in the cleared space below the old Courthouse of Dred Scott memory, symbolizes the epic flow of America toward its "manifest destiny."

Gateway to the West. Jefferson National Expansion Memorial National Historic Site. [*Photo: M. Woodbridge Williams*]

Figuratively, through this shining gate passed the mountain men of the fur trade, the covered wagons of the Oregon emigrants, the eager rushers toward the California diggings, the traders of the Santa Fe Trail, homesteaders and cowboys headed for a vast extent of free cattle range—all, indeed, that we associate with the "winning of the West." Along this riverfront were docked the famous Mississippi steamboats, belching black clouds from their stacks when they fired up; and alongside were the smaller craft that went out to serve the developing towns of the upper Mississippi and Missouri Rivers. The historian Hiram Chittenden said: "It is doubtful if history affords the example of another city which has been the exclusive mart for so vast an extent of country as that which was tributary to St. Louis."

When visitors come to see what modern technology has done, to ascend the arch and gaze out upon the surrounding city and countryside, or, when it is completed, to visit the great museum which the National Park Service will create beneath the arch, they should not forget that there is much of precious history not far from the city itself. Who could fail to be charmed, for instance, by the dreamy allurement of Ste. Genevieve, with its fine old Creole Bolduc house? One can see how the early builders, having first followed the Norman or French Canada design, then added their wide West Indian galleries to fend off the burning summer sun. Or, on the Illinois side of the river, one can visit the Pierre Menard home, the sweet retreat of a man who had made his fortune from the skins of animals, in company with the Chouteaus, Andrew Henry, and other partners.

2. CUMBERLAND GAP NATIONAL HISTORICAL PARK
[Kentucky–Tennessee–Virginia]

THEIR GRACIOUS MAJESTIES (*dei gratia*, etc.) had a quaint way, in the colonial times of North America, of issuing grants of land to those who had influence at court. We grant; you go and find out where it is. It cost the Crown nothing, and it might bring in some pounds sterling in the way of taxes.

Employed by one of these "proprietors" in 1750, Dr. Thomas Walker set out from Albemarle County in Virginia, with five fellow walkers, to locate 800,000 acres of desirable real estate in a wilderness the Indians called Kentucky. Report had it that the grazing lands were incredibly rich, and abounding in bison, deer, and other game. The Cherokees of North Carolina used to cross the Alleghenies and battle with other red men for the hunting rights. That journey was all very well for Indian warriors traveling afoot. But these

Bolduc House. Ste. Genevieve, Missouri. [*Photo: M. Woodbridge Williams*]

same Alleghenies loomed like an impassable barrier against white men with carts and oxen, which required roads. Was there a natural cut somewhere that the "Loyal Land Company" could find and use?

Walker never did discover the rich grazing lands. He did come upon the "levil" gateway to the West that he named "Cave Gap." It was destined to become the main artery through which poured the migrating colonists, first into the Northwest Territory, and finally to the Mississippi River and beyond. And he found a large river which he named the Cumberland in honor of the son of George II. Later the gap was so named too.

It remained for Daniel Boone and his hardy band to reach the "dark and bloody ground," and to blaze a trail. In March 1775, Judge Richard Henderson bought "twenty million acres of land south of the Kentucky River" from the Cherokee Indians. Whatever the Indians got for it was pure velvet, because they didn't own it. But less than two decades afterward, when Ken-

Through this cut in the Alleghenies, America moved westward. Cumberland Gap National Historical Park. [Photo: National Park Service]

tucky became a state, it had a population of 100,000. The end of the Revolutionary War had sent venturesome Americans on a great westward trek.

3. FORT LARAMIE NATIONAL HISTORIC SITE
[*Wyoming*]

IN THE ANGLE formed by the junction of the North Platte and a tributary creek there was a fine location for a voyageur of the fur-trading days. Jacques La Ramie spotted it first, hence the later name of Fort Laramie. He was soon erased by the Indians, but Sublette and Campbell set up a post on the spot, calling it Fort William. The competition in the fur trade was keen, even bitter. The trading posts changed hands oftener than the traders changed shirts, and with less ceremonial observance. Thomas Fitzpatrick, the great mountain man, took over for the American Fur Company in 1836.

When Francis Parkman saw Fort Laramie in 1846 it was a rare sight for a Bostonian. Near the post were clusters of Indian lodges—Cheyennes, Arapahoes, Sioux—ready to trade their coats for doctored alcohol. In the late summer would come bands of bison hunters. The fur trade was declining, and the era of the "buffalo-robe" was waxing.

Here, on the parade ground of the army fort that was abandoned in 1890, visitors can reconstruct in their minds the stirring scenes of its past. It is a long time since the last soldiers had their farewell roaring party, with the officers tilting their glasses to "Old Bedlam." Old Bedlam had well earned its name. There was, among other memories, the memorable Christmas night when the dance was on. Suddenly came "Portugee" Phillips, a veteran scout, out of a wild ride through a blizzard, to summon aid for the besieged troops at Fort Phil Kearny, at the foot of the Bighorns.

Visitors to this monument should push onward over the trail of the Oregonian emigrants to Guernsey, Wyoming—a matter of ten miles or so— and see Register Cliff, on whose chalky face the covered-wagon folks cut their names and left messages for those laboring behind. And nearby are those historic deep ruts in the surface rock cut by the iron-shod wheels of the pioneer wagons. We hear much about the toils of the emigrants, and truly they were heroic souls; but has anyone mentioned the draft animals that here sweated and strained to pull their loads up, up, over this bare limestone rock?

4. SCOTTS BLUFF NATIONAL MONUMENT
[*Nebraska*]

THE COVERED WAGONS of the Oregonians had not proceeded far beyond Chimney Rock when a peculiar geologic formation halted them, saying, "What's your hurry, little men?" The little men well knew what their hurry was. They knew that time was of the essence; they had to pass through the western mountains before the deep snows came. But the badlands, coming right down to the south bank of the North Platte, were not negotiable for wagons. There was a choice: a deep slit at an imposing headland known as Scotts Bluff, and a pass between two ridges named for the squaw-man Roubideaux.

The bluff, looming up eight hundred feet above the river, had received its name from a tragic event of the early trapping days. According to Washington Irving's "Captain Benneville," a pioneer named Hiram Scott, with several other men, had been descending the North Platte in canoes. Caught in eddying currents, their craft overturned, and supplies and ammunition went. Living upon wild fruits and roots, they finally reached Laramie Fork, where Scott was taken sick. A generally accepted story is that Scott was left to die by his companions. It is hard to believe, but the tradition goes on to state that the abandoned man actually crawled and tottered for sixty miles to the base of this bluff, where his skeleton was later found.

From the summit of the bluff there is a revealing view of the badlands which forced the emigrants away from the Platte; to the west can sometimes be seen Laramie Peak, 120 miles distant.

5. CHIMNEY ROCK NATIONAL HISTORIC SITE
[Nebraska]

WILLIAM HENRY JACKSON, a photographer in Vermont, heard the call of the roseate West. With camera and painter's easel he roamed it most widely of all limners. He loved it, to the last days of his ninety-ninth year. Maybe while you were in the museum at Scotts Bluff National Monument you saw Jackson's watercolors, painted in his ripe years from sketches made when he was a muleskinner with a caravan heading west along the Oregon trail.

Once, when I was going down the long but not steep hill near Gering, Nebraska, I came into view of that "earthy sandstone" pinnacle called Chimney Rock (how could it have had any other name!). I happened to have with me a reproduction of Jackson's watercolor of the very scene. In his picture the hill was steeper than now, as the highway engineers of today make easier grades. But there are the covered wagons at the foot of the hill, drawn up in circle for protection; the golden-yellow sunset puts a violet light upon the hills, and I am sure the bullwhacker in the foreground, twirling a rawhide, can be none other than William himself. That's the way Jackson saw Chimney Rock in 1866; the way I see it with the inner eye; the way you and millions of other tourists will picture it till Chimney Rock, inevitably crumbling, shall be a heap of angular blocks.

6. FORT CLATSOP NATIONAL MEMORIAL
[Oregon]

HAVING SEEN AT LAST the blue water of the Pacific, Lewis and Clark looked for a suitable location for fortified winter quarters. They chose a place near

From a distance it is almost like a ruin of the classic age. Fort Laramie National Historic Site. [*Photo: Carl Degen*]

the river which now bears the name of the two Jeffersonian explorers, on a bay, said Clark in his journal, "which I call Meriwether's Bay, the Christian name of Captain Meriwether who no doubt was the first white man who ever surveyed this Bay."

Most of their supplies exhausted, the party settled down to a lean winter diet of fish and "pore elk," with wild roots for vegetables. Lacking salt, they set up a camp on the ocean beach and boiled out three bushels from the seawater. Some families of "Killamuck" Indians made them a friendly gift of "a considerable quantity of the blubber of a whale which had perished on the coast . . . it was white and not unlike the fat of Poark."

There is an Oregon state park at Ecola, "the place of the whale." When I was there, on one occasion, I remembered with delight the story of how little Sacajawea, the Shoshone squaw who had made the long trip with the explorers, begged to be allowed to see that whale. When Clark at first declined to have her go with the group, she said that "she had traveled a long way with us to see the great waters, and now that monstrous fish was to be seen, she thought it very hard that she could not be permitted." Sacajawea had her way. She saw the whale. But the explorers did not get much meat from it to take back to Clatsop. The Indians liked blubber, too.

7. FORT UNION NATIONAL MONUMENT
[*New Mexico*]

WHEN COLONEL EDWIN V. SUMNER selected a spot on the west bank of Coyote Creek as a place where the military could serve and protect the great traffic that was moving over the Santa Fe Trail, one of his purposes was to seek an isolation that would keep the enlisted man from the temptations of the town. What the soldiers thought of this we may conjecture, since a freedom from temptation made life so dull in a frontier post that, lacking activity against the Indians, a new temptation arose: to shoot themselves.

But it was a well-chosen spot nevertheless. Strange indeed how the cobweb of wagon ruts made a century ago are so clear on the face of the land today. As the fort was at the division point of the trails, Fort Union was a welcome haven where travelers could rest and refit. It was the principal quartermaster depot of the Southwest.

All in all, the dragoons and mounted riflemen were not called upon for large-scale operations. They had to knock out Chief Chacon and his Jicarilla Apaches in 1854 and the southern Utes the following year; in 1860 the Kiowas and Comanches were restless, and the following January a column from the fort killed a few rebellious ones and otherwise discouraged them. Yet if Fort Union hadn't been where it was . . . it would have been a different story!

8. BENT'S OLD FORT NATIONAL HISTORIC SITE
[*Colorado*]

THERE WERE MANY TRADERS who set up posts in the Indian country to do a lucrative and often reprehensible business, but none had the phenomenal success of Bent, St. Vrain and Company. Gray Thunder, a potent chief of the Cheyennes, was not loth to give his comely daughter, Owl Woman, in marriage to William Bent. William's brother Charles was the credit man of the firm; St. Vrain was the merchandiser; but the magic touch of friendly relations with the tribes resided in the finesse and fair dealing of William. It was said: "These were mighty men, whose will was prairie law."

On the north bank of the Arkansas River in southeastern Colorado one sees the remains of the way station erected in 1833, which became headquarters for trappers and Indians and the chief point of contact between the whites and their neighbors. Here, springing up from the prairie land like a legendary sky castle, the Bents reared a fortress of mud bricks, fireproof and impregnable. It was a self-contained little barony. If your caravan needed the service of gunsmith, wheelwright, carpenter, or blacksmith, they were here. From this stronghold went General Kearny to Santa Fe in 1846, to raise the American flag over that Mexican possession.

Overtaken by reverses, William Bent abandoned the adobe structure in 1849 and set up a new fort farther down the Arkansas.

9. FORT DAVIS NATIONAL HISTORIC SITE
[*Texas*]

NOT THE LEAST COLORFUL of the memories connected with this best preserved of the Southwestern forts is the experiment with camel transportation from

Century-old wagon ruts are clearly seen around this Santa Fe Trail post. Fort Union National Monument. [Photo: G. S. Cattanack, Jr.]

1857 to 1860. It was Jefferson Davis's pet idea to use these burden beasts to cross the desert country—a sound scheme that came to nought when the Civil War changed all things.

The rush of emigration to the goldfields of California sent a horde of eager Easterners toward the West, and thousands chose the most southerly route to avoid the winter snows. The San Antonio–El Paso road had just been opened. The Indians made this a dangerous trip, for the trail crossed the trails of the Comanches and the Mescalero Apaches, raiders who had long plundered the villages in northern Mexico. Fort Davis was the answer.

The ardor of the Comanches was finally chilled by the United States Army in the Red River War, though troops from Fort Davis were not engaged there; but as late as 1880 the Apaches were making the El Paso road hazardous. It was then that Chief Victorio came up out of Mexico and found Colonel Benjamin H. Grierson and his Fort Davis troopers blocking his progress. There was some hard fighting, but the death of Victorio brought peace at last to West Texas.

10. FORT SMITH NATIONAL HISTORIC SITE
[*Arkansas*]

MAJOR WILLIAM BRADFORD reached Belle Point, a rocky bluff at the junction of the Arkansas and Poteau Rivers, on Christmas Day, 1817. Though white men habitually encroached upon Indian lands, the immediate need here happened to be to quell the warfare between the Osages and the Cherokee invaders, who had come from North Carolina to get a share of the good hunting. The frontier shifted, and this first post gradually melted away. Later another installation was built, and it is of this later Fort Smith that visitors today see the barracks and commissary buildings.

The fort's military career was never impressive. The real drama began when the U.S. District Court moved into the abandoned barracks in 1871 and began sternly to deal with the lawlessness and violence that existed in the territory to which the dispossessed Indian tribes of the East had been moved by that kindly old gentleman Uncle Sam. Here, for more than twenty years, the fearless and upright Judge Isaac C. Parker dispensed justice with a capital J. Three hundred and forty-four men stood before the bar accused of major crimes: seventy-nine were hanged. Hanging having such a strong touch of finality about it, conditions in the region steadily improved.

11. HOMESTEAD NATIONAL MONUMENT OF AMERICA
[*Nebraska*]

DANIEL FREEMAN WAS A MAN who knew a good piece of land when he saw it. He was serving in the Union Army in 1862 when the Homestead Act was passed by Congress. Not far from Beatrice, Nebraska, there was a sweet portion of turf. Cub Creek ran through it, providing an unfailing water supply, as well as a fringe of cottonwood and oak.

I happened to be a visitor at this monument soon after it was established. In the makeshift office of a newly arrived superintendent, I saw Daniel Free-man's "Entry Number One," the classic of homesteading, hanging on the wall. I saw also a cracked and weathered wooden spade, a relic from some-where in the vicinity, dating back to those days of filing on the land. It was not that steel spades didn't exist; many of the homesteaders just didn't have the cash, so they whittled their own. There were hardships.

But the homesteaders could say: "This is only a little cabin, but it is our own. We have only one skillet and we honestly are tired of flapjacks, and come night our muscles are sore . . . but someday we'll have a brick house and Ma will have a hired girl." I doubt if we should pity the pioneers more than they pitied themselves, and I am guessing that wasn't much.

12. WHITMAN MISSION NATIONAL HISTORIC SITE
[*Washington*]

ABOUT THE THIRD DECADE of the nineteenth century there was a great searching of hearts among church folk about carrying the gospel to the be-nighted. The Indians of the Far West were in this category. Not only were their notions of personal hygiene faulty, but they were inclined toward superstitions. It happened that a delegation of Nez Perces and Flatheads had visited St. Louis and suggested that they would like to hear more about the white man's Truth. The Commissioners for Foreign Missions gave ear. They sent Marcus Whitman, a doctor not of divinity but of medicine, to found a mission in the Columbia River Valley. The location, in Cayuse tongue, was Waiilatpu—"The Place Where the Rye Grass Grows."

What a man was this Marcus Whitman! A stubborn and devoted dynamo, he raised the standard of living and the health of the Indians around him. When the fur-trade rivalry was acrimonious and the Hudson's Bay Company was for the moment getting the better of it, someone said, seeing Marcus pass by, "*There* goes a man the British can't drive out of Oregon!" But a sudden burst of primitive passion on the part of the Cayuses spent itself on their benefactors on a night in November 1847, though none of the Christianized Indians were involved. The mission was destroyed; Dr. Whitman, his wife, and fourteen other persons were murdered.

13. McLoughlin House National Historic Site
[*Oregon*]

SIR GEORGE SIMPSON was a Scotsman with a cold gray eye, a boundless energy, and a dislike of deficits. He came into the fur-trade picture in 1821 when the Hudson's Bay stockholders discovered a situation not unknown to-day: that gross sales may be large, business brisk, but net profits nonexistent. The trading posts, remote from London, were staffed by young men with a vast appetite for comforts and delicacies. To Sir George's horror, he found in the warehouses such things as ostrich plumes and coats of mail. His eye fell upon an apprentice surgeon out of Montreal, by name John McLoughlin, a very giant of a man with a booming voice, liable to sudden rages, but scrupulously honest and big hearted. This man, Simpson's manager, was to become "the father of Oregon."

Simpson was a dapper man who felt uncomfortable in the company of this Goliath whose clothing was usually in tatters and who had "a beard that was like the chin of a grizzly bear." He wrote that "McLoughlin is such a figure as I should not like to meet on a dark night in one of the byelanes of London." Yet this was the same man whose hospitality and aid to the missionaries and stranded emigrants was unfailing. When the people of the United States set up a "provisional government" in Oregon, he joined them, and the Hudson's Bay Company lost an irreplaceable servitor.

14. Fort Vancouver National Historic Site
[*Washington*]

THE ORIGINAL FORT VANCOUVER was built on a lovely point of land on the north bank of the Columbia above the confluence of the Willamette. Even so stern a businessman as Sir George Simpson of the Hudson's Bay Company was ravished by the beauty that surrounded it. "I have rarely seen a Gentleman's seat in England," he said, "possessing so many natural advantages."

In 1829 it was decided to shift the location farther west and four hundred yards from the river. This later Fort Vancouver was the one to which American settlers turned for aid against Indian malcontents; it recovered the abducted women and children of the Whitman Mission at Waiilatpu. After the fur trade declined, the post was still conducting a booming business, especially during the California gold rush. It was, in effect, the terminus of the Oregon Trail.

Though the Oregon Treaty gave the Hudson's Bay people "possessory rights," the end of its occupancy could be foreseen. On June 14, 1860, the last load of the company's property was aboard a ship and headed for Victoria on Vancouver Island.

So ended the life of Fort Vancouver—until the day came when the importance of the old post caused it to be "rediscovered." The site was excavated, careful research began, and Fort Vancouver's place in the National Park System was secured.

15. Golden Spike National Historic Site
[*Utah*]

"The last rail is laid, the last spike driven, the Pacific Railroad is completed."

So flashed a telegraphic message to the Associated Press on May 10, 1869, from Promontory Summit, Utah. Two railroad companies—the Union Pacific building from Omaha westward, and the Central Pacific laying rail eastward from Sacramento—had met. The dream of transcontinental direct transportation was now realized.

On the western face of the Promontory Range, the Central Pacific, using Chinese labor, laid down ten miles of track in one day—a record in the history of railroad building that has probably never been equaled.

16. Pipe Spring National Monument
[*Arizona*]

When Joseph Smith, founder of the Church of Jesus Christ of Latter-Day Saints, was murdered by a mob at Nauvoo, Illinois, the embattled Mormon people chose Brigham Young as successor. They could not have found a more resourceful and energetic man. Young's executive force, diverted to profane purposes, would have made him one of the commercial giants. By his sagacity and iron will the Saints achieved their "land of the honey-bee," Deseret, and made it bloom like a rich June meadow. "If the Gentiles will let us alone for ten years," Young had said, "I'll ask no odds of them." On the

[493]

shores of the Great Salt Lake of Utah the Mormons asked no odds, as their descendants do not today.

They had not long been seated at Deseret when they began to fan out into the adjoining country. Their outposts reached to the Grand Wash of the Colorado River. In 1856 the Jacob Hamblin party, sent out to explore the Navajo country, make friends of the Indians, and set up tithing cattle ranches for the church, came upon a spring about fifteen miles southwest of present-day Fredonia. From a dugout of earth and juniper logs, this settlement finally had two red sandstone buildings of two stories each, constituting a fort.

Clothed with juniper, piñon, cottonwood, willow, and desert plants, this national monument is just about a mile above sea level. You will see Lombardy poplars here, too, but they are not native. The Mormons brought them in.

17. BIG HOLE NATIONAL BATTLEFIELD
[Montana]

DURING THE WHOLE SOMBER HISTORY of the expulsion of the Indian peoples from their ancestral homes, the Nez Perces of the Northwest had been singularly docile. They had even joined with the whites against their own color, on occasion, as when they covered Colonel Steptoe's retreat in the "Oregon War." Their intelligent Chief Joseph, not because he loved the whites but because he saw the futility of trying to broom back the ocean, was pacific and yielding.

In early August 1877 the Nez Perces were about to receive their reward for cooperation. It was the old story. The white settlers had moved in upon the fertile lands of the Willowa Valley which, by treaty, were to belong to these Indians in perpetuity. "Perpetuity," in a treaty with the Indians, meant "till we change our minds." Now the Nez Perces were to be moved out to places "just as good." A sarcastic chief once said to an army commander, "You have moved us five times. Why don't you put us on wheels? You could move us with less trouble."

The Indians, planning to migrate to Canada, promised to do so peaceably and were so doing when they arrived at their old campground at Big Hole. There they were attacked by federal troops at night. They rallied and counterattacked with such courage that when they moved on the troops dared not pursue them.

Here Custer's men made their "last stand." Custer Battlefield National Monument.
[Photo: Andrew M. Loveless]

But of course the end was certain. The Nez Perces finally surrendered in the Bearpaw Mountains and became government wards.

18. CUSTER BATTLEFIELD NATIONAL MONUMENT
[*Montana*]

LET US SAY AT ONCE that the whole truth about the slaughter into which the 7th U.S. Cavalry rode can never be known. Custer died; of his surrounded men on the ridge above the Little Bighorn not one survived. One wounded horse, Comanche, survived to become an army pet while he lived—and then was stuffed and preserved to the present day. A century after that battle, military buffs will be shouting vehement opinions at each other at the visitor center of the monument.

For myself, I can never look upon certain widely separated white markers rising from the ungrazed prairie grass without an unashamed tug at the heart, even more than when viewing the fenced cemetery. White slabs that tell where troopers fell upon this uneven ground—the very markers seeming to flee toward a hoped-for refuge. Here one man. Over yonder two men, close together. Two stumbled and died over there . . . that black and white bird just winging past us is a lark bunting . . . what a fluttering of lark buntings there must have been on that June day in 1876!

In death, color differences are washed out. In the cemetery you see headstones that read: Coyote, Indian scout; Bad Heart; Hunts-the-Enemy; Chippewa Indian Woman. Chippewa? So far from home? And one marker says, simply: An Indian Child.

19. CHICAGO PORTAGE NATIONAL HISTORIC SITE
[*Illinois*]

MILO M. QUAIFE, the historian, wrote: "It is no exaggeration to say that Chicago owes her very existence to the fact of her strategic location on one of the most important water routes of North America . . . Chicago Portage was one of the five great 'keys of the continent.'"

The explorer Louis Jolliet had suggested as early as 1673 that it would only be necessary to cut a canal through a mile and a half of prairie "to go in a bark by easy navigation from lake Erie to the Gulf of Mexico." He had reason to know. With Père Marquette, in their return from the Mississippi voyage, he had reached the Great Lakes by way of a little creek and Mud Lake, "portaging" over this very mile and a half of land barrier.

20. THEODORE ROOSEVELT NATIONAL MEMORIAL PARK
[*North Dakota*]

WHEN THE FRENCH VOYAGEURS called these strangely eroded "vast silent spaces" badlands, they did not mean that they might not someday be productive. They merely meant that this country was hard to travel through. Teddy Roosevelt's cattle found good sweet grazing here on the Little Missouri when their owner came from the East and set up as a ranchman in 1883. The Northwest was still a frontier. Only the year before had the Northern Pacific Railroad finally put a bridge across the Missouri at Bismarck.

Totem poles tell a family and tribal story. Sitka National Monument. [*Photo: Josef Muench*]

In the sense that Roosevelt did not have to get his bread and butter from the cattle industry, we shall have to regard the Maltese Cross brand as a dude undertaking. He was there partly for his health, partly because it was a wilderness region of the kind he loved to the end of his life. Nevertheless he aimed to make the business prosperous, and he came through one bad winter without great loss. But the winter of 1886–7 was the most terrible that the white man had ever recorded in the Northwest. It ended the "open-range" delusion which, it must be confessed, had stood up well for a good many years. Roosevelt lost more than half his cattle. He did not give up, and though he was now enjoying his political successes back East, he returned to the Little Missouri nearly every year, until in 1898 he disposed of the dwindled stock before going to Cuba with his colorful Rough Riders. He always regarded his losses as money well spent.

21. CHESAPEAKE AND OHIO CANAL NATIONAL MONUMENT
[Maryland–West Virginia–District of Columbia]

ON THE FOURTH OF JULY 1828, President John Quincy Adams raised the first shovelful of earth to initiate the digging of a canal that was planned to connect the federal capital on the Potomac with Pittsburgh on the Ohio. It was that boom period of canal building when the Eastern states were feverishly attempting to capture the trade of the fast-growing West. Stock-company speculations found ready capital, and this plan of the Chesapeake and Ohio Canal Company for water transport between 360 miles of artificial banks was at first greeted with enthusiasm. George Washington as a young man had been among the first Americans to promote such projects.

Various difficulties, ultimately financial ones, prevented the completion of this ambitious design. At Cumberland, where the canal was to cross the Alleghenies, the stockholders decided to quit. It took twenty-two years to reach that point, and by that time the frenzy for building steam railroads was in full swing. Nevertheless this canal continued to carry freight in its barges until 1924, and in its most active period, in the 1870's, as many as 540 boats were in use.

The right-of-way of the canal is now owned by the government. The western division, from Seneca to Cumberland, constitutes this monument, where the towpath can be walked in surroundings of great beauty and interest. The twenty-two miles from Georgetown to Seneca may be enjoyed by visitors to Washington.

22. GRAND PORTAGE NATIONAL MONUMENT
[*Minnesota*]

Stalwart IS THE WORD for those Canadian French voyageurs—picturesque wilderness figures in their deerskin leggings, moccasins, and red woolen caps—who came paddling out of Montreal in canoes laden with trade goods for the North West Company posts. The word originally meant "with a firm foundation." These indefatigable men with full chests and muscular legs could tote two ninety-pound packs over the "big carry" to the rendezvous on the Pigeon River, undaunted by rocky ledges or trails that turned to grease in the rain and sleet.

They had come from France when Canada was French. The British victories at Quebec and Montreal had changed all that. The names of the fur-trade enterprisers were now McTavish, McGill, Mackenzie, and the like; but the carriers were still Jacques and Armand and Louis.

In July and August the guns and kettles, axes and beads, tobacco and rum were exchanged for beaver and other furs brought to the North West post by other canoe brigades. Along this highway of the voyageurs were many of these carries, and this Grand Portage of nine miles was neither the longest nor the most laborious, but it was at the point where the trading company maintained its Great Hall, held its annual meetings, feasted and bickered, and kept the payrolls. Sometimes a thousand workers were paid off. And then . . . what an odor of West Indian rum!

23. NEZ PERCE NATIONAL HISTORICAL PARK
[*Idaho*]

HERE IS A REGION in our Northwest not only rich in history but still retaining much of its frontier natural beauty. Here is the Lolo Trail of Lewis and Clark, here are told the stories of the fur traders, the gold seekers, the work of the missionaries, and the Nez Perce War of 1877. The area marks rather a departure from the usual in the National Park System. It is a coordination of related sites, in which the large land areas separating those sites will remain under present ownership and control.

Two of the separated historic units deal with the conflict between the Nez Perces and the federal troops: Whitebird Canyon and Clearwater River. These engagements forced the crucial battle at Big Hole.

24. HUBBELL TRADING POST NATIONAL HISTORIC SITE
[*Arizona*]

IT WAS AFTER THE INDIAN of the Western plains and mountains had been subdued and brought into reservations that a new kind of trader came into existence, to run the necessary post exchange where the government wards could dispose of their articles of craftsmanship and obtain the needed goods of white man's fabrication. The Indian trader came to exercise far more influence upon the lives and ways of the native people than could the federal agents, who usually came and went with political change.

These traders might be good or bad; usually those who did business in Navajo lands were genuinely interested in the welfare of their clients—even to a fatherly attitude. Perhaps the greatest and most influential was John Lorenzo Hubbell, whose post at Ganado had distinguished visitors from all over the country and from foreign lands. In the house Don Lorenzo built in

Inside the great wall on Honaunau Bay was sanctuary. City of Refuge National Historical Park. [Photo: Walter Horchler]

1900, next to the trading post, the walls of the big living room and the bedrooms are covered with the works of famous artists who thus showed their appreciation of the Hubbell hospitality.

25. ARKANSAS POST NATIONAL MEMORIAL
[*Arkansas*]

TERRITORIAL CAPITAL of Arkansas in 1819, this military and commercial lodgement in the wilderness then looked back upon a tempestuous career since "Iron Hand" Tonti, the vigorous lieutenant of the adventurer La Salle, had founded it in 1686. Those were the days of the Great Triangle—the struggle among England, France, and Spain for supremacy in the rich new world. The moves on the European chessboard were sudden and sly. Commanders at the post, in a day of tardy communication, were never sure whether they were governors or intruders.

Altogether, the history of this outpost of empire, besides being a reflection of the turbulent struggle for power, reveals a picture of men at their best and worst. You wonder how such a post could be governed at all. There were humorous aspects too. An English traveler, in 1766, found the place a rendezvous for undesirables, including one chap "whose only cargo in his pirogue was a pack of cards by which, and by his skill, he stripped hunters of their possessions." The perennial cardsharp!

26. FORT LARNED NATIONAL HISTORIC SITE
[*Kansas*]

SINCE IT IS the best preserved of all the military posts that protected the Southwestern frontier, Fort Larned is certain to have many visitors, now that it has become part of the National Park System. For years since its abandonment by the army it has been preserved as a ranch headquarters, in parts of which the Fort Larned Historical Society has maintained a museum.

The location of the post in 1859 was strategic. First known as the Camp on the Pawnee Fork and later as Camp Alert, it was the northern anchor of the military protective line. The following year, a new location three miles west was chosen and a sod-and-adobe Fort Larned was built, later to be replaced by stone structures, of which nine are still standing. In 1864 the fort became the agency for the Kiowas and Comanche Indians, and later for the Cheyennes, Arapahoes, and Kiowa-Apaches. Traders flocked in for a rich harvest. When the Santa Fe Railroad was being built, this fort provided protection for the laborers.

[V]

The Civil War

1. Appomattox Court House National Historical Park
[*Virginia*]

THE UNION VICTORY at Five Forks on April 1, 1865, forced General Robert E. Lee to evacuate the long-besieged town of Petersburg, which in turn had so effectively protected the Confederate capital from that quarter. With Richmond doomed, the Confederacy had one last chance of continuing the war. Lee headed his Army of Northern Virginia toward Danville with the hope of uniting his remaining forces with those of General Johnston in North Carolina.

Hot in pursuit, General Grant followed the retreating army. The Union forces cut Lee's line before he could reach Amelia Courthouse, and forced him northward toward Farmville. Downhearted, many of Lee's soldiers left the ranks and took the muddy roads for home. They were no longer even called deserters. Appomattox Station on the Southside Railroad was the last chance of escape. When daylight came on the morning of April 8, at Appomattox Court House, the Confederates found Union infantry in front of them. In the quiet of an informal truce, Lee then arranged a meeting with the Union commander to discuss terms of the surrender of his army.

The two great military leaders met in the red-brick home of Wilmer McLean, who, oddly enough, had seen the battle at Manassas rage around his house in the first days of the war. After the war this Appomattox building was taken down with the idea of making it a museum. Later it was faithfully reconstructed by the National Park Service. In the parlor of this house the two men, who had served in the Mexican War together, began by amiably discussing their old army days. As to the terms of surrender, Grant's attitude

---

... *Enshrined forever: the Lincoln Memorial. National Capital Parks.* [*Photo: W. E. Dutton*]

was one of greatness of spirit. The generous concession by which the common soldiers of the Confederacy were allowed to keep their own horses or mules "to work their little farms" caused Lee to remark: "This will have the best possible effect upon the men. It . . . will do much toward conciliating our people."

The civil strife between North and South was now virtually at an end. But it was necessary for Lee's troops to march past their conquerors, to lay down their weapons, and to receive paroles. Three days later, as eighty thousand Union soldiers quietly watched, the men in gray filed up the side of Clover Hill. Grant had left this final ceremony in the hands of the tough, bullet-scarred Maine schoolmaster General Joshua L. Chamberlain, who proved not less magnanimous in victory than his chief. As the defeated soldiers came opposite the receiving group, with General Gordon at the head, a bugle sounded, and the marching salute, from "order arms" to the old "carry," was given.

And later, Chamberlain was to record a strange aspect of this surrender, as moving as the scene in the McLean house. With the dispersion of the disarmed men in gray, "we are left alone, and *lonesome*. We miss our spirited antagonists . . . and lose interest. Never are we less gay. It was dull, on our march homeward, to plod along . . . without scouts and skirmishers ahead, and reckless of our flanks. It was dreary to lie down and sleep at night without a vigilant picket out . . ."

Thus it was; that four years of savage conflict had created for the armies a way of life, and they found the stillness and the freedom from danger tame.

2. GETTYSBURG NATIONAL MILITARY PARK
[*Pennsylvania*]

THE GREAT NUMBER of Americans who yearly visit the battlefield of Gettysburg is an expression of the consummate interest this engagement will always have for students of our history. Though no immediate military aims were achieved by either side, it still was the great battle of the greatest of civil wars. Here, on the first three days of July 1863, more soldiers died than before or since in an encounter in the Western Hemisphere. More than 172,000 men were involved. It was rightly called "the high water mark" of the efforts of the Confederate States to break away from the Union. Not only that, but

The famous cyclorama is beautifully housed. Gettysburg National Military Park. [Photo: M. Woodbridge Williams]

Warren's figure still surveys that sanguinary field. Gettysburg National Military Park. [Photo: M. Woodbridge Williams]

the imperishable Gettysburg Address of Abraham Lincoln was delivered here.

Once before—in September 1862—General Robert E. Lee had taken an army north of the Potomac River. A salient reason then was that a successful invasion could well have resulted in the recognition of the South by the European powers. The resulting battle at Antietam was a stalemate and a disappointment to the South, but the opportunity of a negotiated peace was still alive. Besides, Vicksburg was in danger of falling to the hammering of Grant, and a single victory might relieve the pressure there.

From early June, Lee's army had been moving through the gaps in the Blue Ridge and into Pennsylvania. It left the back door of Richmond vulnerable, but Lincoln chose to send an army in pursuit of Lee. That the opposing forces met and fought at Gettysburg was really accidental, but a chance contact having been made, the great armies were soon locked in a gigantic struggle in which the fortunes swayed dramatically in favor first of one and then of the other, ending with the magnificent but tragic charge of fifteen thousand Confederates against the Union center. The costly effort failed, and with it went the last hope of a successful invasion of the North.

Lee's Army of Northern Virginia retreated across the Potomac, unpursued by the Union forces; but it was a bitter day for the Confederacy, for on that very Fourth of July came news that Vicksburg had been surrendered.

3. VICKSBURG NATIONAL MILITARY PARK
[*Mississippi*]

FARRAGUT'S NAVAL FORCES in the spring of 1862 had been able to clear the lower Mississippi River and capture New Orleans, Baton Rouge, and Natchez. Union forces could move up the Tennessee and Cumberland Rivers into the very heart of the Southland. But so long as the Confederacy held Vicksburg, with big guns lining the waterfront and the steep bluffs, the problem of dividing the seceding states, East and West, was unsolved. The task of reducing this formidable bastion had been given to Ulysses S. Grant, as commander of the Union Army of Tennessee. And through no fault of his, but

An unusual monument—a pup tent of 1863. Gettysburg National Military Park.
[Photo: M. Woodbridge Williams]

rather because of dismal failures in the eastern theaters of the war, the North was discouraged.

When Farragut took his fleet back to New Orleans and the Union gunboats withdrew to Memphis, it became certain in Grant's mind that the city could not be taken by amphibious operations through the swamps and bayous of the riverfront. Among several possibilities of taking the city from the land side, Grant chose to fix a bridgehead to the south on the west bank, and with the help of Porter's gunboats ferrying them across, to move his troops eastward against the Confederates under General John C. Pemberton, hoping not only to capture Vicksburg but to destroy Pemberton's army. A quick change of plan enabled him to defeat Johnston's forces, which were aiming at a juncture with Pemberton, and to take the vital rail center of Jackson. By the middle of May, Pemberton was besieged in Vicksburg, and the Union forces were ready to storm the city.

Vicksburg finally fell, not to the several costly assaults that were made, but to hunger and lack of supplies. Stubbornly as the city was defended, the net was drawn ever tighter. Cornmeal was gone, and mule meat took the place of salt pork. No help came; and on the morning of July 4, 1863, the Confederates marched out and stacked their arms. There was a tinge of irony in the fact that Vicksburg was surrendered by a Confederate general who had been a West Pointer from Philadelphia and who, following his sentiments at the cost of lifetime friendships, had thrown in his fortunes with the South.

4. MANASSAS (BULL RUN) NATIONAL BATTLEFIELD PARK
[Virginia]

TWO IMPORTANT BATTLES were fought on almost the identical ground at what was an important railroad junction near the little stream of Bull Run, not far from Washington. The green troops on both Union and Confederate sides were not lacking in courage, but panicked easily on the first occasion they clashed in July 1861. There was no conception of the magnitude the civil struggle would attain. The North clamored for a quick finish of the war by the capture of Richmond; and Manassas, on the Orange and Alexandria Railway, was the only direct connection between the two capitals. Quickly after the firing on Fort Sumter this junction had been fortified for defense. A final attack by the Southerners routed the federals and sent them straggling back to Washington. It was in this battle that General Thomas J. Jackson won his famous nickname "Stonewall."

The second battle here, a little more than a year later, was even more of

The Yazoo has changed its course many times since 1863. Vicksburg National Military Park. [Photo: M. Woodbridge Williams]

a crushing defeat for the Union; so much so that General Robert E. Lee now saw the possibilities of a bold invasion north of the Potomac. Only a steady stand by federal troops on that same Henry House Hill where in the first battle the Confederates had put them to rout enabled Pope's army to get back to the shelter of Washington defenses. McClellan's Peninsular Campaign had failed to take Richmond. Now another setback. The clouds in the North looked sullen.

5. CHICKAMAUGA AND CHATTANOOGA
NATIONAL MILITARY PARK
[*Georgia–Tennessee*]

WITH VICKSBURG FALLEN, in July 1863, the major Union strategy next called for creating another dividing line among the states of the Confederacy. The aim now was possession of the great rail center of Chattanooga, in eastern Tennessee. In expectation of this move, the Southern general Braxton Bragg, with a large force of seasoned men, was dug in for its defense. The battle at Stones River, six months earlier, had opened this campaign. Bragg was facing Rosecrans, and both generals showed a good deal of skill in their tactics. Fighting for the key city began with a skirmish on September 18, 1863, and quickly developed into a general battle party in open fields, partly in dense woods, and sometimes waged hand to hand. The first day was indecisive, but on the day following, Rosecrans's army was nearly cut in half and destroyed by a sudden thrust by Longstreet. Only the Union left, on Snodgrass Hill, held its position. It was then that General George H. Thomas, the Union field commander, earned for himself a title somewhat similar to that of Stonewall Jackson. With stubborn determination the "Rock of Chicka-mauga" held against every assault and covered the Union retreat. But now the Union army was trapped in Chattanooga, reduced to near starvation, and it was only later, near the end of November, that Grant, now overall com-mander, after bitter fighting, succeeded in raising the siege and opening the way for Sherman's campaign through Georgia. The famous "battle in the clouds" on Lookout Mountain occurred during the last days of the engage-ment.

6. PETERSBURG NATIONAL BATTLEFIELD
[*Virginia*]

MANY OF THE MEN of the 48th Pennsylvania, the army of Grant at the siege of Petersburg, had been coal miners in civilian life. Though against the city defenders of 50,000 the Union troops numbered at least 112,000, this vital back door of Richmond was so heavily armed against a frontal attack by troops as to make that idea unthinkable. "But," said the miners, "let us drive a tunnel under the Confederate battery opposite us, and let the infantry pour through the breach we shall make." The idea was accepted, and on July 30, 1864, four tons of powder were exploded, leaving a great crater, 170 feet long, 60 feet wide, and 30 feet deep. But this mine, which could have meant the capture of the city, not only failed of its purpose, but because of incompetence and blunders, cost the Union army dearly in killed, disabled, and prisoners.

Most visitors who come to Petersburg Battlefield first ask, "Where is the crater?" Naturally enough: it was a dramatic event. Yet really the great story here is the matching of skill and power of the two great generals, Grant and Lee, from the Wilderness struggle in May 1864 until Petersburg—and therefore the capital of the Confederacy—fell. Every Grant move, to the end, had brought him closer to Richmond, by way of its outpost on the south. In the ten-month siege, the Union losses were far heavier than those of the defenders—but the war was won. Petersburg was the war's largest single battlefield—approximately 170 square miles.

7. Fort Donelson National Military Park
[Tennessee]

It was here that Ulysses S. Grant came into national prominence as a bold and able military leader. At this time a brigadier general, he worked out a plan to break the eleven-mile line between Fort Henry and Fort Donelson, part of the Confederate front which now stretched from Columbus on the Mississippi River to Cumberland Gap. With seventeen thousand men, he moved up the Tennessee River on transports supported by gunboats. Fort Henry, a mudhole at best, could not be defended, and its garrison moved to Fort Donelson.

Grant had twenty-seven thousand men when he arrived before the fort. There were twenty-one thousand men within Donelson, and they were well supplied—except with leaders who could face a man like Grant. Indeed, Grant's position was precarious after the Confederate batteries had knocked out Foote's supporting gunboats. But the Confederate commander, Floyd, was timid, and his associate, Pillow, feared falling into federal clutches. Finally, on the night of February 15, 1862, the decision was made to have the junior commander, Simon Buckner, ask Grant for surrender terms. Pillow and Floyd escaped up the Cumberland River, and the cavalry leader, Nathan Bed-

---

Overleaf: Lookout Mountain stood in Sherman's path. Chickamauga and Chattanooga National Military Park. [Photo: M. Woodbridge Williams]

ford Forrest, who would have no part in the shady business, took his men out safely. When Buckner asked for terms, Grant's reply was: Unconditional and immediate surrender. "Unconditional Surrender Grant" was a slogan that brought fresh spirit to the drooping Union. But in Richmond it was dismal news.

8. KENNESAW MOUNTAIN NATIONAL BATTLEFIELD PARK
[*Georgia*]

WROTE GENERAL SHERMAN, when he was making his drive toward Atlanta and the sea in early May 1864: "Kennesaw, the bold and striking twin mountain, lay before us . . . the scene was enchanting; too beautiful to be disturbed by the harsh clamor of war; but the Chattahoochee lay beyond, and I had to reach it."

Sensitive writing, this, on the part of a military man, who could perceive the loveliness of the north Georgia countryside at a time when he was facing the master of Fabian tactics, Joseph E. Johnston. Sherman had 100,000 well-supplied troops against the Confederates of half that number, but he was in hostile country and had always to take the offensive against adroitly chosen positions. Not till Sherman found Kennesaw Mountain looming between him and his objective, Atlanta, did the Union general decide upon a direct attack.

Up the steep grades of the mountain the federal troops pushed against formidable Confederate breastworks and the deadly rifle fire. Two hours and a half of this vain attempt, and the fighting ended. The breakthrough had failed, with great Union losses. Sherman went back to his flanking tactics that were forcing Johnston steadily, if slowly, back upon Atlanta. Then the Richmond government, tired of retreat, retreat, and wanting something more dashing, replaced the patient Johnston with the eager General Hood. It was what Sherman had wanted. The capture of Atlanta soon followed.

9. ANTIETAM NATIONAL BATTLEFIELD SITE
[*Maryland*]

WHILE THE BLOODY BATTLE that took place here at Antietam Creek and Sharpsburg was not a Union victory, it was essentially a defeat for the Confederacy. Lee's hope of swinging Maryland to the Southern side, and the possibility of getting Great Britain (hit hard in its economy by the lack of American cotton for its mills) to declare the Confederacy a sovereign nation, had to be relinquished for the moment.

It is said that more men were killed and wounded at this battle than on any other single day's fighting during the entire war. Of the 87,000 federal troops under General McClellan the losses were more than 15 per cent. Lee had about 41,000 men in the fight, and 26 per cent were lost. So desperate was the conflict at many points that the soldiers quit from sheer exhaustion. The terrible effectiveness of the firepower can be imagined from what General Hooker wrote of the action north of the town of Sharpsburg: "in the time I am writing every stalk of corn in the greater part of the field was cut as closely as could have been done with a knife, and the slain lay in rows [Jackson's troops] precisely as they had stood in their ranks a few moments before."

The timely arrival of Confederates from Harpers Ferry prevented a Union victory here.

10. SHILOH NATIONAL MILITARY PARK
[*Tennessee*]

THE CAPTURE of Fort Henry and Fort Donelson by Grant forced the Confederate commander, Albert Sidney Johnston, to fall back from Kentucky and that part of Tennessee north of the all-important railroad that ran from Memphis to Chattanooga. The possession of this supply line was to become the reason not only for the battle at Shiloh, but for much sanguinary fighting afterward.

The Tennessee River was now open to Union gunboats and transport. Up to Pittsburg Landing, only a short distance from the Confederate railroad center at Corinth, Mississippi, came 40,000 of Grant's soldiers, and Buell, with 25,000 more, left Nashville to join Grant. Before these reinforcements could arrive, Johnston moved out of Corinth to get between the Union forces and their supply base at Pittsburg Landing. Before daybreak on April 6, 1862, the Southerners made an attack upon the federal camp, which apparently was unaware that Johnston was so near them. It touched off the bloody encounters between the unseasoned but courageous men on both sides, which caused Grant to write in his memoirs that "Shiloh . . . was a case of Southern dash against Northern pluck and endurance . . . the troops on both sides were Americans . . . united they need not fear any foreign foe."

Albert Sidney Johnston died from a wound received in this battle, as he sat on his horse under the oak tree still seen by visitors. And peaches still bloom in the part of the battlefield where some of the fiercest combat took place.

11. RICHMOND NATIONAL BATTLEFIELD PARK
[*Virginia*]

ONLY A LITTLE MORE than one hundred miles separated the capital of the Confederacy from the federal city of Washington. This geographical location constituted a military liability to the seceding states from the first; yet it is easy to understand why the old seat of government of Virginia was chosen. Richmond, on the James, naturally became the symbol of secession. The Northern slogan "On to Richmond!" meant "Put down the rebellion!"

In spite of seven distinct drives to capture Richmond, the city was never actually taken. It fell because Petersburg fell, and only at the very end of the war. It did, though, have two narrow escapes: once during McClellan's Peninsular Campaign in 1862, and again two years later when Grant crossed the Rapidan and came to the very edge of the city. But all the terrific hammering of Grant's forces would not break down the defenses that had been created against the chance of just such a frontal attack. The final effort, at Cold Harbor on June 3, 1864, lasted less than half an hour, but left seven thousand soldiers dead and dying. Grant himself said that the attack was an error of judgment.

As would be expected, the battlefield park, as preserved and administered by the National Park Service, consists of ten different parcels of land, and a complete tour of the battlefields is about fifty-seven miles.

12. FREDERICKSBURG AND SPOTSYLVANIA COUNTY BATTLEFIELDS MEMORIAL NATIONAL MILITARY PARK
[*Virginia*]

FOUR MAJOR BATTLES of the Civil War are represented in this military park—Fredericksburg, the Wilderness, Chancellorsville, and Spotsylvania Court House. As Petersburg was the back door of the capital of the Confederacy, so was Fredericksburg the front door. At the falls of the Rappahannock River, just about halfway between Richmond and Washington, the possession of this city was of the utmost importance. The wide river was a barrier against attack from the Union.

In November 1862, President Lincoln had wearied of McClellan's super-caution and slow movement and replaced him with General Ambrose Burnside. After a long delay while pontoon bridges were procured, Burnside crossed the Rappahannock successfully and captured the city in street fight-

More than a memorial: a heartbreak in stone and bronze. Shiloh National Military Park. [Photo: George Grant]

ing. But the later attack upon Marye's Heights, despite heroic efforts, was a disaster. There was a long lull on this front until Hooker succeeded Burnside and made an attempt to get behind Fredericksburg. The ensuing Chancellorsville was a Confederate victory, but their great leader Stonewall Jackson was killed during the fighting.

In May 1864, Grant, now in supreme command of the Union forces, sent the army of Meade across the Rapidan, and the battle of the Wilderness followed, west of Fredericksburg. The bitter fighting here was indecisive, but the struggle moved on to Spotsylvania Court House, where Lee formed a new strong line which Grant decided not to attack.

13. STONES RIVER NATIONAL BATTLEFIELD
[Tennessee]

THE HOPE OF THE CONFEDERACY, to bring Kentucky under the banner of secession, vanished when the army of General Braxton Bragg was defeated by Buell at Perryville in October 1862. Indeed, with Nashville in Union hands, Bragg needed all his strength to frustrate the clear intention of the northern leaders to cleave the upper from the lower South by thrusting along the line of the west-east rails into Chattanooga from Memphis.

Bragg selected a base at Murfreesboro and placed his troops along the stream called Stones River. Thirty miles northwest was the Union Army of the Cumberland, commanded by Rosecrans. Late in December the two armies were facing each other, and the opposing generals had developed almost identical plans. Each intended to assault the other's right wing and bend it back into the river. The three days of desperate fighting that took place here ended with a sudden reversal of fortunes at the moment when the Confederates were about to achieve a victory. Eight batteries of guns, assembled with astonishing speed and massed on the heights to meet the Confederate all-out attack, poured out a devastating fire of a hundred rounds a minute. An almost certain success changed to a rout in a matter of minutes.

Bragg's soldiers had captured Union cannon in this fighting, as well as more than three thousand prisoners. But it was hardly a victory. The Union troops held the field, and Bragg had to seek another base.

14. FORT SUMTER NATIONAL MONUMENT
[South Carolina]

ON DECEMBER 20, 1860, South Carolina seceded from the Union, and this example, so long threatened and feared, was soon followed by the formation of a Confederate government, with Jefferson Davis of Mississippi as President. Virginia, North Carolina, Tennessee, and Arkansas, though generally sympathetic with the other Southern states, hesitated to make the break. By March 1861 nearly all the forts and navy yards in the seceding states had been seized by the Confederates, but Fort Sumter, in Charleston harbor, remained in federal possession.

Major Robert Anderson, in command of the small garrison at Fort Moultrie on the mainland, moved over to Sumter "to prevent the effusion of blood," as he reported to Washington. The Charlestonians immediately occupied Moultrie and prepared to bombard the harbor fort if necessary. Anderson had only a few months' provisions, and Buchanan, then President of the United States, sent a supply ship to his aid. But it was turned back by the shore batteries. After Abraham Lincoln became President he notified the Governor of South Carolina that Fort Sumter would be supplied and defended.

The Confederate officers did not wait. At four thirty a.m. on April 12 a shell burst over the fort. By daybreak other shore cannon opened fire. A hot shot started a fire. In the afternoon, "the magazines surrounded by flames," Major Anderson agreed to a surrender.

On April 15, Lincoln issued his call for 75,000 volunteers, and Civil War had begun. The reluctant Southern states, including Virginia, now threw in their fortunes with the Confederacy.

15. Fort Pulaski National Monument
[*Georgia*]

AFTER THE WAR OF 1812 the young United States, realizing the vulnerability of its long coastline against a possible invasion by a European power, began the construction of a chain of forts, of which this one, named for its Polish friend of Revolutionary days and located on Cockspur Island, near Savannah, was nearly twenty years in the building. In its massive walls were 25 million bricks, and the superb masonry had not only utility, but also a touch of elegance. One military authority said that "you might as well cannonade the Rocky Mountains as Fort Pulaski."

At the outbreak of the Civil War, Pulaski was not garrisoned by the federal government, and Governor Brown of Georgia ordered it seized just before Georgia joined the Confederacy. Early in November 1861, Robert E. Lee, then in command of defenses in the Southeast, considered the possibility that the fort might be attacked from batteries on nearby Tybee Island.

About eight hundred yards was then considered the distance from which a brick fort could be breached by cannon. Lee said to the fort's chief: "They can make it very warm for you, Colonel, with shells from that point, but they cannot breach you at that distance."

It was true when Lee said it, but the war soon brought refinements of old means, and when federal batteries did open up from Tybee, early in 1862, rifled cannon were used. A thirty-hour bombardment brought about its surrender.

16. BRICES CROSS ROADS NATIONAL BATTLEFIELD SITE
[Mississippi]

AS THE CIVIL WAR dethroned some military idols, so it also unexpectedly created others. Not the least surprising of the latter was Nathan Bedford Forrest, who entered the Confederate service in a humble capacity and proved to be one of the greatest of cavalry commanders. Forrest had no formal military training whatever. He was original, daring, and a natural leader of men. There was a legend that when Forrest was once asked for the secret of his success he replied, "To git thar fustest with mostest." Even if he never said it, this actually described his tactics on many a field.

Brices Cross Roads was the scene of a spectacular victory by this swift-moving leader over a Union force more than twice his numbers. As Sherman was moving toward Atlanta in mid-1864, his supply line, the railway from Nashville to Chattanooga, was in danger from attack by the Confederates located in Mississippi. Sherman ordered: "Hold Forrest . . . until we can strike Johnston." So General Sturgis came out of Memphis headed for Corinth, Mississippi. Forrest attacked him with such swift energy at Brices that soon there was confusion in the Union ranks, then panic. The attempted orderly retreat of Sturgis to Memphis became a rout. Most of the Union artillery and more than 1,500 soldiers fell into Forrest's hands. At points of his own selection, the unschooled tactician had struck first with the most.

17. TUPELO NATIONAL BATTLEFIELD
[Mississippi]

ALTHOUGH IT WAS a vain attempt on the part of the Confederates to keep Sherman from Atlanta—and the ocean—the battle at Tupelo was fought with the courage usual to both combatants, but produced no real honors for anyone. General Stephen D. Lee, the senior commander, had come to the scene without troops. Forrest, the Confederate cavalry genius, had 9,400 horsemen to defend the rich prairie part of eastern Mississippi from an advance by a Union force of 14,000. Actually the Union thrust was aimed to destroy Forrest. After the fight at Brices Cross Roads, where Forrest had humiliated a Union general with a classic display of skill, Sherman had cried: "There will be no peace until Forrest is dead. Follow him to the death, if it cost ten thousand lives and breaks the Treasury."

So Sherman picked two commanders he thought might have better luck and possibly more ability. "Forrest whipped Sturgis fair and square," said Sherman with wry frankness. "Now I will put him against A. J. Smith and Mower." Smith was an old hand with real soldier quality. Mower was "a young and game officer." Together they might finish off this terrible gadfly.

They did not, but neither did they come off badly. The battle, fought in wilting heat, swayed back and forth evenly. The Union forces were turned back, but Sherman's command of his supply line was safe. And that was his main aim.

18. Fort Jefferson National Monument
[*Florida*]

On one of the coral key islands called the Dry Tortugas, about seventy miles into the Gulf of Mexico from Key West, was built the largest of the brick forts intended to secure the nation from invasion. It covered most of sixteen-acre Garden Key. The plan provided for 450 guns, in three tiers, but although thirty years' work was done on it, it was never completed.

Actually Fort Jefferson played no part in the Civil War, save that it was hurriedly garrisoned at the outbreak and was used to imprison Dr. Samuel A. Mudd and others accused of complicity in the assassination of President Lincoln. An insecure foundation and hurricanes gradually made a ruin of this "guardian of the Gulf ports."

What Fort Jefferson lacks in military significance is far outweighed by the amazing wildlife picture presented here. Nesting of the thousands of sooty terns between May and September (with some hundreds of noddy terns among them) is an unforgettable spectacle. Then come in the man-of-war, or frigate, birds to live a life of ease by robbing the terns of their hard-earned catches of fish. Around and around, without moving a wing, these seven-foot-spread soarers circle above the fort, gliders without parallel. Wonderful, too, is the underwater plant and animal life seen in the crystal-clear waters.

19. HARPERS FERRY NATIONAL HISTORICAL PARK
[West Virginia–Maryland]

"THE PASSAGE of the Potomac through the Blue Ridge is perhaps one of the most stupendous scenes in nature . . . this is worth a voyage across the Atlantic." So wrote Thomas Jefferson after many a visit. Peter's Hole, the place was first called. Robert Harper built a mill here, and ferried folks across the river. Then came canal and railroad, and the lower part of the gap, less beautiful than before, was busy and important. Occasionally flood waters of the Shenandoah and Potomac, joining their streams here, scoured the lower town. But Harpers Ferry hung itself out to dry, and trade went on.

It was inevitable that when the Civil War came, both sides in the struggle should covet the possession of this stragetic point. Even before, the place had been dramatically awakened to the coming conflict by the raid of the abolitionist John Brown, who swooped down upon the armory there to obtain weapons for a Negro insurrection. When Brown was hanged at Charles Town, there was a man present, in charge of a state guard, named Thomas J. Jackson. Less than two years later Stonewall Jackson, now a Confederate colonel, would lead a column to capture the entire Union garrison.

Fought over continuously, burned, looted, reduced to a ghost town, Harpers Ferry still retained the spark of life. The loveliness of the surrounding mountains and the inspiring view of the great marrying rivers were beyond the malice of man to spoil.

20. GENERAL GRANT NATIONAL MEMORIAL
[New York]

THIS RUGGED SOLDIER, Ulysses S. Grant, who emerged from the obscurity of a country store in Illinois when the Civil War came and was to be the answer to the harassed Lincoln's prayer for a general who "would do something," lies buried in a gray granite monument on a bluff overlooking the Hudson River. He was, indeed, a West Point graduate, and had served throughout the Mexican War, but he had resigned from the army and was so little considered by the War Department that when he offered his services to the Union he was ignored.

Grant's indomitable drive and tenacity, first demonstrated at Fort Donelson, took him to the supreme command of the Union armies, to the surrender at Appomattox, and inevitably, as a war hero, to the White House in 1868. We like to recall his generous terms to the defeated Lee, his personal integrity, and the frank fairness of his *Personal Memoirs*, written in his final days in an effort to pay off his debts and provide for his family.

In the center of the marble-lined interior of "Grant's Tomb" is an open crypt containing the sarcophagi of Grant and his wife. In niches around the walls of the crypt are bronze busts of his old field comrades Sherman, Sheridan, Thomas, Ord, and McPherson.

21. ABRAHAM LINCOLN BIRTHPLACE NATIONAL HISTORIC SITE
[*Kentucky*]

IN THE WINTER OF 1808, when Kentucky was still "dark and bloody ground," and only the resolute could endure the pioneer hardship, Thomas Lincoln and his wife Nancy Hanks paid $200 in cash for a three-hundred-acre farm, a few miles south of Hodgen's Mill. There was a one-room log cabin there, near the Sinking Spring. Here, February 12, 1809, was born Abraham Lincoln, destined to have many memorials of his great life and tragic death, but none that will be so enduring as the love and hope he inspired in the hearts of people of good will, wherever men exist.

The precise history of that log cabin, now seen within a memorial building that was erected with funds raised by popular subscription and including the pennies of schoolchildren throughout the nation, will always be open to controversy. It makes little difference. The multitude of yearly visitors are not interested in the neatness of historiography. They come to do reverence to the great American who, with patience and humor and steadfastness, saw their country through four years of bitter civil strife, and himself remained with malice toward none, and charity for all.

Since Dr. George Rodman bought this log cabin which stood upon the birthplace farm and moved it to his own property nearby, it has seen long travels. Dismantled, and carefully marked for reassembly, it was exhibited at many expositions throughout the country. In 1909, it came back to a spot near Sinking Spring at last.

22. PEA RIDGE NATIONAL MILITARY PARK
[*Arkansas*]

NOWHERE WERE fiercer passions engendered by the issues of slavery and secession than in Missouri. Sixty per cent of all Missourians of military age served in the Civil War—109,000 in the Union armies and 30,000 with the Confederacy. But these numbers did not tell the whole story. Bitter hatreds arose from internal dissension, political and otherwise. The possession of St. Louis alone, as a base for operations in the West, would be a rich prize for either side.

When General John C. Frémont, fresh from an interview with Lincoln, arrived in St. Louis in July 1861, he found himself, as he said, "in an enemy's country, enemy's flag displayed from houses and recruiting offices . . . St. Louis was in sympathy with the South, and the state was in actual rebellion against the national authority." The fiasco at Bull Run had been a damaging blow to Union prestige.

At Christmas, General Samuel Curtis was given the mission to drive the pro-Confederate forces out of Missouri. His opponent was General Sterling Price, former governor, who, like many Missourians, had been utterly opposed to secession, but also opposed to the invasion of the South. Price, with state troops that had not become part of the Confederate Army, had to pull back across the Arkansas line, where he could join the regular forces. The ensuing two-day battle of Pea Ridge, bitterly contested, with both sides having their successes, was a decisive defeat for the Confederacy. Missouri was saved for the Union. Yet the state continued to be ravaged by guerrilla warfare throughout the war.

23. ANDREW JOHNSON NATIONAL HISTORIC SITE
[*Tennessee*]

THE NATION has had many prominent leaders who rose from humble beginnings, but none whose climb was quite as steep as that of Andrew Johnson, who became President at the death of Abraham Lincoln. When still a boy, in order to help support his family, he became apprentice to a tailor instead of attending school. But, with a devoted wife and invincible determination, he achieved an education, created a prosperous business, and entered politics, rising steadily from mayor of his city to the United States Senate.

A holder of slaves himself, Johnson took his stand with the Union at the outbreak of the Civil War. "I intend to stand by the Constitution as it is," he declared, "insisting upon a compliance with all its guarantees . . . it is the last hope of human freedom." Thus an ideal choice to run with Lincoln in 1864, he became Vice President, and so was called upon to face the vast problems of Reconstruction.

Like the martyred President, Johnson held that the Southern states had never been out of the Union; the secession was a nullity; the Union was indissoluble; so when resistance ended, they could resume their functions. This brought him in conflict with the program of a Congress that aimed to punish rather than to heal. He became the first President (and the last) ever to be impeached. One vote saved him from conviction.

In Greenville are preserved the tailoring shop that saw his lowly beginning, the home in which he later lived, and a monument that records his devotion to his country's Constitution.

24. LINCOLN BOYHOOD NATIONAL MEMORIAL
[*Indiana*]

SOMETIME IN DECEMBER 1816, a seven-year-old boy was trudging into the wilderness in southern Indiana with his emigrating family. The Lincolns were moving again. Indiana was just at that time assuming statehood, but the locality into which Thomas Lincoln was taking his wife and family was wild, and Abraham remembered that they had to make their own road for the final four miles of the trek.

There was land to clear, and a cabin to build, and the boy was expected to help. On the frontier there were no teen-age problems due to idleness. And here Abraham Lincoln went to school, developed a taste for reading worthwhile books, fell in love, fell out again, collected the salty anecdotes of rural life that he narrated with such telling results in political life in the days to come. He read *Pilgrim's Progress*, Ben Franklin's *Autobiography*, and—best guide of all to the use of simple vibrant language—the King James version of the Bible. Out of reading like this came the monosyllabic trenchant quality of the Gettysburg address.

Other than that he was more studious than most of his companions, this youthful Abraham Lincoln of southern Indiana days was not remarkable. At sixteen he was an odd-job worker, earning money by slaughtering hogs or ferrying passengers out into the Ohio River to board a passing steamboat. A few years afterward he came into New Salem, Illinois, "like a piece of driftwood," as he said. His boyhood and youthful years in Indiana were ended.

25. BOOKER T. WASHINGTON NATIONAL MONUMENT
[*Virginia*]

THAT TWO-HUNDRED-ACRE piece of land of James Burroughs, situated south of Roanoke, must have been, when he was cropping it in Civil War days, what Shakespeare called a pelting farm. To get tobacco, corn, and oats out of the worn-down Piedmont soil, it is said that Burroughs himself worked side by side with his slaves. Of these there were at one time ten, inventoried for tax purposes at something over $7,000. A Negro boy named Booker was listed as having a fair-sale value of $400.

Little Booker had just turned nine when the day came in 1865 that the war was over and there were no more slaves. At first a burst of joy: then, as with so many others, came the somber feeling that a fixed and certain way of life was being exchanged for a cloudy unknown. But Jane Ferguson and her children went to West Virginia, where for the first time Booker met the alphabet. "Your full name? Booker what?" asked the schoolteacher. "Booker . . . *Washington*," was the reply. He chose a name for himself; chose gravely.

Hardship could not gravel this Negro youth. Working in the salt furnace, in the coal mine, as a houseboy, as a waiter, he got his education. The time came when he had a college under his own administration and was writing widely read books, the best known being *Up from Slavery*. This memorial to a great man, who helped so many of his people to help themselves, preserves the Burroughs "plantation," with a reproduction of the kind of cabin in which Booker Washington was born.

26. George Washington Carver National Monument
[*Missouri*]

IT SO HAPPENS that another Negro who pulled himself up by indomitable will, achieving a distinction in the sciences that warranted his birthplace being made a national monument, also had in his name a memory of the first President. Although the date of his birth is uncertain, George Washington Carver was probably about five years old when the Civil War ended. He and his mother were the property of Moses Carver, who lived in Diamond Grove in southern Missouri. At the outbreak of the Civil War that region was the scene of merciless guerrilla raiding. George, his mother, and a baby sister were kidnapped. Later, Carver recovered only the boy, who, now orphaned, continued to live with the white family and went to school in the nearby town of Neosho. As he grew, he showed remarkable versatility. Music, painting, mathematics, the natural sciences—he was proficient in all; but he finally devoted himself to agricultural chemistry. Booker Washington had the inspiration to bring Carver to Tuskeegee in Alabama, where he produced many bulletins aimed at teaching Negro farmers how to raise their standard of living.

George Washington Carver once said: "I like to think of nature as an unlimited broadcasting system, through which God speaks to us every hour, if we will only tune in." Carver himself tuned in, effectively for himself and for those who had less skill in listening.

27. WILSON'S CREEK BATTLEFIELD NATIONAL PARK
[*Missouri*]

ACCORDING TO one Civil War buff, there were more surprises at the battle of Wilson's Creek than at any other engagement during the war. "The initial attack of both Lyon and Sigel were complete surprises. In turn, Sigel was completely surprised and defeated by McCulloch. But possibly the greatest surprise was that of Lyon when he encountered the Missouri Militia under Price. These troops were fresh from the farm, without drill or organization . . . but they had led a frontier life . . . and had great skill in marksmanship."

In 1938, at the seventy-seventh anniversary of this battle, it was reported that there were no important changes since '61. "Bloody Hill remains untouched and on its rocky side many bullet-scarred oaks still are mute witnesses. A pile of native stones marks the spot where General Lyon fell . . . across the valley on the east side is the old farmhouse where Lyon lay."

[VI]

March of America

1. Sagamore Hill National Historic Site
[*New York*]

"I WISHED a big piazza . . . where we could sit in rocking chairs and look at the sunset," wrote Theodore Roosevelt when he was describing the home he had built, as a young man, at Cove Neck on Long Island. He had it, as he had most things that he wanted during his life of sixty years. The piazza looked out over Oyster Bay and Long Island Sound. Though he ranched in Dakota for several years, traveled widely, and occupied the White House in Washington, this was his home, and visitors today, especially older visitors, feel his presence in it. "There isn't any place in the world like home—like Sagamore Hill, where things are our own."

The Roosevelt children felt that way about it, too. Father was an outdoorsman, and he carried to them his healthy notion of the vigorous enjoyment of simple pastimes. He said, "They swam, they tramped, they boated, they coasted and skated in winter, they were the intimate friends with the cows, chickens, pigs and other livestock." He saw to it that they could manage a pony or horse as soon as they could sit one. He called his fellow Americans to "the strenuous life," and set the example.

This solidly constructed Victorian house at Cove Neck, with its ample acreage, became a summer White House where newspapermen could always find copy that had country-wide appeal. If there was a touch of the flamboyant in his activities, it endeared him the more to the millions who still retained a feeling that a frontier, and frontier virtues, still existed. They called him, affectionately, Teddy. Of course, as might be expected, he was called other things by those he denounced, in political life, as "malefactors of great wealth."

"Teddy's" family had a happy childhood. Sagamore Hill National Historic Site. [*Photo: M. Woodbridge Williams*]

Though there were not many dull domestic moments during his years at the White House, perhaps Theodore Roosevelt's participation in the international field was even more important. After the war with Spain, in which he had led a cavalry regiment of Rough Riders, his doctrine "Speak softly, and carry a big stick" began to have expression in important ways. An American fleet went around the world, as an advertisement of our naval strength; the Panama Canal was built; the Russian and Japanese envoys had discussed peace on the porch at Sagamore Hill; and Roosevelt had a frank talk with the German Kaiser, which resulted in neither of them becoming fond of the other.

Notwithstanding all this prominence in the affairs of state, somehow visitors to Sagamore Hill leave with the feeling that here was a home where domestic virtues were the normal thing; where children "were never allowed to be disobedient or to shirk lessons or work," but where "they were encouraged to have all the fun possible." Old-fashioned, perhaps. If the idea is to suffer the fate of the dodo, all the better reason for preserving Sagamore Hill, as we preserve the bones of the dinosaur.

2. THEODORE ROOSEVELT BIRTHPLACE NATIONAL HISTORIC SITE
[New York]

NOT AT ALL like Sagamore Hill was the house on 20th Street in New York City where Theodore Roosevelt was born in 1858. It was one of those narrow-fronted dwellings where the first floor was really a basement, English-fashion, and you climbed up a stoop to make a social entrance. Very respectable place for a couple, newly married and of moderate means; and to it Theodore Roosevelt, Sr., brought his Southern bride, Martha Bullock. There was a porch on the rear of the house overlooking the fine gardens of rich Mr. Goelet—almost as good as having gardens of your own, and less upkeep.

The first child born to the Roosevelts was sickly, weak of eyes, not even rugged enough to attend school. His parents called him Teedie, and there is something about that very nickname which suggests weakness. How strange it is that these weaklings sometimes grow up to be so energetic that it is exhausting to the less robust merely to be in their presence. So it was with little Theodore; but it was not until manhood, after he had deliberately sought health and strength by coming in close relation to the raw nature of the Western range, that he really became the Teddy of an admiring public, instead of the Teedie of his childhood.

Roosevelt's own recollection of this middle-class house on 20th Street is graphic enough. "The black haircloth furniture in the dining-room scratched the bare legs of the children as they sat on it. The middle room was a library, with tables, chairs and bookcases of gloomy respectability."

3. HOME OF FRANKLIN D. ROOSEVELT NATIONAL HISTORIC SITE
[*New York*]

THERE IS NOTHING UNCOMMON, in our succession of Presidents, about election for a second term. Indeed, it has almost been a tacit expectation. Franklin Delano Roosevelt was not only elected President for a third term but a fourth, and the November returns suggested that he could have remained in the White House as long as he chose to do so. From the time he was sent to the New York Assembly by his Hyde Park neighbors in 1911, his political career sustained but one setback—an unsuccessful campaign for the Vice Presidency. He was twice elected governor of his state.

In this, his ancestral home overlooking the Hudson River, visited by millions of his fellow Americans, there is a museum label that never fails to elicit a warm and intimate response. It reproduces a telegram sent by the happy father, James Roosevelt, announcing the arrival at Hyde Park on a January day in 1882 "of a bouncing boy, weight 9½ pounds, this morning." He was to be an only son, but a famous one.

Unlike the first Roosevelt in the White House, this boy had a healthy playtime in the woods and fields of a lovely countryside. But in 1921, in the full vigor of manhood, he was struck down by infantile paralysis, which his own courageous battle to overcome resulted in so much benefit to other sufferers.

The shock wave of the sudden death of Franklin Roosevelt in April 1945, at Warm Springs, Georgia, will long be remembered. The month before, he had been at Hyde Park for what was to be his final visit. Perhaps the room in the house that seizes most visitors is the bedroom, in the stone wing over the living room, where the President was at ease among his naval prints, his pictures and family photographs. Scattered about are the books and magazines, just as they were left when he was last there; and the chair and leash and blanket of the scottie Fala, who, in Washington days, was a character better known than many members of Congress.

In the rose garden, nearly surrounded by an ancient hedge of hemlock, Franklin Roosevelt was buried, and beside his grave is that of his wife Eleanor, who survived him by many years. A rose garden was traditional with the family, since the name Roosevelt is Dutch for "field of roses." The white marble tombstone is from the Vermont quarry that supplied the beautiful material that went into the Thomas Jefferson Memorial in Washington.

Next to the site is the Franklin D. Roosevelt Library, administered by the Archivist of the United States.

4. VANDERBILT MANSION NATIONAL HISTORIC SITE
[New York]

HOW DIFFERENT from the ample but unostentatious Roosevelt homes at Sagamore Hill and Hyde Park is this "royal palace" almost literally transported from Europe, one of the finest examples of Italian Renaissance architecture in the United States! Rightly it has been called "A Monument to an Era." The era was that of vast fortunes created by the spectacular growth of the nation in the days following the Civil War. It was the "country home" of Frederick W. Vanderbilt, a grandson of Commodore Cornelius Vanderbilt of steamboat and railroad fame. These giants of commerce seldom went into active political life, choosing to remain silent partners in the art of governing.

When Frederick Vanderbilt bought this imposing site, with its magnificent outlook across the Hudson River to the Shawangunk Range on the west and the Catskills to the north, it was already a place of great distinction. It had been the scene, since early in the eighteenth century, of development and experimentation in gardening and horticulture. The rare and exotic flora seen on lawns and park were the work of a Belgian landscape gardener as early as 1828. And there was a fine mansion there, which was demolished to make a place for the present one, erected at a cost of $660,000, not counting furnishings. Visitors wonder at the elegance, and usually conclude that, for themselves, they would like something simpler.

5. HERBERT HOOVER NATIONAL HISTORIC SITE
[Iowa]

IT WAS THE ILL LUCK of Herbert Hoover, who had acquitted himself so nobly in relief work during and after World War I, to be elected President of the United States just as the economic roof of the country was about to collapse,

Having climbed to great wealth one may climb a staircase like this. Vanderbilt Mansion National Historic Site. [Photo: M. Woodbridge Williams]

due to several years of unbridled popular capitalization of assets that existed only on paper. It was hardly to be expected that a whole generation of eager young people, stunned and disillusioned, would realize the truth that any other Chief Executive in office would have shared the same fate. Hence it was many years before Hoover emerged from eclipse and his great abilities and patriotic devotion were again recognized.

This historic site preserves the cottage in which the President was born in West Branch, and restores, with some minor changes, the neighborhood atmosphere of 1874. Hoover was a great mining engineer, but his scholarship is not so well advertised. With his wife, Lou Henry Hoover, he translated the Latin text of the great *De Re Metallica* of Georgius Agricola, rendering clearly into modern terms the often baffling references to mining and metallurgy of the fifteenth century.

6. SAINT-GAUDENS NATIONAL HISTORIC SITE
[*New Hampshire*]

IT WAS IN 1876 that Augustus Saint-Gaudens, one of America's foremost sculptors, established his home in the lovely region on the Connecticut River in New Hampshire where one looks westward toward smooth-shouldered Mount Ascutney. Other artists loved this spot, too: Maxfield Parrish, the painter whose blue skies rivaled the blue water of Crater Lake; and Percy MacKaye, the poet-dramatist. This significant cultural memorial, administered by the National Park Service, is the donation of the Saint-Gaudens trustees for the use and inspiration of the public.

Among the most important of Saint-Gaudens's works are the Farragut Monument in New York City; the Shaw Memorial in Boston; the Adams Memorial in Rock Creek Park, Washington, D.C.; and statues of General Sherman and Abraham Lincoln. Not so often seen by the public nowadays is the Saint-Gaudens gold double eagle, considered by some the most beautiful coin ever minted in this country. Aside from its artistic merit, the sight of this gold piece arouses wistfulness.

7. EDISON NATIONAL HISTORIC SITE
[*New Jersey*]

BENJAMIN FRANKLIN snatched the lightning from the sky and Thomas Alva Edison put it to work. This is a tickling manner of speaking, so obviously an oversimplification that it can be ignored. But one thing is certain about these two great inventive geniuses: they both had the sketchiest kind of conventional education, and each went to work for his living at the age of twelve. Neither had to be baited with the carrot of opportunity. They went looking.

This inspiring historic site presents two phases of Edison's life and work at Menlo Park and West Orange. In the large library of Glenmont, the estate purchased in 1886, was the inventor's "thought bench," where ideas (whence? how?) came into that diligent searching mind. Not far distant is the "work bench"—the laboratory buildings where the new devices got shape and substance.

"The greatest adventure of my life," according to Edison, was on September 4, 1882, when New York City began the commercial distribution of electricity for light and power over a system designed by him and built under his supervision. "As darkness fell, that day, in the financial district of Manhattan hundreds of little incandescent lamps went on." When you return home after visiting the Edison site and push the button beside the front door, you have brought, so to say, a great man home with you.

Of course Edison was famous for many other inventions that have changed the course of our lives. The phonograph, the motion-picture development, with addition of sound to sight . . . the display of objects at the laboratory-headquarters gives a fascinating picture of the man at work and the almost incredible range of his proficiency.

8. WRIGHT BROTHERS NATIONAL MEMORIAL
[*North Carolina*]

IT FLEW. It flew only twelve seconds; but in the words of Orville Wright, "it was the first [flight] in history in which a machine carrying a man had raised itself by its own power into the air in full flight, had sailed forward without reduction of speed, and finally landed at a point as high as that from which it started." The conquest of the means of air travel, dreamed of by Leonardo da Vinci and perhaps by other engineering minds before his, had arrived. The year was 1903; and today the upper air is so full of transport that the planes are subject to collision.

The scene of the event was Kitty Hawk, on the sand dunes of the North Carolina coast, below Norfolk. The brothers Wright, Wilbur and Orville, had built a camp just north of Kill Devil Hill in 1900, to test a man-carrying glider. Two years later, having solved important problems of equilibrium, they were ready to test a powered machine. They built both *The Flyer*, the craft with a wingspan of some forty feet, and the power plant, a twelve-horsepower engine weighing 170 pounds. The first attempt was unsuccessful, but two days later the plane took off, from a spot visitors now see marked by a granite boulder, and went 120 feet.

The Wright Memorial shaft is a sixty-foot pylon of North Carolina granite on a high dune whose normally shifting sands have been partly tied down by shoreline grasses.

9. Castle Clinton National Monument
[New York]

BEGINNING AS A FORT for the protection of New York City and its harbor, but never called upon to do serious shooting, Castle Clinton has had a strange and varied life. When its military use ceased it was converted to a place of public entertainment. Band concerts, exhibits, an occasional balloon ascension, receptions for distinguished visitors, grand opera; name the type of amusement, and it was there. Here, in 1850, New Yorkers jostled and outbid each other to hear the first concert in America of Jenny Lind, "the Swedish nightingale." In the middle part of the nineteenth century, during the great surge of immigration, the garden was a landing depot, where the newcomers had a shade of protection from the human predators that swarmed for prey at the arrival of each shipload. Then it became a famous aquarium. In 1941 there were plans to destroy the historic building, but an act of Congress preserved it as a sample of our fast-moving development since the time when the guns of the West Battery celebrated the evacuation of New York by the British.

10. Mount Rushmore National Memorial
[South Dakota]

A FEW MILES to the north of Wind Cave National Park is Mount Rushmore National Memorial. Here, carved out of the solid granite of one of the pinnacles that characterize the Black Hills Dome, are the colossal portraits of Washington, Jefferson, Lincoln, and Theodore Roosevelt.

Concerning this astonishing feat, which, in the immensity of the undertaking, compares with the carving of the Great Sphinx of Egypt or the rock sculptures of Babylonia, I confess that, for myself, I was for a number of years a skeptic. I was so sure that art had become enmeshed in engineering, and that the audacity of the conception bordered on pertness, that I would not even go and look at it. Finally I did, however, and found reasons to revise my snap judgment. That it is impressive there is no doubt. There could be no better testimony to its assault on the imagination—which is just what the sculptor, Gutzon Borglum, intended—than the fact that on the day when I was there, when the area was thronged with visitors, there was an unmistakable hushed and reverential attitude noticeable in every group that stood viewing the work from different angles.

Whatever else one may think of it, the memorial now seems to me an unforgettable example of man's will to force nature to take him into at least a junior partnership. He may be a relatively feeble thing on the face of the earth, but he insists on making his presence felt. He may be expelled from the garden at any moment, but he will leave his initials carved on the fig tree.

11. JOHN MUIR NATIONAL HISTORIC SITE
[*California*]

DURING THE LAST twenty-four years of the life of the man who has been described as "the father of our national parks and forest reservations," the old library den on the second floor of this Muir home was the place where most of his published writings originated. Leaders in the conservation field met here with Muir and planned with him many a move toward the saving of precious spots of natural beauty. They were generally successful, though they lost the fight for the Hetch Hetchy in Yosemite—a butchery that we now look back upon as profitless and witless.

In the mid-nineteenth century, Dr. John Strentzel came from Poland to the Alhamora Valley and established a ranch. His daughter became Muir's wife. The "big house," which is being preserved, along with the Vicente Martinez Adobe, is the one John and Louie Muir occupied by invitation of Mrs. Strentzel after her husband's death. The nearby adobe was built about 1849 by a son of the original grantee of Rancho El Pinole.

In 1912, a lonely widower, Muir wrote in a letter to a friend: "I'm in my old library den, the house desolate, nobody living in it save a hungry mouse or two . . . dearly cherished memories [I have] about it and the fine garden grounds full of trees and bushes and flowers that my wife and father-in-law and I planted—fine things from every land."

The place is little changed from Muir's lifetime. It will certainly be a mecca for preservationists who regard him as "one of the great few who have won title to remembrance as prophets and interpreters of nature."

PART

FIVE

[I]

National Capital Parks

"Born of compromise—witness to history—reflection of culture."

Progeny of compromise between Thomas Jefferson and Alexander Hamilton, the Capital of the United States rose from the Potomac flatlands.

With watchwords of order, beauty, and vision, its planner, Pierre Charles L'Enfant, said: "I would not plan for thirteen States and three million people but for a republic of fifty States and five hundred million; not for a single century, but for a thousand years."

In the L'Enfant Plan of 1791, Washington was intended as a city of parks or a city in a park. To L'Enfant, the crown jewel was the Grand Mall stretching from the Capitol to the proposed site for a monument to George Washington. It was envisioned as a formal park, bordered by a canal with broad basins and imposing fountains.

As the public buildings and parks took shape, there came the inescapable association between the city and George Washington. Its name, its monuments, its origin, its importance as the capstone of our representative system of government bespoke of his leadership and his example. This association gave something very special to the Capital, for Daniel Webster once remarked: "America has furnished to the world the character of Washington! And if our American institutions had done nothing else, that alone would have entitled them to the respect of mankind."

As the Capital's parks matured, three principal responsibilities, each significant and together forming an interrelated whole, emerged. These three responsibilities were reflected by the role of the parks as (1) settings for public buildings and national memorials; (2) areas for public recreation; (3) elements in forming the character of the city.

Picture without a title. National Capital Parks. [*Photo: W. E. Dutton*]

The key to the impact of the L'Enfant Plan was the site selection of the public buildings and their enhancement by complementary park settings. The site for the Capitol was selected as the radial center of the plan; the site for the White House chosen; and both structures linked by a broad avenue named for the "Keystone" State. A line was drawn west from the Capitol and south from the White House; at its intersection, a monument to George Washington was proposed. Between that memorial site eastward to the Capitol lay the Grand Mall. Completing the final arm of the cross was a site for a memorial to a second national leader at a point directly south of the Washington Memorial site. The resulting cross—joining living government with heroes of the past—is the heart of the Washington park system. In 1901, the McMillan Park Commission reaffirmed the soundness of the L'Enfant Plan and added a major refinement—an extension of the Mall vista west of the Washington Monument to the Potomac River, where a third memorial, the Lincoln Memorial, rose to enshrine the memory of Abraham Lincoln in the hearts of the people.

Today the mall complex with its east-west, north-south axes epitomizes the initial purpose of the parks as settings for the public buildings and national memorials; and yet, these formal parks are much more. They are places where 16 million Americans and foreign visitors converge each year to feel the impress of this setting—the center of what some call the most beautiful city in the world.

Washington, more than any other city in the nation, reflects the past achievements of our country. First and foremost, as its symbol, stands the Washington Monument, 555 feet tall. The eager eyes of millions of young Americans see this monument. If they but pause to reflect upon its purpose, they will see in its granite the nation's resolve to honor the man who helped to forge the United States of America.

Not far from the Washington Monument, through the green-swathed parks, aglow with pale, misty pink and white cherry blossoms in early April, they will visit the Thomas Jefferson Memorial. Here they can read and absorb the words of a great architect of democratic thought: "I have sworn upon the altar of God eternal hostility against every form of tyranny over the mind of man." And nestled deep in the heart of downtown Washington is the House Where Lincoln Died—the smallest unit of the vast National Park System. Within its walls a brave heart stopped at 7:22 on the morning of

Iwo Jima (the flag half-staffed for ex-President Hoover). National Capital Parks. [Photo: W. E. Dutton]

April 15, 1865. Young citizens of the Union which he saved now come to pay their respect.

It would be difficult to envision many of the great moments in the history of the United States without the historic background of Washington's streets, circles, and parks. Hardly a single period in our proud national history did not have its origin in Washington. Here for almost 170 years the leaders of government and the private leaders of America's economic, social, and cultural development have wrestled with the problems of their times. Many of their actions took place in the historical parks of the Capital—the prime example is Lafayette Park across from the White House, which throughout the nineteenth century was the residential setting for the homes of the great and the near-great. Center of social, literary, and political life, it might have been called Cabinet Park, for around it have lived at different times members of the official families of seventeen Presidents.

"The mission of parks is to make urban life not just bearable but happy" —hence the second major responsibility, to provide active programs to build healthy bodies and nourish eager minds. The parks of Washington appeal to a wide variety of interests and tastes. More than 100 million visitor days per year are spent by people engaged in picnics, hiking, fishing, horseback riding, sailing, organized baseball, football, tennis, soccer, cricket, and just sitting on a park bench as Bernard Baruch so often did in Lafayette Park across from the White House. There are also a host of cultural attractions in the parks—art shows, bands from every branch of the armed services in concerts at the Watergate, Shakespeare on the Washington Monument grounds, and a variegated program of Broadway entertainment at the Carter Barron Amphitheatre in Rock Creek Park. Parks—particularly metropolitan parks—are for the people. As people use them, they bring refreshment to mind and body, awaken interest in nature's omnipresence, and foster greater community spirit as citizens take increased pride in the appearance of their city.

Because of the urban character of many parks in Washington and the geographical features of the area, one would not expect to find exemplary natural parks of outstanding scenic quality. Yet, there are few metropolitan areas in the country that possess an array of natural wooded parks which offer so much in the way of contrast for the city dweller. In them children, who have not known anything but city life, are introduced to the wonders

Just as our ancestors traveled on the Chesapeake and Ohio Canal. National Capital Parks. [Photo: M. Woodbridge Williams]

No pollution in this laughing mountain stream at Catoctin. National Capital Parks.
[Photo: M. Woodbridge Williams]

of the natural world and to the "beautiful," which Goethe said "is a manifestation of secret laws of Nature, which, but for this appearance, had been forever concealed from us."

The third responsibility of the Washington parks stems from the historical legacy of the parks themselves—as basic elements in forming the character of the city. There is the Grand Mall, which impresses because of its monumental character and its broad vista; there are the small circles and triangles which break the boredom of concrete, offering greenery and treating the eye to pleasant floral colors. There are the larger squares where thousands of office workers find welcome respite from their confinement and shaded repose while they listen to a high school band from Ames, Iowa, or some other home-town group in Washington to participate in one of the big parades which are so much a part of the city scene.

And finally, there are Washington's large natural retreats—the 1,700-acre Rock Creek Park, winding its sylvan path along the stream valley of the creek from its mouth northward to Maryland. Established in 1890 as a national park, its charter was worded much the same as that of Yellowstone National Park, created eighteen years earlier and the first national park in the world. Rock Creek Park, with its thickly wooded slopes, shaded glens, and wild flowers, was a favorite haunt of Theodore Roosevelt and his family and has been frequented by statesmen, ambassadors, and millions of plain citizens. Speaking of Rock Creek Park, Teddy Roosevelt said:

> When our children were little . . . each Sunday afternoon the whole family spent in Rock Creek Park . . . I would drag one of the children's wagons; and when the very smallest pairs of feet grew tired of trudging bravely after us, or racing on rapturous side trips after flowers, and other treasures, the owners would climb in the wagon . . .

Bringing visitors and nearby residents into the city are several expressively landscaped parkways. The most spectacular is the George Washington Memorial Parkway—a ribbonlike park passing the high bluffs of the Potomac along the Virginia shoreline, and giving panoramas of Washington. Not far away is Great Falls Park, Virginia, a more recent addition to the National Capital Park System and the site of the remains of the old locks of the Potomack Canal Company, the first corporate work in America, chartered by George Washington in 1785.

Thus parks of many kinds and with many purposes form the character of Washington. And the larger natural parks—changing ecological communities surrounded by man's proud achievements of urban living—bring smiles to little faces as they watch ducks swimming in Rock Creek or turtles sunning themselves on a log along the old canal.

[11]

L'Envoi: Vistas of Beauty

TRUTH, *and goodness, and beauty, are but different faces of the same All.*
Beauty in nature is not ultimate. It is the herald of inward and
eternal beauty . . . it must stand as a part and not yet as the last or highest
expression of the final cause of Nature.

—RALPH WALDO EMERSON

[1]

IN FEBRUARY 1965, President Johnson sent to the Congress of the United
States a message "On the Natural Beauty of Our Country." It was a state
paper probably unique in the history of government. Can anyone recall
a similar instance, when a nation's leader has proclaimed the vital importance
of beauty in human welfare, and moved to salvage what remains of the lovely
heritage which a thrusting, feverish, ruthless technology has dilapidated to
the point of ugliness? This is a Great Chart. And the time to preserve, to
repair, to cease being a nation of prosperous slovens, is now.

The German poet Goethe said: "We should do our utmost to encourage
the Beautiful, for the Useful encourages itself." Indeed, utility needs nothing
other than its physical materials to work upon. We need not quarrel with
that. And it was inevitable that the primeval landscape of America would
be vastly altered; that the rich resources would be eagerly tapped and exploited; that rivers should be harnessed, prairies plowed; that roads should
scar the land surface; that virgin forests should fall. Nor could it be expected that, except for a few souls gifted with insight, a people aiming at a
fuller and more comfortable existence would exercise a philosophic restraint.

Twins are twice as much trouble: white-tailed deer. Blue Ridge Parkway. [Photo:
Leonard Lee Rue III]

[549]

Prancing coyote, Mount McKinley. Mount McKinley National Park. [Photo: National Park Service]

There is no deep villain in this very human drama. There is only a saddening imbalance that was bound to ensue. Man does not live by bread and gadgets alone. Take beauty out of his life: a googol of dollars and a Lucullan luxury will not fill the void.

The imbalance is here. It is shockingly manifest. With an erupting population, we see the places of natural beauty retreating from the millions as fast as they seek and move toward them; urban slums where people feebly degenerate; roadways lined with the horrible corpses of junked automobiles, and with the vulgarities of clamoring commerce; our air polluted with fumes and our rivers and lakes and estuaries so laden with filth and chemicals that fish are killed and humans endangered. The whole drab picture is outlined in President Johnson's message, in measured terms.

Will the President's appeal be effective? There are already signs that it will. The regeneration will take time. Nature repairs ills of the abused human body by slow processes; ills of the spirit even more slowly. There are signs of awakening on all political levels. But it is a warning that must come into the realization of every citizen. Josiah Royce said that the philosopher Immanuel Kant "had small interest in noble sentiments, but very great natural respect for large and connected personal and social undertakings, when guided by ideas." The point is timely. The appeal for the restoration of Beauty to her rightful eminence cannot remain merely a "noble sentiment." It needs action, and not merely in the field of legislation. It must enter the understanding of all of us.

[2]

BUT THE MESSAGE to the Congress has far wider significance than appears upon its surface, or in its words. What *is* natural beauty? What, indeed, is *beauty?*

The wisest philosophers have failed to define or to explain this human emotion to which, in our English language, is given the name of beauty. There is an equivalent word in every language. Paul Shorey, reflecting his study of Plato, said that feeling for beauty is "a touch of noble unrest; the

Falling through thin ice, these creatures are in mortal danger. Grand Teton National Park. [*Photo: National Park Service*]

reaching for something of finer quality than the dailiness of life." The love of beauty, he added, becomes the guide toward the perception of the good and the true. Vague as this may sound, at first glance, it will serve as the path along which our quest for understanding must go. Surely we deal with an essence that is beyond our powers of expression. But we can, and we do, feel its reality.

In the realm of natural beauty, apprehended mainly through the sense of sight, but also by the other organs, we are first overwhelmed by the more spectacular forms. "Breath-taking" is a hackneyed expression; yet it is accurate. The pulse reflects the surge. Beyond that impact, we can come to understand that what we have sensed is only a gorgeous greeting. Behind that curtain lies an infinite world of detailed beauties. As we develop realization of those composing elements, we know that there can be nothing ugly in nature. Nothing. The seeming exceptions are simply facets of beauty we have not yet grasped.

Sometimes we think, in our egotism, that nature has provided these beauties as a special act on our behalf. If I may be allowed a harmless bit of fantasy, I shall imagine a conversation you might have with nature on this point. After hearing you patiently on the subject of Beauty, nature would perhaps say something like this: "I see the source of your error. It derives from your very limited knowledge. You are thinking that I have a Department of Beauty—that I deal with beauty as one of my activities. Really, I do not *intend* beauty. I *am* beauty. I am beauty and many other things, such as you are trying to express by your abstractions like order, harmony, truth, love. What you see in my scenic manifestations is the glamour behind which lies an absolute beauty of which I myself am an expressive part. You do not understand? Naturally it is difficult. But you are trying: I do like *that* in you, little man."

No, we can only shadowly comprehend, and perhaps the mystery will always tantalize us. But fortunately for our spiritual welfare we live with the fact. And this fact is that in the presence of unsullied, unexploited "raw" nature, we are lifted to a height beyond ourselves. Our first physical contact with Yosemite, the Tetons, the redwood groves, the Alps, the falls of the

---

Above, left: Some summer fur shows on this "snowshoe rabbit." Mount McKinley National Park. [Photo: Charles Ott] Right: The raccoon is a resourceful and impudent masked bandit . . . and charming. Great Smoky Mountains National Park. [Photo: Leonard Lee Rue III] Below, left: Mountain goat youngsters. Glacier National Park. [Photo: Leonard Lee Rue III] Right: Nine ounces of shrill defiance. Isle Royale National Park. [Photo: W. W. Dunmire]

Iguazu—with such spectacles wherever they exist—leaves us with an indelible coloring such as has not dominated our thoughts and feelings before. That is the fact. The metaphysical reasoning about it is more engaging than important. We grow in dimension and capacity. Not only that. We become more sensitive to the opposites of beauty: ugliness, defacement, disharmony.

Although the purely aesthetic aspect of this absolute beauty is but the prologue to a whole, its importance must not be minimized. It is as basic as the letters of the alphabet. Without those letters there are no words; and without words, no communication.

[3]

WHILE OUR PEOPLE have been remiss in the sacrifice of beauty to utility, and the time has come to take account of stock, as the President asked, there is still much to our credit. In a period of explosive growth such as few nations have known, possessors of a technological skill which has finally become more than a little frightening, we have yet managed to set aside and wisely to administer a system of national parks that evokes the admiration of the world. It is true that we had rare advantages, and time was on our side. But it is also true that we had from our earliest days a large and articulate group of forward-thinking men and women alive to the need for preserving the treasures of our culture and the integrity of our inheritance before, as in other lands, it was too late. So that, as the case stands, it is not so much that we have been unmindful of spiritual and moral values: we have not been sufficiently alert to the somber truth that "the Useful encourages itself," while the preservation and affirmation of beauty needs a constant renewal of faith and the watchful devotion of a shepherd. Nor can our preserved places of natural beauty and memorials of the historic past prosper and remain inspirational if they become islands in an environment of sanctioned ugliness. This is a very nullification of our reverence for beauty. To paraphrase Lincoln: our cultural and spiritual aspirations must shrivel in a world half beautiful, half loathsome. We shall not expect the impossible. But there must be in our mechanized and controlled ecology, while we confess that we have violated much natural beauty physically, and defend it as unavoidable, a mani-

Above, left: The brown pelican. Everglades National Park. [Photo: M. Woodbridge Williams] Right: Big-eared bat. Jewel Cave National Monument. [Photo: Jack E. Boucher] Below, left: Blacksnake—harmless friend of man. Shenandoah National Park. [Photo: William M. Taylor] Right: The anhinga spears his victim. Everglades National Park. [Photo: M. Woodbridge Williams]

festation that we still retain the spirit, and show it in our national house-keeping. That is where we have failed.

[4]

As I HAVE SAID, this message is something not merely for legislation, though that is imperatively desirable, but for all of us to meditate. What are its implications, for example, in the work of the National Park Service, where so much natural beauty, majestic and awe-inspiring, and so many less obvious beauties, even hidden ones, are the current stock in trade? The very business of the National Park Service is the custodianship and interpretation of beauty. How could it be otherwise? The interpreter, whether naturalist or ranger or historian or mechanic, is a middleman of this precious cultural wealth.

Viewed as an absolute, beauty has numberless aspects. For the purpose of the interpreter I think we need be directly concerned with but four:

1. The park visitor's sensuous contact with scenic or landscape beauty —with "wildness."

2. The beauty of the adventure of the mind: the revelation of the order of nature.

3. The beauty of the artifact: man's aspiration to create beautiful things.

4. The beauty of human conduct, or behavior, of which man has shown himself capable.

It is axiomatic that natural beauty, as perceived by the organs of sense, needs no interpretation: it interprets itself. Here the interpreter acts only as a scout and a guide. He leads his groups to the most alluring scenes he has discovered, and is silent. Would you varnish the orchid? He refrains even from using the word "beauty." To suggest that his visitors are to consider either the scene or the song of the hermit thrush as beautiful is even an affront. They *know*. In this aspect beauty is a precious personal possession. It is the individual's shock, *his* apprehension, *his* discovery: and what he discovers is more than what he sees or hears. He has discovered something of himself, hitherto unrealized. No; we do not interpret that aspect of beauty. It is an exhibit.

Exactly at this point is where the office of the interpreter begins. There is a concealed beauty that does not appear to the senses. Indeed, this aspect takes two forms. It involves a revelation of the natural beauty we think of as order—nature at work—and the beauty of that development of the human

A boxing match; most of the does are unimpressed. Glacier National Park. [Photo: Channing T. Howell]

mind which makes it possible for man partly to understand it. What are the forces that created what one sees, and feels as beautiful?

Whether we call it so or not, the interpreter is engaged in a kind of education. It is not the classroom kind. It is, if you will, a proffer of teaching; but it is not the professorial sort. It aims not to *do something* to the listener, but *to provoke the listener to do something to himself*. It is a delicate job, requiring the greatest discretion. The man on holiday does not wish to be lectured; he did not come to a park to be educated. Even the most discerning, and therefore successful, interpreter must feel conscious of the fact that the materials upon which he works are by their very nature—what shall I say? not *cold*, but certainly *cool*. We appeal to the head, to the mind.

Can we not infuse into this worthy activity an appeal to the heart: to attain something of that impact which nature does so easily and implicitly by presenting the beautiful landscape? Erosion and mountain building, the adaptation of life to its environment, the grand and vital organic community of which man is only a species, however a dominant one; all these entertaining revelations of man's place in nature are at last a presentation of an aspect of the beautiful. If the interpreter feels this to be so, he can project that feeling. Not by a preachment about it. Heavens, no. It is something to be felt, not analyzed. If deeply felt, it can be communicated.

The scenes upon which you have looked, and the natural sounds you have heard, you regard as beauty. How did it all come about? By a process which science aims to know more and more about; but whatever we may discover, one thing is sure about that process—it is even more beautiful than what the eye or ear perceives. This is an appeal to the heart, the soul, or what you wish to call it, whichever yearns to be satisfied. It is warmth. Added to understanding, it is the objective of interpretation.

The other day, a great American chemist, Robert S. Mulliken, received a Nobel prize. This man once wrote something which has deeply affected my thinking about this world of natural beauties. The italics are mine:

The scientist must develop enormous tolerance in seeking for ideas which *may please nature,* and enormous patience, self-restraint and humility when his ideas over and over again are rejected by nature before he arrives at one to *please her.* When the scientist does finally find such an idea, there is something very intimate in his feeling of communion with nature.

When the non-scientist understands what Mulliken meant when he talked of "pleasing nature" he will be on his way to understanding the scientific mind. He will realize what the pure scientist means when he talks of a "beautiful equation"—the statement of an idea in artistic form with an economy of means. We "please nature" when we search for, find, and *feel* beauty. It is as simple as that: and yet it is not simply attained and maintained in a world where the marketplace dominates.

When we come to the beauty of the artifact—man's inspiration to produce with his own hands something of the quality which he has observed in his natural surroundings—we are in a complex and baffling domain. Much we must guess. A paleolithic artist incised on the wall of a cave at Altamira the figure of a running deer. The draughtsmanship, resulting from the acute observation of this prehistoric man, is by modern standards a beautiful thing. But did he intend beauty, or was it a propitiation of the spirit of the chase —a magical device to procure meat, and therefore a matter of utility? We cannot know: surely there is no harm in concluding that it could have been both. I have held in my hand the bowl of a ceremonial pipe made of the red Catlinite claystone which came from southwestern Minnesota, but taken from a mound in northern Mississippi, the work of one of our prehistoric

Left: Prairie dog, almost exterminated by predatory man. Wind Cave National Park. [Photo: Wayne Bryant] Right: The almost extinct blackfooted ferret. Badlands National Monument. [Photo: Robert Powell]

Indian artists. It is the figure of a man sitting and thinking—a forerunner of the famous Rodin sculpture, and not a whit less impressive. Did this early artist intend beauty? I think he did; perhaps also religious significance.

But clearly we are here in a region of taste, tradition, changing standards of judgment. The interpreter of the story of the artifact is not dealing with beauty as such, but with man's attitude toward beauty; and this can be made warmly appealing, for it is an appeal to the heart even more than to the mind. The standards of judgment in architecture change. The filigree gingerbread of the Victorian period is today a matter of mild amusement. Structures that were considered beautiful in their time cause pained surprise now. Yet, worldwide, there are not many people who do not thrill at the classic beauty of the Parthenon, the Maison Carré at Nîmes, or the Lincoln Memorial in Washington. And all of us are sensitive to harmony of structure and environment. The humble adobe dwelling arising from our southwestern desert, created from the desert soil itself and roofed with rush or with tiles shaped on the thigh of the builder, violates no principle of art. The most expensive structure, of architectural merit in itself, but alien to its environment, may be an excrescence—almost an ugliness. Hence the fine current effort around Washington to procure scenic easements. The objection is not so much to the

[559]

artifacts themselves: in relation to the greater natural beauty they may be in the wrong place.

One could go on endlessly in a discussion of the opportunity for the interpretation of man's aspiration to produce beautiful objects. More to the point at the moment is the effort to restore some of the natural beauty we have blighted, and to make resurgent an innate delight in the beauty of our environment: the aim of the program of beautification to which the wife of the President, Lady Bird Johnson, has given her enthusiasm and the prestige of her position.

As the interpreter, in or out of the National Park Service, is not needed to define or explain scenic beauty, neither does its opposite require interpretation. When Alice was in Wonderland, the Mock Turtle told her that he went to school with an old turtle who taught Uglification.

"I never heard of 'Uglification,'" Alice ventured to say. The Gryphon lifted up both its paws in surprise.

"Never heard of uglifying," it exclaimed. "You know what to beautify is, I suppose?"

"Yes," said Alice, doubtfully. "It means to make anything prettier."

"Well, then," the Gryphon went on, "if you don't know what to uglify is, you *are* a simpleton."

Well we know what ugliness is, and the processes that create it. In the haste to gain material welfare we have forgotten, or chosen to forget; and the bill has now come due. To live willingly in tawdry surroundings is to become numb to their baleful influence upon us; they tend to seem as inevitable as climate. It is not so. It is already proved, in city, state, county, and town, that the feeling for beauty can be dramatized and renewed by *beautifying*. The start has been made.

What interpreters can do is to communicate, from their own conviction, *by indirection but with warmth*, this appeal to an always receptive human heart.

In the interpretation of the beauty of conduct of which the human being is capable, we come under the leering squint of the pessimist. We read in Emerson that "the beauty of nature must always seem unreal and mocking, until the landscape has human figures that are as good as itself."

"Perhaps," replies the cynic, "but tell me just when that will be?"

We do not have to go back to antiquity—to Socrates, Jesus, or the Roman general Regulus—for the answer to that. It is here and now, just as it was

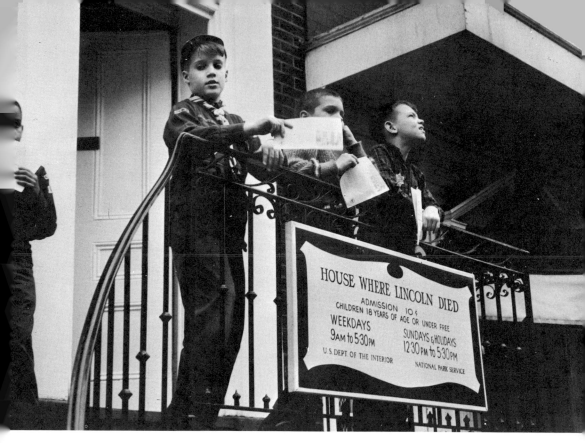

That the young may realize the past. National Capital Parks. [Photo: M. Woodbridge Williams]

yesterday and the day before. The National Park System includes scores of historic memorials, the truest interpretation of which is the evidence that our country has possessed men and women of great moral beauty. And for each one of those a myriad of the humbler unknowns have lived and passed. The birthplace of Washington; the several areas that keep in memory the great-heartedness of Lincoln; the house at Appomattox where Grant and Lee revealed beautiful magnanimity on the one side and a nobility in the acceptance of defeat on the other; the farmer soldiers at the bridge in Concord; an ample preservation of the Civil War battlefields—what are all these but the testimonials that man does transcend his animal boundary?

Just the other day, in Vietnam, a soldier threw himself upon a hand grenade, saving the lives of his comrades. War is a terrible thing; the hope of mankind is that it will cease to be; yet it cannot be denied that out of its shambles have emerged valor and fortitude and self-sacrifice on the part of the individual man and woman. William James, the Harvard philosopher, had this undeniable truth in mind when he wrote his "Moral Equivalent for War"—an attempt to find some other agent in life that would perform the same service to human character. That he failed is less important than that he showed his own beauty of conduct in the failure.

The interpreter in a monument or battlefield of war may thrill his hearer with the account of the mass action, the losses and gains in a swaying conflict, the skill of leadership. This can be made dramatic stuff, exciting the imagination, a capsuled fragment of the national past that must not be forgotten. But these things are an appeal to the mind, to logic and imagination. The appeal to the heart is the story of how in such tragic environment the human being finds the path to beauty of behavior.

The appeal for a renaissance of the appreciation of beauty—in the abstract and in its particular aspects—must not be allowed to falter. It is vital to our moral growth. It is a program of education. Perhaps it is truer to say that it is a program of re-education, for we have always known, in our innermost recesses, our dependence upon beauty for the courage to face the problems of life. We have let ourselves forget. It is the duty of the interpreter to jog our memories.

A P P E N D I X

The New Parks

NORTH CASCADES NATIONAL PARK
& REDWOOD NATIONAL PARK
Created by Act of Congress Since Publication of
THE NATIONAL PARKS in 1968

1. North Cascades National Park
[Washington]

SEVERAL YEARS AGO the commuter-lemmings, surging through the great concourse of the Grand Central station in New York City, were arrested by the sight of an enormous color transparency mounted above their heads. Fifteen by fifty feet in size, the picture was that of a majestic mountain— indeed, a mass of many mountains in one—thrusting its snow-and-ice-mantled head and shoulders up into the blue sky. The photography was by the brothers Bob and Ira Spring, of Seattle, a team deft with camera anywhere, but supremely so in their beloved mountains of the Northwest.

The peak was Shuksan. Now, it happens that Shuksan has had its picture taken often, for it can be seen the year round from a paved highway. But there is a wilderness of snowy and glacier-bearing peaks in this North Cascades region, and most of these other mountains can be viewed only by hikers and climbers who actually enter the fastnesses of our truly American Alps. Before Congress, in 1968, voted to set aside this magnificent 1,053

At the narrows of Diablo Lake. North Cascades National Park. [Photo: M. Woodbridge Williams] square miles of the Cascades Range—the far-northern eighty-five miles of it lying within our country—even the average ardent conservationist had only a dim knowledge of what was there, and few were those who had a first-hand knowledge of its beauty and significance. Yet, even as far back as 1906 a little group of the devoted, the Mazamas of Portland, Oregon, had proposed that it be preserved as a national park.

Weldon Heald gave his impression of the North Cascades in a book published in 1949, and his description serves the purpose well:

> Packed solidly with hundreds of square miles of soaring peaks massed together in lines, groups and knots, the mountains rise steeply thousands of feet from narrow valleys clothed in a jungle-like growth of huge evergreens and tangled underbrush . . . hundreds of glaciers mantle the summits, hang high in cirques under rocky ridges, and stream down the mountainsides into the valleys . . . and hidden away among these twisted convoluted mountains are enough lakes, meadows, waterfalls, alpine basins, and sweeping panoramas, to keep the lover of the outdoors busy for a lifetime.

The Cascades, one of the world's great mountain ranges, extend from northern California to the Fraser River in Canada. In shape these mountains somewhat resemble an hourglass, being about a hundred miles across at the extremities and narrowing to half that distance at the midway point. All but one of the "ring of fire" volcanic cones are on the western flank of the range. Mount Adams is about on the axis.

The rugged southern portions of the Cascades are clearly the product of prodigious volcanic activity. But there is a marked difference readily apparent as one enters that region where the new national park lies. True, there are two mighty volcanoes in this northern end—Mount Baker and Glacier Peak—but the major geologic pattern is that of an uplifted plateau that has undergone great erosion, especially by the agency of ice. Much of the rock is granitic, practically all of it is of a highly resistant order; though the over-all structure is so complex that even the professional geologist sometimes resorts to an informed guess. On the Garden Peak Trail, for example, one traverses a big accumulation of pumice which must have been blown almost twenty miles at a time when Glacier Peak was in eruption. But the main point, after all, is that for the climber of mountains North Cascades offers the safest and most favorable treads.

Mount Shuksan jabs through a cloud ceiling. North Cascades National Park.
[Photo: John M. Kauffmann]

Climatically, here in these northern Cascades, we are in a "rainshadow" of abrupt changes within a few miles of longitude. The moisture-laden winds that sweep inland from the Pacific through the Straits of Juan de Fuca and Puget Sound are pretty thoroughly "milked" by the west-side mountain masses. The rainfall and snowfall on this maritime part of the park is something that has to be seen to become credible. There is a record at Paradise weather station in Mount Rainier National Park, not far to the south of the new park, of a seasonal snowfall of *one thousand inches*, which means better than 83 feet. But every mile, as the winds pass over the Cascades, the precipitation becomes less. You get into the Okanogan Highlands and find the bright sunlight of low rounded hills. Indeed, you don't have to go that far, because you can be in the sun on the heights of the eastern side of the mountains, and see the cloudbanks hovering above the seaward part of the chain. Finally, going eastward, you are in a semi-desert, where the crops require fallowing or irrigation. And all in such a short automobile journey!

The result of such heavy snowfall is certain. When the accretion of snow, year upon year, is greater than the melt, the weight of the growing

The hiker finds abundant white-tailed ptarmigan in the valley brush. North Cascades National Park. [Photo: John M. Kauffmann]

South Pickets, North Cascade Primitive Area. North Cascades National Park.
[Photo: M. Woodbridge Williams]

mass converts the snow to ice; and once the top burden becomes heavy
enough, the underlying ice begins to flow like molasses taffy. Here in our
new national park, then, is the greatest display of ice forms to be seen in
the country, excepting Alaska. The National Park Service says, in its "mini-
folder," that there are "one hundred and fifty active glaciers." I take an
"active" glacier to be one that has movement; is still "flowing," though as
a whole ice mass it might be on the retreat. Harvey Manning of the
Mountaineers of Seattle, says that 519 glaciers have been *identified*. Both
statements could be true, I think, according to how one interprets the word
"active." Aside from glaciers, active or passive, there are innumerable ice-
falls, ice-aprons, waterfalls, hanging valleys, and alpine lakes in glacial
cirques. An astounding example of glacial ice acting as a landscaper is to be
found here in the case of Lake Chelan. Here we may travel by boat a
trench scoured by a Pleistocene glacier seventy miles long, which in some

places gouged an existing valley to a depth of nearly four hundred feet below sea level. Like the Eastern continental glacier which carved out Somes Sound in Acadia National Park in Maine, this five-thousand-foot-thick ice sheet that headed near Cascade Pass and joined another tongue of Canadian ice which descended the Columbia River created waterways which somewhat resemble the Norwegian fjords.

The great range of moisture falling in these North Cascades results in a delightful variation of the forest cover and of the plant communities. Here in this wilderness is seen everything from rain forest to dry shrublands: subalpine conifers, lovely mountain meadows, and tundra. In the eastern parts there are magnificent groves of alpine larch trees—here a timberline tree which, just before it sheds its delicate needles in the autumn, produces masses of golden blaze quite unlike any other forest coloring.

These are not really high mountains, if you think in terms of the peaks of the Rockies and Sierras. Glacier Peak is only 10,541 feet high, and most of the summits are between seven and eight thousand feet. But from the valley bottoms, so deeply carved by ice flows of the past, the climbing is usually steep; the nature of the topography is jagged, the snowfields many. We are told by the professionals that "it is much easier in the North Cascades than in most accessible American mountains to get into difficulty, and hikers who leave the beaten path should be sure they are properly trained and equipped.

For safety it is recommended that climbing parties have three or four members, be provided with internationally recognized climbing gear, and register with the park authorities their destination, the names of their chosen mountain, and the time they propose to spend on the journey. Common sense should suggest that, in case of accident, rescue cannot come to a person who is not known to be in the area.

Among the larger mammals to be seen in this park are mountain goats, deer, and black and grizzly bears. Fortunately these bears have never been degraded into scavengers, so they are shy and unobtrusive; and may we indulge in the hope that they will always remain so? The cougar, or mountain lion, is here, and the moose. You may not see a wolverine, but he is certain to see and scent you. The fur bearers, some of them that have so nearly escaped extinction, are protected here, too: the marten and fisher.

Nooksack Tower, Price Glacier, Mount Shuksan. North Cascades National Park.
[Photo: M. Woodbridge Williams]
Overleaf: Mount Shuksan from Heather Meadows. North Cascades National Park.
[Photo: John M. Kauffmann]

You will probably see plenty of ptarmigans, and if it is winter you will find large numbers of bald eagles gorging themselves on the salmon that run up the Skagit River.

Included within the park are two "wilderness study areas": the Picket Range Wilderness of the north unit, and the Eldorado Peaks Wilderness of the south unit. And here, allied with the new park itself, are two national recreation areas: Ross Lake and Lake Chelan. Ross Lake is twenty-four miles long and two miles wide at most, covering about 12,000 acres. Lake Chelan is fifty-five miles long and from one to two miles in width for most of the distance. The man-made lakes offer fishing in addition to the many natural lakes within the park and the mountain streams. Washington State fishing licenses are required if you are going to take those trout: rainbows, Dolly Vardens, Eastern brook, and cutthroat. Hunting is not permitted, of course, within the park boundaries, but is legal in the recreation areas under licenses from the state.

When Congress finally acted to create, mainly from already existing federal lands, this noble wilderness park, it was a well-deserved triumph for the little band of far-seeing nature respecters who had for so many years labored to such an end. Most of them were naturally of the Northwest, though they had support in all regions. Chiefly, our national indebtedness goes to organizations like the Mountaineers, the Cascadians, the Sierra Club, Mazamas, Spokane Mountaineers, and the Alpine Club of Washington. In the whole body politic they were mice: but they brought forth mountains!

Definitely, here is a national park whose delights and refreshments of soul can never be savored by those persons who want to view unspoiled nature while cruising or sitting in their cars. Indeed, we can go much further than that. I like the brave candor or Harvey Manning when he says: "The well-adjusted, thoughtful person who has completed a full self-analysis *does not* consciously carry the city into the wilds. For example, in the campground he does not abolish night by hanging a gasoline lantern to a tree, but instead enjoys the flames and coals of the campfire, enjoys the moon and the stars, enjoys the darkness."

Manning's theme is that "camping is good fun, but it is even more fun to go 'snooping around.' So, though camper-trucks have their place, those who seal themselves into portable sub-divisions when evening comes, or a

Mount Baker looms over Boulder Creek. North Cascades National Park. [*Photo: M. Woodbridge Williams*]

sprinkle of rain, miss the sound of the river, the brush of the wind, the smell of the trees."

2. REDWOOD NATIONAL PARK
[*California*]

[1]

ON OCTOBER 2, 1968, after many years of deferred hopes on the part of nationwide conservation folks, Congress authorized the creation of a national redwoods park. As described in the Act, which provided more than ninety million dollars for acquisition of suitable forest, the new park is, when completed, forty-six miles long, north and south, and about seven miles wide at its greatest width. It will include thirty continuous miles of coastal acreage, plus hills, ridges, valleys, and streams for an ultimate total of 58,000 acres of redwood forest, bluffs, and beaches.

Implicit in the authorization of the new park is the possibility that three of the superb California redwoods parks—known and enjoyed by millions of Americans over the years—might be included, by transfer to federal ownership. These three parks are: Jedediah Smith, Del Norte, and Prairie Creek, which have a total of more than 27,000 acres. The remainder are now in private hands, including some residences and small business sites, but are mostly represented by redwood groves, coastal bluffs, and beaches. Some cutover redwood stands are included to sustain manageable units.

Well, at last we see that Congress has acted. But I think it well to begin my chapter on the park in this rather pedestrian vein so that our vast journeying public will realize that though the park is authorized it may be some years before it is "ready for occupancy" in the sense that Yellowstone and Glacier are. Though the noble ancient groves will remain intact until purchase arrangements are concluded, that is something which will take time, and while the chance that state parks will be transferred is regarded at this writing as favorable, it is not an accomplished fact. It follows, then, that the public must show patience and understanding. The California state parks, so admirably managed, remain as always offering facilities to the visitor. But you may find "No Trespassing" signs on the lands that lie

---

Jedediah Smith Redwoods State Park, which is proposed to be included in the new Redwood National Park. [Photo: Howard King, courtesy of the Save-the-Redwoods League]

within the planned boundaries of the new park. Logging trucks may be operating, drawing their enormous loads from lumber operations outside the boundaries. Remember that the 349 campsites in the three state parks mentioned above can be reserved in advance, prior to June 30 each year. Campsites not so reserved are on a first-come-first-served basis.

There are four campgrounds along U.S. Route 199 adjoining Redwoods National Park and Six Rivers National Forest to the north. In addition,

Typical wood-strewn seacoast. Redwood National Park. [Photo: Fred Mang, Jr.]

Where the redwood forests come down to the Pacific. Redwood National Park.
[Photo: Fred Mang, Jr.]

there are a number of campgrounds on U.S. 299 and California 96 in Six Rivers, Klamath, and Trinity National Forests. Private trailer parks and motels are available all along U.S. 101 from Eureka to Oregon, and on California highways 299, 96, and 199.

[2]

SAID RALPH WALDO EMERSON: "Whether we are too clumsy for so subtle a topic, or from whatever cause, as soon as men begin to write about nature, they fall into euphuism." He meant the tendency to become ornate, artificial, self-conscious. I have written much about nature, and I know that I have been guilty of Emerson's accusation. It derives no doubt from the simple fact that nobody *can* write adequately about nature. The human

brain works implicitly toward divorcing man from the rest of nature. Writers like Rachel Carson and Anne Lindbergh, from their very sweetness of soul, can make you unaware of this deficiency. Perhaps a man of science like our own John C. Merriam comes out of the challenge best. Merriam went far toward identifying himself with all natural objects. Whether you are observing an animal, a bird, an insect, a rock, or the blue sky, said an ancient writer in Sanskrit, *that art thou.*

I remember, back in the days when the far-sighted conservationists of the Save-the-Redwoods League were soliciting donations to match state funds in preserving some of the finest groves of the ancient trees, that someone wrote a stirring appeal in which he likened the groves of living giants to the great cathedrals of Europe. It was felicitous language. I liked it then, and I still read it with pleasure. But in actual fact it reverses essential truth; which should make us exclaim when we enter a great cathedral: "How wonderfully you have the feeling here that you are in a redwood grove in California."

Similarly, in that vast erosional country of our Southwest, somebody sees a strange rock shape and names it "Queen Victoria." Good fun: no harm done; but it is another case where man's egotism denies the priority. The fact is that Queen Victoria, dressed as she was in her period, managed to resemble a certain rock in Arizona or New Mexico.

Yet all this is not to say that we have not, in these days, a fine body of nature writers who seek the ideal: to place man, in the minds of their readers, in his proper environmental place.

[3]

THE MEANING of the redwoods. The meaning to us humans, not the aesthetic aspect; though they are trees and groves of surpassing beauty. Not that contact with them is not tonic for the wearied, perplexed, and self-hounded mortal—though it is. They have something more valuable to do than this. They can tell us something about ourselves. They are, as Merriam has said, "a living link in history." They were a flourishing genus—this Sequoia—when man was in the process of becoming.

Redwood Creek. Redwood National Park. [Photo: David Swanland, courtesy of the Save-the-Redwoods League]
Overleaf: Roosevelt Elk at Prairie Redwoods State Park, which is proposed to be included in the new Redwood National Park. [Photo: Moulin Studios, courtesy of the Save-the-Redwoods League]

Merriam continues:

Considered in the setting of their history, these great trees open to us one of the most fascinating chapters of the story of life. As you advance into these splendid forests the arches of foliage narrow above you and shade deepens into twilight. Between close-set trunks you look through windows framed in shadow. Here and there behind these openings in a distant aisle faint touches of sun upon a young tree bring out its red-brown glow . . . but woven through this picture is an element which eludes the imagery of art . . . the mysterious influence of these groves arises not alone from magnitude, or from beauty of light filling deep spaces. It is as if in these trees the flow of years were held in eddies, and one could see together past and present. The element of time pervades the forest with an influence more subtle than light, but that to the mind is not less real.

Consider, you venturer into this living past, that within the belt of redwood forest, near Calistoga, you may see a prostrate redwood that was felled and covered with volcanic ash and mud, perhaps in a mighty explosion of Mt. St. Helena, not far away. That redwood log which has been exposed to our view by excavation is, of course, now stone. But in all details of form and structure, even to the microscopic formation of the cells of growth, the petrified logs are identical with the redwoods that rear their heads toward the sky today.

Consider too, that as living formations, over the aeons during which sequoia has flourished, it has had a tiny companion. Several associates, no doubt; but this frail Sugar Scoop, with pure-white flower and threadlike stem, is as much a part of the forest scene as the great trees themselves. Acres and acres of the humble flowers may be seen, and the botanist Willis Jepson speaks of this flowery expanse at its peak as "giving back a soft, strange light such as never was seen elsewhere on land or sea."

Why are the redwoods where they are, and nowhere else in the world growing in a natural state? Now they exist in a narrow strip from the general vicinity of Monterey northward along the coast and just lapping over into Curry County in Oregon. The paleobotanist knows the answer to that. Thirty or forty million years ago the climate in what is now the western United States had gradually changed from nearly tropical to temperate, and most of the mahogany and figs and palms had disappeared. The redwood

Seedlings spring up at the feet of the giants. Redwood National Park. [Photo: Fred Mang, Jr.]

came down from the north; not the redwood you gaze at today, but a "dawn redwood," a type that shed its leaves in autumn. By unusual chance a "living fossil" of this "metasequoia" was discovered in the province of Szechuan by a Chinese forester named Wang. The fossil remains of this species have been found over an area extending from Washington and Oregon eastward into Montana. They lived in those now lava-covered lands east of the Cascades, where the John Day and other rivers flow through a semi-desert.

The redwoods we see today represent the development of a species adapted to the climatic conditions that exist along the northern California coast: moderate temperatures, heavy rainfall during the winter months, and dry summers with considerable fog. Indeed, all those who have been in the redwood forests associate them with fog—and far from being annoying, there is something about those fleecy invaders that makes the experience more worthwhile. But it is not definitely known whether *Sequoia sempervirens* is "dependent" for its life on fogs. One thing is certain: the magnificent ancient groves were certainly produced under optimum conditions, the likes of which we cannot know will exist again in any time we can foresee. *As a tree* the redwood is not likely to become extinct—on the contrary, it grows with astonishing rapidity. But *groves of giants* like these? We would wisely preserve all we can, while we can.

The stillness of the redwood forest is extraordinary, and even a little frightening to the urban visitor. The bird watcher at first wonders whether birds ever visit these trees, and may conclude that in this respect he is in a sort of wooded desert. But of the 141 species of birds that have been reported, at least sixty-five are known to breed in the coastal forest and at least twenty in the forest itself.

When the crowns of the trees, where birds would naturally spend their time, are from two hundred to more than three hundred feet above a person on the ground the chance of seeing them or hearing them is not great.

Not to be neglected is the beautiful shoreline of the park. Because of the rocky promontories that finger into the sea, the beaches are relatively short, and in many cases their rocky boundaries cannot be rounded even at low tide. It is not a shoreline for safe swimming and surfing. But there is much to be seen. Sea lions have their colonies here, and migrating whales are not uncommonly observed. The entire area of the park is in the path of the Pacific Flyway of aquatic birds. The offshore rocks make ideal havens for them in nesting time.

The silence of the forest: the pounding of the sea. You may have both.

INDEXES

(An index to the Appendix begins on page xix. Illustrations are indexed under the national park, etc., to which they appertain.)

[iii]

Index

INDEX TO THE APPENDIX

About the Author

FREEMAN TILDEN, a native of Massachusetts, quit a successful career as a writer of fiction and plays to devote his talents to the cause of conservation, with particular reference to the role of the National Park System in American life. He has served as consultant to four Directors of the National Parks. Beginning with his standard work *The National Parks,* of which this present volume is a completely revised and enlarged edition, Mr. Tilden has produced a series of books devoted to the preservation and interpretation of natural and historic places: *The State Parks, The Fifth Essence, Interpreting Our Heritage.* Part of his volume *Following the Frontier* deals with the early days in Yellowstone National Park. When he is not traveling in the parks Mr. Tilden continues a pleasant association with nature in the woods and fields of his farm in Warren, Maine.

A Note on the Type

The text of this book was set on the Linotype in Janson, a recutting made direct from type cast from matrices long thought to have been made by the Dutchman Anton Janson, who was a practicing type founder in Leipzig during the years 1668–87. However, it has been conclusively demonstrated that these types are actually the work of Nicholas Kis (1650–1702), a Hungarian, who most probably learned his trade from the master Dutch type founder Kirk Voskens. The type is an excellent example of the influential and sturdy Dutch types that prevailed in England up to the time William Caslon developed his own incomparable designs from these Dutch faces.

Composed, and bound by The Colonial Press, Inc.,
Clinton, Massachusetts, printed by Halliday Lithograph Corp.,
West Hanover, Massachusetts.

Typography and binding design by
GUY FLEMING

NOTES

NOTES

NOTES

NOTES

NOTES

NOTES

NOTES

NOTES

NOTES

NOTES